The Play of TRUTH & STATE

Matthew H. Wikander

The Play of
TRUTH & STATE

HISTORICAL DRAMA FROM
SHAKESPEARE TO BRECHT

THE JOHNS HOPKINS UNIVERSITY PRESS *Baltimore & London*

This book has been brought to publication with the
generous assistance of the Andrew W. Mellon Foundation.

The Johns Hopkins University Press
701 West 40th Street
Baltimore, Maryland 21211
The Johns Hopkins Press Ltd, London

*The paper in this book is acid-free and meets the guidelines for
permanence and durability of the Committee on Production Guidelines
for Book Longevity of the Council on Library Resources.*

LIBRARY OF CONGRESS CATALOGING-IN-PUBLICATION DATA
Wikander, Matthew H.
  The play of truth and state.

  Includes index.
    1. Historical drama—History and criticism.   2. History in
literature.   I. Title.
PN1872.W55   1986   809.2'514   85-23128
ISBN 0-8018-2979-8 (alk. paper)

To my parents

Contents

Acknowledgments

The extent of my debt to previous scholars is suggested, but by no means fully discharged, in the notes. Conspicuous omissions and unwarranted intrusions into others' preserves are both risks of this kind of study; I hope that what is here justifies its presence and that what is absent is not unduly missed.

Grants from the Columbia University Council for Research in the Humanities and a Columbia College Chamberlain Fellowship provided me with the time and travel I needed to pursue this project. The argument of part 1 first appeared, in shorter and simpler form, in *Genre* (University of Oklahoma) 9 (1976); some portions of chapter 2 initially appeared in *JEGP* 78 (1979). I would like to thank the editors of these journals for their permission to draw upon these materials.

Libraries whose librarians have made me welcome include: the Sawyer Library and the Chapin Library at Williams College; the Cambridge University Library, the British Library, the Libraries of the University of Michigan, the Columbia University Libraries, the Swedish Royal Library, the Clark Art Institute Library, and the New York Public Library.

Among individuals I owe much to the teachers who started me to thinking about drama and history: especially George Pistorius, the late Clay Hunt, Philip Edwards, Anne Barton, and J. L. Styan. The following colleagues read the manuscript at various stages of its development and offered timely encouragement and helpful misgivings: Michael Goldman, Martin Meisel, Harry Carlson, Daniel Gerould, and Bernard Beckerman.

Beatrice Terrien typed and retyped the manuscript with tireless panache. Richard Sacks offered wisdom and friendly counsel; Christine Child, fortitude and good cheer.

The Play of TRUTH & STATE

Introduction

"He shows a history couch'd in a play": so John Ford summarizes his enterprise in the prologue to *Perkin Warbeck,* a history play written in 1634. Such plays had long ceased to be popular on the English stage, and Ford characterizes his own, along with the old Elizabethan plays it imitates, as a "study." He praises his "wise industry," and throughout the prologue—radiating sobriety and seriousness, repudiating "antic follies"—John Ford the playwright plays the historian. "On these two rests the fate / Of worthy expectation," he promises, "Truth and State." But the word *couch'd* is troublesome: history hides in the play, lurking in ambush, ready to pounce. In his role-playing, Ford reveals a special awareness. As he pretends to be a historian, he concedes that he is not one. Thus he acknowledges, backhandedly, the wide gulf that opened up, early in the seventeenth century, between historian and playwright.

No such gulf had bothered Shakespeare. Admiring his ease and authority, generations of later playwrights would apotheosize the Shakespeare of the history plays as the natural, national genius of Britain. Yet when historical drama became popular again in England in the last decades of the seventeenth century, the legacy of Nicholas Rowe and his successors was a body of English historical tragedy that is formulaic to an extreme. Essential to the formula was a denigration of history: English dramatists of the eighteenth century had arrived at a consensus. History reduced all human action to politics; politics was a sordid, dirty business; historians reduced human beings to machines; dramatists could only counter historians by probing the private secrets of the heart.

Dramatists in other European countries, however, found Shakespeare's histories radically inspiring. Romantic and revolutionary movements in Germany and France looked to Shakespeare for liberation from the stiff formalities of classical style. His immediacy—again celebrated as untutored natural genius—challenged the narrative history of the age. As a political ideal no less than an aesthetic one, Shakespeare's histories, accorded mythic status, attracted great dramatists like moths to a flame. England may have failed to sustain an indigenous tradition of historical drama, but the myth of such a tradition retained a powerful allure. Schiller, Musset, Büchner, Strindberg, and Brecht all tried their hand at a form that seemed to imitate the past most perfectly in its formlessness. The two parts of this study examine first the English failure and second these later playwrights' experiments. From architect of a kind of popular entertainment despised by the learned in his own age, the Shakespeare of the history plays came to be enshrined as the dramatist of the real, whose plays embodied life itself.

The decline of historical drama in England and its transmutation into mythic ideal in Europe took place against the backdrop of academic history's encyclopedic unassailability in the late-eighteenth and early-nineteenth century. Yet as Ford reveals in *Perkin Warbeck,* the historian's shadow darkens the playwright's endeavor as much as Shakespeare's does. The humanist historian's ideal of "truth and state," persistently questioned in Ford's play, eludes and worries all the playwrights in this study. Brecht, declaring himself to be a historian and his theater to be history, arrogates to himself total authority. For Shakespeare and Brecht, the incompatible roles of dramatist and historian are one. R. G. Collingwood's famous definition of history as the imaginative reenactment of past experience suggests the same kind of integration through its theatrical metaphor.[1] But historical drama's difficult relations with the discipline of history reflect instead confusion and rivalry. The ancient tradition of the poet's vatic mission as custodian of the past died hard in the three centuries between Shakespeare and Brecht. The historian's increasing reliance upon facts led playwrights to assert authority over a whole range of higher truths.

Shakespeare shows remarkable freedom from later playwrights' confusion about historical fact and ultimate truth. But the image of the world as theater and history as drama—an image central to the Augustinian, providential view that predominated in the chronicles Shakespeare used as his sources—was open to skeptical question in Shakespeare's own time and in Shakespeare's own plays. In Shakespeare, as in his sources, providential language and a desire to see human action *sub spaeculo aeternitatis* ("through the glass of eternity") coexist with Machiavellian clarity of vision about why men do what they do. "We are much beholden to Machiavelli and other writers of that class," pronounced

Francis Bacon, indefatigable promoter of the new, "who openly and unfeignedly declare or describe what men do, and not what they ought to do."[2] Shakespeare's dramatizations of the past partake both of the Augustinian model of history as a series of emblematic rises and falls, demonstrating the vanity of human ambition, and of the humanist ideal of political science, "truth and state." Like the Elizabethan playhouses, where the action took place upon a platform just below a canopy called the "heavens" and ghosts emerged from a trapdoor leading to a "hell" beneath the stage, Shakespeare's history writing retains strong connections to old, medieval forms. E. M. W. Tillyard's great contribution to the study of Shakespeare's history plays was his recognition that Shakespeare wrote history just as the historians of his time did—moralizing the spectacles of the historical record, peopling it with theatrical archetypes drawn from mystery and morality drama, pointing its lessons with authority. Yet Tillyard failed to recognize the degree of tension between the humanist and providential ways of looking at the past in both Shakespeare's sources and Shakespeare's own dramatic technique.

The sense of immediacy that Shakespeare's histories conveyed to other dramatists derives directly from the playwright's recognition of tension between these two ways of seeing the past and his constant arousal of both kinds of seeing in his audience. Emblematic morals are offered and confuted; charged language transforms mundane negotiations into allegorized psychomachias. Shakespeare's dramatic history writing reveals a profound mistrust of traditional homiletic clarifications of past events—a mistrust Shakespeare shared with the humanist historians—linked with an equally profound mistrust of the humanist ideal. "The humanist historian," Donald J. Wilcox has argued, "did not see himself as a collector of facts but as an artist who organized the facts into a coherent and attractive form."[3] The activity is essentially fictive, easily as fictive as the old invocations of divine providence. But the alternative, that events in the past might make no sense at all, threatens Shakespeare's history in the form of repeated images of chaos. Shakespeare is thus able to tempt and frustrate his audience through the fluidity of the shifting moral patterns his action seems to take. Forced actively to make sense out of what they see, the audience become historians. Shakespeare's skepticism about the ways of looking at the past available to him furnishes both the tension and excitement—the elusive immediacy—of his mature history plays (in chapter 1, *1 Henry IV* will serve as a model) and the nostalgic, passivist mood of *Henry VIII*.

The elegiac pageantry of that late historical romance is both a challenge to the historical record and a confession of defeat. In *Henry VIII,*

Shakespeare anticipates the later decline of English historical drama. Where Ben Jonson (as we shall see in chapter 2) fought censorship and struggled to establish historical drama as a new light of truth, Shakespeare came at the end of his career to dismiss history's ability to master the mysterious operations of time. In the second chapter, we examine Jonson's attempts, and the attempts of George Chapman, to illuminate the past with lessons for the present and the rejection of their embrace of humanist discipline by playwrights of a younger generation, Philip Massinger and John Ford. Ford turns back to Shakespeare, questioning the truth of historical fact and offering countertruths that assert the power of theatrical illusion. Ford may adopt wholesale from his source—Bacon's *History of Henry VII*—a battery of sneers at Warbeck's theatrical posturing; but the dramatist makes the impostor kinglier than Henry VII. Nor, as we shall see in chapter 3, is there any interruption in dramatists' mistrust of history despite the twenty-year suspension of legal theatrical activity. After the restoration of Charles II in 1660, there was no outburst of enthusiastic patriotic drama. Rather, such plays as told English stories continued Ford's exploration of a kind of nobility outside politics, wholly personal, wholly ethical, utterly secret. Heroic drama shared Ford's contempt for mere fact. John Banks's history plays, in the 1680s, hit upon a durable formula: concentrating on the private sufferings of monarchs in love, Banks left politics in the hands of serviceable villains. Some dramatists of the Restoration, most notably John Dryden and Nathaniel Lee, essayed serious political dramas, history plays that touched on the issues of their own times, but they achieved only inflammatory topicality. Rowe, in the early eighteenth century, successfully combined providential rhetoric, party propagandism, and erotic voyeurism in a blend that held the stage for at least a century and a half.

Thus if Shakespeare sets a standard in *1 Henry IV,* his failure in *Henry VIII* to achieve the electrifying balance of responses demanded by his mature histories foreshadows this later passivism. For the problem in *Henry VIII* (subtitled as it is *All Is True*) is precisely that of resolving a record of sordid and petty doings to what Shakespeare regards as a providential end: the same problem Rymer solved with the idea of poetic justice. The divorce of Katherine of Aragon, after all, makes possible the succession of Elizabeth. The sufferings of Katherine are subsumed into the onward march of the autonomous, happy event: the result is an uncertainty of tone that most critics find jarring and for which many blame John Fletcher. But the playwright's sense of historical event as autonomous and inevitable reflects a sense of powerlessness over historical story (as fable or plot) that is wholly characteristic of the later English drama. Banks and Rowe carry passivism and reliance upon familiarity with the stories they stage to sadistic extremes: trapped in circumstances utterly out of control, queens suffer and lovers die. What happened in the past has to happen in the play. History becomes an analogue for fate.

Distaste for historical fact thus combines with a total relinquishment to historical discipline of authority over the past. Between Shakespeare, at the beginning of this study, and Brecht at the end, lies the great age of history writing. In England, Bacon was followed by Clarendon, Hume, Gibbon, Robertson, Hallam, Macaulay; side by side there developed historical drama of appalling bathos. Continental dramatists— enlisting the aid of the Shakespeare of *1 Henry IV* rather than *Henry VIII*—more eagerly attacked the historian's monolithic assertion of authority. Schiller and Strindberg, strange bedfellows in most regards, both engaged in the struggle, and their assertions of higher truths than history's are the subject of chapter 4. The tension between playwright and historian is legendary in Schiller's case: he practiced both vocations at once while composing his *Wallenstein* trilogy. Ultimately, Schiller's idealistic distaste for facts won out over the dialectic balance he struck in *Wallenstein*. Strindberg, too, began his career as a historian: where Schiller studied Kantian "universal" history, Strindberg in his youth was a devotee of Thomas Buckle and a scientific positivist in his own right. Yet Strindberg came at the end of his career to dismiss all "pragmatic" history as *gudlös och därför värdelös* ("godless and therefore worthless"), a pack of lies.[4] Both Schiller and Strindberg offered transcendental alternatives to history, in contrast to the English dramatists, whose antihistorical pastoral yearnings and providential rhetoric aimed merely at pathos. Shakespeare suspended his audience between medieval and Renaissance ways of seeing the past; Strindberg openly adopted a self-conscious, medievalistic providentialism, seeing the hand of God everywhere. Schiller no less than the English dramatists disliked history's unpleasant record of deceptions, but he systematized yearning for higher truth into a coherent philosophical idealism.

The scientific history that Strindberg first admired and then rebelled against supplanted humanist history in the nineteenth century, primarily as a result of the archival researches of Leopold von Ranke. Schiller and historians he admired like Robertson could still see history as a branch of literature rather than as a discipline in its own right; debate between antiquarians and "philosophical" historians raged through the eighteenth century. Ranke, however, urged his successors to avoid humanist moralization and to tell history, in the famous phrase, "as it really happened"—(*wie es eigentlich gewesen war*). He rejected the "high office" of history, the "task of judging the past, of instructing the present for the benefit of ages to come." Instead, as he put it in his English history, "I have wished to extinguish my own self, as it were, and to allow only things to speak and to allow the mighty forces to appear which in the course of the centuries have risen and grown alongside and across one another."[5] The study of history could reveal laws akin to the natural law discovered by science. By the 1870s, Lawrence Stone points out, "the theory of historicism was triumphant, and it was seriously believed that all that was needed to establish Truth was to cleave faithfully to the facts gleaned from the archives."[6] A true believer in historicism in the 1870s, Strindberg after his Inferno crisis descried in world history, not natural laws, but the hand of God. In his *Blue Books* he clamored that archivists lied and that kings falsified records to make themselves look good; but Strindberg nonetheless found in history evidence of a conscious will. *The Mysticism of World History,* a series of essays published in 1903, juxtaposed facts and dates in different times and places to reveal God's purpose. The idea that the facts could reveal laws—as in the natural sciences, with which Bacon had identified the new discipline of history in the early seventeenth century—attracted Strindberg as it attracted his contemporaries. His application of it, characteristically, is unique.

Other dramatists subscribed more conventionally to the secular, scientist tenets of historicism. Georg Büchner, preparing his drama of the French Revolution, searched the records and emerged appalled at history's horrid fatalism, its ineluctable laws. For Musset too, as for Büchner, history seemed to annihilate the individual, draining human choices of all significance. Where Schiller and Strindberg could challenge the notion of historical necessity through their own highly personal versions of providentialism, Büchner and Musset reached a dramatic and historical impasse: the anomie and paralysis of Danton and Lorenzaccio, examined in chapter 5, figures this impasse.

Büchner and Musset followed contemporary fashion in imitating Shakespeare's staging. But his potent and useful recognition that the historians of his own time offered no single way of understanding the past went unnoticed in the nineteenth century. Strindberg, in the twentieth century, could argue that both he and Shakespeare were providentialists, but for Büchner and Musset imitating Shakespeare was a matter of staging crowd scenes, mixing tragedy and comedy, seeking the elusive Shakespearean grotesque. For dramatists during the period no questioning of history's authority and prestige was possible. The alternative, the temptation to which the English dramatists succumbed and which Musset and Büchner avoided, was trivialization. Scribe perfected this kind of historical drama; he and his emulators, Wagner sneered, "have thrust into the inmost recesses of the whole historic mechanism, and have discovered its heart to be the antechamber of the prince, where men and the state make their mutual arrangements between breakfast and supper."[7] As in the dramaturgy of Banks and Rowe and Bulwer-Lytton, famous events are shown to have trivial causes—a glass of water, a mislaid handkerchief, and a kingdom is lost. Resisting the lure of this kind of playwrighting, Musset and Büchner took the opposite position: individuals in their dramas have no effect whatsoever upon the autonomous development of the event. As a discipline, history seemed utterly antipathetic to ideas of human agency that made drama possible; the drama of individual heroes gave way, as Herbert Lindenberger argues, to the operatic expression of "history as sheer power."[8]

The notion of history as a science deriving laws from the records of state came under fire at the end of the nineteenth century. In Hayden White's words, "the contributions of Marx and Nietzsche to the 'crisis of historicism' of the late nineteenth century consisted in their historicization of the very concept of objectivity itself."[9] Shakespeare before the great age of history could entertain alternative ways of looking at the past; Brecht too—his lessons learned from Marx—could with wildly different results force his audience to become historians. "Alienation," his favorite theatrical strategy, he defined as "historicization": in his theoretical writings, Brecht demanded an audience of scientists, historians, sports fans, who would evaluate not only what they saw but also their ways of seeing it. "C'est un théâtre qui invite, oblige à l'explication, mais qui ne le donne pas;" wrote Roland Barthes of Brecht's ideal, "c'est un théâtre qui provoque l'Histoire, mais qui ne la divulgue pas: qui pose avec acuité le problème de l'Histoire, mais qui ne le résout pas" ("It is a theater that invites, requires explanation, but does not give it; it is a theater that provokes History, but does not reveal it, that poses with acuity the problem of History, but does not solve it").[10] Brecht adopted a whole range of Elizabethan staging techniques, but his real link to Shakespeare lies in his scrutiny, not his acceptance or rejection, of history.

Shakespeare is a touchstone for historical drama, then, not in terms of direct influence—blank verse, crowd scenes, mixed styles—but in terms of the equal footing he takes with his sources. For Shakespeare, neither the historian nor the dramatist has a monopoly on truth; both are involved in the same activity, imposing patterns that may well stifle life as they organize it and lend it significance. Just as the dramatists in this study react against the authoritative posture of historical discipline in a wide variety of ways, so too do their responses to Shakespeare's freedom from history's authority range from worship to contempt. Brecht, like Ford, poses as a historian; secure in the role, he recasts the events of the past to fit his vision of the future. But he reaches beyond Ford in the freedom he, too, arrogates to himself. Brecht historicizes not only Renaissance science in *Galileo* but also the whole humanist idea of important historical individuals. Suspended between providential and humanist models of history, Shakespeare chose neither: Brecht assaults the idea of individualism in *Galileo* while at the same time personally blaming the historical Galileo for the atom bomb. The freedom to engage contradictory ways of looking at the past eluded the English playwrights; likewise, Schiller and Strindberg celebrated higher truths by denigrating interests of state. Musset and Büchner despaired at history's imperatives. But the devaluation of individual action and responsibility that these playwrights saw in history offered to Strindberg evidence of the hand of God and to Brecht a way to revitalize European theater. Strindberg's idiosyncratic syncretism helped him to write some great historical dramas; Brecht's enthusiastic rejection of individualism is fully tested by his plays. With *Galileo* as a case in point (chapter 5), we can examine the implications of this self-criticism in some detail.

Brecht does not mark an end to the confusion about the nature and purpose of historical drama discussed in this study. Shakespeare and Brecht may share common dramatic techniques and a mistrust of ideological authority, but they mainly share a clarity of vision about the limitations of dramatic form. In Brecht's case this led, not to a new drama of "truth and state," but to persistent ironic self-questioning in which most audiences do not willingly participate. The popular image of Brecht's Mother Courage is not that of a hyena of the battlefield; *Galileo* is more often praised as a traditional "martyr play" than as a critique of the form.[11] Nonetheless, Brecht's experiments in theory and drama show Shakespeare still to be a powerful critical force. What Shakespeare did, as a dramatist, can be studied to help us understand the difficulty later playwrights had with history, both as subject matter and as a discipline. The critical scrutiny to which Shakespeare subjects the kind of history writing prevalent in his day makes clear how much all historical drama, whether playwrights want it to or not, must challenge our preconceptions about the very act of understanding the past. The best history plays immediately engage audiences in the challenge; the second part of this book is devoted to some of these. The worst submit feebly, redefining the proper sphere of drama as ahistorical, private, outside time: this is the story of post-Shakespearean historical drama in England.

In contrast to this drama, the efforts of Schiller, Musset, and Büchner stand in bold relief; grappling with the past, they actively engaged the main issues of early modern historiography—times and men, necessity and freedom, *Dichtung und Wahrheit* ("poetry and truth"), truth and state. Strindberg and Brecht too sought to write responsible public drama. The difficulty audiences have with Strindberg's medievalist mysticism and Brecht's riddling historicism is a pungent commentary on the crisis in modern theater.

Shakespeare created a genre and defined its standards. What Brecht shows is that the modern theater too can entertain radical questioning of the relationship between historical and dramatic ways of portraying the past. The discipline of history is no longer the authoritative monolith it appeared to dramatists of the eighteenth and nineteenth centuries; Brecht's ironic historicist stance partakes of historians' own self-criticism. "In my view," Hayden White has said, "history as a discipline is in bad shape today because it has lost sight of its origins in the literary imagination. In the interest of appearing scientific and objective, it has repressed and denied to itself its own greatest source of strength and renewal."[12] Paradoxically, Brecht sought to rejuvenate theater by declaring it to be history itself, and by decrying "Aristotelian," "dramatic" aesthetics. Whether a mutual renewal is possible remains to be seen. Riddles about historical and dramatic truth and confusion about the drama's proper place in the secular state will always trouble history plays. But the particular advantage Shakespeare held over the other dramatists that this study examines—his recognition of the essentially fictive nature of history writing—no longer holds. The problem of truth is once again incapable of resolution. The historian no longer enjoys the advantage of authority that so troubled the dramatists between Shakespeare and Brecht. Free to populate the stage with alternative pasts and alternative futures, dramatists must now ponder the institutional role historical drama can play in contemporary society. Three hundred and fifty years after John Ford, "worthy expectation" still waits on a drama of truth and state.

I

THE PATHOS OF POWER

ENGLISH HISTORICAL DRAMA
AFTER SHAKESPEARE

1

Shakespeare's Dramatic Historiography
1 HENRY IV *TO* HENRY VIII

i

Right in the middle of *1 Henry IV* a memorable sequence of three scenes—the tavern scene (II.iv), the Welsh scene (III.i), and the royal interview (III.ii)—forces the audience into a shift of attitude essential to the play's success as a dramatization of the English past. The range of response Shakespeare demands is astonishing: in the tavern scene, the tired slapstick of baiting Francis gives way to the exuberance of Falstaff's boasts, the half-serious, half-comic rehearsal for Hal's interview with the king, and finally the muted comedy of ransacking the sleeping fat man's pockets. The Welsh scene is as various as the tavern scene. Hotspur provokes Glendower into monstrous Falstaffian boasts, all in good fun until tempers flare over the division of the map; peace and quiet descend as the Welsh lady sings. Hard upon her strange lyricism follow the stately rhythms of the royal interview and Hal's self-dramatization, before a wholly serious audience this time, as returned prodigal, hero, and warrior-prince. The audience's laughter must give way, at the end of this sequence, to an endorsement, however qualified, of Hal's vow to kill Hotspur and win his honors.

The prince's effort to convince the king of his good faith is equally Shakespeare's effort to convince the audience to accept his difficult and confusing portrait of the prince. The techniques employed here are characteristic of Shakespeare's dramatic construction, especially the tripartite design in which analogous situations in a beginning (the tavern) and an end (the interview) are played off against each other and also against an apparently unrelated middle (Wales). Hence the true prince / false thief dichotomies spoofed by Falstaff receive utterly serious expression after, rather than before, their comic deflation. Hal's promise to tear a "reckoning" from Percy's heart follows our last view of him searching

Falstaff's pockets, exclaiming over unpaid bills, and promising to pay back with advantage the money stolen at Gadshill. Both promises recall, with enriching ironies, Hal's troublesome soliloquy, his paradoxical vow to "pay the debt [he] never promised" (I.ii.197) and his theatrical challenge to the audience: "I'll so offend to make offense a skill / Redeeming time when men think least I will" (lines 204–5).[1] Between the two scenes in which Hal figures, we see Hotspur quibbling over a contract.

Fathers confront sons in all three scenes. Falstaff plays father and son to Hal, and Hal plays himself and his father. The same reversals and readjustments animate the royal interview, as Hal offers to "Be more myself" (III.ii.92). In between, just after Hal, in mockery—with serious overtones—has banished his grey-beard Satan, we see Hotspur, his father curiously not present (and he will be absent again at the play's end) match wits with a self-avowed Satanist (undoubtedly bearded) only to be brought to heel by that "notorious misleader of youth," Worcester. Worcester's mixture of Machiavellism and fatherly advice carries over into the king's advice to his son.

The thematic, structural, and theatrical centrality of these three scenes to *I Henry IV* cannot be denied, whether we call them the central triptych (with Mark Rose), the climactic plateau (with Bernard Beckerman), a sequence of mirror-scenes (with Hereward T. Price), or merely a Freytagian turning point.[2] In all the critical attention that has been lavished on the play, the Welsh scene has been somewhat slighted; partly to redress the balance, we can use this scene as a key to understanding *I Henry IV* and as an epitome of Shakespeare's historical drama. Hotspur's appeal to an audience must be subordinated to the larger design of the whole play, and the subordination takes place here, in a scene most frequently characterized as a kind of intermission, an interlude instructive of the folly of civil division, a lull before the storm.[3]

As the central scene in the central sequence of scenes in the play, however, III.i should be expected to reach out beyond the system of echoes and anticipations that link it to II.iv and III.ii. Given the centrifugal nature of Shakespeare's art, we should be surprised if the scene did not. Glendower, who appears only here, in a magnificent gust of theatrical exuberance, is talked about throughout the play. His fantastic speech and appearance make his failure to show up at Shrewsbury as much a theatrical disappointment to the audience as it is a political disappointment to the rebels. His eccentricity, for a few moments, challenges Falstaff's. Also introduced here, and vitally important to the politics of the play, is Mortimer, as pale and languid a presence as Glendower is vivid. As "next of blood" whose claim to the throne supposedly legitimizes the rebellion, he should be of great interest to an audience. In a play so full of counterfeit kings, here apparent heirs apparent, and thieves of thrones, one would expect Mortimer to take his proper place among the false princes and player kings. It is perhaps revealing that he does not.

But the linkage of the scene to the design of the play has to be tighter than its mere presentation of two figures much discussed by other characters. Shakespeare's usual practice is to anticipate a play's center in its beginning, echo it at the end. Wales looms distressingly large in both. "A post from Wales" (1.i.37) breaks off the council's discussion of Henry's favorite project, a penitential and politically desirable crusade. Welsh troubles cloud the horizon at the end of the play; Glendower's absence from the field at Shrewsbury means that while the battle may be won, the war is not. "Myself and you, son Harry, will towards Wales," says the king, "To fight with Glendower and the Earl of March" (v.v.39–40). Wales becomes a metaphoric backdrop against which the rest of the play's English action takes place. The play's Welsh frame suggests that the problems that have frighted peace at the beginning remain to be solved at the end.[4]

Wales is particularly important as an idea in *1 Henry IV* because it is nominally Hal's principality. The title itself becomes the name for Hal's reformed personality. "Tell your nephew," he instructs the unreliable Worcester, "The Prince of Wales doth join with all the world / In praise of Henry Percy" (v.i.85–87). The name enhances the formality of the challenge. Throughout the final act of the play, Hal insists upon it. With another direct echo of his soliloquy in 1.ii, he pounces on the Douglas and rescues his fainting father: "It is the Prince of Wales that threatens thee, / Who never promiseth but he means to pay" (v.iv.41–42). Again, in the confrontation with Hotspur, the name becomes all-important: "Thou speak'st as if I would deny my name," he answers to Hotspur's denigratory reference to him as Harry Monmouth (v.iv.60). His challenge to his rival is itself a formal assertion of identity:

> I am the Prince of Wales, and think not, Percy,
> To share with me in glory any more.
> Two stars keep not their motion in one sphere,
> Nor can one England brook a double reign
> Of Harry Percy and the Prince of Wales.
>
> (v.iv.62–66)

James Black has suggested that the "favors" (line 95) that Hal lays on Hotspur's face are the traditional emblems of his principality: the ostrich feathers associated with the motto *ich dien* ("I serve"). Hal's reformation is, at this point, emblematically complete.[5]

One of several ironies attendant upon this emphatic identification of Hal not only as Prince of Wales but as a Welsh prince (picked up later in *Henry V*) would be more immediately apparent to an audience member familiar with Holinshed and the *Mirror for Magistrates* than it is to us. In response to the tradition of Merlin prophecies derided by Hotspur in III.i (but Percy gets them confused[6]), the historical Owen Glendower had had himself named Prince of Wales by a rebel Welsh parliament in 1404. The historical Prince Henry had been given the title in 1401, but of Wales a French observer reported "I think he must conquer it if he will have it."[7] Shakespeare deliberately obscures the political situation in Hal's Wales in favor of a larger metaphoric significance. But the emphasis on the Welshness of Glendower and the reference, through Hotspur, to the vaticinatory tradition to which Owen Tudor and Henry VII also appealed provides the central scene of *1 Henry IV* with a Tudor resonance.[8] Harry Monmouth becomes by extension a true Tudor prince; Glendower, a monstrous counterfeit.

Wales stands not only outside the play's politics but also outside civilization itself. Our first news from there suggests brutality of a most savage kind. The fate of Mortimer's troops—

> Upon whose dead corpse there was such misuse,
> Such beastly shameless transformation,
> By those Welshwomen done as may not be
> Without much shame retold or spoken of
>
> (1.i.43–46)

—may draw no strong response from the king, but it establishes Wales in an audience's mind as a primitive, horrible place. Black has pointed out that the wound that Falstaff inflicts upon the dead Hotspur's "thigh" is a visual enactment of the Welsh women's mutilations, reinforcing an identification between rude Glendower and Falstaff.[9] Hotspur derides Welsh language as crude—Glendower's translation and the Welsh lady's song belie him—and jokes that "the devil understands Welsh." His last remark rings truer than he knows.

Precisely where in Wales the scene takes place has puzzled Shakespeare's editors since Nicholas Rowe. The Tripartite Indenture was signed by Glendower, Mortimer, and Northumberland after the battle of Shrewsbury at the house of the archdeacon of Bangor, so this traditional stage direction is obviously incorrect. There is no historical source for an agreement before Shrewsbury involving Hotspur.[10] While we are clear-ly on Glendower's turf, this is a metaphorical Wales, set apart from the rest of the play by tradition and suggestion as a location for the enact-ment of moralized spectacle.

In fact, this Wales is something of a theater. "These promises are fair, the parties sure, / And our induction full of prosperous hope," in-tones Mortimer (III.i.1–2). The language suggests a self-contained play-let. Unlike the world of the court, bustling with news, or the world of Falstaff, rowdy and idle, the world of the Welsh scene is magical, ancient, primitive. Glendower's musicians, at the end, "hang in the air" (unless we remember that they are sitting in a gallery above the stage). "A plague upon it," says Hotspur, "I have forgot the map" (lines 4–5), and the remark begs emblematic interpretation.

Glendower produces the map (by sleight of hand?), and the fencing begins. His long-winded compliment draws from Hotspur a cleverly disguised insult in response: "And you in hell, as oft he hears Owen Glendower spoke of" (line 11). The language of heaven and hell may remind us of Falstaff's unholy trinity—"that fiend Douglas, that spirit Percy, and that devil Glendower" (II.iv.351)—and it persists in Glen-dower's blasphemous boasts about his "nativity." Hotspur attempts to bring the scene back down to earth with medical, rationalistic explana-tions ("Diseased nature oftentimes breaks forth / In strange eruptions," lines 27–28), which draw laughter partly because of their common sense but mostly because of their veiled scatology. Glendower's wrath and boasts mount; Hotspur threatens to go to dinner; Mortimer must intervene.

A few observations about this first portion of the scene are in order. First, the comic sparring has its political dimension: this is a struggle for dominance in the rebel camp, another falling-out among thieves. Fur-ther, it reminds us in its give-and-take of the interaction between Falstaff and the prince. Glendower's insistence upon a supernatural birth and a miraculous life that exempts him from "the roll of common men" (line 43) is a curious exaggeration of Falstaff's doctrine of "instinct. The lion will not touch the true prince" (II.iv.257). Bearing in mind Glendower's identity in the *Mirror* as an impostor Prince of Wales, we can see in Glendower's claims of astronomical portents at his birth a challenge to Hal's vision of himself in his soliloquy as a restorer of astronomical regularity, imitating the sun. King Henry calls the armies of civil war "meteors of a troubled heaven" (I.i.10). As both sun of heaven and son of England it is Hal's job, Falstaff suggests, to resolve cosmic and civil unrest:

> Shall the blessed sun of heaven prove a micher and eat
> blackberries? A question not to be asked. Shall the son of
> England prove a thief and take purses? A question to be
> asked.
>
> (II.iv.389–92)

The mingling of comic and serious, public and private, cosmic and
domestic in the tavern scene receives further expansion and qualification
in the posturing of Glendower.

The relationship of II.iv to III.i is one of what Robert Merrix and
Arthur Polacas call "proleptic parody"; the relationship becomes more
complex, however, when we realize that both scenes stand together as
parodic anticipations of III.ii, the royal interview.[11] Bardolph, for example, anticipates Glendower:

> My lord, do you see these meteors? Do you behold these
> exhalations?
> *Prince:* I do.
> *Bardolph:* What think you they portend?
>
> (II.iv.303–6)

Like the Welsh magician, Bardolph invokes menacing portents; like
Hotspur, the prince deflates his rhetoric with a medical image: "Hot
livers and cold purses" (line 307). "Choler, my lord, if rightly taken" (line
308), responds Bardolph, with mounting anger. "No, if rightly taken,
halter" (line 309) is the prince's answer, an anticipation (like "I do") of
the sudden change into seriousness that marks his vow ("I do, I will") to
banish Falstaff later in the scene. The language of portents—and the
danger of trifling with them—recurs with multiple irony in III.ii as the
king describes his own miraculous popularity:

> By being seldom seen, I could not stir
> But, like a comet, I was wond'red at;
> That men would tell their children, "This is he!"
> Others would say, "Where? Which is Bolingbroke?"
>
> (III.ii.46–49)

Verbal echoes ("seldom seen" / "wond'red at") link the king's speech
back to Hal's soliloquy; Hal promises to imitate, not a comet, but the
sun. Association back to the tavern scene and the Welsh scene suggest
links between the king and Bardolph, Glendower, Falstaff, and the meteors of civil war.

Bardolph's "choler" and the "halter" awaiting him have another
proleptic function, too, in suggesting the fate that awaits the choleric

Hotspur. Hotspur's temper flares and spoils his teasing of Glendower: "I think there's no man speaks better Welsh. I'll to dinner" (III.i.50). The lame joke heightens the tension, and as Mortimer vainly attempts to make peace, Hotspur recovers to get off his best joke yet:

> *Glendower:* I can call spirits from the vasty deep.
> *Hotspur:* Why so can I, or so can any man;
> But will they come when you do call for them?
>
> (lines 53–55)

Glendower's alliance with the powers of darkness—treated lightly in II.iv but no joke to Henry and his messengers in I.i and I.iii—is here openly mocked. If Falstaff as a "white-bearded Satan" (II.iv.440) anticipates the Welsh magician, Hotspur imitates Hal. He forthrightly dismisses the evil old man—"O, while you live, tell truth and shame the devil!" (line 62)—just as Hal promises to banish plump Jack. To Mortimer, this is "unprofitable chat" (line 63).

Glendower, however, shifts from demonic boasts to military ones. His account of his victories over Henry comes straight out of the chronicles (although, again, we can quibble about dates: one of the defeats has yet to happen). In effect, he has been shamed into telling truth. Hotspur has won the first point, but Glendower now shifts strategies: "Come, here is the map" (line 70). The negotiations that follow take on a distinctly Faustian coloring.

For Shakespeare has clothed the historical Glendower in diabolic robes. From the first, the "shameless transformation" performed by the Welsh women has had its overtones of witchcraft; Mortimer's marriage is narrated by Henry in a way that suggests enchantment. In Glendower's conflicting claims that he is self-taught ("Where is he living . . . which calls me pupil or hath read to me," lines 44, 46) and that he was "trained up in the English court" (line 123), we can hear an echo of the equivocating Lucifer of the mystery plays, who instead of framing ditties with the other angels conspires against God's throne and falls from the sky like a meteor or comet.[12] Hal, as Prince of Wales, "never promiseth but he means to pay" (V.iv.42); Glendower's "promises are fair" (III.i.1), but he never arrives at Shrewsbury. The chronicles tell us he was never expected there; in Shakespeare, "overruled by prophecies" (IV.iv.18), he deliberately stays at home. Glendower's language, too, is charged with images of night and chaos. The conspirators "must steal and take no leave" (III.i.93) from their wives: we may recall Falstaff's perverse proposal to rename thieves "Diana's foresters . . . minions of the moon . . . under whose countenance we steal" (I.ii.27). "The moon shines fair, you may away by night," promises Glendower, later in the scene (III.i.140). He emphasizes the wild passion of Hotspur's and Mortimer's wives; their tears of parting become an apocalyptic "world of water shed" (line 94).

Thus, through charged language, echoes of medieval tradition, and distortion of source material, Owen Glendower becomes transformed into a devil. The process is analogous to the creation of Falstaff from padding and old theatrical traditions.[13] The next action of the scene, the quarrel over the map, also has a long tradition behind it. From *Gorboduc* on, division of the kingdom had been an unpleasant thing for Elizabethan theatergoers to watch. When Richard II, in *Woodstock,* asks his sycophants to "reach me the map" (IV.i.220) so that he can divide the plundered realm among them, he marks himself an irresponsible leader, following in the foolish steps of Gorboduc and the King Leir of chronicle and stage. "All this division business is fictitious," fulminated A. P. Rossiter in his edition of *Woodstock.* So is this division: the signers of the real Tripartite Indenture "planned to slice the country into petty kingdoms," but Hotspur, already dead, was not among them.[14] Yet it is Hotspur in this scene who quarrels most, sacrificing much audience sympathy as he behaves like a greedy child, even to the point of endorsing Worcester's inflammatory suggestion of diverting the channel with "a little charge" (line 112). Disregard for the unity of the land, dramatized by dividing the map and urging explosive alterations, evokes all the horror of civil war.

After a seemingly pointless discussion of poetry with Hotspur, Glendower gives way, and Hotspur praises himself as a sharp bargainer: "But in the way of bargain, mark ye me, / I'll cavil on the ninth part of a hair" (lines 137–38). The Faustian folly of this is clear enough, and the discussion of court poetry condemns Hotspur yet further. Glendower may be a fallen court poet, but Hotspur's repudiation of his language is too broad. The problem with his insensitivity becomes clear after Glendower has left to fetch the ladies—and "haste the writer" (line 141) of the pact. In his impatience, Hotspur derides the Welsh prophecies as "skimble-skamble stuff" (line 152). To a Tudor audience, however, the Welsh tradition is not to be taken lightly, and Hotspur has failed to realize how dangerously misapplied it is in this situation. Misreading of Merlin is no longer possible after Henry VII.[15]

But Hotspur's error is greater than this. He goes on to recount dozing off while Glendower chanted "the several devils' names / That were his lackeys" (lines 155–56). This is dangerous neglect at any time. Mortimer's praise of his "worthy" father-in-law ("profited / in strange concealments . . . bountiful / As mines of India," lines 164–67) is full of exotic menace. Yet Mortimer is under Glendower's spell—as we see later on—and he has it backwards:

> I warrant you that man is not alive
> Might so have tempted him as you have done
> Without the taste of danger and reproof.
>
> (lines 171–73)

Reproof will come at Shrewsbury. And the temptation remains at hand: playing Mephistophilis to Glendower's Lucifer is Worcester.

His only previous contribution to the scene has been the proposal to turn Trent with explosives. Otherwise he has stood silent by, watching.[16] Now he moves in to instruct Hotspur in "good manners" (as Hotspur calls them). His instruction anticipates the lesson in Machiavellian image management that the king will offer Hal, a prince who, as we know from the soliloquy, needs no such instruction. Hal's skillful offense is part of a program; his fault serves as foil to a planned and promised reformation. Hotspur's faults taint rather than set off his goodness, and Worcester must warn him of the impression they make:

> The least of which haunting a nobleman
> Loseth men's hearts, and leaves behind a stain
> Upon the beauty of all parts besides,
> Beguiling them of commendation.
>
> (lines 184–87)

Again we see the king's confrontation with his son played out in rehearsal, as a kind of parody. For while Worcester enacts Henry's attitude towards Hal in his chiding of Hotspur, Hotspur utterly rejects the kind of self-awareness Hal comes to embody in the play. He brusquely dismisses Worcester: "Well, I am schooled. Good manners be your speed" (line 188). Sitting up late with Glendower he "cried 'Hum' and 'Well, go to,' / But marked him not a word" (lines 156–57). Where Hal is acutely aware of the moral dangers that surround him, Hotspur is wilfully blind.

The entrance of the wives marks a complete change of pace and mood in the scene. Hotspur ceases to challenge Glendower's preeminence, and the Welsh magician dominates the stage. A non-Welsh-speaking audience must rely for information upon their eyes as the Welsh lady speaks: what they see is a strange triangle indeed. Mortimer and the Welsh lady gaze at each other, hold hands, kiss. Glendower, between them, interprets and controls. His daughter's grief, singled out for our notice by Glendower, and Mortimer's despairing passion ("O, I am ignorance itself in this!" line 210) emphasize the young couple's total dependence on the old wizard. The language of Mortimer's bondage is conventionally erotic:

> thy tongue
> Makes Welsh as sweet as ditties highly penned,
> Sung by a fair queen in a summer's bow'r,
> With ravishing division, to her lute.
>
> (lines 205–8)

The language also evokes the dispute about courtly lyric earlier in the scene, and the pun in line 207 offers a perversely Spenserian echo. *Division*, a word central to the play and the scene for its political significance, is here applied to music, sensuality, ravishment.

Mortimer is under a spell, bewitched. As Glendower describes the effect the lady's song will have upon him— "Charming your blood with pleasing heaviness" (line 215)—Mortimer's response links his sensual bondage to the indenture: "With all my heart I'll sit and hear her sing. / By that time will our book, I think, be drawn" (lines 220–21). Spell and contract merge; Glendower calls for music. The abrupt reminder of the political purpose for this gathering switches our attention back to the Percies: Hotspur, his wife, and uncle Worcester have been present on the stage throughout.

As an onstage audience, they transform the love scene and the love song into a cautionary play-within-a-play. Mortimer, tearful, uxorious, lyrical, is a far cry from the images of him as valiant and noble (according to Hotspur) or rebellious and treacherous (according to the king) that were promulgated in 1.iii. The vanity and folly of a conspiracy to restore his title is hammered home. In the previous scene, we have seen Hal "depose" Falstaff and "banish" him; here we see Mortimer, "next of blood" though he may be, utterly lost to vanity. The language barrier insists upon his helplessness; Hal's language—"I do, I will"—is the emphatic and solemn language of a vow in which word and deed agree. The echo of marriage vows in the tavern scene—in effect, Hal vows to divorce Falstaff and marry his kingdom—receives added emphasis in the stage picture of Mortimer's absorption into Glendower's enchanted, empty realm.

Mortimer's problems with Welsh highlight Hal's fluency, his potential of becoming (in Joseph A. Porter's words) "a many-tongued monarch." Language jokes dominate the last moments of the Welsh scene, just as they did the first. As the Percies mock the lovesickness of the other couple, Glendower illustrates the power of his words by calling for music. David Woodman has it that Glendower hereby "silences" Hotspur with his magical prowess, but Hotspur chatters on, unconcerned.[17] His only response is another Welsh joke: "Now I perceive the devil understands Welsh" (line 228). In this context, the relevance of Hotspur's double-edged sex banter and volubility on the subject of a "good mouth-filling oath" (line 252) becomes both clearer and more complex. Kate's refusal to sing ("Not mine, in good sooth," line 244) echoes Hal's refusal to continue playing along with Falstaff. Hotspur's jests raise once again that abundance of doubts about the connection between word and deed, promise and performance, that plagues the play from the very beginning. In fact, King Henry's "holy purpose—now twelve month old"—introduces the play only to be forgotten, thrust aside by news of civil strife. Hal's vow to redeem himself and his country plays off against this first unkept promise, as does Hotspur's demand in the third scene that his uncle and father redeem their "banished honors." The quarrel at the beginning of III.i—like Hotspur's quarrel with the king over the denial of his prisoners and like the exposure of Falstaff's lies in II.iv—is animated by warring notions of language as power and language as vanity.

In Glendower, as in the resourceful Falstaff, these apparent oppositions merge. As he is a magician, his language is incantatory and demonstrably spellbinding; as he is an ally in the rebel cause, he is boastful and unreliable. The paradox is emphasized by verbal and theatrical pointers that link Glendower to an alter ego, the Father of Lies, a presence who lurks behind Falstaff as well. The suggestion that Hotspur has signed a damnable pact is playfully made by Glendower himself:

Come, come, Lord Mortimer. You are as slow
As hot Lord Percy is on fire to go.
By this our book is drawn; we'll but seal,
And then to horse immediately.

(lines 260–63)

Hotspur hurtles headlong to destruction. Hal's oaths in the next scene are validated by the empty contract of the Tripartite Indenture.

But not for long: Shakespeare does not neglect in the final scene the ambiguities he has labored so hard to rouse here. Hal's triumph in deed over Hotspur and his eulogy over the fallen Falstaff are both swallowed up by the fat man's resurrection. Furthermore, Falstaff's outrageous tale of dueling counterfeits makes the prince into Falstaff's "factor / To engross up glorious deeds on my behalf" (III.ii.147–48). Falstaff's appropriation of the corpse of Hotspur parodies the most serious promise of the royal interview, and Hal permits the transfer of honors to take place: "For my part, if a lie may do thee grace, / I'll gild it with the happiest terms I have." (v.v.153–54). The prince's retreat into falsehood sabotages the neat equations of the moralized spectacle in which he has bid farewell in turn to Hotspur (vanity of spirit) and Falstaff (vanity of the flesh).[18]

The technique of speaking pictures, iconic images, moralized spectacle, that Shakespeare inherited from medieval and Renaissance traditions of theatrical practice and theory is here used with uncommon force against itself.[19] Each moment seems potent with emblematic resonance, loaded with significances religious, political, historical, and yet the lessons apparently to be drawn are confuted and questioned by the action of the rest of the play. In the Welsh scene, there is an iconic center in which two moments of strong visual impact play off against each other: the quarrel over the map and the love scene between Mortimer and the Welsh lady. Each draws upon a tradition in visual and verbal art. The map scene reaches back into a homiletic tradition as an emblem of the "Serpent of division";[20] the splitting of a single Edenic Britain by vanity and ambition into warring parts is the essence of the Leir story, of *Gorboduc,* and of the map scene in *Woodstock.* The love scene is equally traditional: the pastoral bower in which Mortimer is invited to repose is the same abode of sensual self-abandonment that Guyon must destroy in book 2 of the *Faerie Queen.* The unchaste chatter of Hotspur and Lady Percy reinforces the picture of Glendower's castle as a place of incontinence. These lessons, the one political and the other moral, work together to show in different ways the folly and evil of rebellion. The "polyphonic" or "prismatic" complexity of technique forbids the drawing of simple conclusions from the scene.[21] Rather, the actions of the characters take place in a context charged with multiple historical and religious meanings.

The centerpiece of the learning experience in III.i is Glendower. He produces the map; he introduces the ladies. He "stages" both parts of the scene, even to the point of announcing the moral of each. We are invited to see him at once as a damnable magician and a lyrical framer of ditties. As a creature compound of vanities, Glendower should be dismissed, shamed, banished by the telling of truth. Hotspur knows this, but he blindly rushes on; Hal, acutely conscious of his own moral status, elects to gild Falstaff's lies at the end. And the chaos of Wales frames the whole play.

Shakespearean history, as we see it in this scene and in *1 Henry IV* as a whole dramatic experience, is history moralized even as the act of moralization is sharply questioned. The key technique is the emblematic scene, with its host of traditional associations, but Shakespeare, like the banished duke in *As You Like It,* is of two minds about its efficacy. "Did he not moralize the spectacle?" asks the duke of the lords who tell the story of Jaques and the deer (II.i.44). The lessons Jaques draws from the deer are trenchant, the activity of extracting them ridiculously compulsive. Similarly, the Welsh scene of *1 Henry IV* demands and confutes moralized interpretation. Hotspur palters with the devil; Mortimer is in his thrall. Together these would-be princes are associated with Glendower's monstrous imposture. Hal's vow to his father in the royal interview plays off against this foil and against the tavern scene; but with equal force these two rehearsals for the true prince's self-revelation call into question its spontaneity and authenticity. Somehow, too, Hotspur retains his attractiveness, even though he dies irrepressibly vain. Glendower and Wales remain to be tamed. Falstaff, his banishment promised in II.iv and the spectacle of his death moralized in v.iv, rises again, graced with the prince's lies.

ii

The evocation of moral patterns and rhetorical lessons is more straightforward and less qualified in Shakespeare's earlier history plays. Nonetheless, even in *1 Henry VI* the lessons of history are put to severe tests. A key scene in this play is II.iii, in which the nature of Talbot's heroism receives emblematic demonstration when the countess is surprised to find herself face to face with "this weak and writhled shrimp" (II.iii.23). But Talbot matches his unconventional appearance with a startling revelation of his true greatness:

> You are deceived, my substance is not here;
> For what you see is but the smallest part
> And least proportion of humanity.
> I tell you, madam, were the whole frame here,
> It is of such a spacious lofty pitch
> Your roof were not sufficient to contain't.

> (lines 51–56)

This powerful speech identifies the heroic ideal outside of Talbot's body and in his humanity; the gigantic whole to which he refers is a community, a united, fighting England, represented on stage by the troops who answer his call on the horn. The demonstration is, however, futile. From the play's first scene the "whole frame" has threatened to disintegrate from the pressure of faction, as the nobles quarrel over Henry V's bier. The abandonment of Talbot by York and Somerset (IV.iii) gives the lie to

Talbot's noble vision; in a last, grating irony, Shakespeare recapitulates the Auvergne scene after Talbot's death.

This time it is the English messenger, Lucy, who makes the mistake of identifying Talbot with Hercules:

> But where's the great Alcides of the field,
> Valiant Lord Talbot, Earl of Shrewsbury,
> Created for his rare success in arms
> Great earl of Washford, Waterford, and Valence,
> Lord Talbot of Goodrig and Urchinfield,
> Lord Strange of Blackmere, Lord Verdun of Alton,
> Lord Cromwell of Wingfield, Lord Furnival of Sheffield,
> The thrice victorious Lord of Falconbridge,
> Knight of the noble order of Saint George,
> Worthy Saint Michael, and the Golden Fleece,
> Great Marshal to Henry the Sixth
> Of all his wars within the realm of France?
>
> (IV.vii.60–71)

Again, a French woman, wily and deceitful, boasts over the feebleness of Talbot's body, but with a difference, for Talbot now belongs to the community of the dead:

> Here's a silly stately style indeed!
> The Turk, that two and fifty kingdoms hath,
> Writes not so tedious a style as this.
> Him that thou magnifi'st with all these titles,
> Stinking and flyblown lies here at our feet.
>
> (lines 72–76)

Here the mirror-scenes that are the basic building block of Shakespearean drama cast a gruesome reflection. Talbot's generous and human heroism, his recognition of himself as a small part of a great and glorious endeavor, is recalled just as it is brutally confuted by the structural similarity of the two moments.

In another basic dramatic strategy, scenes play off, not against a memory of previous scenes, but against traditional scenic patterns. Emrys Jones demonstrates parallelisms between York tormented on the molehill in *3 Henry VI* and the crucifixion plays in the old mystery cycles.[22] Humphrey, in *2 Henry VI,* gives a morality-play coloring to his demise: "Virtue is choked with foul ambition," he warns the king (III.i.143). He portrays his doom as a theatrical one:

But mine is made the prologue to their play,
For thousands more, that yet suspect no peril,
Will not conclude their plotted tragedy.

(lines 150–52)

When Warwick confronts the king and the conspirators with
Humphrey's body—and through the technical vividness of his language
forces the audience to see it as well—the metaphoric choking of virtue by
ambition becomes concrete:

But see, his face is black and full of blood;
His eyeballs further out than when he lived,
Staring full ghastly, like a strangled man.

(III.ii.168–70)

A rhetorical trope becomes a dramatic reality.

The grisly images of flyblown Talbot and strangled Humphrey are
epitomes of the plays in which they appear; what is striking about a
mature historical play like *1 Henry IV* is the evocation, as we have seen in
III.i, of multiple epitomizing images of this kind. The damnation of
Hotspur is acted out as a kind of cautionary drama for Hal, who also
trifles dangerously with Satan; but Hotspur becomes himself audience
to the morality play of Mortimer's bondage. Traditional patterns and
images refuse to stay put as they do in the earlier history plays. Hal,
Hotspur, Mortimer, and Glendower merge as pretenders to princehood;
Falstaff, King Henry, Worcester, and Glendower merge as misleaders of
youth. The clear rhetorical lesson that each scene seems to offer is undercut and questioned even as it is taught.

This dramatic complexity is not unique to the histories, but it is
historical in its very nature. The revolution in Renaissance historiography in which Shakespeare's history plays figure prominently centers
around the problem of how to moralize the past. The medieval position,
as enunciated in Augustine's *City of God*, is strongly providential: history
is the arena of God's judgment; the falls of proud kings are cautionary
tales played out in a divine theater before His watchful eye. Undeserved
sufferings are merely felt to be undeserved; if we cannot understand why
bad men prosper, it is because we do not have God's omniscience. The
humanist challenge to Augustinian providentialism came from Machiavelli and in England from historians and antiquaries like Bacon and
Selden. Though perceived as such in the sixteenth century, Machiavelli's
attitude is not basically incompatible with a Christian view. Accepting
the impossibility of detecting with certainty God's judgments before the

Last Day, Machiavelli searched history for mortal lessons, examples of successful and unsuccessful statecraft, the nuts and bolts of politics. Shakespeare's historiography incorporates elements of both attitudes.[23] Actions in the world of *1 Henry IV* are, as we have seen, charged with religious significance, but it is a world governed by manipulation, deception, and division. Just as Shakespeare's theater is a mixed medium—a secular, professional, illusionistic theater with roots in a religious, amateur, typological tradition—so is the chronicle history he used for his sources. However providential their rhetoric, the authors of Holinshed and other historians, especially Hall and Polydore Vergil, have a strong partisan bias and a worldly mistrust of the professed piety of their characters.[24] Because of its scriptural tradition, providential history is necessarily the history of God's chosen people or favorite nation; the old language provides theoretical justification for the emerging doctrine of centralized national authority.

Renaissance historians invoked and revoked providential explanations at will, usually in response to the political preferences of their patrons. The divinely ordered and hierarchically arranged Elizabethan world picture that has been so severely debunked by recent critics remained, through the seventeenth century, a useful propaganda tool, even as contemporary historians departed more from the humanist or providential models and patterned their craft upon the new sciences.[25] In Shakespeare's history plays we find the same kind of coexistence: hard analysis of policy and character takes place *sub spaeculo aeternitatis*. Both the political folly and the damnability of rebellion receive equal stress.

The one factor that tends to sabotage serious discussion of Shakespeare as a dramatic historian is his cavalier attitude towards his sources. In III.i, he dramatizes a meeting that never took place, confusing it with an agreement reached years later. Mortimer is a conflation of two people, himself and his uncle; the ages of principal characters have been readjusted at will. Hotspur, in history a little older than the king, becomes the same age as his son. The reasons generally given for these readjustments stress their antihistorical nature: dramatic economy demands a single Mortimer; dramatic impact demands a negotiation between Hotspur and the Welsh leader; dramatic construction demands that the prince and his rival be of the same age. But the historians from whom Shakespeare drew his material were guilty of the same faults: the drawing of parallels and analogies, the allegorization of historical personages, the telescoping of a lifetime into a fable.

We should be chary of seeing these rhetorical strategies as medieval holdovers; Plutarch's parallel lives of the Greeks and Romans served as a model for humanist historians. Machiavelli's *Discourses* mined Roman history for instructive analogies; Tacitus's *Annals* were understood to "shadow" in their accounts of earlier tyrannies the more recent depredations of Domitian.[26] In a sense, Shakespeare's alterations are in keeping with contemporary ideas of acceptable historical practice. The pointing up of lessons through traditional homiletic devices, where Shakespeare, unlike the historian, has a whole popular stage tradition behind him, is responsible history writing, as is the drawing of connections between seemingly unlike personages in different eras. The evocation of the Welsh prophecies in III.i is as historical in impulse as the co-optation of Arthurian legend by Polydore Vergil; legendary material received serious consideration even from those seventeenth-century historians who, like Milton, denied its historicity.[27]

Thus if it is critically dangerous to describe, in terms of a world picture, *what* the Elizabethan audience believed, Tillyard's system nonetheless helps us to understand *how* they believed. The mirror-scenes and verbal anticipations and echoes that animate Shakespeare's plays were used by his contemporaries as well; the tendency to draw homiletic conclusions from juxtaposed parallel lives seems pretty nearly universal. Shakespeare merely heightens it to an unheard-of degree. Each scene in *1 Henry IV* is, as we have suggested, a little play in its own right, grounded in morality tradition;[28] once we begin to look at these playlets closely, emblematic units within each begin to proliferate like Chinese boxes. Hotspur becomes audience to the drama of Glendower's enchantment of Mortimer; Hal's soliloquy uncomfortably suggests that he is consciously playing the roles of lusty Juventus, Prodigal Son, warrior-prince that we see him play.[29]

One might expect this self-conscious theatricality to heighten an audience's sense of the artificiality or fictiveness of Shakespearean history. But what instead results is a sense of the essentially fictive quality of historical endeavor itself. For Shakespeare turns his audience's tendency (whether the audience is considered to be Elizabethan or modern) to rationalize and moralize the spectacle before them against itself. Falstaff's destruction of Hal's paradigmatic triumph over vanity insists on the intractability of life. The historian's desire to find articulate moral patterns in the past—indulged in throughout the play by the audience—remains unsatisfied. Hal must reform all over again in *Part 2,* and in *Henry V* the epic, historical, narrative voice of the Chorus is severely challenged by the very actions it glorifies and presents.[30]

The desire to make order out of the past is most horribly exploited in *King Lear. Lear* relies more heavily than any of the tragedies upon chronicle tradition, and the most striking feature of the play as history is Shakespeare's total rejection of the story as the tradition invariably presents it.[31] The shifting of the Tripartite Indenture ahead in time to include Hotspur is a pardonable lapse; the killing of Cordelia is not. All of the sources—and they reach back to ancient legends of Brute—allow, where there is a good daughter or son, for the king's reunion with the good child. And Shakespeare's play forces its audience to expect this traditional ending, just as Kent and the Gentleman, in III.i, seem to expect the civil war between the sons-in-law that the tradition describes but the play does not provide.

The emblematic description of Cordelia as a redemptive presence— "There she shook / The holy water from her heavenly eyes" (IV.iii.30)— and its fulfillment in the kneeling together of father and daughter in IV.vii, are presented with such poetic and dramatic power as to make its refutation unconscionable. Lear's vision of life in prison is a return to that speechless moment of reunion in: "When thou dost ask me blessing, I'll kneel down / And ask of thee forgiveness" (V.i.10–11). It is a vision outside time and politics, similar to Lear's earlier vision of retirement as an "unburdened crawl toward death" (I.i.41). "Take them away," Edmund orders after this speech (V.iii.19); the reminder that the world exists in time and is governed by governors is blunt and brutal. The delays, the false endings, the ceremonious circumlocutions of Edgar's self-vindication all drag on until— "Great thing of us forgot!"—Albany (V.iii.237) and the audience remember that this elaborate tying up of loose ends is not to the main point. The theatrical and religious ironies of Kent's "Is this the promised end?" (V.iii.264) have been so extensively explored that only a word on their historical resonance is in order.

The desire, on the part of all the "good" characters in the play, to vindicate the gods and prove them to be just tempts them into providential readings of the sufferings they endure. Albany's response to the death of Cornwall—"This shows you are above, / You justicers" (IV.ii.78–79)—is a reflex, like Edgar's attempts to provide stoic rationalizations for his plight and cure his father's despair. The patterns Albany, Kent, and Edgar seek to apply to the play's experience are theatrical, conventional, homiletic, and, most importantly, historical.[32] The reunion of Lear and Cordelia, and the restoration of Lear to his throne is the "promis'd end" of history itself. Shakespeare permits the reunion. But it is not so much Edmund's unscrupulousness that sentences Cordelia to death as Edgar's long drawn-out morality play of restoration and Albany's moralization of the deaths of Goneril and Regan as a "judgment of the heavens." History itself—truth itself, for this is what Cordelia embodies from the first—is destroyed, "ended," by moralizing it; silent Cordelia monopolizes our eyes ("Look there, look there," v.iii.312) while Edgar (at least in the Folio) articulately (and falsely) moralizes the spectacle: "Speak what we feel, not what we ought to say," v.iii.325). The paradox of the experience of *Lear* is that somehow the play's failure to fulfill its historical pattern seems more "true" than the pattern itself. Tate's *Lear,* which, after all, does go back to the source in restoring a happy ending, is now derided, the old *Chronicle History of King Leir* unread.

The lessons of history, both political and religious, pale in a context that holds that the teaching and deriving of lessons from experience is as foolish an endeavor as dividing a kingdom or seeking to quantify love. Elements of this tragic rejection of historical practice can be found in the history plays as well. In the first tetralogy, the plays explore a period in history that the Tudor apologists and chroniclers had understood as a kind of morality drama about the need for obedience to lawful monarchs and the dangers of civil strife. Such lessons do indeed seem to be taught in the three Henry VI plays, but *Richard III* poses special problems. Wilbur Sanders has complained, "If [Shakespeare] was planning to exemplify the simplified monarchic theory of Tudor propaganda, it was a singularly unhappy choice of subject. One might as well try to justify papal infallibility by writing a play about the Avignon schism."[33] His affinities with the ever-popular Vice of morality tradition alter utterly the monstrous usurper of More's Richard III. Shakespeare's Richard performs the same crimes, but delights the audience while doing so; his loss of zest upon gaining the kingship loses the audience's sympathy. The theatrical experience of the play challenges the historical lesson: where the chroniclers celebrate the coming of Richmond as an end to civil unrest, Shakespeare leaves the audience flat.

The tension between theatrical experience and historical moral is higher in the second tetralogy. Richard II's image of twin buckets in a well (IV.i.185) provides an epitome of the dialectical pressure of the play: Shakespeare provides us with a vacillating, vain, corrupt, and contemptible king through the first half of the play and then reverses his strategy, transforming these faults, not into virtues, but into irrelevancies. Bolingbroke's peremptory "lopping off" of Bushy and Green (II.iv) is a literal, historical anticipation of the highly figural garden scene (III.iv). Following as it does upon the execution, the homiletic lesson the Gardener draws from his "commonwealth" seems reductionist. As in the writing of history, the event precedes the moral; and the two do not really match.

The multiple ironies of *1 Henry IV* come to a climax on the battlefield with the proliferation of counterfeit kings and with Falstaff's
counterfeit death. The patterns of restoration and reformation that the
play, its sources, and its central actor, the prince, have promised from the
outset are fulfilled only to be overturned. Rumor, "stuffing the ears of
men with false reports" (I.i.8), introduces *Part 2;* the affirmations of
Hal's heroism in the first play give way to the chicanery of Prince John in
Gaultree Forest. The unreliability of Rumor, the falsehood of John, the
misunderstanding between prince and king when Hal mistakes his father
for dead and takes his crown, all spin out of the retrospective central
scene in which Henry and Warwick discuss the uncertainties of history
and the inexorability of time. Henry's vision of history is apocalyptic:

> O God! That one might read the book of fate
> And see the revolution of the times
> Make mountains level, and the continent,
> Weary of solid firmness, melt itself
> Into the sea!
>
> (III.i.45–49)

The threat of watery chaos, embodied, as we have seen in *1 Henry IV,* in
Falstaff and Glendower, is immanent, from the beginning, in the book of
history—a book that in Henry's speech is both Genesis and Revelation, a
chaos of beginning and end. But Henry's religious reading of Richard's
prophecy is answered by Warwick's secular, historical perspective:

> There is a history in all men's lives,
> Figuring the nature of the times deceased,
> The which observed, a man may prophesy,
> With a near aim, of the main chance of things
> As yet not come to life, which in their seeds
> And weak beginnings lie intreasured.
>
> (lines 80–85)

The terms of discussion here at the center of *2 Henry IV* echo Renaissance
debates about history. Henry's language is providential, scriptural; Warwick explains Richard's prophecy in secular, Machiavellian terms.

The second part of *Henry IV,* then, brings to the surface questions
latent in the first part and central to a discussion of historical drama.
Warwick's historical counsel seems to answer Henry's immediate question about prophecy, but a far larger question goes unanswered: "Are
these things then necessities?" (III.i.92). Henry's portrayal of himself as a
humble agent of providence—"But that necessity so bowed the

state / That I and greatness were compelled to kiss" (lines 73–74)—begs judgments that historians, and audiences of history plays, are bound to make. Whether the four plays were designed as a tetralogy or not, certainly this scene looks back on the events of *Richard II* and *1 Henry IV,* and the king's self-image here is not altogether borne out by his actions in the earlier plays. But the mood of retrospection and resignation evoked in the scene is so powerful, and the king's despair so palpable, that the repetition of his futile purpose—"We would, dear lords, unto the Holy Land" (line 108)—draws compassion.

The question whether it is possible to understand a life lived, like Henry's, in the political arena in religious terms is important not only to Shakespeare but to all Renaissance historians. Humanist historians, following Machiavelli's example, eschewed religious judgments, with the consequence, in Sanders's rather harsh words, that they "abdicated a whole province of historical thought—the province of ultimate significance."[34] Rejection of moral, traditional patterns of understanding, based upon Christian typology, leads too easily to a vision, like Henry's, of a watery world of chance and flux. Henry's despair arises from the knowledge that in Christian terms his acts are sins demanding expiation and that in secular terms the fact that they can be seen as political necessities offers no consolation or explanation of their importance. If, in Shakespeare's histories, the moral patterns of traditional judgment are contradicted by the flux and variety of life itself, life, although constantly threatening to dissolve into Henry's chaos, does not do so. Henry does die in "Jerusalem."

Henry V picks up these speculations on historical understanding more explicitly through the demands the Chorus makes of the audience. Here the challenge is not latent in the play's design (as in *Richard II* and *1 Henry IV*) or engaged primarily by a character (as in *2 Henry IV*), but is explicitly thrown into the spectator's lap. The prologue's demand that we supply the scenery for this pageant insists upon the vanity of the whole project:

> But pardon, gentles all,
> The flat unraised spirits that hath dared
> On this unworthy scaffold to bring forth
> So great an object.
>
> (lines 8–11)

Traditional apologies for history plays, like Heywood's, relied upon the audience's identification with the heroes of the past, defined in an illusionistic way:

> What English prince should hee behold the true portrature
> of that [f]amous king Edward the third, foraging France,
> taking so great a king captive in his owne country,
> quartering the English Lyons with the French flower-delyce,
> and would not bee suddenly inflam'd with so royal a
> spectacle, being made apt and fit for the like atchievement.
> So of Henry the fift.[35]

The preconceptions here deserve some scrutiny: Heywood assumes, as Sidney does in his famous discussion of the usefulness of tragedy, that the proper audience for a history play is a royal one, and that the play's lessons will lead to imitative action.[36] Shakespeare's prologue toys with the figure, invoking this ideal—"a kingdom for a stage, princes to act / And monarchs to behold the swelling scene" (prologue, 3–4)—and debunking it. The stage is a wooden *O;* the actors professionals of the trade; the audience, at best, made up of "gentles." And it is the task of their "imaginary forces" to make the action seem important.

Thus we have, as many critics have pointed out in different ways, two plays going on: the Chorus introduces as glorious, epic, and brilliant, actions that belie the buildup. Again, as in the previous history plays, tension is drawn between the events themselves and the ways in which they are interpreted. Here, however, the burden of interpretation falls upon the audience itself; the simple contrast the Chorus paints between "true things" and "mock'ries" is not that simple—radiating out into questions about relationships between staged illusions of reality and historical truths, between historians' accounts of the past and the events themselves, between epic inflation and comic deflation.[37] In its explicit questioning of the assumptions implicit in such formulations of the usefulness of heroic historical dramas as Heywood's, *Henry V* is a fitting end to the series of Lancastrian plays. But its explicitness poses certain theatrical problems. Where, in *1 Henry IV,* the desire to perceive actions as morally and aesthetically resonant according to preconceived patterns is simultaneously stimulated and confuted, here the Chorus's demands are blunt and unmediated. Instead of being forced to reenact the experience of making sense of the past, the audience is asked only to place the Chorus's formulations and the events it witnesses side-by-side.[38] "Behold, as may unworthiness define, / A little touch of Harry in the night" (lines 46–47), urges the Chorus to act IV: what we see instead of the king bestowing a "largess universal, like the sun" (act IV, chorus, line 43) is the king skulking about the camp in disguise, quarreling with Bates and Williams and getting the worst of it, and bemoaning the "hard condition" of royalty in language reminiscent of Henry IV's despair. The irony is as blunt as the ironies of the first history plays. In *1 Henry IV* the sense that life simultaneously arranges itself into morally articulate patterns and confutes them animates the whole play; *Henry V* is dominated instead by the skepticism about the usefulness of moral history and moralized spectacle that later achieves its fullest expression in *King Lear*.

Shakespeare's discontent with historical practice has political as well as philosophical dimensions. Henry V, like Edward IV, caused problems for historians who wanted to depict the years between the deposition of Richard II and the coronation of Henry VII as an uninterrupted dark age of civil war. Prince Hal in *1 Henry IV* prefigures in some ways Henry Tudor; here in *Henry V,* on the other hand, the analogy is drawn to Essex, "from Ireland coming / Bringing rebellion broachèd on his sword" (act v, chorus, lines 31–32). The change in perspective is significant. One need not agree with Evelyn May Albright's vision of Shakespeare's audience as a circle of Essex supporters to recognize the topicality of the reference. Where the reference to contemporary politics in the other Lancastrian plays is oblique, these lines draw attention to themselves. The relationship between the Lord Chamberlain's Men and the Essex rising is lost in the murky reaches of Privy Council deliberations; we know the actors revived *Richard II* at the request of Sir Gilly Meyrick, one of Essex's followers, and that they were not punished for it.[39] But before dismissing *Henry V* as partisan propaganda, we should recognize that the two opposed readings are latent in the words themselves. Rebellion can be broached ("transfixed") or broached ("set on foot, started, introduced") on Essex's sword: wordplay of this kind may bespeak caution on Shakespeare's part, or the pun may be designed to frustrate any attempt to read the play as propaganda at all.

The issue of contemporary reference itself is explicitly raised in the play, suggesting that the selection of the double-edged word may not be merely playful. The pedant Fluellen is a military historian and a drawer of parallels: "If you mark Alexander's life well, Harry of Monmouth's life is come after it indifferent well; for there is figures in all things" (IV.vii.29–30). The analogies are ridiculous; the only one that strikes home is the one that Fluellen has most trouble with, that between Alexander's drunken murder of his old friend Cleitus and Hal's sober dismissal of the drunkard Falstaff. Through Fluellen, Shakespeare mocks the contemporary practice of using history as a source of specious heroic parallels, yet Fluellen's failure to remember Falstaff's name suggests that the parallel has an unpleasant validity. When we remember that Essex was likewise paralleled to Alexander by his supporters, we recognize that Shakespeare is again teasing the tendency to draw historical analogies even as he critiques it.[40]

The devious double meaning of *broached* and the simultaneous debunking and suggesting of historical analogies through Fluellen partakes of the doubleness of a play that is at once patriotic pageant and antiwar satire. Instead of resolving its complicated political vision, the play retreats into domesticity as King Henry woos Katherine. But there is no real conflict between the public and private man in this play: just as, after the debate with Bates and Williams, Henry presents himself as a king in a private moment, here he plays the role of bluff, wooing soldier almost to excess. Critics who become indignant at the king's apparent lack of a private self miss the point: Hal has become a wholly public man.[41] Like Alexander, he is essentially unknowable but infinitely adaptable to different situations; he is a figure, a rhetorical device.

The protean nature of King Henry V disappoints because the prince of the earlier plays could be seen making morally significant choices; here none occur. The reasons for invading France are so obscure as to be ludicrous; victory is foreordained. In the prologue to the play, the Chorus, celebrating the victory before it occurs, promises the fulfillment of the kind of clear historical pattern that Shakespeare undermines in the earlier plays. The series of triumphs that culminates in the wooing of Katherine is qualified only by the epilogue, reminding us of the infant Henry VI:

> Whose state so many had the managing
> That they lost France and made his England bleed:
> Which oft our stage hath shown.
>
> (lines 11–13)

In *2 Henry IV*, Glendower dies and Falstaff is rejected; their destructive powers are subsumed into the conventional historiography of *Henry V*. Instead, Shakespeare's unease with historical patterns shows itself in his deviousness about contemporary applications and in his opaque protagonist. In both respects, *Henry V* anticipates the last history play, *Henry VIII*, more clearly than might be expected.

iii

The controversy over this late play's authorship reaches beyond the metric tests applied by Spedding, Alexander, and Partridge (with widely varying results) to debate about the structure, mood, and historiography of the play. Ornstein, the strongest modern proponent of Fletcherian authorship, derides those who, like Foakes, Kermode, and Felperin, portray Henry "as the Prospero of the history plays": "Critics cannot debate, . . . whether Henry is compassionate or callous, noble or contemptible; they can only debate whether the amorphousness and ambiguity of his characterization are artistically defensible or appropriate."[42] Henry VIII shares the opacity of Henry V; the late play, like its predecessor, refuses us an understanding of the public man.

More explicitly and more belligerently than *Henry V,* the play goes beyond ambiguous portrayal of the king to challenge, not the players' ability to stage the glories of the past—as in the *Henry V* prologue—but the audience's ability to make imaginative sense out of it. "I come no more to make you laugh" (line 1), says the Prologue, dismissing out of hand comparison between this play and the comical histories in which a disguised Henry VIII has been appearing recently upon the stage.[43] "Such noble scenes as draw the eye to flow, / We now present" (lines 4–5), runs the promise; the Prologue insistently warns the audience not to laugh:

> For, gentle hearers, know
> To rank our chosen truth with such a show
> As fool and fight is, beside forfeiting
> Our own brains and the opinion that we bring
> To make that only true we now intend,
> Will leave us never an understanding friend.
>
> (lines 17–22)

Linked to the solemnity and sobriety of the Prologue is the play's "truth": unlike the merry, bawdy plays it displaces, in *Henry VIII,* as the subtitle reminds us, *All is True;* all we need do is sit quietly and watch.

We are even told explicitly how to understand what we see:

> Think ye see
> The very persons of our noble story
> As they were living. Think you see them great,
> And followed with the general throng and sweat
> Of thousand friends. Then, in a moment, see
> How soon this mightiness meets misery.
>
> (lines 25–30)

The pattern is moralistic, traditional, and homiletic. The falls are emblematic and instructive. The audience is not asked, as in the Lancastrian plays, to indulge in its own search for historical meaning; the meaning is already distilled.

Yet the complicated expression of the players' intention—"the opinion that we bring / To make that only true we now intend"—is curiously ambiguous. It can suggest the author's and actors' belief that the play will contain only true facts. Or the lines can be read as a solipsistic insistence that the audience must accept whatever "opinion" the actors dramatize as true. The second reading suggests mere perverseness; yet, comparing the promises of the Prologue to the practice in the play, even Tillyard complained of the Prologue's "wanton lies."[44]

Despite its demands that the audience weep and its delineations of a tragic *de casibus* structure for the play, the Prologue introduces a play whose basic rhythm is comic: the falls of the mighty are subsumed into the more glorious process of the birth of Elizabeth. The last challenge is particularly grating: "And if you can be merry then, I'll say / A man may weep upon his wedding day" (lines 31–32). Whether or not *Henry VIII* was designed as a commemoration of Princess Elizabeth's wedding, the wedding of Henry and Anne Boleyn is the central event of the play.[45] The scenes devoted to this wedding do belie the Prologue by demanding a mixed response of pity and mirth. The pageantry of Anne's coronation procession (IV.i) and the Third Gentleman's description of the full ceremony take place immediately after Wolsey's fall and just before Katherine's farewell to life. Furthermore, the Gentlemen in IV.i remind us of Buckingham's fall ("'Tis very true, but that time offered sorrow / This, general joy," lines 6–7), of Katherine's sickness (line 35), and of the king's seizure of Wolsey's palace (lines 94–96). All this sorrow is displaced by more timely mirth. "These are stars indeed," sighs the Second Gentleman as the countesses bring up the rear of the procession. "And sometimes falling ones," quips the first, drawing for his bawdy remark a sharp "No more of that" (lines 54–55). This levity is coupled with jests about the divorce—"I cannot blame his conscience" (line 97)—that verge on poor taste.[46] In fact, both laughing and weeping are the only possible responses to this wedding day. The sad falls of Buckingham, Katherine, and Wolsey are mentioned in the same breath as the falling stars of the court. In its stress on the uniform solemnity of the tale, the Prologue seems to forget that the play will ask us to rejoice in the royal wedding and celebrate the birth of the royal child.

The discrepancy here is too fundamental to be the result of mere sloppiness. There are other instances in which the promises of the Prologue are disregarded. "Those that come to see / Only a show or two," we are assured, "may see away their shilling / Richly in two short hours," (lines 9–10, 12–13); the affinity between the pageantry of *Henry VIII* and the spectacular staging of court masques has received much discussion from critics.[47] But the play offers as well some examples of pageantry foregone: the opening scene contains Norfolk's lengthy descriptions of the shows and masques accompanying the peace between Henry and Francis. He stresses the visual splendor of the event, dubbing himself "ever since a fresh admirer / Of what I saw there" (lines 3–4). Seeing is believing, as the Prologue suggests, and chivalric fiction is validated by spectacle in Norfolk's account of the passage at arms:

> they did perform
> Beyond the thought's compass, that former fabulous story,
> Being now seen possible enough, got credit,
> That Bevis was believed.
>
> (lines 35–38)

"O you go far," marvels Buckingham; like the audience, he is staggered, not by sumptuous spectacle, but by sumptuous description. Similarly, we are not permitted to view the glorious coronation of Queen Anne, though we do see the procession pass by. But the Third Gentleman did see it, and he teases his interlocutors:

> *1 Gent.:* God save you sir. Where have you been broiling?
> *3 Gent.:* Among the crowd i'th'Abbey, where a finger
> Could not be wedged in more. I am stifled
> With the mere rankness of their joy.
> *2 Gent.:*   You saw
> The ceremony?
> *3 Gent.:*   That I did.
> *1 Gent.:*   How was it?
> *3 Gent.:* Well worth the seeing.
> *2 Gent.:*   Good sir, speak it to us.
>
> (IV.i.56–61)

Again, the spectacle is spoken, not seen. There is pageantry aplenty in the play, but these descriptions of more splendid pageants again challenge the blunt declarations of the Prologue.

If the Prologue's statements about the play's uniform seriousness and visual splendor are undercut, we may expect qualifications of the more basic promises, that the play will "draw the eye to flow" (line 4) with pity and that

> Such as give
> Their money out of hope they may believe
> May find here truth too.
>
> (lines 4–6)

The play's whole design puts these impulses in conflict: in order to celebrate appropriately the birth of Elizabeth, we must believe in the "truth" of Henry's scruples about his first marriage, scruples that are openly ridiculed by the courtiers. The strong appeal of the discarded Katherine herself forces us to question, if not the legitimacy, the justice of her divorce.

A more jarring conflict between pity and belief animates the scenes of Buckingham's fall; ii.i particularly merits close attention as wholly characteristic. Like most of the scenes in *Henry VIII*, it is a set piece, an emblematic playlet. The Gentlemen, on stage at the beginning of the scene, discuss Buckingham's trial; the unhappy duke enters, delivers his famous farewell orations, and departs; the Gentlemen complete the frame by remaining behind and discussing the impending divorce. We are set up to expect a morally instructive play-within-a-play, an interlude for reflection, like iii.i of *1 Henry IV,* or the simpler emblematic scenes in the earlier histories. The sense of metadramatic Chinese boxes is heightened by the presentation, again through secondhand narrative, of the trial of Buckingham. As in the later case of Anne's coronation, the Gentleman is forced to rely for information on one eyewitness:

> *2 Gent.:*   Were you there?
> *1 Gent.:* Yes indeed was I.
> *2 Gent.:*   Pray speak what has happened.
> *1 Gent.:* You may guess quickly what.
>
> (ii.i.5–7)

The coyness of the First Gentleman anticipates that of his counterpart in iv.i; so does the eagerness of the listener. The audience, like the Second Gentleman, is convinced that Wolsey "is the end of this" (line 40), but the First Gentleman, who appears to be wholly sympathetic to Buckingham, also seems to accept the conviction upon its merits. "The great Duke / Came to the bar," he reports,

>   where to his accusations
> He pleaded still not guilty, and alleged
> Many sharp reasons to defeat the law.
> The king's attorney, on the contrary,
> Urged on the examinations, proofs, confessions,
> Of divers witnesses.
>
> (lines 11–17)

The series stresses the orderly progression of evidence presented by the crown. Buckingham's "sharp reasons," on the other hand, have as their purpose "to defeat the law." His defense begins to crumble when he demands that the witnesses be "brought viva voce to his face" (line 18):

> All these accused him strongly, which he fain
> Would have flung from him, but indeed he could not;
> And so his peers upon this evidence
> Have found him guilty of high treason. Much
> He spoke, and learnedly for life; but all
> Was either pitied in him or forgotten.
>
> (lines 24–29)

The accusations stick to the duke; it is hard to reconcile the Gentleman's account of the just and orderly trial with the notions of Wolsey's malicious manipulations that the earlier scenes have encouraged. Buckingham's eloquence evokes from his peers only pity; the charges still stand.

The Gentlemen step aside, becoming an audience in their own right, as we are asked to judge for ourselves Buckingham's skill as an orator; Henry himself has warned us that "the gentleman is learned, and a most rare speaker" (1.ii.111). The duke's entrance is staged with full pomp. The Second Gentleman recalls that the commons call Buckingham "the mirror of all courtesy" (line 53), and on this highly charged phrase the duke's procession enters. The Gentlemen stress the conventional, theatrical quality of what we are about to witness:

> *1 Gent.:*   Stay there sir,
>   And see the noble ruined man you speak of.
> *2 Gent.:* Let's stand close and behold him.
>
> (lines 53–55)

Discussion of the proofs urged by eyewitnesses at the trial gives way to our own witnessing; we are presented, not with the course of the king's justice in the trial, but with Buckingham's flowery self-exoneration.

Buckingham's farewell is a controlled oratorical display, a self-dramatization that explicitly fits him into the pre-existing pattern of "noble ruined man," leading up to an emblematic conclusion: "And when you would say something that is sad, / Speak how I fell" (lines 135–36). The appeal throughout is to the pity of "all good people" (line 55)—both the audience onstage and, by extension, the audience in the theater—yet the tone frequently descends to bitter self-pity as Buckingham snobbishly recalls that he was betrayed by his own servants:[48]

> Yet I am richer than my base accusers,
> That never knew what truth meant: I now seal it;

And with that blood will make 'em one day groan for it.

(lines 104–6)

Coming hard upon the torrent of forgiveness Buckingham directs at Lovell—"I as free forgive you / As I would be forgiven: I forgive all" (lines 82–83)—the remark is jarring; throughout the speech Buckingham both forgives and denigrates his accusers:

> The law I bear no malice for my death,
> 'Thas done upon the premises but justice:
> But those that sought it I could wish more Christians.
> Be what they will, I heartily forgive 'em.

(lines 62–65)

The forgiveness here, too, is short-lived; speculation on his enemies' ambition leads Buckingham to portray himself as a wronged Abel: "For then my guiltless blood must cry against 'em" (line 68). Buckingham's unscrupulous and inconsistent employment of religious figures lends an air of falsehood to his exculpations.

But Buckingham's challenge to the process of the king's justice is not merely emotional. His definition of truth clearly conflicts with the law's. To the duke, truth consists in loyalty; as a result, his servants "never knew what truth meant," although from the account we hear of the trial it appears that they did not lie. His offer of his own blood to "seal" (line 105) his oaths confirms the archaic notion of truth as troth.

Since Buckingham sees truth in terms of social fealties, he depicts his betrayal as an inversion of the social order. "A beggar's book / Outworths a noble's blood," he complains earlier (1.i.117–18), as Wolsey passes by reading his surveyor's testimony. Buckingham's oration attacks the version of "truth" arrived at by the law—in a process the audience is not permitted to witness—with a strong emotional appeal to the truth of blood, breeding, and sworn oaths. The speech displaces the narrative of the trial purely by dint of its theatrical appeal to attractive aristocratic abstractions.

The First Gentleman responds as Buckingham would desire: "O this is full of pity!" (line 137); the Second Gentleman is less swayed by the duke's rhetoric: "If the duke be guiltless, / 'Tis full of woe" (lines 139–40). On this note the subject of Buckingham is dismissed, and the two rush on to close the scene with gossip about Katherine's fall. Their talk is again charged with confusion about truth.

The First Gentleman dismisses rumors of a separation as idle, and in fact forbidden by royal order; the Second disabuses him. "But that slander, sir, / Is found a truth now" (11.i.153). The Gentleman's difficulties in distinguishing truth from scandal in this case match the audience's difficulties in resolving the contradictory truths of Buckingham's appeal, juggling the false promises of the Prologue, and reconciling a discordant sympathy for Katherine with the play's triumphant mood. Felperin has expressed doubts as to "whether Shakespeare is not ironically hinting that we revise our conventional notions of historical truth, even of mimetic truth itself," in the play's subtitle, *All Is True;* confusion about the word itself is a major part of our experience of the play.[49] The disparity between limited, human, emotional truths and providence's ultimate purposes animates the discordant demands made especially by the fall of Katherine.

"And every true heart weeps for't," says the lord chamberlain of the queen's dilemma (II.ii.38). At her hearing, Katherine protests her truth—her fidelity and love: she has always been a "true and humble wife" (II.iv.21). The word *true* figures significantly in Henry's own testimony:

> That man i'th'world shall report he has
> A better wife, let him in naught be trusted
> For speaking false in that. . . .
>   She's noble born,
> And like her true nobility she has
> Carried herself towards me.
>
>   (lines 132–34, 139–41)

Her first appearance in the play is on her knees, as a suitor on behalf of the subjects "of true condition" (I.ii.19) who oppose the onerous taxes imposed on them by Wolsey.

Yet Katherine's "truth," unlike Buckingham's, is distinguished by her high regard for candor. Her main objection to Wolsey at her trial is that he is "not / At all a friend to truth" (II.iv.82). Before her death, she reiterates this judgment:

> His own opinion was his law: i'th'presence
> He would say untruths, and be ever double
> Both in his words and meaning.
>
>   (IV.ii.37–39)

When Griffith, her gentleman-usher, offers to point out Wolsey's good qualities, however, she willingly listens and concludes by accepting Griffith's assessment:

> After my death I wish no other herald,
> No other speaker of my living actions

To keep mine honor from corruption,
But such an honest chronicler as Griffith.
Whom I most hated living, thou hast made me,
With thy religious truth and modesty,
Now, in his ashes, honor: peace be with him!

(IV.ii.69–75)

Her rapid change of attitude has been attacked as Fletcherian, but the sudden shift is typical of the play's structure, and it dramatizes an important feature of the play's historiography.

Katherine is swayed by an argument that is based closely upon the facts of Wolsey's public career; her condemnation of the man centers upon his malice towards her and failure to match his promises with performance. Griffith's account of Wolsey, which follows closely the evaluation of the cardinal in Holinshed, is tempered with charity. Both accounts are true, in different senses of the word, as are the Gentleman's account of Buckingham's trial and the duke's self-dramatization.

Katherine's problem becomes the audience's because of the way in which Shakespeare manipulates our own responses to Wolsey. First presented as "lofty and sour" (IV.ii.53), he moves through the early parts of the play with ruthless Machiavellism; he orchestrates the frustrating "dilatory sloth and tricks of Rome" (II.iv.235) that hinder the divorce; he amasses a vast personal fortune "indeed to gain the Popedom / And fee my friends in Rome" (III.ii.212–13). In all ways a conventional Italianate cardinal, Wolsey has no call upon our sympathy.

Yet his fall is sympathetically depicted: stripped of his titles, Wolsey piously meditates upon the vanity of worldly pursuits. To Cromwell, he discloses his new state of mind:

Never so truly happy, my good Cromwell.
I know myself now, and I feel within me
A peace above all earthly dignities,
A still and quiet conscience.

(III.ii.377–80)

Discordant as this image of the cardinal turned hermit may be, more jarring yet is the language in which Wolsey asks a blessing upon his successor:

May he continue
Long in his highness' favor, and do justice
For truth's sake and his conscience.

(lines 395–97)

Both words have by now been so abused in the play—mostly by Wolsey himself—as to be utterly meaningless.

Wolsey's advice to Cromwell, similarly, founders in self-contradiction. Cromwell's promise of loyalty to "so good, so noble, and so true a master" (line 423) brings tears to his eyes; Wolsey, like Buckingham, appeals blatantly for pity as he presents himself and paints the lesson of his case. He teaches Cromwell a curious "way . . . to rise in / A sure and safe one" (lines 437–38): "fling away ambition!" (line 440). The preposterous paradox in the moral compounds the ambiguities that already encircle ideas of truth in this play. The ideal of service that Wolsey now recommends to Cromwell is the path that he admits he "miss'd" (line 338): he has not been true to his master. He urges Cromwell to make his goals "thy country's / Thy God's and truth's" (line 447–48); his famous last words resound with like irony:

> Had I but serv'd my God with half the zeal
> I serv'd my king, he would not in mine age
> Have left me naked to mine enemies.
>
> (lines 455–57)

An exemplary lesson, but patently false. Throughout the play Wolsey has been shown to be disloyal, hypocritical, overweeningly ambitious. His advice to Cromwell includes the admission of disloyalty to the monarch. His aspiration to the papacy, not his enemies, stripped him of his glories.

The cardinal's evaluation of his moral situation (a favorite showpiece for declamatory actors) is totally unreliable. After urging Cromwell to shun ambition and serve the king well, Wolsey sees himself as a loyal servant undeservedly cast off and condemns all worldly service. The scene's last lines, in which Wolsey takes his "hopes" (line 459) to the court of Heaven are again paradoxical. The ultimate effect is to force a suspension of judgment: like Surrey and the lord chamberlain, we must balance sympathy for Wolsey with recognition of his guilt and moral confusion. Katherine's response to Wolsey's death and Griffith's chronicle is a dramatization of this desired balance. With Wolsey as with Buckingham, we are confronted with a homiletic, "stagey," pious farewell to the things of this world that we cannot endorse at face value. Buckingham's forgiveness founders in curses; Wolsey is unable to avoid courtly double-talk.

Both, as well, have been convicted in accordance with the king's justice; their unacknowledged guilt silently confutes their pathetic appeal. Similarly, in Katherine's case, the justice of the divorce, upheld by Cranmer and other "learned and reverend fathers of his order" (IV.i.26) is acknowledged without question. Whatever resentment Katherine feels is expressed not against the decree but rather against Henry's unkindness as a husband. Nor is justice allowed to miscarry in Cranmer's trial. Assured of his innocence, the king suspends Gardiner's persecutions.

But Cranmer's danger points to weaknesses in the processes of justice themselves. The king himself warns him:

> Your enemies are many and not small; their practices
> Must bear the same proportion, and not ever
> The justice and the truth o'th'question
> Carries the due o'th'verdict with it.
>
> (v.i.128–31)

The phrase *not ever* is certainly disturbing: the king can mean that verdicts do not always reflect truth, or that they never do. At any rate, all Cranmer can do is throw himself on the king's mercy; and the king, convinced by his tears of his "true heart" (v.i.152–53; v.ii.208), presents him with the fairy-tale ring that later saves him. Called into doubt here are the very principles of orderly procedural justice that, despite pathetic appeals to the contrary, have shaped our responses to the falls of Buckingham and Wolsey and have allowed us to accept without question the divorce and remarriage of the king. The result is a deepening confusion, in which, somehow, the right ends are still achieved.

Henry sweeps aside the charges against Cranmer out of sheer faith in the man, just as questions of right and wrong, guilt and innocence, truth and falsehood, are all forgotten in the final scenes. Warring sympathies are overridden. Inconsistencies of characterization force the audience simply to accept the people before them as unknowable. Most problematic is Henry himself. He sways from the awesome to the comic, the majestic to the clumsy. Again the Prologue's promise of a solemn, true story is proved inadequate: the monarch is shown to be doing in a casual, whimsical manner things that will eventually prove important.[50]

Thus the play's pageantry and descriptions of pageantry seem to glorify the past, while comic moments, like the sessions between Anne and the Old Lady and the preparations for the christening, debunk and belittle famous events and people. The result is a presentation of the complicated religious and political issues of the age that is oblique, tangential, vague. The atmosphere of nostalgia and forgiveness breathed by the falling characters—Buckingham, Wolsey, Katherine—befogs the play's historiography. Ribner accuses Shakespeare of "slavishly" following Holinshed, while Felperin finds that he "departs from history" here "more radically" than ever before.[51] Both are right: in *Henry VIII* the chronicles are extensively used, but radically rearranged. Shakespeare celebrates the stability and continuity of the monarchy in a manner even more providential than that of the Tudor chronicles. The deliberate and ironic evocation of uncertainties about the nature of truth, the contradictory and incomprehensible behavior of the characters, the distortion of source material into a grand pattern, all lead an audience into a kind of historical despair from which the only release is total acceptance. The Prologue's lies demand that we be skeptical of what we see; the play's pageantry demands that we believe its affirmations without question. Katherine's pious response to Griffith's dialectical account of Wolsey epitomizes the process: she forgives him as we forgive history itself for the messy way in which Elizabeth has been brought to light.

The implications of this passivist historiography are worth some consideration. Isaiah Berlin has distinguished two primary ways in which history can be seen to fulfill its function of instruction: either through providing examples of choices made by men in the past for the benefit of those who must make choices in the present, or through claiming to uncover the immutable laws that govern human action with an ultimate view to revealing the future.[52]

The first complex of attitudes can be readily associated with Machiavelli and the humanist historians; the second, with providential chroniclers. We have shown how both attitudes balance and qualify each other in *1 Henry IV* and the rest of the Lancastrian plays; in *Henry VIII*, characters' actions seem irrelevant to the unfolding of the great, happy event. To Berlin, such an assumption of historical inevitability makes moral evaluation of human activity impossible, since it denies the possibility that individual actions can alter the real picture (except to the extent of clarifying or obfuscating an immanent truth). The result is a complacency that expresses itself in visionary and skeptical terms. Where Hotspur in III.i of *1 Henry IV* is shown in the action of choosing bondage to Glendower, Henry VIII never chooses Anne Boleyn. The divorce is inevitable; the king's conscience is a joke; Katherine's plight is sad. Shakespeare refuses to explore the religious, moral, or historical ramifications of the divorce; what makes this play most disturbing, of course, is the fact that recognition and evocation of historical issues in their full moral complexity is the hallmark of Shakespeare's mature dramatic style.[53]

The antihistorical attitude of the play is, however, not totally anti-Shakespearean. The skepticism about historical understanding that leads, in *King Lear*, to total refutation of source and tradition, motivates the deliberate confusion of the audience in *Henry VIII*. The play demands that we believe what we see and then presents us with a series of lies and contradictions; it is a theatrical conundrum, like the living statue of Hermione in *The Winter's Tale* or, like the double Cesario at the end of *Twelfth Night*, "a natural perspective, that is and is not" (v.i.209). The ending of *1 Henry IV* holds comic and tragic ways of understanding in a precarious balance: Hotspur is dead, Falstaff rises, and the morality play of the prince's reformation is proved both true and false. Shakespeare permits history to validate traditional patterns of moral understanding even as he sees human life as infinitely variable. Falstaff embodies the chaotic energies that challenge articulate arrangement of the past; his resurrection suggests that historical arrangement of life's raw material can be as fictive as playacting.[54] *Lear* takes this further: Cordelia's death and Edgar's lame moralizations demonstrate that the fables that organize and give meaning to life falsify human suffering. *Henry VIII*, like the comedies and late romances, urges an audience to experience the folly, not the horror, of judging. The theatrical miracle of Elizabeth's birth, like the comic resurrections of Hermione and Sebastian, redeems time; its mysterious operations have healed the wounds of history.[55]

Shakespeare's providentialism, in *Henry VIII*, is not the propagandist whitewash Felperin suspects or the consummation of Tudor myth that Tillyard celebrates; rather it is the result of a skepticism about history so searching that, incapable of discovering any truth that is not relative, it blurs over moral and factual distinctions to assert that "all is true." No one in *Henry VIII* is a morally responsible agent; the contrast to the charged atmosphere in which decisions are made in *1 Henry IV* is extreme. Where the earlier play succeeds in suggesting both that human life is significant on a cosmic scale and that our conventional ways of expressing this significance are untrue to experience, *Henry VIII* refuses to pass judgment. History is fate; conceding the ultimate happy issue, we are set free to concentrate upon the feelings of the individuals caught up in the process without attributing to their actions any significant consequences. The result is a total denial of Renaissance notions of the utility and validity of history through a skeptical juxtaposition of history's truths to the variousness and unknowability of life itself. The pageants of *Henry VIII*, like Stuart court masques, translate politics onto an idealized, abstract plane.[56] *1 Henry IV* forces its audience to reenact the historian's efforts to make sense out of life; *Henry VIII* simply declares the significance of the event and presents, as spectacle, the joys and sufferings of characters who have no moral agency at all. History is full of surprises in the earlier play; the ending of *Henry VIII* is a foregone conclusion.

The career of Shakespeare himself, then, runs from the creation of the history play in the first tetralogy, through its fulfillment in the Lancastrian plays, to its dissolution into pageant and spectacle in *Henry VIII*. Shakespeare's skepticism about the ability of historical understanding to master the chaos of human experience leads, at once, to the greatness of *1 Henry IV* and the pettiness of *Henry VIII*. As a dramatist, Shakespeare challenges and defeats his historical sources by staging, with full credibility, events that did not occur in the recorded past but that must have occurred if human experience is at all coherent. Hotspur signs the Tripartite Indenture; Lear loses Cordelia. The suggestion that poets communicate a higher truth than mere historians is a commonplace in Renaissance Platonism.[57] Shakespeare puts it to the test, like so many other ready formulations, in the mature history plays; in *Henry VIII* he allows the fictive spectacle wholly to override mere historical truth.

Shakespeare's mistrust of his sources is symptomatic of a movement away from historical material not only in his own career but in all of seventeenth-century English drama. In fact, as historical discipline is defined more clearly by its practitioners through this period, dramatists show themselves less and less interested in historical subjects for plays. Those who do dramatize the past—Ford, Orrery, Banks, Rowe—do so in a manner more reminiscent of *Henry VIII* than of *1 Henry IV*: skeptical, spectacular, nostalgic, and pathetic. The alternative of a humanist historical drama was essayed only, with characteristic force and perverseness, by Ben Jonson and George Chapman, whose plays about Roman and French histories are learned attempts to bring the new art of history to the English stage.

2

Humanist History and Theatrical Truth

JONSON, CHAPMAN, MASSINGER, AND FORD

By playing off providential and humanist ways of understanding the past against both each other and the chaos of life itself, Shakespeare takes a position that is critical and finally dismissive of history's ability to master the mysterious operations of time. In this regard he shows himself to be both more firmly rooted in medieval modes of seeing the past and more adventurous in his historiography than the hard-line humanists among his contemporaries. Ben Jonson and George Chapman use the past, as Machiavelli does, to point lessons for the leaders of the present; the technique of parallel lives, as practised by Fluellen in *Henry V,* animates *Sejanus* and *The Conspiracy and Tragedy of Byron.* These plays are English history plays insofar as they attempt to bring the lessons of history to bear upon issues of recent domestic concern: in both cases, the central problem for the historian-dramatist is the Essex crisis of 1601. Both Jonson and Chapman are acutely self-conscious about their responsibilities as historians and about the problems of government interference they face in dealing with sensitive issues.

Government censorship, in fact, plays a large role in the disappearance of English history plays from the stage early in the seventeenth century.[1] Out of fashion as they may have been, chronicle history plays in the first decades of the century received special attention from the growing Office of Revels. After 1610 and before the closing of the theaters in 1642, if we define English history plays as narrowly as we do in distinguishing history plays from tragedies, comedies, and romances in the 1580s and 1590s, we find only three extant: *Henry VIII* (1612), Thomas Drue's *The Life of the Dutches of Suffolke* (1624), and John Ford's *Perkin Warbeck* (1634).[2] Jonson's *Mortimer His Fall,* left unfinished at the poet's death, would have made a fourth. We have already discussed the peculiarities of *Henry VIII;* of interest here is the fact that both *Perkin Warbeck* and *The Dutches of Suffolke,* like *Sejanus* and *Byron,* suffered some kind of governmental interference before being allowed upon the stage. What happened in the case of *Perkin Warbeck* is not clear, but *The Dutches* was licensed only after Sir Henry Herbert had received two pounds for his pains in excising "dangerous matter" on 2 January 1624.[3] The play rather crudely parallels the wanderings of the duchess, persecuted through the Low Countries by vengeful Catholics, to those of James I's daughter, Princess Elizabeth, after her husband Frederick's assumption of the title of King of Bohemia and the outbreak of the Thirty Years' War. The issue of James's (and later Charles's) refusal to help Frederick figures prominently in Philip Massinger's *Believe as Ye List,* a play that, in manuscript, can be seen to have begun as a drama treating the historical wanderings of Sebastian, king of Portugal, before Herbert refused to license it, again on the grounds of "dangerous matter," on 11 January 1631.[4] The wanderings of Perkin Warbeck in Ford's play can likewise be seen to "shadow" those of the Winter King and his English queen.

While Jonson's and Chapman's plays about the Essex crisis, and Massinger's and Ford's treatments of English noninvolvement in the struggles of Continental Protestantism may seem at the outset to be specimens of the same type of political parallel drawing, the plays of the later playwrights reveal a mistrust of historical understanding and a denial of ultimate significance to politics that goes far beyond Shakespeare's. The Essex plays of Jonson and Chapman show a firm faith in the moral usefulness of history; as well as embodying historical lessons, both plays are full of discussion of the ways these lessons should be taught. The "Pretender plays" of Massinger and Ford (the phrase is Philip Edwards's), however, emphasize the unverifiability of fact and the mysteriousness of identity. Tiberius's identity in *Sejanus* is made known by his "times," and the play's Romans hold him accountable; Antiochus and Perkin are kings without kingdoms. Their private, personal royalty challenges a political understanding of kingship; Ford goes further, and defies, in his Perkin's heroic death, Bacon's masterpiece of humanist "civil" history, his primary source.

i

A playwright who shared Bacon's sense of the usefulness of history and was undaunted by Shakespeare's crushing precedent would hardly be discouraged from activist history writing by the increasingly vigilant censors. It is not surprising that Ben Jonson should rise to the challenge on both fronts: *Sejanus* has long been recognized, and condemned, as a wholly un-Shakespearean tragedy; and in both form and matter, the play is an outspoken critique of censorship. When it first took the stage in 1603, *Sejanus* provoked the wrath of Northampton, who summoned Jonson before the Privy Council, where he accused him of "poperie and treason." Some critics (notably Palmer and Bryant) take at face value Jonson's explanation, to Drummond, that personal malice alone motivated Northampton.[5] But the 1605 Quarto, bristling with notes to Jonson's sources, both announces the historian's integrity and challenges censorship by stressing the remoteness of the subject. As the historian in the play, Cremutius Cordus, protests at his trial:

> What could be aimed more free, or farther off
> From the time's scandal, than to write of those
> Whom death from grace or hatred had exempted?
>
> (III.446–48)

Jonson too demonstrates his innocence and respectability by citing his sources. In the Quarto edition, he renounces the performed play: in this, he says, "a second hand had a good share," and *Sejanus* has now been revised "in all numbers" for publication.[6]

Like Cordus's apology to the Senate, Jonson's conduct is disingenuous. The government's recent experiments in book burning at the height of the Essex crisis made it acutely aware of the embarrassments attendant upon censorship. At Essex's trial, Bacon went so far as to accuse him of initiating the suppression of Hayward's *History of Henry IV* to enhance its appeal, because "forbidden things are most sought after." Cordus, in the play, sounds the same note in his defense of the slanders alleged to appear in his *Annals:*

> for such obloquies,
> If they despised be, they die suppressed;
> But if with rage acknowledged, they are confessed.
>
> (III.439–41)

The rhyme "points" the Tacitean moral ("For things unnoticed are forgotten; resentment confers status upon them"); the word *suppressed* suggests the English context, not the Roman.[7]

In its design, Jonson's play emphasizes the fate of Cordus; the historian's trial, at the very center of the play, follows hard upon the dramatic suicide of Silius. According to Tacitus, the two incidents happened a year apart; here they combine to emphasize the intolerability of Tiberius's rule. Earlier on, Jonson takes pains to dramatize forcefully both the danger and the necessity of writing history in corrupt times. As

Cordus and Arruntius join Sabinus and Silius in one corner of the stage,
the informers Natta and Latiaris watch the gathering of good men. The
audience's attention is drawn towards the spies as they whisper:

> *Natta:* Who's that salutes your cousin?
> *Latiaris:*   'Tis one Cordus,
>   A gentleman of Rome, one that has writ
>   Annals of late, they say, and very well.
> *Natta:* Annals? Of what times?
> *Latiaris:*   I think of Pompey's
>   And Caius Caesar's, and so down to these.
> *Natta:* How stands h'affected to the present state?
>   Is he or Drusian, or Germanican?
>   Or ours, or neutral?
> *Latiaris:*   I know him not so far.
> *Natta:* Those times are somewhat queasy to be touched.
>   Have you seen or heard part of his work?
> *Latiaris:* Not I; he means they shall be public shortly.
> *Natta:* Oh, Cordus do you call him?
> *Latiaris:*   Aye.
>
>   (1.74–85)

Natta's oblique approach, his careful questions as to Cordus's party affil-
iation, his noting of the historian's name, are rich with menace. As the
two move off, righteous anger bursts out at the other side of the stage:

> *Sabinus:*   But these our times
>   Are not the same, Arruntius.
> *Arruntius:*   Times? The men,
>   The men are not the same! 'Tis we are base,
>   Poor, and degenerate from th'exalted strain
>   Of our great fathers. Where is now the soul of
>   Godlike Cato?
>
>   (1.86–91)

Through his split-stage technique, Jonson shows both sides to be obsessed utterly with the past, a glorious past that demands comparison
with the present. Even the informers are well aware how much their age
suffers by contrast to "those times"; Arruntius's outburst, with curious
irony, brings the positive characters, the Germanicans, down to the same
"base, / Poor, and degenerate" level as the spies.[8] Both sides are impotent, paralyzed by historical memory.

Where the Germanicans struggle to understand the relationship between men and their times, the emperor's supporters see history as nothing more than slander. Afer the orator, at Cordus's trial, reproaches the historian for failing to praise Caesar:

> Nor is't the time alone is here dispriz'd,
> But the whole man of the time, yea, Caesar's self
> Brought in disvalue, and he aimed at most
> By oblique glance of his licentious pen.
> Caesar, if Cassius were the last of Romans,
> Thou has no name.
>
> (III.401–6)

Tiberius's identity, fascinating to both Jonson and Tacitus, infects the whole age. His inactivity breeds "monsters" (K. M. Burton) like Sejanus; his Rome is a headless state, veering from one form of tyranny to another, imbued from top to bottom with riot and disorder. The imagery of "dismemberment of the body politic," detailed by Ricks, enhances the horror of Tiberius's absence; to Evans, Jonson evokes a "Machiavellian state, in which government is conducted by violence and fraud," lacking "the sole guarantee of social stability, . . . a strong and consecrated monarchy."⁹ The great names of history resonate in the emptiness of the present.

History is a weapon in *Sejanus,* and a dangerous one. Jonson makes it clear that its lessons should not be carelessly applied. As the noble Romans mourn the passing of Germanicus, Cordus suggests a possible application:

> I thought once,
> Considering their forms, age, manner of deaths,
> The nearness of the places where they fell,
> T'have parallel'd him with great Alexander.
> For both were of best feature, of high race,
> Yeared but to thirty, and in foreign lands,
> By their own people, alike made away.
>
> (I.136–42)

The parallel may seem as pedestrian as Fluellen's, but it is otherwise thoroughly conventional. Sabinus, however, reacts angrily:

> I know not, for his death, how you might wrest it,
> But for his life, it did as much disdain
> Comparison with that voluptuous, rash,
> Giddy, and drunken Macedon's, as mine
> Doth with my bondman's. All the good in him,

His valor and his fortune, he made his.
But he had other touches of late Romans,
That more did speak him: Pompey's dignity,
The innocence of Cato, Caesar's spirit,
Wise Brutus' temperance; and every virtue
Which, parted unto others, gave them name,
Flowed mixed in him.

(lines 143–54)

Sabinus rejects Cordus's parallel because it is inaccurate, but he, too, insists upon seeing Germanicus in a historical light. His virtues are not self-generated, but can be furnished with precedents.

The play as a whole is similarly cautious, from the precedence given to "truth of argument" in the Preface to the Readers to its tenuous and slippery applicability to the confusions of its own times. As in the conversation between Cordus and Silius, parallels are consistently suggested and revoked. Sejanus can be seen to figure the earl of Essex: as a grandiose, boasting, ambitious favorite he corresponds perfectly to the Essex portrayed by Bacon in his prosecution of his former patron. But curiously, both of the Alexanders mentioned above can be wrenched to fit Essex's mold. Sabinus's description of Germanicus's mission abroad and of the conspiracies at home to destroy him "and work to put him out / In open act of treason" (1.171–72) rehashes Essex's complaints about his mission to Ireland. Jonson distorts the charges against Silius to remind his audience of the prosecution of Essex, but he depicts Silius's self-defense (again, the terms recall more clearly Essex than the Tacitean original) with full sympathy. Jonson thus dramatizes on the one hand the harshest government attitudes toward Essex, while at other times attitudes far more sympathetic to the earl are given full expression. As Sabinus suggests, allegory of persons is naive and simplistic; what he offers, for Germanicus, and what Jonson, too, offers for Essex, is a mosaic of references. Germanicus is a composite of the virtues of a number of great Romans. The play's relationship to the Essex crisis is similarly prismatic. Jonson multiplies parallels in order to evoke the whole range of discussion evoked by Essex.[10]

The ostensible subject of the play does not "parallel" the English subject in a direct way; rather, the audience is forced to draw connections and perceive correspondences in ways that will enrich their understanding of both. A simplistic reading of Sejanus's fall as a slander against Essex founders on Jonson's sympathetic presentation of Sejanus in the fifth act, but other attitudes to Essex have been presented throughout.[11]

The correspondence is one of "times," not men: seen in this way, *Sejanus* becomes not an antiquarian exercise but, like so many of Jonson's plays, a demonstration. It is a truthful history play, based upon the reliable model of Tacitus, not upon the frequently fraudulent chronicles. For the murky legendary background of the native historical drama, *Sejanus* substitutes a sharp Machiavellian glimpse of the mechanics of political power. Sejanus falls, not because his Marlovian boasting upsets the gods, but because, with his head in the clouds, he fails to notice Macro digging away at the foundation of his power. In its avoidance of simplistic and inflammatory parallels to recent memory, the play forces its audience to function as careful historians, making appropriate connections and rejecting false ones.

The age of Tiberius figures the last years of Elizabeth, then, the same way Sejanus figures Essex: history provides exaggerated images of what might have been. The past is worth studying because it hints at possible alternative futures. At the time of its performance in 1603 and its publication in 1605, *Sejanus* presented an image of government paranoia that magnifies only slightly the kind of repression that accompanied the rising of Essex and, later, the Gunpowder Plot. The message of the play is that the chaos of Tiberian Rome threatens in the absence of a strong monarch, and that Elizabeth in her last years, delegating authority to an upstart favorite and to faceless bureaucrats like Marco, came perilously close to fulfilling the parallel. But the humanist historian addresses himself to his prince: Jonson's play warns James I about the kingdom he has inherited and serves, in this particular sense, as a cautionary tale.

Good history, in Jonson as in Shakespeare, is, consequently, prophetic. But where in Shakespeare's histories a dense fabric of prophetic lore clothes the actors in the nation's past, Jonson's fable is adorned only with sufficient modern instances to make its relevance clear. Hal's fulfillment of the Prodigal Son pattern speaks to a whole body of significance that Tiberius's sloth and tyranny might address but do not. The play's secularism, like Arruntius's insistence that men make their times and that Germanican and Drusian alike are responsible for the degeneracy of the age, is ostentatiously humanistic. There is no place in Jonson's scientific, serious historiography for the popular traditions that permit the existence of Falstaff and make of Hal something more (and less) than an ideal Renaissance prince.

Jonson is not merely secular in his idea of history, for, as Barish has pointed out, he reverses Sidney's priorities and sees history as communicating the higher truth that Sidney reserved for poetry. Claiming for history the "light of Truth, and life of Memorie," Jonson rejects the

Augustinian and Platonic distinctions between historical truth and truth itself.[12] The facts of the past, directly related, teach lessons that can and must be acted on if we are to avoid the chaos of Tiberian Rome, where history terrifies the corrupt and paralyzes the virtuous. Fact has all the force of revelation.

When the facts about Sejanus are dramatized in such a way as to evoke also the facts about Essex, however, we see differences as well as similarities. The parallel will only become complete if we fail to overcome our fear of historical truth and act as the Roman Senate does:

> Let 'em be burnt! Oh, how ridiculous
> Appears the Senate's brainless diligence,
> Who think they can, with present power, extinguish
> The memory of all succeeding times!
>
> (III.471–74)

The folly of tyranny is exposed in the oxymoronic language Arruntius uses: book burning cannot extinguish the light of truth. But if present power cannot suppress the memory of liberty, it can suppress present liberty itself; this is the danger that *Sejanus* points to in its attack upon censorship. Jonson was wrong, of course, in his belief that his audience, unlike the brainless Romans of his play, would respond correctly to the light of his historical truth. As a prophet, if not as a historian, Jonson could take some cold comfort from the increasingly ruthless vigilance of the Office of Revels in succeeding years.

One of the most notorious examples of this kind of interference in historical drama is the case of Chapman's pair of two five-act plays, *The Conspiracy and Tragedy of Charles Duke of Byron*. The play took the stage in the absence of the court, but it was faithful enough to French fact to provoke the French ambassador into taking legal action:

> April 8, 1608, I caused certain players to be forbid from
> acting the history of the Duke of Byron; when, however,
> they saw that the whole court had left town, they persisted
> in acting it; nay, they brought upon the stage the Queen of
> France and Mademoiselle de Verneuil. The former, having
> accosted the latter with very hard words, gave her a box on
> the ear. At my suit three of them were arrested, but the
> principal person, the author, escaped.[13]

When the censor finally did pay attention to *Byron*, the results were disastrous. The ear-boxing scene of which the ambassador complained was removed; Byron's conversation with Queen Elizabeth, in which she warns him to shun Essex's fate, was forbidden, and the scene is lamely narrated at second hand. Numerous other passages seem to be missing: Parrott, Chapman's editor, complains, "The wounds made by the censor's hand remain unhealed today" (p. 592). The fact that the government's mangling of the play so far exceeded simple courtesy to an ambassador clearly indicates that the Essex affair was still "somewhat queasy to be touched" (1.82) in 1608. The ear-boxing scene is not only an affront to the French queen: Elizabeth Bridges, a lady-in-waiting to Elizabeth, had "suffered 'a good beating at the queen's own hand' for dallying with Essex."[14]

Elizabeth boxed Essex's ears once as well, in an incident that is also suggested in the play (*Conspiracy*, V.ii). The earl had rudely turned his back to her, and smarting from the blow he drew his sword part way in the royal presence. Byron, enraged by King Henry IV, "offers to draw" (v.ii.29, SD) and is restrained by Auvergne, just as Essex's hand was held back by Nottingham, the lord admiral. A few lines later, the king returns, and Byron pointedly turns his back:

> Turn, I pray.
> How now, from whence flow these distracted faces?
> From what attempt return they, as disclaiming
> Their late heroic bearer? What, a pistol?
>
> (*Conspiracy*, v.ii.39–42)

Byron's petulance, half-drawn sword, turned back, and threat to the king with a weapon (not in the French sources, according to Parrott) are all reminiscent of Essex's bad behavior.[15]

There may have been more of this kind of theatrical parallel in the play as performed, as may also be the case with *Sejanus*. But Byron's failure in the play to apply the parallel with Essex correctly is central in spite of the censor's mutilations. As his doom approaches, Byron remarks upon the coincidence:

> All these things are indeed ostentful,
> Which, by another like, I can confirm:
> The matchless Earl of Essex, whom some make
> (In their most sure divinings of my death)
> A parallel with me in life and fortune,
> Had one horse, likewise, that the very hour
> He suffer'd death (being well the night before),
> Died in his pasture.
>
> (*Tragedy*, IV.i.131–38)

Essex's fate has been set before the duke as a lesson he must learn. Yet Byron in his speech is unwilling to concede the close connection that his horse's death confirms. Similarly, as he awaits execution, he twists Elizabeth's advice to his own advantage:

> the Queen of England
> Told me that if the wilful Earl of Essex
> Had us'd submission, and but ask'd her mercy,
> She would have given it past resumption.
> She like a gracious princess did desire
> To pardon him, even as she pray'd to God
> He would let down a pardon unto her;
> He yet was guilty, I am innocent;
> He still refus'd grace, I importune it.
>   (*Tragedy*, V.iii.139–47)

Byron stubbornly refuses to accept any responsibility for his own treasons: he blames his rebellion on witchcraft and reproaches Essex for not indulging in self-pity at the moment of death.

The story of Essex is for Byron a cautionary tale that he chooses to misinterpret at his own peril. Early in *The Conspiracy*, Henry expounds upon the educational merits of a voyage to England:

> I therefore mean to make him change the air,
> And send him further from those Spanish vapours,
> That still bear fighting sulphur in their breasts,
> To breathe a while in temperate English air,
> Where lips are spic'd with free and loyal counsels,
> Where policies are not ruinous, but saving;
> Wisdom is simple, valour righteous,
> Human, and hating facts of brutish forces;
> And whose grave natures scorn the scoffs of France,
> The empty compliments of Italy,
> The anyway encroaching pride of Spain,
> And love men modest, hearty, just and plain.
>   (*Conspiracy*, II.ii.46–57)

Byron finds no charm in the moderation he might learn across the Channel; instead, he bestows his admiration upon the king of Spain. Not surprisingly, he parallels this ambitious monarch to Alexander, by now almost a byword for irresponsible applications. The king's lust for conquest is misunderstood; he "desir'd t'extend" his empire

> so that he might withal
> Extend religion through it, and all nations
> Reduce to one firm constitution
> Of piety, justice, and one public weal;
> To which end he made all his matchless subjects
> Make tents their castles and their garrisons;
> True Catholics, countrymen and their allies;
> Heretics, strangers and their enemies.
>
> (*Conspiracy*, IV.ii.147–54)

Montigny, who hears this encomium, chooses to point its lesson another way:

> The greatest commendation we can give
> To the remembrance of that king deceas'd
> Is that he spar'd not his own eldest son,
> But put him justly to a violent death,
> Because he sought to trouble his estates.
>
> (*Conspiracy*, IV.ii.158–62)

"That bit, my lord, upon my life," murmurs the chancellor to Montigny as Byron gasps, "Is't so?" (line 163).

Byron's susceptibility to the falsehoods of Spain (as opposed to England's moderate truths) carries over into his fanatical Catholicism. As epitaph, "he never wish'd more glorious title / Than to be call'd Scourge of the Huguenots" (*Tragedy*, v.i.75–76). Dragged off to prison, he protests: "Ye see all how they use good Catholics!" (*Tragedy*, IV.ii.290). Essex's personal chaplain thought him to be "either an atheist or a papist";[16] Henry has a similar attitude to Byron: "Come, you are an atheist, Byron, and a traitor / Both foul and damnable" (*Tragedy*, IV.ii.250–51). The chancellor offers the most balanced summary of Byron's piety: "Suppose it true, it made him false; but wills / And worthy minds witchcraft could never force" (*Tragedy*, v.ii.285–86). Byron has a "Spanish heart," like Essex and Raleigh before him.

The classic fear of Spain is called upon to clarify the danger Byron poses to the state. Henry IV has been seen as Chapman's ideal ruler— wise, tolerant, protective of his country's unity.[17] Henry is willing to allow Byron to profit from another's mistakes by sending him to England, but his hatred of divisiveness and religious faction is such that he shows no mercy when Byron proves to be irremediably lost. The king's desire for peace and civil stability transcends differences of religion; Byron's main danger to the state is a religion that ignores national boundaries.

The fall of Essex, whose grandiose ambitions parallel Byron's, should warn Byron away, as should the king's admiration of English stability and moderation. But Byron refuses to learn history's lesson, and he dies for his opposition to a reasonable and decent king. The Essex story plays out Byron's fate in the face of his blindness; ambitious men are doomed to repeat each other's folly. Like Samuel Daniel's closet Senecan tragedy about Essex, *Philotas,* Chapman's play adopts a general and sententious perspective upon Byron's fall. Unlike Jonson, Chapman upholds the primacy of poetry, as he points out in the dedication of his utterly fictive *Revenge of Bussy d'Ambois* (1613):

> And for the autentical truth of either person or action, who
> (worth the respecting) will expect it in a poem, whose
> subject is not truth, but things like truth? Poor envious souls
> they are that cavil at truth's want in these natural fictions:
> material instruction, elegant and sententious excitation to
> virtue, and deflection from her contrary, being the soul,
> limbs and limits of an autentical tragedy.
>
> (Parrott, *Tragedies,* p. 77)

But although Chapman's tendency is to generalize the fate of Byron, his use in the play of the Essex story as a "material instruction" that Byron rejects lends greater authority to "autentical truth" than we might expect from the author of *Bussy d'Ambois.* While both Sejanus and Byron fill out the generalized homiletic pattern of Blind Ambition, Jonson's and Chapman's use of the Essex story as a background lends a historical particularity to their sentand purpose.

For neither dramatist is the past dredged up purely for its own sake, or for inflammatory partisan aims; rather recent and ancient history provide a framework for relevant moral argument. The use of historical parallels by both Jonson and Chapman underscores their confidence in the continuity of history, in the universality of the moral laws discoverable in the past human experience. In this sense, Jonson's insistence upon "truth of argument" and Chapman's defense of "natural fictions" can be seen, not as two opposed attitudes to historical scholarship, but as expressions of the same optimism about the educability of their audiences and their leaders. The tragedy, in both plays, results from the failure to learn: the Roman mob submits to the greater monster Macro after rending Sejanus; Byron persists in misunderstanding what people tell him about Essex. While the moral stance of each playwright is clear, doubts about the efficacy with which historical understanding can be communicated persist at the close of each play.

Nonetheless, both Chapman and Jonson, at the end of their careers, continued to explore the possibilities of humanist historical drama. Chapman's *Tragedy of Chabot,* licensed 39 April 1635, almost a year after his death, and published only in 1639 in a version reworked by Shirley, draws a parallel between the fall of Chabot and the fall of James's first favorite, Robert Carr, earl of Somerset. Norma D. Solve, who has argued that "the tragedy in question presents an action which agrees more closely with the English situation than with the story in the French source," goes on to suggest that Chapman designed the play as an "appeal to James for mercy" for Somerset, Chapman's friend and patron.[18] The tendency to see in plays of this kind a personal political bias extends to studies of Jonson as well: DeLuna's contention that in *Catiline* Jonson portrays himself in Quintus Curius and thus dramatizes his own key service to the government at the time of the Gunpowder Plot, while more ambitious, follows similar lines.[19] One risk for the authors of historical dramas based upon contemporary applications is the charge of partisanship. This weakness is more apparent in *Chabot* than in *Catiline,* a play that attacks faction and divisiveness and celebrates political stability. Even so, Chapman presents in Francis a most unflattering portrait of a bungling, testy, and vain monarch: and the Chabot family's aggressive righteousness, proclaiming "the duty of the absolute monarch to respect the liberty of the loyal subject" would hardly be likely to appease James's anger at Somerset. Readings of the plays as partisan or personal manifestoes, like Solve's and DeLuna's, founder because the playwrights, as we have seen in *Sejanus* and *Byron,* deplore simple one-dimensional parallels. As an appeal to James, *Chabot* is a failure: as Burton says, "the pattern is clear: the evil is disseminated by an imperfect King, whose pride encourages intrigue and who uses intrigue to eject the virtuous man from office."[20] Chapman's perspective in *Chabot* is once again moralistic and historical, but the direction is different: whereas, in *Byron,* the lesson of Essex must be learned by the doomed protagonist, the lesson of *Chabot* is directed to the royal audience.

Jonson's last play, the *Mortimer* fragment, is a similar attack upon the degenerate Stuart monarchy itself. First printed in the 1640 Folio of Jonson's *Works, Mortimer His Fall* consists only of an Argument and a brief first scene. The piece is generally acknowledged to date from late in Jonson's career; the comment in the Folio that he died and "left it unfinish'd" suggests that he was working on it shortly before his death.[21] The story of Mortimer's ascendancy over Edward II and continued dominance over his son, Edward III, is certainly a suggestive one in the context of the duke of Buckingham's remarkably swift rise to power over both James and Charles. His assassination in 1628 might have given the author of *Sejanus* cause to meditate once again on ambition's "slippery height" (*Sejanus:* V.895). As conceived by Jonson, *Mortimer* would have been a tragedy more regular than *Sejanus:* each of the acts is followed by a Chorus that sententiously comments on the events the audience has witnessed or describes events that Jonson, for reasons of decorum, chooses not to stage. The turning point of the action is the Chorus after the third act:

> The *Chorus* of Countrey Justices, and their Wives,
> telling how they were deluded, and made beleeve, the old
> King liv'd, by the shew of him in *Corfe* Castle; and how they
> saw him eat, and use his knife, like the Old King, &c. with
> the description of the feigned Lights, and Masques there,
> that deceiv'd 'hem, all which came from the Court.

The equation of Mortimer's deception with the artificial glories of the court masque puts the ambitious favorite on a level with Jonson's victorious rival on the court stage, Inigo Jones. The young king must learn to see through these deceptions, which, the Chorus to the fourth act makes clear, he eventually does:

> Mortimer's *securitie, scorne of the Nobilitie, too much*
> *familiaritie with the Queene, related by the* Chorus, *the report of*
> *the Kings surprizing him in his Mothers bed-chamber, a generall*
> *gladnesse, his being sent to execution.*[22]

Central to both *Sejanus* and *Mortimer* is Jonson's faith in historical truth: where the early tragedy dramatizes the struggle of truth against a corrupt state, the late fragment pits truth against shows, deceptions, masques—impostures that the king dispels as he bursts into his mother's bedroom.

The image of the king as discoverer, unmasker, can be seen as a thinly veiled reproach to the real king, Charles I, for isolating himself from his kingdom in an increasingly theatrical court. Further, the attack upon "feigned Lights" and artificial shows in *Mortimer* suggests Jonson's own disenchantment with the court masque. In his hands, the masque had served not merely as a glorification of the monarchy but also as an educational experience for its royal audience. The primacy of stage machinery and spectacle over humanistic message that Inigo Jones's ascendancy over the poet carried with it can account for the antitheatrical climax of *Mortimer*. *Mortimer* not only rejects English dramatic tradition in its rigidly Senecan design, it also attacks the court's own sponsorship of theatrical illusion as an evasion of truth.

Thus the message of the fragment is not simply the political one that Charles should grow out of his embarrassing dependency upon favorites but a broader demand, expressed in theatrical terms, that he should act like a king. In enunciating the problem this way, Jonson taps a deep vein of contemporary confusion about the nature of monarchy. Shakespeare's Henry IV promises: "I will from henceforth rather be myself, / Mighty and to be feared" (*1 Henry IV*, I.iii.5–6); his own career and Hal's growth suggest that the relationship between king and self is not so easy, but in the historical plays of the Stuart period this problem becomes an absolute conundrum. Philip Edwards has defined *Believe as Ye List* and *Perkin Warbeck* as "Pretender plays," "exploring the meaning of the terms 'counterfeit' and 'natural' in the period of perturbed and perplexed relationships between monarch and people about the year 1630." Anne Barton too has seen in these Caroline plays a tension between real kings—"practical, cautious, unheroic . . . greatly occupied with questions of cold cash"—and idealized, folk-ballad kings, "just, shrewd, and personal." In an age in which historians "had withdrawn all imagination from their observations," in Cope's phrase,[23] a Shakespearean dramatic historiography, with its blend of magical and practical elements, no longer seemed possible. Jonson and Chapman suggested an alternative: a humanist historical drama stressing the importance of enlightened rule. The best king is the historian, like Chapman's Henry, or the unmasker, like Jonson's Edward III. But censors found enlightenment distressing, and audiences seem to have found the aggressive righteousness of these two playwrights unattractive. At any rate, the reign of Charles I is characterized by the evolution of plays (culminating in Ford's *Perkin Warbeck*) that reject the humanist ideal of responsible kingship and replace it with pure fairy tale.

ii

In this context, Thomas Drue's *The Life of the Dutches of Suffolke* is of some importance; hardly a neglected masterpiece, this play, after the difficulties of licensing in 1624, was "divers and sundry times acted, with good applause"—so the title page of the 1631 Quarto announces. The play is unique in that it draws its ostensible story from the recent English past—the duchess flees from England to escape the Catholic persecutions of Mary Tudor—and is susceptible of application to events of more immediate concern. On a superficial level, the duchess's resolute Protestantism and homelessness are reminiscent of Princess Elizabeth's condition after the destruction of the palatinate; in the play, the duchess is wooed by the county palatine, who arrives to announce that he has unexpectedly been elected king of Poland. She does not marry this obvious embodiment of the Bohemian king, however; but she owes her deliverance from the pursuivants who at last catch her in the fifth act to the palsgrave's miraculous appearance on the scene. Most of the play operates on this jolly level. When forced to choose between her noble suitors, Erbaigh and the palsgrave, the duchess instead marries her servant, Bertie. The only person who objects to the situation, Fox, another servant who wants her for himself, quickly reforms and devotes his time to foiling the duchess's enemies.

These are portrayed as crazed, foolish fanatics: at his release from the Tower after Edward's death, Bonner boasts

> Then let our Suffolkes Dowager expect
> Answere for her scorn'd taunts she threw on me of late,
> That hot spirit, fire and flax, Madam fagot stick,
> If she recant not I will fagot her,
> If all the wood in Middlesex can doo't,
> Or London's Bishopricke have means to pay fort.[24]

Against the insanity, incoherence, and brutality of the Catholics is set the resourcefulness and cunning of the duchess's friends, who engineer a series of farce escapes. It is all good fun, but from time to time the play waxes serious and reminds its audience of the plight of that other "sweete Princes, wrong'd Elizabeth"(sig. C2r):

> You people happy in a land of peace
> That joy your consciences, with the world's increase,
> Look with indifference into my sad life,
> Here my poore husband, dares not know his wife,
> And I a princes, to avoid like danger,
> Must use my owne deere husband, as a stranger.
>
> (sig. F1r)

The reproach chides Stuart indifference to the cause of Protestantism. More forcefully, the play concludes with a direct challenge to the successor to the throne, couched in the form of a prayer for the new queen:

> Or if it be thy gracious providence,
> For to remove her to a happier place,
> Let in her Stead arise, and from her ashes come,
> A Phenix may enlighten Christendome.
>
> (sig. I1r)

The implications are clear: like Jonson in the *Mortimer* fragment, Drue is asking the monarch to unveil himself, to act, in this case to join the growing and popular war party. With its farce action, *The Dutches of Suffolke* insists upon a comic reading of the interval between Edward and Elizabeth: Atkinson's announcement of Mary's death and the duchess's restoration accompany her deliverance at the palsgrave's hand. The play cheerfully suggests that a true Protestant monarch is duty bound to "enlighten Christendome"; the curious scene in which Erasmus of Rotterdam happens upon the duchess and Bertie and chats with them in Latin epitomizes Drue's lighthearted humanism (sig. F3r-v).

Naive as it is, *The Dutches of Suffolke* is not merely comical history, in which the true prince, Elizabeth, finally assumes the throne and restores order. It draws upon contemporary dissatisfaction with Stuart monarchy and does so in terms of the English past. The mistrust of the king that shows through in the last plays of Jonson and Chapman finds even more inflammatory expression in the plays of Massinger. While Jonson, Chapman, and even Daniel draw parallels in order to illustrate the laws the govern human experience, Massinger often simply adds a "political element" to spice up a flat romance. *The Bondman,* licensed 3 December 1623, calumniates Buckingham and Middlesex and decries English unreadiness for war. The famous historian S. R. Gardiner was first to point out this applicability: "we have a treatment of the politics of the day so plain and transparent, that anyone who possesses only a slight acquaintance with the history of the reigns of the first two Stuarts can read it at a glance." But the play itself is a romance; the center of dramatic interest remains Pisander's love for Cleora. Similarly, *The Maid of Honour's* connection with the problems of the palatinate is tenuous and of no importance to the action of the play.[25]

In only two of the many plays in which Massinger was involved do we find a sustained treatment of foreign affairs: *The Tragedy of Sir John van olden Barnavelt,* which survives in manuscript with the notes of the censor, Sir George Buc (Master of Revels from 1610 to 1623), still intact, and *Believe as Ye List,* which Herbert refused to license on 11 January 1631. The first play, a collaboration with Fletcher, is unquestionably inflammatory, as Wilhelmina P. Frijlinck has pointed out: the prince of Orange is celebrated as an ideal warrior-king, and Barnavelt is reviled as a Machiavellian religious hypocrite.[26] His striving for religious freedom becomes, in English terms, violent fanaticism:

> Examine all men
> Branded with such fowle sins as you now die for,
> And you shall find their first step still, Religion:
> Gowrie in Scotland, 'twas his maine pretention:

Was he not honest too? his cuntries father?
Thos fiery Sperritts next, that hatched in England
That bloody Powder-plot: and thought like meteors
To have flashed their Cuntryes peace out in a Moment,
Were not their Barrells loden with Religion?
Were they not pious, just, and zealous Subjects?

(V.iii.2938–47)

So does a lord chide Barnavelt with English examples as he goes to the scaffold. In fact, the play portrays Barnavelt's Arminian followers indiscriminately as Papists and Puritans; the censor complained not only about the play's dangerous subject, but also about its authors' inaccuracy. When Barnavelt inflames the States General to deny the prince admittance to their assembly, Buc rose in protest: "I like not this," he comments in the margin, "neither do I think y^t the pr. was thus disgracefully used" (I.iii).

As an attempt to use recent foreign history to dramatize an English problem, *Barnavelt* is slipshod and irresponsible; ostensibly chiding Barnavelt's divisiveness, the play works in the opposite direction to promote unease and dissension. The events it comments upon are still fresh in memory, and its judgments of them are unhampered by any serious effort to understand or evaluate either the Dutch or English situation.

Believe as Ye List must have started its career as the same kind of play; Herbert refused to license the play because of its subject matter: "the deposing of Sebastian king of Portugal, by Philip the [Second,] and ther being a peace sworen twixte the kings of England and Spayne."[27] Examination of the manuscript has revealed the name *Sebastian* rubbed out and replaced by *Antiochus* several times; "his very nose" has been substituted for the more specific "his German nose," and other elements of physical description have been altered. The prologue admits, cautiously of course, the author's worries that the play may be seen as topical:

> If you find what's Romane here
> Grecian or Asiatic, draw too near
> A late and sad example, 'tis confessed
> He's but an English scholar at his best,
> A stranger to cosmography, and may err
> In the countries' names, the shape and character
> Of the persons he presents.[28]

Gardiner lept upon the suggestion that lurks here and identified the reluctance of the Carthaginians to shelter Antiochus and the vacillation

of Prusias, King of Bithynia, as reflections, not upon Sebastian of Portugal, but of Frederick's cool reception in exile. Of the scene in which
Prusias succumbs, Gardiner proclaimed, "Then, as if Massinger saw into
the very heart of the man who was to deliver up Strafford to the block,
we have the poor, helpless King exclaiming, when Flaminius proudly
offers peace or war; 'How can I / Dispense with my faith given' *Phi.*: 'I'll
yield you reasons.' *Pru.* 'Let it be peace then.' "[29] In his eagerness to see
Massinger as a faithful and consistent adherent to the policies of his
patrons, Gardiner disregarded the implications of the play's whole action: English and Dutch reluctance to help Frederick may be satirized in
the Carthaginians and Bithynians, but Antiochus himself shows no
urgent desire to recapture his kingdom. The play revolves around his
attempts to convince others of his true identity—an identity that is
personal and private, not political. The action is resolved when his royal
identity, not his royal position, is restored to him by Marcellus; what he
gains is recognition as an enemy of Rome who must be punished:

> Then 'tis easy
> To prophesy I have not long to live,
> Though the manner how I shall die is uncertain.
> Nay, weep not: since 'tis not in you to help me,
> These showers of tears are fruitless. May my story
> Teach potentates humility and instruct
> Proud monarchs, though they govern human things
> A greater power does raise, or pull down, kings!
>
> (v.ii)

Rising literally from a heap of dead bodies on the battlefield, Antiochus
wins his quest for recognition when he earns his death.

The relationship to the court of Charles I is not purely satirical here:
Edwards sees Antiochus, like Ford's Perkin Warbeck, as "a luminous
figure appearing from the mists announcing he is the dead past, newly
come alive in order to bring succour to an ailing nation." This helps to
explain the appeal of Antiochus to an audience who "looked on the
occupant of the throne as the dried husk of a king";[30] yet significantly,
the pretender in this play wins penal servitude, not restoration. The
decisive actions, the dramatic, phoenixlike self-revelations demanded of
monarchs by Jonson, Chapman, and even Drue are subtly transformed in
Believe as Ye List. Antiochus recovers his death when he recovers his royal
name: he rises from his own ashes only to be consumed. Massinger
suggests in this play what Ford is to explore most completely in *Perkin
Warbeck:* that kingship itself is a personal matter, a maiming, terrible

secret that exists wholly outside of history and politics. The solution to the question of Antiochus's royal identity rests in his royal demeanor, not in the political dimensions of his rule. The evocations of Sebastian and Frederick in the play raise a larger question, the question of the extent to which a deposed king, a king without a kingdom, can be said to be royal at all. Massinger finds the answer not in the traditional distinction between the king's two bodies but in the stoicism and courtly behavior of the man himself.

iii

The play's skeptical title, *Believe as Ye List,* emphasizes the riddle lurking in its treatment of kingship: so too does the title of the most important English history play of this period, John Ford's *Chronicle History of Perkin Warbeck, A Strange Truth.* The impostor's challenge to the traditional connection between royalty and power provokes, as in *Mortimer,* some confusion about the truth of dramatic illusion itself. Ford's play, dialectical to the end, offers no resolution of the contradictory truths voiced by Perkin and Henry VII. Scholars have suggested various relationships between the two plays, including the notion that *Perkin Warbeck* is counterpropaganda to *Believe as Ye List:* but both plays approach the problem of Bohemia's Winter King as a theatrical one.[31] Frederick's misfortunes provoked in Ford and Massinger renewed speculation on an idea and image that had intrigued Shakespeare—the player king. Cope calls *Perkin Warbeck* "a species of actor's agon: the question it puts is one of negative identity: that is, who is the player-king, the mocking lord of misrule who shakes a Falstaffian sword of lath?"[32] In the context of Ford's play, the answer is not as simple as it seems.

Ford's major change from his sources (Bacon's and Gainsford's histories of Henry VII's reign) has the effect of leaving ambiguous the validity of Warbeck's claims. Both historians vilify Perkin's humble origins, and Warbeck himself is reported to have confessed that his father was in fact John Osbek, not Edward IV. Warbeck, in Ford's play, goes to death with his royal bearing and confidence in himself unshaken, leaving the audience in what T. S. Eliot called "the right state of uncertainty, wondering whether his kingly and steadfast behaviour is due to his royal blood, or merely due to his passionate conviction that he is of royal blood." Jonas Barish dubs the play "anti-history": Ford "invites us throughout . . . to entertain the hypothesis that Perkin may be telling the truth."[33] By refusing to accept history's judgment as final, Ford gives us an impostor whose language and bearing proclaim him a king and pits him against a skillful administrator who happens to hold a throne. The result is a somewhat perverse restaging of the confrontation that animates Shakespeare's *Richard II*. For Ford as for Massinger, the theory of the king's two bodies is a riddle to be toyed with; but Ford goes further, parodically engaging Shakespearean models and ironically echoing the language of Bacon's history, to find a riddle at the heart of the idea of historical truth itself.

The prologue to the play, in its deadpan way, hardly prepares an audience for the strangeness of the truth they are about to witness. The author portrays himself as a diligent scholar:

> Studies have of this nature been of late
> So out of fashion, so unfollowed, that
> It is become more justice to revive
> The antic follies of the times than strive
> To countenance wise industry.

> (lines 1–5)

This pose has led many critics to see *Perkin Warbeck* as a "study," a throwback to an old form, "bookish" and quaint.[34] But Ford has been careful here to evoke Shakespeare's own troublesome prologues: like that to *Henry V,* Ford's prologue apologizes for the limitations of the stage; like that to *Henry VIII*, it chides those who revive "antic follies." "Wise industry" characterizes the endeavor here, and the phrase echoes Bacon's history: *wise* serves there as a key adjective, denoting Henry's political skill. In this atmosphere of solemnity, Ford addresses his play to the "clearer judgments" he has singled out as the play's proper audience. To them:

> He shows a history couch'd in a play,
> A history of noble mention, known,
> Famous and true: most noble, 'cause our own,
> Not forged from Italy, from France, from Spain,
> But chronicled at home.

> (lines 14–18)

Ford stresses the relationship between this play and both the chronicle histories of the past and Bacon's "learned and . . . honorable pen" (dedication). "On these two rests the fate / Of worthy expectation," he promises: "truth and state." (prologue, lines 25–26) The phrase suggests a rigorous historical method; on the face of it, "truth and state" are the concerns of responsible historians like Jonson and Chapman. In this play, the substance of Warbeck's claims should be of some importance, if we are to rely upon Ford's sober invocation of his illustrious predecessors.

But the play's title reminds us that "truth" here will be "strange"; Ford eschews research into Warbeck's origins and summarily dismisses him from consideration as a contender for the throne. His incompetence and cowardice in battle, his reliance upon foolish advisors, his ignorance of politics all establish his inadequacy in contrast to Henry. At his death, Warbeck defines his kingdom in distinctly different terms: "Even when I fell, I stood enthroned a monarch / Of one chaste wife's troth pure and uncorrupted" (v.iii.125–26). As in *Henry VIII,* we find ourselves confounded by puns that toy with "truth" and "troth"—fidelity to fact as opposed to fealty itself.

Thus the phrase *truth and state* sets up a ruthless dialectic. The demands of "truth and state"—as historical truth and good statesmanship—enunciated by Henry and his advisors confront Perkin's imposture and political incompetence. Contrariwise, Perkin's "truth and state"—truth to ideals and royal bearing—plays off against Henry's opportunism and undignified delight in his own cunning. Both complexes of values are rigid: the schematic design of Ford's play makes any serious political discussion impossible. Henry is the more competent ruler; Perkin the more regal. James, as Anderson has pointed out, falls somewhere between these two poles, developing from an impressionable admirer of Perkin to a skilled political operator. From the riddling equivocations of this phrase in the prologue, through the shifts of scene from England to Scotland and back again in the exposition, to the uncertainties of the end, Ford strives for a balance of sympathies in his audience.[35] The demands of humanist history for factual and moral truth are counterpoised by the imperatives of theatrical illusion. Neither can claim exclusive authority: fact is not the same as truth, nor is pure belief.

At issue is the possibility of illusionistic historical drama itself. Henry's contempt for Perkin, rich in phrases borrowed from Bacon, is witheringly antitheatrical:

> first Ireland,
> The common stage of novelty, presented
> This gewgaw to oppose us.
>
> (I.i.105–7)

Perkin is a "colossic statue," a "smoke of straw," a "pageant majesty": but these sneers are undercut by fear. Henry reveals himself to be "haunted," "pursued," "frighted with false apparitions." Peter Ure and Jonas Barish have pointed out the echoes of *1 Henry IV* in these opening lines;

politically, they can remind us of the shakiness of Henry Tudor's title, but theatrically they conjure up that world of counterfeit kings in which Hal must find his way.[36]

Henry's distaste for the language of theatrical illusion colors his response to the captured Perkin. He cannot marvel: "Dawbney, / We observe no wonder" (v.ii.36–37). To Perkin's unshakeable conviction of his royal birth, Henry responds as to a performance "oft rehearsed / Till, learnt by heart, 'tis now received for truth" (v.ii.78–79). For Barish, "the wooden inadequacy of this as a response to the total phenomenon of Perkin stamps Henry as the smaller, drier, more prosaic personality," but it is worth remembering here that the explanation Henry offers is Bacon's own: "Nay himself with long and continual counterfeiting and with oft telling a lie, was turned (by habit) almost into the thing he seemed to be; and from a liar to a believer."[37] Bacon's ironic mockery of the "mists" and "sparks" of imposture troubling Henry's realm is turned against the king himself in the play.

Glorying in his own theatricality, Perkin spectacularly defies Henry's merely political power:

> But let the world, as all to whom
> I am this day a spectacle, to time deliver
> And by tradition fix posterity,
> Without another chronicle than truth,
> How constantly my resolution suffered
> A martyrdom of majesty.
>
> (v.iii.70–75)

He expresses his triumph in terms of theatrical tradition. Accepting Henry's premise that he is an actor playing a part, Perkin asserts the power of illusion, even to the point of suggesting that he is himself a figment of the haunted king's imagination:

> Our ends, and Warwick's head,
> Innocent Warwick's head—for we are prologue
> But to his tragedy—conclude the wonder
> Of Henry's fears.
>
> (v.iii.190–93)

Ford's interest in abnormal psychology surfaces here in the tantalizing notion that Perkin embodies a repressed other side of the practical Tudor monarch.[38]

Henry is portrayed throughout the play as tough, practical, merciful, and just; but curiously enough, Ford stresses the ways in which the king's manipulation of his royal image can also be seen as playacting. The scene in which he learns of Stanley's perfidy is a good case in point. He excuses himself from confronting Sir William on the grounds that

> If 'a speak to me
> I could deny him nothing. To prevent it,
> I must withdraw.

> (II.ii.42–44)

The confrontation that follows raises some serious questions about the justice of Stanley's conviction. Clifford, the informer, draws only scorn from Stanley when he appeals to "my truth and the state's safety" (line 81). Contemptuously, Stanley puns on the prologue's slippery phrase as he marks on Clifford's cheeks "a state-informer's character, more ugly / Stamped on a noble name than on a base" (lines 90–91). Clifford's "truth" is linked to images of counterfeiting; Stanley, on the other hand, prophesies that his reputation will emerge unblemished "In chronicles writ in another age" (line 102). The confusion provoked by Stanley's dignified bearing is like that provoked by Buckingham's farewell in *Henry VIII*: how can an informer, who betrays like Cain or Judas a sacred trust, ever speak true? Stanley's valedictory tag, "Subjects deserve their deaths whose kings are just" (line 109), is similarly riddling; especially because the doubts seeded by it are far from dispelled on the king's return, when he banishes Clifford from the court. Henry now treats Stanley's death as the result of Clifford's private malice:

> We have given credit
> To every point of Clifford's information,
> The only evidence 'gainst Stanley's head.
> 'A dies for't; are you pleased?

> (lines 114–17)

This seems a bit harsh, especially since the execution of Stanley has already been described as a political necessity by Durham, who has argued against a pardon:

> You may, you may;
> And so persuade your subjects that the title
> Of York is better, nay, more just and lawful
> Than yours of Lancaster; so Stanley holds:
> Which if it be not treason in the highest,
> Then we are traitors all, perjured and false
> Who have took oath to Henry and the justice
> Of Henry's title—Oxford, Surrey, Dawbney,

With all your other peers of state and church
Foresworn, and Stanley true alone to heaven
And England's lawful heir.

(lines 14–24)

The issue is not so much one of guilt as (Durham makes clear) "truth,"
which is, in terms of Henry's title, a far from certain commodity. Earlier
in the play, Stanley himself endorses the executions of Simnel's supporters as the sure way to establish

Precedents sufficient to forewarn
The present times, or any that live in them,
What folly, nay, what madness 'twere to lift
A finger up in all defense by yours,
Which can be but impostorous in title.

(I.i.96–100)

The vagueness of the syntax here suggests Stanley's true attitude toward
the king's title; the madness and folly of opposition to the king is purely
political. In II.ii the king "stages" Stanley's death as an example of his
justice: he officiously does not involve himself, and he turns on Clifford.
"Let Justice / Proceed in execution," (lines 39–40) he announces, with-
drawing, and the display of his "chancery of pity" (line 12) is wholly
successful: "'Tis a king / Compos'd of gentleness—" says Surrey; "Rare
and unheard of!" exclaims Durham (lines 49–50).

Henry's assertions about divine right are similarly undercut, usually
by the king's own biting wit. Lambert Simnel's claim to royal birth, for
example, draws Henry's scorn:

Lambert, the eldest, lords, is in our service,
Preferr'd by an officious care of duty
From the scullery to a falc'ner; strange example!
Which shows the difference between noble natures
And the baseborn.

(I.i.64–68)

Henry mocks the rhetoric of kingship in his own case as well:

A guard of angels and the holy prayers
Of loyal subjects are a sure defense
Against all force and counsel of intrusion.
But now, my lords, put case some of our nobles,
Our "great ones," should give countenance and courage
To trim Duke Perkin, you will all confess

Our bounties have unthriftily been scattered
Amongst unthankful men.

(1.i.73–80)

Following the satirical "character" of Simnel, the speech suggests an ironic equation between the two player kings. Like Lambert, Henry holds his office by virtue of "officious care of duty"; the "angels" that guard his throne are coins, "bounties" well bestowed.

Royal mystique is rhetorical dressing up of administrative good sense, and its language rings hollow in Henry's mouth:

Thoughts busied in the sphere of royalty
Fix not on creeping worms without their stings,
Mere excrements of earth. The use of time
Is thriving safety, and a wise prevention
Of ills expected.

(IV.v.94–98)

The effect is as jarring as Bacon's rare shifts into providential rhetoric in his history. Henry's talk of royal prerogatives always includes awareness of the need for action, for a concrete plan. Only to his advisors does providence have anything to do with the hunting down of Warbeck. Not admitted to the king's confidence, they can only marvel.

Wise Henry
Divines aforehand of events; with him
Attempts and execution are one act,

(IV.iv.66–68)

Dawbney tells us as the clever monarch acts decisively on the latest news from the front. Earlier, Urswick, praising "the powers who seated / King Henry on his lawful throne" (III.i.14–15), promptly misses the point when Henry discloses to him the real source of his power:

Money gives soul to action. Our competitor,
The Flemish counterfeit, with James of Scotland,
Will prove what courage, need and want can nourish
Without the food of fit supplies; but, Urswick,
I have a charm in secret that shall loose
The witchcraft wherewith young King James is bound,
And free it at my pleasure without bloodshed.

(III.i.29–35)

"Your majesty's a wise king, sent from heaven / Protector of the just" (lines 136–37), marvels Urswick, still left in the dark. Henry is teasing his advisors here: the secret charm, of course, is his politic offer to James of marriage to his daughter. Henry is God-given only in so far as he can think ahead and make plans. For him, whatever magic Perkin might possess is empty posturing, witchcraft. Only at the end does he grudgingly allow: "Perkin, we are inform'd, is arm'd to die; / In that we'll honor him" (v.iii.214–15). But the language is again revealing: Perkin's heroism reaches Henry's ears as news, as information.

Perkin Warbeck does not share Henry's (or Bacon's) distaste for the language of royal divinity. His first appearance at the Scottish court, amidst considerable pomp and pageantry, prompts an admiring linguistic response from James: "He must be more than subject who can utter / The language of a king, and such is thine" (II.i.103–4). Crawford, a Scot skeptical of Warbeck's story, is nonetheless amazed at the skill with which it is told:

> 'Tis more than strange; my reason cannot answer
> Such argument of fine imposture, couch'd
> In witchcraft of persuasion, that it fashions
> Impossibilities, as if appearance
> Could cozen truth itself; this dukeling mushroom
> Hath doubtless charmed the King.
>
> (II.iii.1–6)

Crawford's bafflement at Perkin's ability to "fashion impossibilities" reflects the audience's reaction to his strange tale; in relation to the prologue's promise, which this speech echoes, of "history couch'd in a play" we are again confronted with the possibility that reason and fact are not the sole arbiters of truth. For *couch'd* here means "lying hidden or concealed, covert" (*OED*): Crawford raises the issue here that we might be dealing, not with antihistory, but with a mystifying, baffling, irrational alternative truth. The idea, exploited by Jonson and Chapman, that an historical play can covertly embody a contemporary political issue is met by the suggestion in *Perkin Warbeck* that what public history hides is something alien to it, private, and wholly incomprehensible. As Warbeck tells the story of his years in exile to James, we recognize it for the fiction that it is. Ostentatiously he promises the king that he is "reserving the relation" of its circumstances "to the secrecy of your own princely ear" (II.i.94–95).

Perkin demands that his Scottish audience accept his story on faith and endorse the secret of his kingship with pity. His self-presentation is both archly formal and nakedly pathetic:

> Most high, most mighty king! that now there stands
> Before your eyes, in presence of your peers,
> A subject of the rarest kind of pity
> That hath in any age touched noble hearts,
> The vulgar story of a prince's ruin
> Hath made it too apparent.
>
> (II.i.40–45)

Warbeck reminds the Scots of his sorrows

> whose true relation draws
> Compassion, melted into weeping eyes
> And bleeding souls.
>
> (II.i.54–56)

Perkin cozens truth with pathos; the "softness of my childhood," he tells us, deterred the hardened murderers (line 62), and this is the level of the appeal he makes throughout. He glosses over the facts—"registered already in the volume / Of all men's tongues" (lines 54–55)—and dwells instead upon the pathetic scene of his brother's death. The prologue's puns recur in Perkin's account of the murderers' lies:

> Great king, they spar'd my life, the butchers spar'd it,
> Return'd the tyrant, my unnatural uncle,
> A truth of my dispatch.
>
> (II.i.65–67)

Warbeck's account of his childhood is wholly internal, uncircumstantial. He recalls the growth in him of "disdain / Of living so unknown, in such a servile / And abject lowness" (lines 71–73). He emphasizes the mysteriousness of his origins here, through fairy-tale account of his deliverance and his spontaneous "recollecting who I was" (line 75), prompted by the stirrings of his royal blood.

Put to the test, Warbeck's conviction of the "divinity / Of royal birth" (IV.v.56–57) rings true later in the play. He lashes out at Frion's suggestion that he observe moderation "If you will appear a prince indeed":

> What a saucy rudeness
> Prompts this distrust! If, if I will appear!
> Appear a prince! Death throttle such deceits
> Even in their birth of utterance; cursed cozenage
> Of trust! Ye make me mad; 'twere best, it seems,
> That I should turn impostor to myself,

> Be mine own counterfeit, belie the truth
> Of my dear mother's womb, the bed
> Of a prince murdered and a living baffled!
>
> (IV.ii.22–30)

With full conviction he invokes the most secret authenticators of kingship: the mother's womb and the royal bed. Like Henry, he derides Simnel's pretension, even to the point of using Henry's own sneering tone. "Perkin a king? a king!" (IV.iv.93), cries Henry in utter disbelief; Perkin echoes the insult in his disdain of Lambert Simnel, "Thou an earl?" (V.iii.56). The imagery of infectious vapors that the royal party inherits from Bacon and applies to Perkin ("This smoke of straw was packed from France again / T'infect some grosser air," I.i.115–16) finds its way into Perkin's mouth when Simnel urges him to recant:

> A dunghill was thy cradle. So a puddle
> By virtue of the sunbeams breathes a vapour
> To infect the purer air, which drops again
> Into the muddy womb that first exhal'd it.
>
> (V.iii.60–63)

Henry jokes about Simnel's "noble nature" (I.i.67), but for Perkin, heredity is no laughing matter:

> But sirrah, ran there in thy veins one drop
> Of such a royal blood as flows in mine,
> Thou wouldst not change condition to be second
> In England's state without the crown itself.
> Coarse creatures are incapable of excellence.
>
> (lines 65–69)

Perkin's snobbery immediately sets him apart from the "officious" (as Henry puts it, I.i.65) Simnel; Henry fails to recognize this fundamental difference in the two claimants. To him, Perkin is merely more polished in performance.

But to James of Scotland polish is everything. James is immediately susceptible to Perkin's performance, and he admits the impostor into the international community of kings:

> The right of kings, my lords, extends not only
> To the safe conservation of their own,
> But also to the aid of such allies
> As change of time and state hath oftentimes
> Hurled down from careful crowns.
>
> (II.i.18–22)

This notion of mutual support among monarchs goes well beyond Henry's identification of kingship with the national interest alone. When Huntly begs that James not marry Katherine to "a straggler," the king of Scots is quick to invoke this principle:

> Kings are counterfeits
> In your repute, grave oracle, not presently
> Set on their thrones with sceptres in their fists.
> But use your own detraction. 'Tis our pleasure
> To give our cousin York for wife our kinswoman,
> The lady Katherine. Instinct for sovereignty
> Designs the honour, though her peevish father
> Usurps our resolution.
>
> (II.ii.37–44)

The contemporary argument about the status of Frederick of Bohemia echoes in this speech, as does the premise of Massinger's *Believe as Ye List* that one may be a king and yet not rule. But the political application is undercut by another of Ford's deft borrowings from Shakespeare: James's "instinct for sovereignty" sounds curiously like Falstaff's "instinct" for detecting a "true prince." As the play goes on, James comes to overrule his instinct, make politic deals with Henry, and dismiss Perkin from his court.[39]

James's notion of kingship is portrayed as comically high-handed. When Huntly protests the expense in Scottish lives of James's proposal to invade England, the king curtly responds:

> Then shall their bloods
> Be nobly spent. No more disputes; he is not
> Our friend who contradicts us.
>
> (II.iii.63–65)

Later in the play, worried about "waste of blood" (IV.i.25), James offers to meet Surrey, the English general, in single combat, an offer whose import Durham clearly understands:

> Sir, you find
> By these gay flourishes how wearied travail
> Inclines to willing rest. Here's but a prologue
> However confidently utter'd, meant
> For some ensuing acts of peace.
>
> (IV.i.59–63)

The theatrical metaphor emphasizes the anachronistic impropriety of James's offer.

James's change of heart is pivotal to the play, but not because he grows to fulfill an ideal of practical kingship. Rather he is unable to sustain belief in the charismatic pretender once he is exposed to the political pressures of high office. The two cannot mix. The Scottish court, as we see it early in the play, is an unworldly place that provides the only atmosphere in which Perkin can thrive. While the English, in the first scene, worry about national security, Huntly and Daliell, in the second, discuss questions of love and honor. Katherine's father allows his daughter to decide for herself the question of marriage to Daliell, and he is delighted when her choice is made in thoroughly courtly terms:

> It shall be my delight that worthy love
> Leads you to worthy actions, and these guide ye
> Richly to wed an honorable name.
>
> (1.ii.51–53)

James himself offers chivalric recreation to Perkin:

> Come, we shall taste a while our court delights,
> Dream hence afflictions past, and then proceed
> To high attempts of honor.
>
> (11.i.113–15)

James may awaken from his dreaming, and forsake "high attempts of honor," but Perkin's adventure in the play is explicitly dramatized as a courtly trial, a test of love and honor.

Perkin is well aware of this. When James dismisses him from the shelter of the court, he comforts his wife:

> Should I prove wanting
> To noblest courage now, here were the trial:
> But I am perfect, sweet.
>
> (IV.iii.123–25)

As Warbeck remains constant to his inner conception of his own nobility, so Katherine is "perfect" in her faith to her husband. Huntly marvels at the end:

> I glory in thy constancy:
> And must not say I wish I had missed
> Some partage in these trials of a patience.
>
> (IV.iii.163–65)

Perkin's royalty and Katherine's constancy are seen as courtly values; their marriage is seen as his kingdom.

The paradox, strangely enough, derives from a remark in Bacon: speaking of Lady Katherine Gordon, the historian indulges in an ironic play on words: "The name of White-Rose, which had been given to her husband's false title, was continued in common speech to her true beauty."[40] Ford picks up this hint and develops it in the play into a full-fledged confrontation between Perkin's truth as husband and lover and the public truth of civil history. Daliell, Katherine's rejected suitor, initiates a further complication of the paradox as he grumbles:

> 'A courts the ladies,
> As if his strength of language chained attention
> By power of prerogative.
>
> (II.iii.6–8)

The political pun cuts two ways: Perkin's claim is belittled to mere skill in courting ladies, but the phrase "strength of language" also reminds us of logocentric notions of kingship, in which the king's word, like his creator's, is law. Katherine, likewise, firmly locates the seat of Perkin's power in his language: "You have a noble language, sir; your right / In me is without question" (III.ii.163–64). In the marriage vow itself, word becomes one with deed:

> For when the holy churchman joined our hands
> Our vows were real then; the ceremony
> Was not in apparition, but in act.
> Be what these people term thee, I am certain
> Thou art my husband.
>
> (V.iii.113–17)

Divine-right rhetoric, which Henry uses ironically or opportunistically as it suits him, fuses with religious ceremony and the language of vows to provide Perkin with a "real" identity: but the identity is a private, domestic one—"Thou art my husband."[41]

Perkin's kingdom, in this light, is likewise private. Katherine points this out early on. She promises:

> however
> Events of time may shorten my deserts
> In others' pity, yet it shall not stagger
> Or constancy or duty in a wife.
> You must be king of me. And my poor heart
> Is all I can call mine.
>
> (III.ii.164–69)

Perkin's defeats are merely trials of constancy: "events of time"—history itself—cannot change a stubbornly held inner truth. "It is decreed," Katherine pronounces at the end,

> and we must yield to fate,
> Whose angry justice, though it threaten ruin,
> Contempt and poverty, is all but trial
> Of a weak woman's constancy in suffering.
>
> (v.i.1–4)

Fate is embodied not only in Henry and his faction but in the known facts of public history.

Ford's presentation of history as a force inimical to love is thoroughly characteristic. His major plays—*Lovers Melancholy, The Broken Heart, 'Tis Pity She's a Whore,* and *Love's Sacrifice*—all show him to be profoundly interested in the aristocratic lover's behavior under stress. Lovers defy convention and society, speaking the language, in Leech's phrase, "of an ideal court, dignified above that of James or Charles."[42] Like the incestuous pair in *'Tis Pity,* or the more numerous unhappy lovers in *The Broken Heart,* Perkin and Katherine find themselves trapped in an impossible world that they can only transcend through death. But in *Perkin Warbeck* the conditions that stifle heroic love are not those of social convention, as in *'Tis Pity,* but of historical fact.[43] Ford thus goes beyond testing love alone: on trial here is a whole complex of aristocratic, courtly values—the aesthetic and mystical accoutrements of kingship, which, to the play's political realists, come across as imposture, witchcraft, and delusion. The play is paradigmatic in its statement of Ford's aristocratic ideals.

Like the omission of Perkin's confession, Ford's other alterations of his sources serve to recast the story into this frame. As a model of fidelity, Katherine challenges "events of time": in history, Lady Katherine Gordon remarried. Ford stages a confrontation between Perkin and Henry that the real Henry VII avoided. His alterations extend, in a different way, to his "parasitic"[44] use here of Shakespeare's histories—a technique that Ford also used in his inversion of *Romeo and Juliet* in *'Tis Pity.* Recent editors of *Perkin Warbeck* have pointed out that the play echoes *Richard II* and *1 Henry IV;* in its basic situation, it also mirrors *Richard II,* even to the extent that the roles have been reversed.

These changes do more than offer "subtle questioning" of "the excesses of King Charles" on the issue of divine right, as Ribner has suggested they do.[45] While it is true that an impostor enunciates this doctrine, the early identification of Henry with the "shaken" king of *1*

Henry IV cuts the other way, lending a greater validity to Warbeck's words. Thus while the values of aristocratic love and divine kingship are defined as anachronistic fictions, endorsed only by the Scots and the lovers, these fictions expose the limitations of a merely factual, purely political version of truth. While in his other plays, Ford relies upon strained contrivances of plot and character to try the nobility of his lovers, here he finds in Bacon and dramatizes in Henry VII a vocabulary and attitude towards history that is wholly antipathetic to the language and truth of the heart.

The issue here, then, is that of self-definition in the face of hostile historical inevitability. As in Shakespeare's *Henry VIII,* the processes of history are perceived as fate: both plays are antihistorical in rejecting humanist preconceptions about scientific, political history writing as irrelevant to a higher order of truth. In *Henry VIII* celebration of the monarchy overshadows the inconsistencies of human action. Where Jonson and Chapman almost stridently announce the accountability of men for their times, characters in *Henry VIII* rise and fall as a great destiny fulfills itself in spite of their activities. In *Perkin Warbeck,* Ford's forceful dramatization of the political context serves mainly to lend shape and specificity to Perkin's "strange truth" through relentless dialectical opposition. A humanist historian like Bacon may admire Henry VII, and Ford's king is a historian himself, the custodian of the play's facts; yet the wise king lacks the charisma of royalty that the foolish impostor possesses. Humanist history, stripping providence of its role in shaping human experience, judging kings solely in political terms, fails to satisfy the dramatist. In part this shift in emphasis is attributable to the unpopularity of James and Charles; as Anne Barton puts it, "as visible kings are reduced to petty and undistinguished private men, private men of a certain kind may come to seem like kings as kings once were."[46] The problem with this formulation, though, is that Henry VII in *Perkin Warbeck* is not private at all: his behavior is throughout controlled, stage-managed, public. As public men, both Henry and Perkin are false men, player kings, impostors: real royalty is private, inexpressible, inhering in the secret of Perkin's identity that itself is wholly bound up in the ceremony and sacrament of his marriage.

What we witness, in the history plays stretching from *Sejanus* to *Perkin Warbeck,* is first an engagement and then a rejection by dramatists of the growing discipline of history writing modeled upon Machiavelli and popularized by Bacon in his *History of Henry VII.* The lessons of this kind of history are both practical and general, as its applications can be both specific and universal. Where Shakespeare in his history makes his audience experience the activity of making sense out of the past itself, playing off the chaos of life against the patterns we habitually impose upon it, Jonson and Chapman present an organized past, made relevant to the present, "illuminated" by the poet's skill.[47] It is taken for granted by them as much as by Shakespeare that we will reason historically, make the appropriate connections between past and present, avoid the inappropriate ones, and derive a moral lesson. But where Shakespeare rarely permits the unquestioned survival of the moral, Jonson and Chapman see sententiousness in itself as the end of tragedy. And this sententiousness is wholly secular; their humanist ideas about history forbid the evocation of the old providential patterns discredited by Machiavelli and ridiculed by Bacon.

Censorship discouraged this kind of activist history writing, as we have seen: the avoidance of ostensible English stories by these playwrights derives from government displeasure. As Stephen Orgel has pointed out, and as Shakespeare suggests in *Henry VIII,* the court masque is the only acceptable kind of political drama in the age of the early Stuarts: its "Platonic Machiavellism" posits a kind of idealized, allegorized notion of royal power outside time, outside history.[48]

In *Perkin Warbeck,* the playwright pits theatrical illusion against historical fact and finds "truth" firmly ensconced in the former. The implications for historical drama are devastating. For what Ford suggests here is that the illusionistic power of the stage is so great as to make its claim to truth exclusive and unverifiable. In this, as in so many other respects, Ford revises Shakespeare to exaggerated and distorted extremes. Whereas in Shakespearean dramatic historiography both history and drama are scrutinized as patterns we somewhat arbitrarily apply to life, in Ford history is rejected as inadequate and ceremony is celebrated as truth. Ford's enhancement of Shakespeare's mistrust of history is clearly a reaction to the lofty humanist claims made by Jonson, Chapman, and Bacon: the wise, moderate, skillful monarchs they envision fail to engage the dramatist's imagination. Ford's royal pretender, on the other hand, is mythic, mysterious in his origins, glorious in his language, constant in his martyrdom.

The linkage in *Perkin Warbeck* between monarchy and marriage, the merging of "apparition" and "act" in the vows Katherine has taken, also has large implications for later dramatic historiography. Perkin's royalty is that of a lover and a husband: in this sense, Ford shows himself less out of touch with Charles's uxorious court than critics have suggested him to be. Henrietta Maria's cult of French romances like *L'Astrée* and the Platonic love dialogues attendant upon it share Ford's ethical bias. Nobility in *Perkin Warbeck,* as in Ford's early pamphlet *Honour Triumphant* and in the plays Harbage groups together as "Cavalier drama," is a matter of manners; aristocracy entails, not political responsibility (as in humanist programs of education), but rather social grace and constancy in love.[49] Politics in *Perkin Warbeck* is reduced to a pressure upon personal behavior: Perkin's heroism consists in his defiance, to the end, of historical fact. But the play transcends Ford's usual glorification of love in its dialectical tension: its celebration of Perkin's "strange truth" to his noble fictions plays off against a hard-edged cynicism about courtly values that is not totally dispelled at the play's end. In this significant respect *Perkin Warbeck* differs from the court masque, the form that, in Davenant's hands, had ceased to fulfill the didactic, humanistic potential envisioned for it by Jonson. When the theaters reopened in the Restoration, Davenant's influence remained predominant. In the heroic historical dramas of that period, nobility is a personal attribute, created introspectively and sustained in the face of the demands of truth and state.

3

The Pathos of Power

THE RESTORATION AND AFTER

"It was that memorable Day," John Dryden situates *An Essay of Dramatick Poesie,* "in the first Summer of the late war, when our Navy ingag'd the *Dutch:* a day wherein the two most mighty and best appointed Fleets which any age had ever seen, disputed the command of the greater half of the Globe, the commerce of Nations, and the riches of the Universe."[1] Not since the drinking party on the day after Agathon's first victory in the tragic competition has historical placing been so important in a philosophical dialogue. The immediate context of the discussion of poetry here is the English victory over the Dutch, and its background is war—emptying the town, sending its inhabitants down the river to hear "the noise of distant thunder" (p. 8). "Both the naval triumph and Neander's arguments serve English patriotic interests," declare the editors of the California Dryden (p. 357). More importantly, the debate about poetry arises spontaneously as the noise of war ceases: the journey back up the Thames to Somerset House, where the barge stops and Neander must break off his remarks about rhyme, is a journey from the "depth of silence" (p. 8) back to the civilized environs of the "Town." The situation of the essay figures the Restoration. Neander makes the point clear later in the dialogue. "Be it spoken to the honour of our *English,*" he proclaims, finishing his "examen" of Jonson's *Silent Woman,* "our Nation can never want in any age such who are unable to dispute the Empire of Wit with any people in the Universe. And though the fury of a Civil War, and Power, for twenty years together, abandon'd to a barbarous race of men, Enemies of all good learning, had buried the Muses under the ruines of Monarchy; yet with the restoration of our happiness, we see reviv'd Poesie lifting up its head, & already shaking off the rubbish which lay so heavy on it" (p. 63). Thus the restoration of monarchy is a recovery of civilization; the "riches of the Universe" that the English and Dutch contest correspond to the "Empire of Wit." While the duke of York bests England's commercial opponent, Neander in his barge will rout the French. The endeavor is doubly heroic, vindicating, as Dryden puts it, *"the honour of our* English *Writers, from the censure of those who unjustly prefer the* French *before them"* (p. 7). At the end of the *Essay,* the four friends go "up through a crowd of French people who were merrily dancing in the open air, and nothing concern'd for the noise of Guns which had allarm'd the Town that afternoon" (p. 80). In their cheerful obliviousness, they do not know that their future conqueror passes among them.[2]

The design of the *Essay* makes clear the great political and historical significance that Dryden at this phase of his career ascribed to the restored monarchy and to himself, as Neander, the new man destined to serve as its poet. The drama in the *Essay* is not only heroic but historical, for the main purpose of the argument here is to locate precisely in time and space the kind of poet and the kind of drama that the restored court culture requires. The answer reached is the rhymed heroic drama—with what Dryden would later repudiate as its "mistaken Topicks" of love and honor (in the preface to *Don Sebastian,* 1690)[3]—a form that would hold the stage for about ten years, from the late 1660s to the late 1670s. The Popish Plot panic of 1678, the parliamentary attempts to exclude the duke of York from succession to the throne in 1679, 1680, and 1681, and finally the Glorious Revolution of 1688 revealed the tenuousness of the Restoration settlement and also confirmed, unhappily for him, Dryden's perception, triumphant in the *Essay,* that poetry is made not only for but also by its political context.[4] The replacement of heroic drama by a drama that focused on the pathos of royal station, seeing kings and queens as victims of irresistible historical process, happened in direct response to these upheavals. In the *Essay,* Dryden portrays the Restoration as cultural and social renewal, a return, with improvements, to the glories of Renaissance court culture—*Astraea Redux,* in short. Modern historians, on the other hand, see Dryden's age precariously perched on "a kind of San Andreas fault" running through English polity, and the victory over the Dutch at Lowestoft as a "disaster for the Crown," not the herald of a new age, as Dryden thought.[5]

Dryden's failure to produce an English heroic play mirrors "in little" (as he declared heroic drama should mirror epic poetry) his failure to write the English epic.[6] But the context of this failure is not individual. In this chapter we can trace a widespread rejection of visions of monarchy as triumphant and history as heroic in favor of portrayals of monarchs as victims and history as an occasion for tears. What emerges at the end of the process, in the nineteenth century, is a full-fledged drama of the pathos of power. The dominant Whig historiography of that period, best exemplified by the narrative of Macaulay, portrayed the Stuart monarchs as engaged in a futile effort to impose absolutism in the face of an innate English drive towards liberty, property, progress, science, and industry. In the drama, the heroic and romantic desires of kings and queens became occasions for pity, not contempt, and as Gardiner's remarks on *Believe as Ye List* (quoted in part ii of chapter 2) suggest, even hardened Whig historians would occasionally shed a tear for Charles I. Responses to Charles I, in fact, offer a skeletal anticipation of the development this chapter examines in detail. The heroic drama, glorifying as it did the mystique of royalty, did not, and would not, engage the topical problem of regicide. The political tragedies that accompanied the crises of 1678–81, on the other hand, abounded in unveiled references to the miseries of civil war; Nahum Tate recast Shakespeare's *Richard II* (1680) to make the king wholly admirable, deposing himself as a type of royal martyr. Charles I emerged in his own person on the English stage in 1737, in William Havard's *Tragedy of Charles I:* devoted husband, loving father, he succumbs philosophically to the evil machinations of the villain-statesman Cromwell. The same character persists in W. G. Wills's *Charles I* (1873); the only functional difference between the Victorian and the eighteenth-century play is that now (as Wills explains in an appendix) Cromwell is permitted "a measure of remorse for his great crime."

Accompanying the emergence of this consensus is the emergence of the Shakespeare that German and French playwrights of later generations would adore, the rough, anticlassical, natural British genius. In this regard, Dryden's attempts to come to grips with "the giant race before the flood" in the *Essay of Dramatick Poesie* and in his later critical writings are prophetic. Imitation of Shakespeare accompanied a larger movement toward the homiletic and domestic in English tragedy. Historical settings and stories were reintroduced into the mainstream of English drama as homely, pathetic, quaint, along with pseudo-Shakespearean language ("Avaunt, base Groom!"). Nicholas Rowe, Shakespeare's first editor, delivered, in *Jane Shore,* an "imitation of Shakespeare's style"[7] that effectively institutionalized consciously archaistic blank verse as the language of the past (Maxwell Anderson's verse plays of the 1940s simply follow in this tradition). Dryden found no effective way of implementing his discovery that language could change from age to age; for Rowe and his own imitators, the language of Shakespeare was the language of the past.

Rowe also systematized the formula that, like the political stability reached in the early eighteenth century, would long endure. By accommodating providential rhetoric to the pastoral nostalgia of pathetic tragedy, Rowe was able to suggest a wider Christian context to history. At the same time, by concentrating on the powerlessness of his characters in the grip of passion and political intrigue, he created a form in which the sexual politics of triangular love intrigue governed politics at a national level. Later historical plays would offer voyeuristic glimpses of courtiers and monarchs in love; famous crises of the past were shown to have secret sources in the unacknowledged passions of the court.[8] In *Sir Thomas Overbury, A Tragedy* (1777), a reworking by William Woodfall of an unfinished play by Richard Savage, that unpleasant episode from the reign of James I is emphatically regularized. "O Love!—O Friendship! / Sustain me!" cries Overbury as he dies, poisoned, a victim of secret love and jealous rage. "Ruin and death, on ill-plac'd love are built," moralizes Somerset at the end, "And passion, sprung from weakness, ends in guilt."[9]

The powerlessness of historical figures in the throes of passion has a political resonance, like the abundance of weak, vacillating, or lustful kings in the earlier heroic drama. The uncontrollable passions of a lover-queen like Elizabeth in John Banks's *The Unhappy Favourite* (1681) make her utterly susceptible to the machinations of Nottingham and Burleigh, the play's villains. Thus, she can lose Essex—recorded history can run its necessary course—without being responsible for his death. The pathos of royal station in the plays reflects contemporary confusions about the status of the monarch in the English system: Elizabeth enjoys absolute power in this instance, but her passions, skillfully agitated by the villains, so becloud her judgment she cannot use it. This formula, too, will endure as another essential ingredient of the drama of the pathos of power.

Nostalgia about the past, pity for the passionate ruler, assertions of pastoral and domestic longings are all features of historical drama throughout the nineteenth century. Despite lip service to authenticity and historicity—in practice, usually limited to pedantic accuracy in set design—playwrights like Bulwer-Lytton and Tennyson devoted their attentions to love intrigue rather than to the rich historical contexts available to them in the age of Macaulay.

Dryden saw revived poesy emerging out of the rubble of civil war: a more tangible consequence of the war and the constitutional struggles before it had been the development of the discipline of history. The new science Bacon celebrated was called into service by both sides in the debate about royal prerogatives. The whole process of recovering the

"Ancient Constitution" was linked with antiquarian research through records and documents.[10] By the eighteenth century, the historian's claim to absolute authority over the past—trumpeted earlier by Jonson and Bacon and derided by Ford, as we have seen—had been tacitly conceded by dramatists. Practitioners of the age's newest form, the novel, on the other hand, played the historian with aggressive irreverence. "Fielding in *Tom Jones*," Leo Braudy argues, "implies what Hume, seemingly secure in his detachment, never considered: only by admitting that his general pattern is arbitrary can the historian be free to demonstrate what he believes to be specifically true." Like Shakespeare's mature history plays, Fielding's novels "attack and qualify the false orders of public history and the inflated rhetoric of causal connection." To Shakespeare as well as to Braudy's Gibbon, "history is what the mind has made of the past."[11] Hayden White describes the great eighteenth-century historical works themselves as fundamentally "Ironic, . . . with the result that they all tend toward the form of Satire, the supreme achievement of the literary sensibility of that age."[12] In this context, the historical drama is shockingly naive. By locating the tension between public and private truths exclusively in amorous intrigue, English dramatists of the eighteenth and nineteenth centuries wholly abdicated the critical function that Shakespeare, Jonson, Chapman, Ford, and finally Dryden sought to perform.

In the Victorian revivals of Shakespeare, massive, accurately detailed scenery dwarfed the helpless protagonist as surely as the inscrutable power of history crushes individual agency in nineteenth-century dramaturgy. But as Herbert Lindenberger has pointed out, this shift towards operatic depictions of history as "sheer power" is European in its scope; discussion of that phenomenon awaits in part ii.[13] This chapter engages the problems of seventeenth- and eighteenth-century English dramatists as exemplary of the kinds of problems early modern dramatists had to face when approaching history. First, discussion of Dryden's *Essay of Dramatick Poesie* as heroic historical drama can offer an appropriate theoretical background to the question of "history" in seventeenth-century criticism of drama, not only English but also French. Next, we can examine the uncomfortable survival of humanistic ideas about history in the extravagant historical pageants of Roger Boyle, first earl of Orrery. The difficulties of accommodating historical material and goals to dramatic decorums are acute in Orrery, but no less so in the most ambitious historical play of the period, Dryden and Lee's *Duke of Guise*. In that play, and in the political tragedies of the period, we can see the identification of political power with heartless Machiavellism. The proliferation of villain-statesmen, who, like historians, dive into the springs of human action and reduce humans to machines, betokens a violent general distaste for humanist political history among dramatists. The plays of John Banks can serve as ample demonstration; Rowe's providential eroticism builds on this distaste to suggest the dramatist's mastery over the secret higher truths of passions unrevealed and the mysteries of the marriage bed. Finally, this chapter concludes with a few examples of the pathos of power in dramatists and historians of succeeding generations. The dramatists' systematic, wholesale belittlement of politics and trivialization of history anticipates Eugène Scribe's "Glass-of-water" dramaturgy ("Great effects from small causes . . . that's my system") by a century and a half.[14] And the image of Shakespeare as a rough, national genius, the embodiment of the unaccommodated and irrecoverable past itself, that emerged out of the cauldron of Restoration poetic politics is another phenomenon of European importance. The Restoration dramatists' problems with decorum epitomize the problems of any dramatist attempting to impose a shape on the events of the past. Their failures, and especially Dryden's failure, to improve upon Shakespeare through creating new forms appropriate to their more sophisticated age can serve as cautionary tales.

i

We begin with *An Essay of Dramatick Poesie* as a key document because of the acute sense of potentiality and possibility that animates Dryden, as both recorder of that "memorable Day" and alter ego of Neander. What makes the *Essay* historical drama is not merely the specificity of its "placement" in time and space but also its preoccupation with history itself. The whole movement of the *Essay* is historical: Ancients are bested by Moderns in the first of its confrontations, that between Eugenius and Crites. When Lisideius praises the French, in the second debate, Neander counters by showing that his examples are out-of-date. What Dryden stresses through this sequence—and through the dialogue's climax with discussion of the day's most immediate and pressing problem, that of rhyme—is the new idea of progress. "For if Natural Causes be more known now than in the time of Aristotle," Eugenius argues, "it follows that Poesie and other Arts may with the same pains arrive still neerer to Perfection" (p. 22). The analogy with science is revealing: in his *Defence of An Essay* (1668), Dryden identifies the enterprise with "the modest Inquisitions of the Royal Society."[15] Thus it is as a modern, scientific historian that Neander can crush Lisideius: "since the death of Cardinal

Richelieu," he notes pointedly, "which *Lisideius* and many others not observing," the French have been "imitating afar off the quick turns and graces of the *English* stage" (p. 45). Neander even historicizes the long tirades and Messengers' speeches of the French drama: "When the French stage came to be reform'd by Cardinal Richelieu," he argues, "those long Harangues were introduc'd, to comply with the gravity of a Churchman" (p. 48). Neander's historical denigration of the French leads into his "examen" (modeled on Corneille's practice) of Jonson's *Silent Woman.*

At this juncture, Eugenius interrupts to ask Neander if he does not agree that "all writers, *French* and *English,* ought to give place to" Jonson. But if Neander considers *The Silent Woman* the "pattern of a perfect play" (p. 55), he is nonetheless forced at the very moment of analyzing its excellence into praising Shakespeare. "If I would compare him with *Shakespeare,*" Neander says, "I must acknowedge him the more correct Poet, but *Shakespeare* the greater wit" (p. 58; earlier he has remarked on Shakespeare's "comprehensive soul" [p. 55], which gives a clearer idea of what *wit* means here). Then he offers the famous analogy that anticipates by some years Schiller's distinction between naive and sentimental poets: "Shakespeare was the Homer, or Father of our Dramatick Poets: Jonson was the Virgil, the pattern of elaborate writing; I admire him, but I love Shakespeare" (p. 58). The intrusion of Shakespeare into Neander's Cornelian examen reveals again the historical complexity of Dryden's *Essay.* Where Corneille, in his *Trois discours,* contrasts his French audiences and their tastes to hypothetical Athenians, with the conclusion that tastes change over the centuries, Dryden deals with much smaller units of time. Not only must Ancients meet Moderns in the journey of the Thames, and the French meet the English among the Moderns: finally, the English must confront their own past. Acutely aware of the horror of civil war, Dryden sees the great gulf it has interposed between his age and Shakespeare's: and he cannot find a systematic way to justify why he "loves" Shakespeare when by the standards of his own time he should prefer Jonson.

Third in Dryden's pantheon of English dramatists is Fletcher; there is nothing disruptive about his presence there. Fletcher's elegant language is an "improvement" on Shakespeare's and Jonson's—an improvement upon which Dryden hopes to improve. The greatness of the plays of the former age, according to the scientistic notion of progress that informs the essay, promises for the next age greater yet. This idea leads Neander to conclude his examen with a boast of heroic proportions: "Onely I think it may be permitted me to say, that as it is no less'ning to us to yield to some Playes, and those not many of our own Nation in the last Age, so can it be no addition to pronounce of our present Poets that they have far surpass'd all the Ancients, and the Modern Writers of other Countreys" (p. 64).

This is a declaration that causes some consternation in the boat, as Lisideius, champion of the French, rises to his own defense only to be cut off by the brusque and belligerent Crites. He is dismayed by the current fashion for plays in rhyme; as the attention shifts to this issue, we can see clearly the progress of the *Essay* from most remote and distant—the Ancients—to the pressing issue of the day—rhyme in drama. Crites' blunt insistence on verisimilitude leads Neander to engage a central tension in neoclassical criticism, its demand for decorum on the one hand and for consistent illusionism on the other.[16] For Neander, "imitation of common persons and ordinary speaking" is appropriate only to comedies: a serious play, "to be like Nature, is to be set above it; as Statues which are plac'd on high are made greater than life, that they may descend to the sight in their just proportion" (p. 75). Finally, Neander demolishes Crites' objection that rhyme hinders "fancy": luxuriant fancies need hindering, he argues. As for the fact that Jonson did not use rhyme, first, his fancy was far from luxuriant; but, more importantly, "Neither was Verse then refin'd so much to be an help to that Age as it is to ours, Thus then the second thoughts being usually the best, as receiving the maturest digestion from judgment, and the last and most mature product of those thoughts being artful and labour'd verse, it may well be inferr'd, that verse is a great help to a luxuriant Fancy; and this is what that Argument which you oppos'd was to evince" (p. 80). At this moment the dialogue ends: the boat has arrived at Somerset stairs, and Neander has to be called to "twice or thrice." The luxuriance of Neander's fancy is dramatized. The merrily dancing French, as we have said before, are oblivious to Neander's challenge. Where Eugenius, Lisideius, and especially Crites are all out-of-date, Neander, the new man, is on the leading edge of taste. He knows the latest trends in France; he praises "second thoughts"; he gets the last word. Neander embodies a resurgence of English drama—a second generation greater than the first—out of the rubble of war. The drama he will write will be victorious, heroic, revealing the improved language of his day in elegant rhyme.

What Dryden advocates here is a drama similar to Corneille's, expressive, as Robert J. Nelson puts it, of a "positive Baroque," a "seemingly obvious confidence that the self can fulfill the injunctions of society and the gods to submit love to duty."[17] Yet by the date of Dryden's *Essay,*

Corneille was already fighting a rear-guard action to defend his kind of heroic historical drama against the assaults of a critical establishment that also enjoyed the protections of the court. Chapelain had demonstrated the French Academy's *maîtrise* over the arts by handing down its "opinion" of *Le Cid* in 1638; the play's greatest flaw had been its violation of *vraisemblance*. This quality is not merely verisimilitude as bare illusionism, parodied by Dryden in Crites' objections to rhyme, but rather an adherence to appropriate decorums of moral psychology, in accordance with which Chimène's apparent willingness to consider marriage to Rodrigue a few hours after he has killed her father is not merely repellent or unlikely but quite simply impossible. In 1657, the doctrine was codified and argued with chilling pedantry by François Hédélin, abbé d'Aubignac, in his *La pratique du théâtre* (published in English translation in 1684 as *The Whole Art of the Stage*). Corneille's *Trois discours sur le poème dramatique,* published to accompany his collected works in 1660, are full of malicious digs at d'Aubignac, whose practical experience of the stage consisted of one disaster. Corneille calls upon his own thirty years' experience as a man of the theater; in the 1682 edition of *Trois discours,* he increased the figure to fifty without changing his combative stance.

For Corneille the idea of *vraisemblance* was particularly troublesome. Tragedy required great subjects, extraordinary individuals, monstrous crimes: often history records events that are shocking, improbable, but nonetheless true. Heroic action, Serge Doubrovsky argues, can only take place for Corneille in a clearly defined, politically understood, historical context:

> Telle est, en définitive, la signification de la fameuse
> distinction cornélienne du "vrai," garanti par l'histoire et
> supérieur, en matière de tragédie, au "vraisemblance," qui ne
> repose que sur la ressemblance psychologique à des modèles
> médiocres. C'est que l'histoire a une valeur essentiellement
> métaphysique: *lieu de la vérité* pour l'homme, elle constitue le
> terrain unique où se joue son existence, et où se décide sa
> perte ou son salut.

> Here, definitively, is the meaning of the famous Cornelian
> distinction between the "true," guaranteed by history and
> superior as subject of tragedy, and the "verisimilar," which
> relies upon psychological resemblance to mediocre models.
> It is that history has a value that is essentially metaphysical:
> as *ground of truth* for man, history is the only space where his

existence is played out, where his salvation and damnation are decided.

Or as Robert McBride puts it, history provides an arena in which the hero can demonstrate the "mastery over himself and others which results in his personal and public *gloire*."[18] There is much common ground between Corneille's insistence on truth and Jonson's humanistic ideals; and Corneille proved less malleable to changes in poetic fashion than Dryden. Love, he argued in the first *Discours,* is a proper subject of comedy, not tragedy. "Sa dignité," he goes on, "demande quelque grand intérêt d'État, ou quelque passion plus noble et plus mâle que l'amour, telles que sont l'ambition ou la vengeance, et veut donner à craindre les malheurs plus grands que la perte d'une maîtresse." ("Its dignity demands some great interest of State, or a passion nobler and more masculine than love, like ambition or revenge, in order to make us fear miseries greater than the loss of a mistress.")[19] We have already seen the displacement of historical truth by the passion of love in Ford; the English fashion, like the French, reversed Corneille's priorities. Honor is completely devoured by love (as we shall see) in Orrery's plays, and the monarch's fitness to govern is validated by his skill in Platonic debate. When Katherine Philips (the "matchless Orinda") removed all *raison d'état* from her version of Corneille's *Pompée,* Orrery responded in a dedicatory poem with enthusiasm: *"If he could read it, he like us would call / The copy greater than th'Original."*[20] Yet to the end of his career, Corneille resisted the fashion both for amorous intrigue and for easy morality: immediately after the first edition of the *Discours,* he was attacked by d'Aubignac for his *Sophonisbe.* Mairet's *Sophonisbe,* d'Aubignac argued, treated this episode from history better, for it provided a more excellent moral; Corneille countered that his version was far closer to chronicled truth.

Saint-Évremond, almost Corneille's only defender by the end of his career, praised him for his sense of history, but concluded ruefully, "Corneille, qui, presque seul, a le bon goût de l'antiquité, a eu le malheur de ne plaire pas à notre siècle" ("He who almost alone could enter into the spirit of past ages had the misfortune not to please our own").[21] Racine's introspective drama of passion struck Corneille right at his point of attack on d'Aubignac: it succeeded on the French stage. Corneille's insistence (*moderniste* in its relativism) that times and tastes changed and that the rules could do with an *élargissement* based upon standards of contemporary success foundered. Racine was not above turning his older rival's insistence upon historical truth and astounding incident against him: "Il n'y a que le vraisemblance qui touche dans la tragédie," he says in the preface to *Bérénice*, "toute l'invention consiste a faire quelque chose de rien." ("Only verisimilitude moves us in tragedy, . . . all inventive skill consists in making something of nothing.")[22] Corneille's particular problem was the arrival of Racine at the right place at the right time; the consequence was a movement away from the public realm to the private, from interests of state and monstrous crimes to intrigues of love as the mainsprings of tragedy.[23] Racine's drama is unique in managing to be ahistorical and apolitical without trivializing the public realm: nor do his tragedies quite furnish the "excellent morals" prescribed by the age's fabulist critics. Boileau, Dacier, and finally Voltaire argued the inferiority of a plot drawn from history to one that more precisely mirrors the justice of divine providence; the notion that history needed help, as Voltaire put it in his article on "Fable" in the *Encyclopédie,* lest it seem to "accuse providence," had already been established as a commonplace by Rapin and by his English translator, Thomas Rymer, by the middle of Dryden's career.

But if Dryden's *Essay* shows a more complex grasp of changing times and changing tastes than does Corneille's dogged resistance to the shifting taste of his own time, his heroic drama lacks the sense of historic depth that Saint-Évremond praised in Corneille. Dryden follows Neander's Cornelian program most closely in *The Conquest of Granada,* that massive ten-act drama introduced by the essay "Of Heroique Plays" and followed by an epilogue praising the wit of the new age and sneering at the poets of the last: "Fame then was cheap, and the first commer sped, / And they have kept it since, by being dead" (Epilogue, 11–12). Dryden's hero here, too, is a new man: Almanzor, whose first image in the poet's mind "was from the *Achilles* of *Homer;* the next from *Tasso's Rinaldo,* (who was a copy of the former:) and the third from the *Artaban* of *Monsieur Calprénède:* (who has imitated both.)"[24] The progression is not, whatever we may think it today, a decline: rather, Dryden is suggesting a consistent improvement in manners and language from Homer to the modern French, at the end of which process he places himself and his new hero. "As free as Nature first made Man" (1.i.207), Almanzor challenges the feeble king of the Moors throughout the play. His wild nature is finally subdued by love, and at the end of the play we realize what we must always have known as a Restoration audience: he was born royal. The weak king he has been defying all along is proved a usurper; the play itself is a restoration. Any threat of disorder the heroic hero may pose is subsumed into a higher order.[25]

By avoiding the political dimension of the heroic play, so important to Corneille, Dryden and the English playwrights showed that distaste for history that, in *Perkin Warbeck,* found expression as a wholly introspective notion of heroism. When Dryden's Adam, in his operatic adaptation of *Paradise Lost,* awakes and reasons out his existence in Cartesian terms—"What am I? or from whence? For that I am / I know, because I think"—the skepticism of what L. C. Knights called the "best thought of the time" is echoed with almost ridiculous literalness. Critical debate about the seriousness of Dryden's heroic plays has yet to die down. Some critics, like Anne Righter and Bruce King, see the philosophizing in the plays as essentially irrelevant or satirical; others argue, with Anne Barbeau and Geoffrey Marshall, that these are "plays of ideas" in which the heroes and their enemies are abstractions represented, rather than living people dramatized. The plays can be denigrated as trivial entertainments or praised as aspects of a large providential argument. Their lack of a clearly defined public dimension makes both positions possible.[26]

Thus Almanzor, as a heroic hero, can by light of reason alone define his own personal nobility and, by extension, formulate from it a consistent political philosophy. When he first arrives on the scene in *The Conquest of Granada,* he is able to deduce from his own mastery over himself (and doubtless with some help from the royal blood coursing unknown to him through his veins) the true nature of kingship. He instructs the vacillating Boabdelin:

> If thou pretendest to be a Prince like me,
> Blame not an Act, which should thy Pattern be.
> I saw th'opprest, and thought it did belong
> To a King's office to redress the wrong:
> I brought that Succour which thou ought'st to bring,
> And so, in Nature, am thy Subjects King.
>
> (I.i.216—21)

Almanzor's first kingdom is himself; only once that is mastered, at the end of the play, does he recover his throne.

In the process of defining personal nobility, the courtly values of love and honor are not subject to question. The premises from which heroic reasoning develops, love and honor, are innate and inflexible. Both make demands that are absolute and imperative; heroes in Dryden and in Orrery live in a state of suspense and shock. Almanzor's description of his first sense of love, when he glimpses Almahide, is characteristic:

> Ev'n while I speak and look, I change yet more;
> And now am nothing that I was before.

I'm numm'd and fix'd, and scarce my eyeballs move;
I fear it is the Lethargy of Love!
'Tis he; I feel him now in every part:
Like a new Lord he vaunts about my Heart;
Surveys in state each corner of my Brest,
While poor fierce I, that was, am dispossest.

(III.i.334–41)

Almanzor's love, like his innate sense of honor in his reproaches to
Boabdelin, finds expression in political terms, and again his status as
foundling, as dispossessed king, emerges spontaneously as he explores
his feelings. *The Conquest of Granada* may be the paradigmatic heroic
play, but the restoration it portrays, unlike that in the *Essay of Dramatick
Poesie,* takes place in a context that is only figuratively English.

The imposing critical tradition to which Dryden assimilated his
heroic plays has led to the commonplace that heroic drama failed because
artificially imposed foreign criticism stifled the "independent temper of
the national drama."[27] Yet the fate of Corneille's heroic drama and criticism in France shows the problem to be more complex. Without question, the Dryden of the *Essay* wanted to write uniquely English dramas;
in 1693, embittered, sick, and exiled from the town that was the center of
civilized life in the *Essay,* stripped of his companion titles as poet laureate
and historiographer royal, Dryden in his "Discourse concerning the
Original and Progress of Satire," continued to nurse his dream of an
English epic. The desire remains heroic: the poem would be composed
"chiefly for the honour of my native country, to which a poet is particularly obliged." In addition to portraying the "magnanimity of the English hero . . . together with the characters of the chiefest English persons," Dryden assures us he "would have taken occasion to represent my
living friends and patrons of the noblest families, and also shadowed the
events of future ages, in the succession of our imperial line." This piece of
heroic history painting would never be achieved.[28] Nor did Dryden,
except in collaboration with Nathaniel Lee in *The Duke of Guise* (1682),
which will be discussed in detail later in this chapter, attempt on stage the
kind of historical parallel-drawing that animates *Absalom and Achitophel.*

Dryden, says Guibbory, "found the indifference of the government
ultimately responsible" for this failure.[29] And certainly the political situation of the late Dryden neatly reverses that of the fanciful Neander:
after the Revolution of 1688, he had to suffer the installation of Shadwell
as poet laureate and Thomas Rymer as historiographer royal. When in
alliance with the power of the court, Dryden could confidently mock

Shadwell's dullness, but he was tongue-tied by Rymer's brusque dismissal of Shakespeare and earlier English dramatists as inferior to French and Ancient models. Rymer's translation of Rapin's *Réfléxions sur la poétique d'Aristote* had appeared in 1674; in 1677, *The Tragedies of the Last Age Consider'd and Examin'd by the Practice of the Ancients and by the Common Sense of All Ages* staked out his claim to be the age's leading critic. Nor did Dryden challenge this claim, pronouncing it "the best piece of Criticism in the English tongue; perhaps in any of the modern." Secretly he seems to have been preparing his *Heads of an Answer to Rymer* at this time; this he never printed in his lifetime, averring a mortal fear of Rymer's awesome learning and considerable pugnacity.[30]

The disagreement on the matter of the Ancients is substantially the same as that in the *Essay;* the emphasis is on improvements the Moderns have "added to their beauties: As for example, not only more Plot, but also new Passions; as namely that of Love." Dryden had not been behindhand in sensing the trend towards the tender passion on the stage. *Aureng-Zebe,* though still in rhyme, is far less boisterous than *The Conquest of Granada. All for Love,* which Dryden curiously praised for the "excellency of its moral," concentrated on amorous intrigue. In the Preface to *Troilus and Cressida,* Dryden points more clearly to what, for him, had become the keynote of the new blank-verse tragedy: its object is pity, "the noblest and most godlike of the moral virtues."[31] Admiration, the goal of heroic drama, came to be replaced by pity: Eric Rothstein sees in this a general shift from a fabulist to an affective notion of tragedy.[32] Plays came to be judged, not by the excellency of their moral, but instead by the flow of tears they could provoke among the benevolent spectators. Yet in Rymer's work it is clear that there is no contradiction between tears and morality. The spectator of *Othello,* Rymer argues in his *Short View of Tragedy* (1692), gets neither. Rather "What instruction can we make of this Catastrophe? O whither must our reflection lead us? Is this not to envenome and sour our spirits, to make us repine and grumble at Providence and the government of the World? If this be our end, what boots it to be Vertuous?" Better, Rymer says, if the "Fairey Napkin" had "started up" from the sheets while Othello strangles Desdemona: "Then might she (in a Traunce for fear) have lain as dead. Then might he, believing her dead, touch'd with remorse, have honestly cut his own Throat, by the good leave, and with the applause of all the Spectators. Who might thereupon have gone home with a quiet mind, admiring the beauty of Providence; fairly and truly represented on the Theater." Shakespeare's handling of the fable permits neither pity nor fear: the "tragical part" of *Othello,* Rymer concludes, "is, plainly none other, than a Bloody Farce without salt or savour."[33]

Dryden, in his *Heads of an Answer,* shifts the ground of argument. He defends Shakespeare on the basis, not of morality, but rather of what he calls "the Writing": "the raising of Shakespear's Passions is more from the Excellency of the Words and Thoughts than from the justness of the Occasion; and if he has been able to pick single Occasions, he has never founded the whole reasonable, yet by the Genius of Poetry in Writing, he has succeeded" (p. 190). Finally, he cites Rapin, Rymer's master, against him: "Rapin's words are remarkable: 'Tis not the admirable Intrigue, the surprising Events, and Extraordinary incidents, that make the Beauty of a Tragedy, 'tis the Discourses, when they are Natural and Passionate. So are Shakespeare's" (p. 193). *Genius, Natural, Passionate*—these are the words of eighteenth-century Bardolatry. In 1693, Dryden wrote to John Dennis, apropos of Shakespeare and Rymer, "that Genius alone is a greater Virtue (if I may so call it) than all other Qualifications put together"[34]—anticipating later developments that would find their fullest expression in Dr. Johnson's *Preface* and in the Continental discovery of Shakespeare.

In the same letter, Dryden deplores the "success this learned Critick has found in the World, after his blaspheming Shakespear." As spokesman for the literary establishment, Rymer in his blunt assertiveness set a tone that Dryden, tentative in the *Heads,* could not meet. Furthermore, Dryden's strong historical relativism, which we have met in the *Essay,* could not match Rymer's systematic belittlement of history. Exaggerating Aristotle's description of poetry as more philosophical than history, Rymer declared in *The Tragedies of the Last Age Consider'd* (1677) that the Ancients found history "neither proper to *instruct,* nor apt to *please*" in the incidents it offered of virtue oppressed and bad men rewarded. Imitating the justice of divine providence through "contriv'd" fables, thus, is not only more pleasing than history, he declared, but "more *philosophical* and more *accurate.*" Rymer condemns "particular *yesterday-truths*" (p. 22). "Poetry," he argues in *A Short View of Tragedy,* "is led more by Philosophy, the reason and nature of things, than History; which only records things higlety, piglety, right or wrong as they happen" (p. 163). "Il faudra aussi condamner l'Histoire," Dacier concurred, in *La poétique d'Aristote* (1692), "car l'Histoire est bien moins grave, & moins morale que la fable en ce qu'elle est particulière, au lieu que la Fable est générale & universelle & par conséquent plus utile" ("Thus it also becomes necessary to condemn History, because History is much less serious and less moral than the fable insofar as it is particular, whereas the Fable is general, universal, and therefore more useful"). Dennis too, in his *Remarks on Cato* (1713), endorsed the position: "The creation of the fable is that which distinguishes the poet from the historian and philosopher." "Pour qui ne regard qu'aux évènements," Voltaire warned in his *Encyclopédie* entry, "l'histoire semble accuser la Providence." ("For those who only pay attention to events, history seems to find fault with providence.") In Boileau's enormously influential "L'art poétique," as Gordon Pocock points out, "factually accurate history is rejected in favour of parabolic pseudo-history." "Dryden," declares William Myers, "was the last English poet to be interested in history, and possibly only Shakespeare before him united the gifts of a true historian with those of a major poet."[35] Yet a poet so sensitive to the pressures of the "world" and of his "age" could not be expected to resist so universal a movement away from relativism, circumstantiality, and critical particularity.

ii

Near the end of Orrery's *Henry V* (1664), the king and his closest counselors, Exeter and Tudor, meet to discuss the importance of keeping the navy fit:

> *King:* This high success at Sea, which Heav'n has sent
> Has made me Master of that Element.
> When Monarchs have at Land a Battel lost,
> It may, to raise new Troops, some Treasure cost.
> But to repair lost Fleets is not so cheap;
> Woods are a Crop which Men but once can reap.
> That Prince, whose Flags are bow'd to on the Seas.
> Of all Kings shores keeps in his hand the Keys;
> No King can him, he can all Kings invade,
> And on his Will depend their Peace and Trade.
> Trade, which does Kings and Subjects wealth increase;
> Trade, which more necessary is than Peace.
> *Exeter:* If the Worlds trade may to our hand be brought,
> Though purchas'd by a War, 'tis cheaply bought.
> *Tudor:* He who an Island rules, and not the Sea,
> Is not a King, and may a Pris'ner be.[36]

This passage clearly puts its author on the side of the duke of York's policies of aggressive expansionism; what is startling is that a few lines later the king breaks down. "Oh *Tudor*," he cries, "though my Sword at Land and Sea / Does conquer others, Love does conquer me" (V.75–

76). Dryden identifies commercialism with heroic endeavor in the *Essay of Dramatick Poesie;* what Orrery does here is set the valor of that sort of activity into dialectical conflict with love. This is in accordance with Dryden's assertion that love and valor are the proper subjects of heroic poems and plays. Dryden may have used rhyme because it imitated nature at a higher pitch; Orrery did so, he said, at the request of the king, for he "found his majty Relish'd rather the French Fassion of Playes, then [*sic*] the English." This suggests a closeness to the center of the court that a Neander could not enjoy. Later, the king himself "conjur'd" Orrery to finish his second English history play, *The Black Prince* (1667), "which if he could not do till he had a Fitt of the Gout, he wish'd him a Fit presently, yt he might the sooner finish it." Orrery's refined Platonism breathes the atmosphere of a court where "there is no other plague . . . but the infection of love," according to a visiting Frenchman.[37]

But the interchange about ships is striking because, until the king reverts to love-and-honor dialectic, the playwright seems to be offering his audience solid political counsel, entertaining the monarch, as K. M. Lynch, Orrery's biographer, puts it, "while at the same time advocating the nobler pursuits of responsible kingship."[38] Despite his personal friendship with the king, Orrery, like many at court, had served under Cromwell, and his career never bore fruit. His mistrust of the French and his militant anti-Catholicism led him to advocate war against Louis XIV and to support attaching Protestant conditions to James's succession; he withdrew from politics in 1675, and from then until his death in 1681, his Protestant counsels and discoveries of Papist conspiracies went generally ignored. His views coincided with those of the increasingly obstreperous Cavalier Parliament.

Thus his English history plays share with his 1677 *Treatise on the Art of War*—dedicated to Charles, with a frontispiece depicting him as a warrior king—a desire to promote a kind of heroism that is not exclusively Platonic. The models Orrery chose are those suggested by Heywood in his *Apology for Actors,* Edward III, "foraging France," and Henry V; his end, like Heywood's, is to inspire the English prince. In *Henry V,* even the French realize that "Fame can want no theam when she does sing / Of English swords led by an English king" (1.192–93). "Once more invade the French," Orrery urges in the prologue to *The Black Prince;* in both plays, English "beauties resistless as English swords" (*Henry V,* 1.441; *Black Prince,* III.38) contribute to the conquest.

Henry's invasion of France, in *Henry V,* is a gesture of heroic self-definition in the areas of both honor and love. As defined by Orrery, the political situation is unambiguous: the realm is Henry's by right. After the defeat at Agincourt, Chareloys concedes that

> Justice is more than an empty word.
> Therefor, whilst that assists the *English* sword,
> Success will always to their side resort
> And every Field will be an Agin-court.

(II.218–21)

At the play's conclusion, the bishop of Arras supports this basic instinct with historical precedent:

> But, searching our Records, we found at last,
> That a long errour as a truth has past:
> For he who flyes, now justice does advance,
> Is *Charles* of *Valoys,* not the son of France.

(V.523–26)

The dauphin's bad behavior suggested his blood was not royal; the records prove it. The dilemma of the French hero, then, is to resist just enough to preserve honor without erring in the opposite extreme by supporting too fiercely an unjust cause. Burgundy's refusal to accept Henry's right is an aspect of his villainy: "This Duke does all my faculties amaze," marvels Constable, "Yet still he lov'd to walk in crooked ways" (IV.173–74). Even the dauphin comes to recognize the folly of his pretense to an English throne: "Revenge and pride my reason have betray'd," he confesses, "And both have rul'd what both should have obey'd" (V.437–38).

But Henry cannot negotiate, any more than the French can concede his right: his victories are tests of his love. He scorns the idea of political settlement, not as the French do, on the grounds of honor, but on the grounds of love. As he explains to his friend, "She justly, Tudor, might my passion hate, / If love's high interest I should mix with state" (II.128–29). Katherine, reasoning out her attraction to Henry and rejection of Tudor, shows a firm grasp upon this kind of politics:

> Since Glory is the Souls most proper Sphear,
> It does but wander when it moves not there.
> This makes that King, who Courts me, *France* subdue,
> And makes me flye what else I would pursue.

(II.368–71)

By dramatizing the king's conquest as a restoration to a rightful throne, Orrery is capable also of making it a demonstration of model royal behavior.

In the play's climactic scene, the king woos Katherine for Owen Tudor, elevated by Orrery into the necessary role of lover and friend. Katherine's response makes clear her attitude to Tudor's loyalty to his royal rival:

> He who resigns his Love, though for his King,
> Does, as he is a Lover, a low thing:
> But, as a Subject, a high Crime does do;
> Being at once, Subject and Rebel too:
> For, whilst to Regal pow'r he does submit,
> He casts off Love, a greater pow'r than it.
>
> (V.331–36)

The concatenation of heroic and political language here is elaborate: Tudor's generous deference to his friend and king becomes a crime against absolutism itself. The sweeping denigration of valorous enterprise and of politics in the language of Orrery's plays is so extreme as to raise some questions. "Every reader of Restoration plays in our century must be struck with their institutional naivete," says Geoffrey Marshall; but the complete absorption of politics into love in Orrery is even more striking in light of the fact that the author himself was a skilled politician and no stranger to the complexities of court intrigue.[39] The emphasis on love as the mainspring of political activity looks like a displacement, an avoidance of unpleasant truths, an erection of a fictive barrier to the unpleasant realities of court life. Staves has argued that the irreconcilable pressures on Orrerian heroes—particularly the king's "friends," such as Owen Tudor and Delaware in *The Black Prince*—reflect the kinds of pressures endured by less heroic subjects during the interregnum.[40] In projecting the dilemma of the loyal subject as insoluble, Orrery shows himself to be neither naive nor optimistic. Orrery's plays represent politics as paradox: for Delaware and Tudor, personal integrity can only be maintained through acts of betrayal. What looks magnanimous—Delaware's publication of his "secret," Tudor's refusal to woo Katherine—is really cowardice, weakness of a special type that distinguishes subjects from kings.

For if, in Laura Brown's words, the plays are "contests," they are rigged contests: only Orrery's idealized monarchs, Henry V and the Black Prince, are capable of meeting the standards of love.[41] Its absolute demands, which lead the characters to ravel out, sometimes with astounding speciousness, the conflicting ethical dimensions of any situation, can only be fully met by kings. *Henry V* demonstrates this fact with precision and clarity; the rival kings in *The Black Prince*—King Edward of England and King John of France—both falter, deflected from their true course by the dazzling widow Plantagenet, but the prince himself shines the brighter as a model of constancy. The plays demonstrate this innate superiority; we can only marvel at the monarch's model behavior.

The paradox is Orrery's main verbal trick, and his characters' adeptness in this kind of wordplay defines their nobility. But the plays' basic situations are themselves conceived as paradoxical: the demands of love and honor, which appear to be in conflict, must be reconciled into a Platonic identity. The "foolish truth" of history has no relevance here, although it is evoked to create complications whose importance is their gratuitousness itself. Public life is by definition irrelevant. Those who scruple at "interest of state" have the consciousness of subjects, not kings; friends, not lovers. Tudor, like Delaware in *The Black Prince,* accepts his relegation to this lower order reluctantly but fully. "Be but my Friend" (v.404) is Katherine's sentence upon Tudor. As a failure in heroic love, he can hope for nothing more. But in being merely unworthy, the friends—Tudor and Delaware—escape being disloyal. Only the heroic kings are capable of constancy. The terms in which personal nobility is defined—constancy in particular—are reminiscent of *Perkin Warbeck,* but the contrast is equally striking. While in Ford's play the demands of personal nobility and self-definition collide outright with the pressures of time and historical truth, here the process of self-definition so dominates the action that history is wholly absorbed into heroic rhetoric. The distinction between sovereign and subject is made wholly abstract. Thus, where there is specific historical content, as in the discussion of the navy, the tendency towards generalization is so strong that even Orrery's own humanist goals and political aspirations must be subsumed into the play's love-and-honor rhetoric. Contemporary context is evoked in such a way as to figure the utter irrelevancy of all context. In Ford's play, Perkin Warbeck's kingdom is his wife: the heroic lover-king rules only over himself.

The solipsism of the heroic drama is in part attributable to the uncertainties of the Restoration political settlement. The aggressive absolutism of the politics of love in these plays refines the terrible issues of allegiance and sovereignty of the decades before into mere turns of wit. Escapist and didactic at once, the heroic drama purveys a vision of chivalry, in Mrs. Evelyn's famous words on *The Conquest of Granada,* "designed for an Utopia rather than our stage." J. Douglas Canfield describes the plays as "politically reactionary," and "anti-Modern": "They are also Re-storation in the sense that they are a re-storying of the feudal, hierarchical, Classical-Christian *Weltanschauung,* which like a nova was blazing most brightly as it expired."[42] An important qualification must be added to this analysis: for Mrs. Evelyn as for John Ford in *Perkin Warbeck,* the fictiveness, as well as the attractiveness, of the old values is never in doubt. Orrery's dismissal of politics and history is a rear-guard action; the political crises of the late 1670s and early 1680s would violently reanimate the debate about sovereignty and allegiance that heroic rhetoric had stultified and inverted into the catchwords of love and honor.

iii

The Pope-burning processions and street violence that accompanied the Popish Plot panic of 1678 were matched in theatrical activity. "The stage absolutely foamed with politics," exclaimed Sir Walter Scott of the years 1679–82. Audiences disintegrated into rival claques, shouting down each other's views; censorship scanned new plays with revived vigilance.[43] Fears of Jesuit conspiracy led to the publication of histories of the French religious wars: Bishop Burnet issued his *Barbarous and Bloody Massacre* in 1678, and a new English edition of Davila's history of the religious wars appeared in the same year. Nathaniel Lee dramatized *The Massacre of Paris* (loosely based on Davila) in the following year; the play was suppressed unperformed, probably because of its subversive portrayal of the king as drugged into moral insensibility by his popish mother. Lee's *Caesar Borgia, Son of Pope Alexander the Sixth,* an exposé of bungled popish murders, was hissed and booed by a hostile claque. Both plays went on to become staples of the anti-Catholic stage after the Glorious Revolution. To these revivals Lee owes his reputation as a Whig playwright—as to his *Lucius Junius Brutus* (1680), suppressed after a run of six straight days, for its "very Scandalous Expressions & Reflections upon ye government." Read as an endorsement of the people's right to rebel against a libertine monarch, Lee's play does indeed verge upon treason. But he hedged his bets: as Brutus sentences his sons to death, Lee offers a vision of strong rule and political stability reminiscent of Edward Filmer's *Patriarcha.*[44]

The collaboration of Lee with Dryden on *The Duke of Guise* came to their contemporaries as a surprise. "I cannot believe the first Author of himself guilty of such evil intentions, because I have heard better things of him," marveled Shadwell at Lee's conversion; "but the old Serpent *Bays* has deluded him." Lee's biographer, Roswell G. Ham, agreed with Shadwell, suggesting that Lee was already insane (he was to spend the years from 1684 to 1689 in Bedlam), and that Dryden pieced Lee's sections of the play together from *The Massacre of Paris* and other fragments available to him. Ham's diagnosis of Lee's madness is not, however, convincing: "To combine thought and Restoration tragedy was questionable for anyone," he wrote of the effort of composing *Lucius Junius Brutus,* "for Lee it was madness."[45] But Lee went on to write *Constantine the Great,* a thoroughly "Tory" play—Ham felt that Dryden had filched it from the helpless madman's "trunk"—and was clearly at the height of his highly erratic powers in 1681.

The collaboration was thus an important one. More of a theatrical chameleon than a systematic political thinker, Lee timed his shift to coincide with the great shift of public opinion that accompanied Charles's routing of the Whigs after the Oxford Parliament of 1681. Dryden emphasizes that the original idea was Lee's in his *Vindication,* to take full advantage of his colleague's change of heart, and in the play Henry's summoning of the Estates to Blois reflects the Oxford Parliament. "I must do a common right both to Mr. Lee and myself, to declare publicly, that it was at his earnest desire, without any solicitation of mine, that this play was produced betwixt us," Dryden proclaims.[46] Yet this ringing declaration is problematic in light of the opening sentence of the *Vindication:* "In the year of his majesty's happy Restoration, the first play I undertook was 'The Duke of Guise;' as the fairest way, which the Act of Indemnity had then left us, of setting forth the rise of the late rebellion; and by exploding the villainies of it upon the stage, to precaution posterity of the like errors" (p. 146). The play was "damned in private," Dryden says, by his friends, and was set aside. If we are to take this polemical and disingenuous writer at his word, Dryden had cherished the idea of a play on the French religious wars for the past twenty years, and Lee's part in the overall conception of the drama becomes clearly subordinate. The play works on two levels of historical parallel: first there is the occasion of its production itself—the Oxford Parliament, the London mob, and the king's offensive against the City Charter in the summer of 1682—and the play's comparison of the French League with the Exclusionist "association" of Whig Peers; second, as Dryden insists, is the parallel of the French League to the Solemn League and Covenant that preceded the English Civil Wars.[47]

The first scene—which, along with "the whole fourth act, and the first half, or somewhat more, of the fifth" (p. 149), Dryden acknowledges to be his own—sets out the parallel in fine Whig-baiting style. The curate of St. Eustace, whom we later discover to be a demon disguised, presents arguments derived from "A Calvinist minister of Orleans" to the effect that "irreligious kings / May justly be deposed and put to death."

"To borrow arguments from heretic books, / Methinks, was not so prudent," observes Bussy (1.i, p. 24). Dryden thus manages to insist upon identification of the Catholic League with the Protestant Association proposed by Shaftesbury and the earlier covenant: "Heaven is itself head of the Holy League; / And all the saints are cov'nanters and Guisards," confirms the cardinal of Guise (1.i, p. 26). The traditional charge that Catholicism excused the murder of protestant kings is shifted over to Calvinism; Guise, when he appears in this scene as head of the Council of Sixteen, takes Shaftesbury's place at the head of the Sixteen Whig Peers. The tone of the scene is comic; antiroyalist arguments are forced to the limits of absurdity; the hypocrisy of the conspirators is lampooned. By 1682, Shaftesbury's pension from the French king was a matter of common knowledge: "'Tis true," says Guise, acknowledging that he is in the pay of Spain, "a pension, from a foreign prince, / Sounds treason in the letter of the law, / But good intentions justify the deed." "Heaven's good," agrees the Curate, "the cause is good; the money's good; / No matter whence it comes" (1.i, p. 27). Patently satirical, unabashedly partisan, the first scene clearly delineates Dryden's Tory view of the Exclusion crisis and of the French religious wars. The attitude to Guise is mocking; his grandiose rhetoric consistently undercuts itself with logical absurdities, up to his closing couplet in which he portrays himself as "Impatient to be soon recalled, to see / The king imprisoned, and the nation free" (1.i, p. 29). This Guise is a stage Shaftesbury, logic-chopping, scheming, devious; Dryden's indignation at the Whig readers who interpreted the play to be a slander on Monmouth seems well-founded.

Lee's portions of the play, however, offer a different Guise. Marmoutier's reproaches seem clearly directed toward Monmouth: "You have your writers too, that cant your battles, / That style you, the new David, second Moses, / Prop of the church, deliverer of the people" (1.iii, p. 34). Guise becomes a double figure, a composite Whig—Monmouth and Shaftesbury, Absalom and Achitophel. This permits Dryden to evade the charge of personal libel leveled against him by Hunt and Shadwell: "So then it is not (as the snarling authors of the Reflection tell you) a parallel of the men, but of the times; a parallel of the factions, and of the leaguers" (*Vindication*, p. 150). The fusing of Monmouth with Shaftesbury is indeed awkward, and despite Dryden's efforts to discount it, the personal parallel remains important to the play. By the time of the delayed production of *The Duke of Guise*, stage lampoons of Shaftesbury abounded, from Aphra Behn's Sir Timothy Treat-all in *The City Heiress* (1681) to Thomas Southerne's Ismael in *The Loyal Brother* (1682). According to Thomas d'Urfey's dedication of *Sir Barnaby Whigg* (another Shaftesbury figure), the Tories were well in possession of the stage:

> *As to this Comedy, it had the Honour to please one party, and I am only glad, that the St.* Georges *of Eighty-one got a Victory over the old hissing Dragons of Forty-two; 'tis a Good Omen, and I hope portends future successes . . . for in this age 'tis not a Poet's Merit but his party that must do his business.*[48]

Shaftesbury could be easily recognized in the garb of Puritan knight and Guildhall orator or in the more exalted costume of corrupt counselor, turned sour by restless ambition. Both types appear in Thomas Otway's Tory play *Venice Preserv'd* (1682), where Antonio figures the lewd Puritan and Renault the sly (but no less lecherous) statesman. Shaftesbury serves to disgrace both sides in the Venetian story: corruption in power and treason out of power are two sides of the same Whig medal. Otway dramatizes, as does Dryden in the first scene of *The Duke of Guise,* the logical impossibility of Whiggism.

But the play's heroic action belies this satiric intent. Where Otway's virtuous characters are depicted as hopelessly adrift in a republic in which Whigs govern corruptly even as other Whigs conspire to subvert them, Guise, Marmoutier, and King Henry form a typical triangle of heroic love. The tone of Dryden's first scene does not carry over into Lee's second and third acts: Marmoutier's confrontation with Guise in I.iii (Lee's work) moves quickly from public issues to private ones. She hands Guise a letter "from one at court, who tells me, the king loves me"; with this she hopes to urge Guise not to join his forces in Champagne. Guise's response, of course, is jealous rage:

> Ha! Can it be! "Madam, the king loves you."—
> *[Reads.*
> But vengeance I will have; to pieces, thus,
> To pieces with them all.
> *[Tears the letter.*
>
> (I.iii, p. 37)

Love, not ambition, comes to motivate Guise's treason. The climax of the play is Dryden's scene in which the king and Guise confront each other (IV.i): but the buildup to it is wholly Lee's. Guise abandons himself to passion and the result is disaster. Malicorne works the duke into a jealous frenzy before his interview with the king:

> I'll wait him in his cabinet alone,
> And look him pale; while in his courts without,

> The people shout him dead with their alarms,
> And make his mistress tremble in his arms.
>
> (III.i, p. 68)

This initial erotic rage, provoked by the devil's agent himself, leads the duke into open disobedience and treason. Despite her astonishing virtue, Marmoutier also forgets state affairs when she bids Guise farewell, promising a reunion in the apolitical world of death:

> Farewell for ever; ah, Guise, though now we part
> In the bright orbs, prepared us by our fates,
> Our souls shall meet,—farewell!—and Ios sing above,
> Where no ambition, nor state-crime, the happier spirits
>   prove,
> But all are blest, and all enjoy an everlasting love.
>
> (v.iii, pp. 125–26)

What Guise wins at the end of the play is Marmoutier, emblematic of virtue and love; the king, on the other hand, achieves a heroic self-mastery. He unmasks over the body of Guise:

> Yes, I'll wear
> The fox no longer, but put on the lion;
> And since I could resolve to take the heads
> Of this great insurrection, you, the members,
> Look to it; beware, turn from your stubbornness,
> And learn to know me, for I will be king.
>
> (v.v, p. 131)

The image is drawn from Machiavelli, as is the notion of kingship as the raw exercise of power.

This makes the ending of the play unpleasant; assassination is a tyrant's tool, as the stage direction *"The Guise is assaulted by eight. They stab him in all parts, but most in the head"* (p. 130) (drawn literally from Davila) makes abundantly clear. The Whigs decried the glorification of murder in the play; Saintsbury judged the heroic amplification of Henry to be a "flagrant and almost ludicrous travesty" (*The Duke of Guise*, p. 10). Dryden evaded the charge of imputing merit to murder poorly in his *Vindication,* and in the play he himself raised the issue of Henry's Machiavellism—only to dismiss it. The king assures his mother of his ability to deceive:

> I know, he'll make exorbitant demands,
> But here your part of me will come in play;
> The Italian soul shall teach me how to sooth:

Even Jove must flatter with an empty hand,
'Tis time to thunder, when he gripes the brand.

(IV.i, p. 78)

The problem is openly dramatized in the scene between Henry and
Crillon (again, Dryden's) in which the king presents his plan as a pro-
digious birth:

My vengeance, ripened in the womb of time,
Presses for birth, and longs to be disclosed.

(V.i, p. 109)

Crillon refuses: as a soldier he has killed and plundered, but murder is
beneath him. "As for cutting off a traitor," he says, "I'll execute him
lawfully in my own function, when I meet him in the field; but for your
chamber-practice, that's not my talent." "Is my revenge unjust, or tyran-
nous?" Henry asks; "Heaven knows I love not blood" (V.i, p. 110). What
happens next is a severe displacement (and, to Scott, a disappointment):
the blunt soldier reveals that he vowed to spare Guise's life when Guise
spared him on the barricades. The scruple of conscience is reduced to a
soldier's bargain; the dilemma disappears. Henry dismisses Crillon
affectionately:

Make much of honour, 'tis a soldier's conscience.
Thou shalt not do this act; thou art even too good;
But keep my secret, for that's conscience too.

(V.i, p. 110)

Crillon agrees to this, and to watching the doors, which he calls "the
honest part of the job" (p. 111).

The dilemma is endemic to parallel histories. Certain correspondences—between the Oxford Parliament and the summoning of the
Estates to Blois, between the council of Sixteen and the Sixteen Whig
Peers—attracted Dryden and Lee to the subject. Other correspondences
provoked wrathful responses from the Whigs and had to be sidestepped
by Dryden in his *Vindication*—Henry III is not Charles II, he argued;
Guise is not Monmouth. Dryden and Lee could not successfully merge
an attitude towards Guise that was originally satiric—as in the first
scene—with a pathetic, tragic dramatic form that insisted that Guise
should be sympathetically depicted as a lover of Marmoutier. Similarly,
their desire to praise Charles for his display of authority at Oxford and in
revoking the City Charters forced them to dramatize the assassination of
Guise as "speedy justice" rather than to explore its moral and political
implications.

They further sought to reduce Henry's complicity in the death of Guise by introducing into the play the subplot of the diabolical bargain between Malicorne and Melanax. The purpose, originally, is again satirical: faction is the devil's work, so the demon is seen agitating the crowd while "dressed in his fanatick habit," and he acknowledges that the logic-chopping curate is a devil too. But the scene in which Melanax drags Malicorne down to hell is intended to have a larger resonance: the devil prophesies of Guise "If he goes / To council when he next is called, he dies" (v.ii, p. 118). Guise disregards this prophesy—the archbishop plays upon his ambition—as he does the portentous nosebleed that precedes his entrance to the council chamber. His defiance of these omens evokes a whole chain of horrors:

> I come;—down, devil—ha! must I stumble too?
> Away, ye dreams! What if it thundered now,
> Or if a raven crossed me in my way?
> Or now it comes, because last night I dreamt
> The council-hall was hung with crimson round,
> And all the ceiling plastered o'er with black.
> No more!—Blue fires, and ye dull rolling lakes,
> Fathomless caves, ye dungeons of old night,
> Phantoms, be gone! If I must die, I'll fall
> True politician, and defy you all.
>
> (v.iv, p. 126)

Swooning and somnabulistic, he stumbles to his doom; the last boast is utterly hollow. The hardware of occultism in the play serves a dual purpose, at once satirical and evasive. The alliance between Guise and his faction tars him with the devil's brush, but we are forced to take the damnation of the hero as tragic. Dryden changes gears in Malicorne's final scene, in which the joke of the diabolical contract becomes serious: "Thus men, too careless of their future state, / Dispute, know nothing, and believe too late" (v.ii, p. 120), exclaims the damned magician as he descends into hell. Guise is likewise doomed: the playwrights dress his death in all the trappings of hell to make it seem inevitable, fated.

The play's failure as historical parallel can account for the reluctance of the government to release it for performance, but its supernatural dabblings reveal a more important failure. The decision to make the duke a sacrificial victim at the end subverts the desire to portray Henry as a good king forced to drastic action by subversion, just as the decision to recast the struggle between Guise and the king into the shape of a love triangle subverts the play's satirical parallel. Dryden indulged in satiric parallel with great success in the Varronian poem *Absalom and Achitophel*, and the *Vindication* suggests that he conceived *The Duke of Guise* as another such satire. But the result—encumbered by the spectacular hardware of stage damnation and subverted by notions of dramaturgy that made love into the motive force of tragedy—is confusion.

The blessing Marmoutier confers upon Guise belies the rattling of the devils' chains; he dies with her name on his lips, to meet her in the "bright orbs . . . / Where no ambition, nor state crime, the happier spirits prove" (v.iii, pp. 125–26). Beside this triumph of love and pity, Henry's restoration of order seems utterly irrelevant. The impossibility of virtue and honor in the world of *The Duke of Guise* takes the paradoxes of heroic self-definition to a logical extreme. In *Venice Preserv'd*, the sympathetic characters react desperately to the impossible demands of their context; Marmoutier retires to the convent. The duke's passivity at the end—announced by omens as definitive as those that announce Antony's end in *All for Love*—bespeaks the same kind of escape and deliverance.[49] Despite the efforts of the playwrights to the contrary, Henry's world at the end remains a Machiavellian chaos.

Thus the play's Tory purpose—celebration of a monarch's reassertion of strength—founders. The king's phoenixlike unmasking can only be described in Machiavellian terms, a putting off of the fox for the lion, and the audience's sympathy goes out to the virtuous Marmoutier and the doomed Guise. Pitiable and middling virtuous throughout the play, Henry at its end descends to brutality. His action cannot be presented as an epiphany like David's in *Absalom and Achitophel*; and in the last analysis, Lee's efforts in magnifying Marmoutier and Dryden's in baiting the rabblement are both diversionary tactics. Nonetheless, the implications of their portrayal of Henry III are bleak; inactivity dooms the state to chaos; activity dooms the king to the solitary life of the politician.

iv

The same double drive towards both inflammatory applicability and regular romantic intrigue can be seen in the spate of Shakespeare adaptations that appeared in the early 1680s. John Crowne's *Misery of Civil War* (1680) introduced jealous rivalry into the tension between Warwick and Edward in Shakespeare's *Henry VI* plays. In his *Henry VI, the First Part*, Crowne described his adulteration of Shakespeare as the dressing of a salad:

> How'ere to make your Appetites more keen,
> Not only oyly Words are sprinkled in;

> *But what to please you gives us better hope,*
> *A little Vineger against the* Pope.[50]

Crowne regularizes Shakespeare and points his lessons clearly for his own age. *The Misery of Civil War* concludes with scenes that supply the want of explicit Tudor orthodoxy in the Shakespearean originals: the ghost of Richard II appears to Henry VI before his death and explains that the torment of civil war is a just punishment on England for his deposition. In *Henry VI,* Crowne devotes most of his energy to heightening parallels between the murder of Duke Humphrey and the contemporary sensation, the murder of Sir Edmund Berry Godfrey, and the play was suppressed before it could be performed. Crowne forgoes heroic decorum to mix comic and tragic scenes in these plays, but his specifically topical satire jars against, without qualifying, the larger heroic design. Crowne relies upon Shakespeare's prestige to confer legitimacy upon his purposes, but sets himself apart from his model by polishing language and suggesting in his dedication of *Henry VI* that the original author *"hudled up"* (sig. A3v) the true popish nature of Duke Humphrey's death. He repairs Shakespeare's deficiencies as a playwright and as a historian: Godfrey's murder confirms Shakespeare's poor judgment in the case of Duke Humphrey. The adaptor poses as historian, exposing the real truth about Humphrey's death and reviving the providentialism of Shakespeare's sources, which Crowne apparently did consult.

An approach different in emphasis to the problem is that of Nahum Tate, whose adaptations of *Richard II* (suppressed 1680, although it did run for a few performances as *The Sicilian Usurper*), *King Lear* (1681), and *Coriolanus* (*The Ingratitude of a Commonwealth,* 1681), also appeared in these years. Like Crowne, Tate provides a Tory Richard II: this monarch only borrows Gaunt's revenues, promising prompt repayment. *"Not one alter'd page but what breaths Loyalty,"* complained Tate in his dedication, *"yet had this play the hard fortune to receive its Prohibition from the Court."* He adorned his *"Prince with such Heroick vertues, as afterwards made his distrest Scenes of force to draw Tears from the Spectators"*; and commenting on the staging of the play as an Italian rather than English history, Tate adds, *"which, how much more touching they would have been had the Scene been laid at Home, let the Reader judge."*[51] Tate's martyred Richard, sacrificing himself lest his country's blood be spilt in civil war, is characterized as a pitiable reminder of Charles I, and the play warns against, as Crowne does, the misery that follows disobedience. Where Shakespeare's Richard issues blank charters and sneers at the prophecies of the dying Gaunt, Tate's is confused and misunderstood; Tate's Bolingbroke, yet another stage Shaftesbury or villain-statesman, connives vigorously at his fall.

Richard's uxoriousness and Tate's regret that the "scene" in the performed play could not have been "laid at home" points towards an identification of the historical with the domestic that becomes characteristic of later historical drama. "To your own Fathers, sure, you will be kind," John Banks urges the audience in the prologue to *Vertue Betray'd* (1682).[52] Tate's creation of a love interest between Edgar and Cordelia in his *History of King Lear* not only makes the old monarch's rage psychologically plausible but also furnishes a good Tory ending: the installation of Cordelia and Edgar on the king's throne makes the play's resolution a restoration. The greater to torment Coriolanus in Tate's adaptation of that play, Aufidius is just barely forestalled from raping his wife; his henchmen maim the hero's son and in the process drive his mother mad. Thomas Otway's Romeo and Juliet—romanized in his *Caius Marius*—enact their doomed love against a backdrop of civil war rather than family feud (1681). While this change adds to the play as a whole a political dimension Shakespeare's lacks, it also insists on the utter disjunction between the public world and the domestic, pastoral possibilities of love it destroys. Where the Shakespeare adaptations of the period point—like *The Duke of Guise*—to the difficulties of staging politically activist history, they also point in the direction of the new drama of the pathos of power.

v

John Banks made it possible for English history to reappear on the English stage: the whole seventeenth century, as we have seen, up to the 1680s, is a period in which history plays were experimental anomalies, always subject to government attention.[53] Banks shifted from imitative heroic dramas (*Cyrus the Great, The Rival Kings*) in the 1670s, to plays based on English history (*The Unhappy Favourite*, 1681; *Vertue Betray'd*, 1682; *The Island Queens,* suppressed in 1682, revised in 1704 as *The Albion Queens;* and *The Innocent Usurper,* suppressed in 1693, but probably written in 1683). Banks's record suggests no decline in government sensitivity to history; despite their heightened pathos, most English history plays through the eighteenth century earned special scrutiny. Banks's formula thus offered no solution to the continued tendency of audiences to see history as primarily topical. Yet that he devised a formula that made historical drama acceptable and popular cannot be questioned. The main features of Banks's drama are the villain-statesmen who provide the impetus for his plots. Where Dryden and Lee are forced, despite themselves, into endorsing a wholly Machiavellian view of kingship, Banks is able to effect a total separation of the monarch from the world of power politics. Villains propel the story to the conclusion recorded in history; a brutally manipulated monarch yearns for escape. It is the identification of the villain with the force of history itself that makes Banks's drama interesting. In depicting the events of the past as manipulated violations of what is noblest and most human about his protagonists, Banks goes beyond Otway's pastoral visions of "Nature outside of human organisation"—"a condition more authentic than that allowed by merely historical life."[54] Secular, humanist history itself becomes, in the dramas of Banks, Nicholas Rowe, and the eighteenth- and nineteenth-century dramatists who follow them, a malevolent force that destroys and violates humans by reducing them to passionate machines.

Eighteenth-century commentators were baffled by the badness of Banks's plays and by the popularity they enjoyed. Colley Cibber observed that it was not Banks's "barren, barbarous stile," but rather the "intrinsick, and naked value of their well-conducted tales" that drew tears from audiences. To Steele, Banks provided "a remarkable instance that the soul is not to be moved by words, but things."[55] The "things" that Steele's contemporaries found moving constitute a whole arsenal of theatrical tricks and clichés.

The opening scene of *The Unhappy Favourite*—familiar now only through Fielding's parody of it in *The Tragedy of Tragedies*—can be taken as a model of Banks's theatrical shorthand. "Help me to rail Prodigious-minded *Burleigh*," cries the Countess of Nottingham. This famous first line works its crude purpose through an egregious historical error. Queen Elizabeth's hunchbacked counselor at the time of the Essex crisis was the first Lord Burleigh's son, Sir Robert Cecil, and the title had passed to his older brother. But for Banks the name serves only too well to emphasize the politician's awkward bulk. Nottingham's address to Cecil's deformity is set up to satirize both characters:

> Then I'le Caress thee, stroak thee into shape.
> This Rocky dismal Form of thine that holds
> The most Seraphick Mind, that ever was;
> I'le heal and Mould thee, with a soft Embrace;
> Thy Mountain Back shall yield beneath these Arms,
> And thy pale wither'd Cheeks that never glow
> Shall then be deck'd with Roses of my own.[56]

The unrepressed sexuality that colors Nottingham's and Burleigh's malice shows both to be failures in love. Nottingham craves revenge for her rejection by Essex, while Burleigh's "Hot Blood," because of his deformity, "Burn't with continual thought, does inward Glow" (p. 2). Banks's female villains are inevitably consumed with jealous spite; his male villains divert their sexual energies into statesmanship.

Burleigh's hunchback is emphasized so much by Banks for another purpose. Nottingham praises Cecil's acumen:

> Let none presume to say while *Burleigh* lives
> A Woman wears the Crown; Fourth *Richard* rather,
> Heir to the Third in Magnanimity,
> In Person, Courage, Wit and Bravery all,
> But to his Vices none, nor to his End
> I hope.
>
> (1.i, p. 2)

Relying upon his audience's familiarity with Richard III as a theatrical type, Banks forces the countess to undercut herself too blatantly with this clumsy parallel. Cecil's ecstasy at the compliment is repulsively comic. Through his reliance upon the name Burleigh and his reference to Richard III, Banks epitomizes careless and crude stagecraft.

Banks relies upon prepackaged theatrical units not only in the characterization of his villains. His heroes and heroines too communicate in set, formulaic speeches. While a comic dimension is added to the ranting Burleigh and the passionate Nottingham by this technique, an uncomfortable stiffness is the result when Banks attempts to generate pathos. His positive characters invariably turn to a rhetoric of pastoralism. Elizabeth's complaint in the second act shows Banks at his most monotonously homiletic:

> but oh, how heavy
> A Load is State where the Free Mind's disturb'd!
> How happy a Maid is she that always lives
> Far from high Honour, in a low Content,
> Where neither Hills, nor dreadful Mountains grow,
> But in a Vale where Springs and Pleasures flow;
> Where Sheep lye round instead of Subjects Throngs,
> And Trees for Musick, Birds instead of Songs;
> Instead of *Essex,* one poor faithful Hind,
> He as a Servant, She a Mistress kind,
> Who with Garlands for her Coming crowns her Dore,
> And all with Rushes strews her little floore,

> Where at their mean Repast no Fears attend
> Of a false Enemy, or falser Friend;
> No care of Cepters, nor ambitious Frights
> Disturb the quiet of their sleep at Nights.

(II.i, p. 18)

Lessing threw up his hands in despair at Banks's inconsistencies of style: "He is at the same time so ordinary and so precious, so low and so bombastic, and that not from person to person but all throughout."[57] Banks's counterposition of a pastoral ideal to the Machiavellian chaos of politics is wholly conventional; the clumsy terms in which it is expressed—"Sheep lye round instead of Subjects Throngs"—originate with him.

James Sutherland's reaction to this kind of crude pastoralism— Banks is "attempting . . . to make his characters speak the language of the heart"—points towards the severe separation of public and private worlds and languages in Banks.[58] The monarch's yearning to be out of the public world, and to be out of politics, corresponds to a weariness of political intrigue in the audiences of the 1680s. "Damn the State-Fop," Banks urges in the prologue to *Vertue Betray'd*:

> Give us a Pit of Drunkards and Lovers,
> Good sanguine men, who mind no State Affair,
> But bid a base world of itself take care.

(sig. A4r)

Clearly Banks's appeal is not only to the "Ladies," to whom he offered *The Unhappy Favourite*. Rather, his female protagonists embody a feeling of helplessness in the midst of political crisis that is shared by all members of the audience. The powerless queen is Banks's paradigm of the individual trapped in history.

For as Orrery, Dryden, Lee, and the Shakespeare adaptors show, history was still understood in this period to be a topical political science, however incompatible its goals might be to the demands of dramatic form. History, in Banks, reaches its end in spite of the sufferings of his protagonists: his villains embody the autonomy of fact. The familiarity of Banks's story lines is important. "Benevolence requires at least the illusion of a specific response to a specific person or persons," argues Rothstein: presented with familiar figures from the past, spectators pity as they identify with them. But the identification of the villains with the story, and the exclusion of the lover-monarch from responsibility for its consequence, points towards a deep resentment of mere fact.[59]

We have met this resentment in Rymer's contemporary strictures on the inadequacy of history—its "higlety, piglety" disregard of the higher value of divine providence.[60] There is no poetic justice in Banks's plays: historical figures must be either villains or victims. The audience's sympathies are evoked for characters who yearn for a state of being outside politics and outside time, which the historical framework of the drama makes impossible. Because the outcome is already known, and because Banks's persistent eroticism makes his characters seem so naked, so vulnerable, so defenseless, the enterprise is gratifyingly brutal. The prolonged farewells between Essex and his countess in *The Unhappy Favourite* are intolerable: Banks insists that we savor each moment of agony. What Banks portrays and what Rymer decries is history with no congruence to divine providence. As in *The Duke of Guise,* political action is by definition evil; lovers, in their verbal pastoral paradises, do nothing. Banks's hostility to history and his portrayal of monarchs as victims of villainous conspiracies is, in the last analysis, sadistic. People in the public world suffer, and there is no escape from this necessary pain.

Tate's *Lear* and Crowne's *Misery of Civil War* come closer to meeting Rymer's strictures by offering appropriate providential commentaries on the action: Lear is restored, and the virtue of Edgar and Cordelia rewarded; Richard II's ghost helps Henry VI understand the great pattern into which his death fits. Repairing Shakespeare's faults involves regularizing his vision: Banks is unique in finding no consolation for suffering. In the plays of Nicholas Rowe, the disjunction between private and public is as acute as in Banks, but the overriding vision is, as Rymer and later eighteenth-century critics would counsel, theodicean. His plays abound in providential rhetoric and epiphanic demonstrations of the coincidence between divine and poetic justice. Vitiated by its use on both sides of the seventeenth-century's political debates, the language of providence comes in Rowe to be charged with fierce partisanship on the one hand and melting eroticism on the other. For Rowe, all politics reduces to sexual politics. State crimes are analogized to private, personal violations; these offenses trigger the charged language that invokes the justice of God.[61]

The tyranny and duplicity of Bajazet in Rowe's *Tamerlane* (1701), for example, are sexual: he practices fraudulent marriage, and when that fails he descends to rape. The excellence of Tamerlane is similarly localized: falsely accused of adultery, he portrays his vindication as divine justice. In a play designed to celebrate William III's suppression of the ambitions of Louis XIV, the key metaphors for aggression are those of private violation. The greatness of Tamerlane—his refusal to be goaded or tempted into tyranny—is dramatized as control over jealousy and wise repression of awakening desire.

When Rowe turned to English history in *Jane Shore* (1714), he retained the technique of validating political concepts by the evocation of intense personal emotions, opposing male oppression to female beneficence. Tyranny, treason, and providence all find expression in private terms. Hastings's attack on Jane demonstrates not so much his tyranny— he goes on to become a model of pious behavior—as Jane's female isolation and helplessness. "Help! Oh, gracious heaven!" she cries (II.239); Dumont, really her husband in disguise, appears and delivers her. The divine, the political, the domestic merge: the adulterer is foiled by the husband, the prince by the peasant, the would-be sinner by the all-seeing eye of God. As the death scene at the end shows, Dumont/Shore functions on all these levels. Jane sees him as divine—"Arm thy brow with vengeance; and appear / The minister of heav'n's enquiring justice" (V.329–30)—but her perception of his mercy draws on intimate personal memory: "How can you be so good? / But you were ever thus" (V.363–64). The final stage picture has a double meaning: Jane dies the victim of the "tyrant's will," (V.433) but Bellmour moralizes the spectacle differently: "Let those, who view this sad example know / What fate attends the broken marriage vow" (V.435–36). Through political injustice God punishes Jane's sin; the Eden that Dumont/Shore proposes to Jane at the end of act II—"No faction, or domestic fury's rage / Did e'er disturb the quiet of that place" (II.316–17)—is explicitly located outside of history and politics.

Hastings, too, falls because of both his sexual misconduct and his defiance of the tyrant: like Jane's, his end is depicted as privately just and publicly unjust. His defence of the little princes is heroic: "Stand forth, thou proxy of all-ruling Providence," Jane apostrophizes her would-be rapist, "And save the friendless infants from oppression." The division of Rowe's world into tyrants on the one hand and helpless victims on the other presupposes from Rowe's audience identification with the women and the "forsaken, royal little ones" (IV.122) whose fate parallels theirs. Yet as fallen beings, Hastings and Jane must also perish; hence, she cannot eat the "rich conserves" (V.363) that Shore offers her at the end.[62]

But the congruence between divine justice—which rationalizes Jane's fate—and political injustice—figured in Gloster, the scourge-of-God—is challenged by Shore's presence. His boundless mercy suggests the relativity of the punitive justice to which Jane has resigned herself.

From this challenge grows a wider religious dimension of the play. Jane's prayers are reminiscent of the language of the Psalms:

> Yet, yet endure, nor murmur, O my soul!
> For are not thy transgressions great and numberless?
> Do not they cover thee, like rising floods,
> And press thee like a weight of waters down?
> Does not the hand of righteousness afflict thee;
> And who shall plead against it?
>
> (V.142—47)

They are answered by Shore's New Testament forgiveness, which sees Gloster less as "the hand of righteousness" than as the "hand of pow'r" and "proud oppression." As Dumont, Shore gives expression to the play's most trenchant attacks upon "wicked greatness"; and his self-annihilation through disguise gives the lie to Jane's constant expectation of ruthless heavenly vengeance.

As in *Venice Preserv'd,* we are confronted with an immense gulf between society and nature, rendered here in terms of the conflict between political and divine justice. The play's ending is disturbing: the moral intelligibility of Jane's sufferings is withdrawn. Jane is a "sinner-saint," but her sin is never dramatized;[63] and if we are to accept Shore's Christian vision, responsibility for her sufferings falls, as it does in the world of Banks, upon the shoulders of the hunchbacked politician. The audience is left to ponder whether Bellmour's pious homily about marital fidelity really offers an adequate justification of the suffering it has seen.

Rowe's eagerness to address the problem of suffering in a Christian universe does suggest the persistence of something like an Elizabethan "world picture" in Rowe's most Shakespearean play. Private, public, divine levels comment on each other; the appeal to the emotions is strengthened rather than vitiated by religious and political speculation. Yet the shift of focus from the powerful—in Elizabethan plays—to the powerless here carries with it a loss of historical context. The world of *Jane Shore* is generalized and timeless; her dilemma is universalized to such an extent that even the propagandistic specificity of Rowe's early plays has been lost. The simplification of politics into a pattern of ravishing tyrant and ravished victim betrays also an impoverishment in the treatment of love and sex. Rowe's dramas give marriage a central importance; but in all the plays, marriage strives towards privacy, seclusion, pastoral isolation. Against it is pitted the generalized menace of power, of faction, of the tyrant. From Rowe's perception of adultery as the worst of crimes and tyranny as adulterous rape naturally arises the anti-Catholic paranoia of his last play, *Lady Jane Grey* (1715).

Designed to capitalize upon anti-Jacobite feeling, the play's Christianity is not the generalized piety of *Jane Shore*. The idea of Protestant usurpation (supported, of course, by Parliament) is here strongly endorsed, although Banks found the subject too hot to handle in the 1690s, when his *Innocent Usurper* was suppressed. With the passage of time, the Stuarts can now be regarded as priest-ridden pretenders. Mary Tudor, "a blinded Zealot," has been educated abroad by "proud, presuming Romish Priests."[64] But Rowe claims a historian's detachment in his preface. He agrees with the Whig poet Edmund Smith, who had also planned a tragedy on this story, that the "horrible Cruelties" for which Mary has been blamed were less her fault than "the charge of that Persecuting Spirit by which the Clergy were then animated," and cites Burnet's *History of the Reformation in England* for support (pp. 12–13). Rowe notes with some satisfaction that Smith did not, like Banks, hesitate to introduce Mary to the stage. Yet in his own play, Rowe follows Banks's lead, keeping Mary invisible in the background. Gardiner ("whose Head is grown thus Silver White / In Arts of Government and Turns of State" [IV.i, pp. 59–60]) stage-manages the condemnation of Jane and Guilford.

Despite Rowe's pose of objectivity, the play is sensationally didactic. The moral is pointed by the epilogue:

> If from these Scenes, to guard your Faith you learn,
> If for your Lawes to show a just concern,
> If you are taught to dread a Popish Reign,
> Our beauteous Patriot has not dy'd in vain.
>
> (p. 93)

A paragon of virtue, Jane only accepts the throne at the insistence of Parliament; her conscientiousness carries over into domestic affairs as well. Alfred Jackson, who finds this play "less true to history" than Banks's, points out the stress that Rowe lays upon the happy marriage of the protagonists. But Jackson finds her ostentatious goodness annoying: "the effect is weakened by the intrusiveness of her moral utterances."[65] Rowe's key images of marriage and violation figure importantly in the speech with which Suffolk persuades her to take the crown:

> Persecution,
> That Fiend of *Rome* and Hell, prepares her Tortures;
> See where she comes in *Mary's* Priestly train.

Still wo't thou doubt? 'till thou behold her stalk
Red with the blood of Martyrs, and wide-wasting
O'er *England's* Bosome? All the Mourning Year
Our Towns shall glow with unextinguish'd Fires;
Our Youths on Racks shall stretch their Crackling Bones;
Our Babes shall sprawl on Consecrated Spears;
Matrons and Husbands, with their New-born Infants,
Shall burn promiscuous; a continu'd Peal
Of Lamentation, Groans and Shrieks shall sound
Through all our Purple Ways.

(III.ii, p. 53)

The mixture of lurid propaganda with the insistence upon Jane's piety, wisdom, and forbearance is hard to swallow, but the message is clear. Gardiner's spot providentialism is exploded by Pembroke: "And canst thou tell? Who gave thee to explore / The secret Purposes of Heav'n, or taught thee / To set a bound to Mercy unconfin'd?" (v.ii, p. 91). The large religious questioning that colors the ending of *Jane Shore* finds its answer in Rowe's narrow Anglican perspective.

Another important feature of Rowe's historical drama is the playwright's insistence upon spectacle. We are asked to "view" Jane's "sad example"; the ending of *Lady Jane Grey* replaces Banks's grisly language with the block itself. As Gardiner urges Jane onwards, she angrily retorts:

Cease, thou Raven;
Nor violate with thy profaner Malice
My bleeding Guilford's Ghost—'tis gone, 'tis flown,
But lingers on the Wing and waits for me.
  (The Scene draws, and discovers a
  Scaffold hung with Black, Executioner,
  and Guards)
And see my Journey's End!

(v.ii, p. 89)

Like Banks, Rowe assaults his audience's sensibilities relentlessly; his greater insistence upon the machinery of spectacle points ahead, towards the ambitious pageantry of Victorian historical plays.

After the efforts of Banks and Rowe, historical drama ceased to be an anomaly on the English stage. These playwrights brought to an end a century of attempts to resolve the conflict between humanist history and providentialism and to find dramatic forms more congenial to a secularized age. Despite the persistence of providential language in Rowe's work, Banks and Rowe achieve their end by wholly embracing a Machiavellian view of history. The complete gulf between political activity and nature that their pastoral rhetoric insists upon denies, as Machiavelli and the humanist historians did, any ultimate significance to human activity in the political sphere. Thus, the poetic justice of the end of *Jane Shore* is accompanied by an equal and opposite political injustice. The villainous politicians in the plays of Banks and Rowe carry the responsibility for bringing the plays into line with recorded history; the audience's resentment of them is a resentment of known fact.

Canfield's notion that Rowe's plays explicitly engage the problem of despair in a Christian universe is highly suggestive. Rowe's audience is asked to reject the dramatized world of power politics in favor of an idealized, recoverable paradise. The weakness of this dramaturgy is apparent: the alternative to the political world cannot be dramatized. Unless we attribute to Rowe and subsequent eighteenth-century dramatists a very high degree of self-conscious irony, we must see the pastoral pieties of their plays as purely rhetorical. Thus, the action of the plays takes place in a ruthlessly Machiavellian world. The fatalism of the pathetic tragedians comes from their recognition that power, which they identify as evil, is also resistless. The audience's perception of the historical process as an inexorable brutalization of suffering lovers reflects a larger kind of despair that Rowe's plays, dramatically, cannot console.

In denying religious significance to political actions, and in effecting a complete divorce between the virtuous, passive, loving monarchs and their historical context, Banks and Rowe brought to an end the process of questioning begun by Shakespeare. In their plays, all activity has become meaningless, and all meaning resides outside the realm of human activity. The attractions of the old hierarchical systems are as apparent to them as to earlier generations, but they are now wholly nostalgic attractions. Power does not simply corrupt: those who exercise it are tyrants, rapists, machines incapable of love.

But as Rowe demonstrates, this contempt for the political world is not incompatible with the expression of partisan political views. Since Rowe sees politics as having no larger, otherworldly resonance, it is no surprise that the political lessons he wants to teach are wholly local ones. Dryden and Lee met the same difficulty in *The Duke of Guise,* where their political purpose is so clearly confined to immediate context that their ideal monarch becomes a Machiavellian tyrant. Rowe concentrates only on the tyrant's victims (avoiding this problem) but he is forced in consequence, as in *Lady Jane Grey* and *Tamerlane,* to express his political views in the language of sexual violation. Rowe's most public ideas can only be dramatized in private terms.

vi

In the generations to follow, we can see how firmly Rowe's techniques of dramatizing history took hold. William Havard's *King Charles the First: An Historical Tragedy,* published in 1737, is a good case in point. There is the requisite emphasis on pathetic spectacle: the published version of the play carries a frontispiece depicting the scene in which the king bids farewell to his children. Princess Elizabeth and James, duke of York (brought on stage, Havard confessed in his preface, "to heighten the Distress in the last Act"[66]), hold handkerchiefs to their faces as Charles, at peace with himself, bids his youngest son, Henry, farewell. Bishop Juxon looks on, sadly; through an arch at the rear of the stage, Round-heads with pikes and staffs march by. Their bristling presence suggests the enormity of the violation of domesticity that history, through its villainous agents, is about to perform. The engraving bears the caption: "At this sad SCENE who can from TEARS refrain?" Clumsy as he may be, Havard is clearly in Rowe's tradition.

In his preface, Havard confessed that the queen was "in France at the Time I have laid the Action of the Play, but it being a Story barren of female Characters, I was induc'd to make her appear" (sig. A3r). Similarly, the virtuous but helpless Fairfax, depicted here as Cromwell's dupe, functions to repair the defects of history: "I am not conscious of any other Liberties I have taken, except heightening the Characters of *Fairfax* and his Lady, which has added a warmth to the Piece, and in some measure supply'd the Want of real Matter to constitute Five Acts" (sig. A3v).

"Real Matter," in dramatic terms, is something recorded history lacks. Havard is uninterested in dramatizing the public record of Charles's trial and death: he devotes most of his attention to the vacillations of Fairfax, to the "pleasing Distress" of Charles's farewells to his queen and family, and to the gloating villainy of Cromwell. In staging the trial—the scene "draws and discovers the High-Court" spec-tacularly—Havard uses the record once. "May I not speak—? I may, Sir, after Sentence," cries the condemned king, "Your favour, Sir, I may, Sir, after Sentence" (IV.ii, p. 44). Where history records sufficient pa-thos, the dramatist will quote verbatim.

This nod in the direction of documentary authenticity suggests the kind of influence historical discipline exerted on this drama. An advertisement for the 1 March 1737 performance of the play promises that we shall see "The Characters Dress'd After the Manner of the Time."[67] Such claims became commonplace in the eighteenth century, as did the issuing of historical narratives to accompany plays. *Jane Shore* stimulated the publication of a *Life and Character of Jane Shore,* (1714) and of a *Life and Death of Jane Shore: . . . containing the whole account of her amorous intrigues with King Edward the IVth and the Lord Hastings: her penitence, punishment and poverty, to which are added, other amours of that King and his courtiers,"* and supporting material, *extracted from the Best Historians* (1714). Ambrose Philips's play, *Humphrey, Duke of Gloucester,* was printed in 1723 with historical background "proper to be bound up with it."[68]

But Philips's tragedy was meant to be inflammatory: pathos did not force politics utterly off the stage, and unflattering parallels to contemporary events continued to be drawn in historical plays. The denial of ultimate significance to the political realm led playwrights, not to ignore, but to heighten immediate applicability. Rowe's plays work in both directions; they are at once antihistorical and sharply partisan. *Humphrey, Duke of Gloucester* set off a paper war by virtue of its applicability to the trial of Francis Atterbury, bishop of Rochester, before the House of Lords. William Hatchett's adaptation of John Bancroft's *The Fall of Mortimer* (1731) offered in Mortimer a crude satire of Walpole. The play's prologue stresses its relevance:

> The *British* Constitution, so much priz'd
> You'll see, by *one bad Man* was almost sacrific'd.
> Grinding Oppression large Advances made,
> And foul Corruption was become a Trade.
> Our darling Liberty, our Rights, our Laws,
> Subverted to support the Minion's cause,
> Commerce abroad, Science at Home declin'd,
> And every honest, *English,* Heart repin'd.

The catchphrases of the opposition—"Corruption," "Trade," "Liberty"—make the playwright's bias clear. The favorite's fall is described in the same language: "The Laws revive—the Monster is cast down." Both dramatic formula and historical authority are invoked: "Our Faithful Annals thus Transmit to Fame / A Villain-Statesman, not the *King,* to blame."[69]

The serviceable politicians of Banks and Rowe became, in the age of Walpole, opposition representations of the great man himself. Henry Brooke's *Gustavus Vasa, or the Deliverer of his Country* (1739) was the first play to be suppressed under the new stage licensing act of 1737.[70] Brooke was one of the Patriot poets who gathered around Prince Frederick in the days when he set up an opposition court, and the play's first scene is set underground ("The Inside of the Copper-Mines in Dalecarlia" [p. 1]), where Gustavus, incognito, awaits his country's call. Liberty, of course, is his cause:

> O Liberty, Heav'n's choice Prerogative!
> True Bond of Law, thou social Soul of Property,
> Thou Breath of Reason, Life of Life itself!
> For thee the Valiant Bleed.
>
> (III.viii, p. 46)

Here the Whig view of an ancient constitution, grounded in liberty and property, finds explicit expression.

But the action of the play itself is amorous intrigue. Vasa's delivery of his country is also a renunciation of love, a mastery over his passions. "O I will," he announces at the end, "Of private Passions all my Soul divest, / And take my dearer Country to my Breast" (v.vii, p. 81). Trollio, the villain-statesman of the piece, understands how dangerous passion can be, and Cristiern, Denmark's ambitious king, praises his acumen:

> Your Observation's just, I see it, Trollio:
> Men are Machines, with all their boasted Freedom,
> Their Movements turn upon some fav'rite Passion;
> Let Art but find the latent Foible out,
> We touch the Spring, and wind them at our Pleasure.
>
> (IV.i, p. 50)

In its design, the play assents to this mechanistic view of human nature. Arvida is easily wrought up to treason by Trollio, who expertly plays upon his jealousy; from faithful friend, he becomes rival in love to Gustavus, ready through murder to supplant him in Christina's heart. "I know thy Error," says the forgiving Gustavus,

> but I know the Arts,
> The Frauds, the Wile that practis'd on thy Virtue;
> Firm how you stood, and tow'r'd above Mortality;
> 'Till in the fond unguarded Hour of Love,
> The wily undermining Trollio came,
> And won thee from thyself—
>
> (III.vi, p. 42)

Trollio is not only a politician but also something of a scientist: "I know thou hast a serpentizing Genius," says the tyrant, "Can'st wind the subtlest Mazes of the Soul / And trace her Wand'rings to the Source of Action" (II.vi, p. 22). The villain is the historian; the "Source of Action" is his province. While decrying the politician's wiliness, Brooke validates his psychology by permitting only the heroic Vasa to control his barely governable passions.

The thoroughgoing hostility to statecraft in this drama challenges the contemporary humanist idea of history as "the education of the statesman."[71] Instead, in its emphasis upon searching the mainsprings of human activity, history threatens, like the villains of the drama, to turn men into machines. The emphasis on love in the later historical drama can be seen at first view as a challenge mounted against history's public truths by the dramatist's private ones. Yet a typical complaint by the anonymous author of *Courtnay, Earl of Devonshire* (1705) suggests that the material of history is utterly unsuitable for dramatic treatment: "*But it is certainly agreed by all hands that it is one of the hardest things in the world to make an Historical Play regular or diverting.*" The obstacle to regularity and diversion is erected by the authorities, to whom the playwright finds himself deferring almost obsequiously in explaining the love interest in his play: "*the Transactions of the Dramma were all done in her Minority and during the beginning of Queen Mary's Reign, when she was a Princess and certainly young, nay, if we may believe some Authentick Historians of that time, very Amorous, too.*"[72] The authorities are enlisted to validate the playwright's concentration on love. This unhappy author (his play was rejected by the Drury Lane company) does not challenge history, as Ford did in *Perkin Warbeck*. If, for Sidney and Rymer, the poet enjoys a distant advantage over the historian preoccupied with foolish truths, these playwrights accept, however uneasily, the historian's predominance. In fact, their concentration on milking tears from pleasing distress reveals in action their villains' mechanistic psychology. Brooke accepts Trollio's mechanistic view of human nature even as he vehemently deplores it.

Richard Brinsley Sheridan's prologue to Richard Savage's *Sir Thomas Overbury* links this play to another important tradition in eighteenth-century drama. Sheridan deplores neoclassical tragedy's concentration on monarchs:

Too long the Muse—attach'd to regal show,
Denies the scene to tales of humbler woe;
Such as were wont—while yet they charm'd the ear,
To steal the plaudit of a silent tear,
When Otway gave domestic grief its part,
And Rowe's familiar sorrows touch'd the heart.[73]

Sir Thomas Overbury is a tale of private woe; the historical setting permits identification and pity. History is not only regularized but reduced to a universal domesticity:

> On kindred ground, our Bard his fabric built,
> And placed a mirrour there for private guilt;
> Where—fatal union!—will appear combin'd
> An Angel's form—and an abandon'd mind?
> Honour attempting Passion to reprove,
> And Friendship struggling with unhallow'd Love!

Sheridan's debunking of tragedy that features the "scepter'd traitor," the "bleeding hero," the "falling state" as "too great for pity" reflects a larger antiheroic and antimonarchical tendency that can also be seen in the history writers of the late eighteenth century. The Scottish historian William Robertson argued for a shift in focus:

> . . . it is a cruel mortification, searching for what is
> instructive in the history of past times, to find that the
> exploits of conquerors who have desolated the earth, and the
> freaks of tyrants who have rendered nations unhappy, are
> recorded with minute and disgusting accuracy, while the
> discovery of useful arts, and the progress of the most
> beneficial branches of commerce, are passed over in silence,
> and suffered to sink into oblivion.[74]

Tamburlaine and Macbeth and their ilk have dominated the stage and history long enough. Robertson's desire to celebrate the obscure, industrious, and hardworking is, like Sheridan's, a desire to localize and domesticate history. Robertson wishes to divorce history from the conventions of tragedy; Sheridan wishes to replace the pomp of tragedy with more deeply moving private pangs.

The tendency towards domesticity and pathos in historical drama, after beginning with Tate and Banks in the dark days of the Exclusion crisis, gained force and authority after the Revolution of 1688 and the Hanoverian Act of Settlement. Just as we can correlate the skepticism and uncertainty of early seventeenth-century historical drama to the political confusions of the years leading up to the civil war, we can draw some connections between the vision of history in eighteenth-century drama and the emerging Whig version of the events of the last century. All these plays share a vision of the world of politics as harshly antipathetic to and exploitative of human passion; the playwrights strongly identify the discipline of history with cold political analysis. The desires of characters in the plays to escape into insular domestic and pastoral retreats are wholly sympathetic to the playwrights but are inevitably frustrated by evil politicians and by the facts of the story. Whether monarchs or commoners, characters in these plays are represented as victims of inexorable process: even a hero like Gustavus Vasa does not choose to be his country's deliverer and must sacrifice his happiness. The salient features of a Whig view of history, on the other hand, are an optimism like Robertson's about "progress," and a view of English history as a struggle between the people's ancient rights—liberty and property—secured by law, and the royal prerogative. Early statements of this view abound in the Patriot poems of the late 1730s; it received explicit elaboration in Henry Hallam's *Constitutional History of England* (1827). The historians and the dramatists share a sense of the futility of human agency: the Crown's efforts to increase its power in the face of liberty's irresistible (if occasionally interrupted) growth cast the individual monarch in the role of tragic victim or dupe.

Hallam's attempt to arrive at a balanced assessment of Charles I reveals something like the pastoralism of pathetic tragedy:

> The station of kings is, in a moral sense, so un-
> favourable, that those who are least prone to servile
> admiration should be on their guard against the opposite
> error of an uncandid severity. There seems no fairer method
> of estimating the intrinsic worth of a sovereign, than to treat
> him as a subject, and to judge, so far as the history of his life
> enables us, what he would have been in that more private
> and happier condition, from which the chance of birth has
> excluded him.[75]

Treating royalty as a misfortune of birth, and suggesting that private life is "happier" than the life of public responsibility, is as far as Hallam can go towards indicating sympathy for Charles. But the grounds of his sympathy are the same as those in the drama: we pity monarchs and heroes because they are forced, all unwilling, out of their private retreats to suffer before us. This helps to explain the persistent imagery of violation in the plays of Rowe and his successors.

Leo Braudy has described a shift in attitude that distinguishes historians of the eighteenth century from humanist historians of the century before. Clarendon, he argues, "accepts without question the belief that the historian is appropriately a public man dealing with public materials"; "Hume, Fielding, and Gibbon" on the other hand, "are private men contemplating without much pleasure the public world." Like Hallam, Hume "asserts finally the greater moral and historical significance of the private man, who stands in detached contemplation of public life." When we add to Braudy's argument the primitivism that Peardon says colors Hume's "delight in being 'transported into the remotest ages of the world,'" we can see a dim reflection of the more vehement escapism of pathetic tragedy.[76] The more remote the history, the more complete the escape.

Historical drama's disengagement from public life became complete in this period. The suppressions of *Gustavus Vasa* and James Thomson's *Edward and Eleonora* in 1739 show some persistence of the humanist use of history to comment on public issues, but in both cases the comment is limited to partisan sloganeering and the main action of the play is amorous intrigue. More typically, audiences had come to expect pageantry and escapism from historical plays. A case in point is Shakespeare's *Henry VIII,* revived with great success in 1727. So great was the popularity of the coronation scene that audiences insisted on its addition "as a separate Entertainment, to any other Play the Town may be inclin'd to see."[77] This led to performances of *Wit Without Money, The Relapse,* and *The Albion Queens*—each with the coronation of Anne Boleyn as an afterpiece—in the month of December at Drury Lane. The rival theater at Lincoln's Inn Fields, of course, countered with a *Harlequin Anna Bullen.* In the nineteenth century, historical accuracy and authenticity reposed exclusively in the spectacle of the drama: actor-managers like Macready and Charles Kean costumed their actors with pedantic accuracy. James Robinson Planché described the effects of his antiquarian labors into assuring that Kemble's revival of *King John* in November 1823 at Covent Garden would be dressed in twelfth-century costumes. The actors grumbled:

> They had no faith in me, and sulkily assumed their new and
> strange habiliments, in the full belief that they should be
> roared at by the audience. They *were* roared at; but in a
> much more agreeable way than they had contemplated.
> When the curtain rose, and discovered King John dressed as
> his effigy appears in Worcester Cathedral, surrounded by his
> barons sheathed in mail, with cylindrical helmets and correct
> armorial shields, and his courtiers in the long tunics and
> mantles of the thirteenth century, there was a roar of
> approbation, accompanied by four distinct rounds of
> applause, so general and so hearty, that the actors were
> astonished; and I felt amply rewarded for all the trouble,

anxiety, and annoyance I had experienced during my labors.[78]

Charles Kean's aggressive didacticism in historical staging, like Planché's desire for correctness, is a reaction against the irrelevant splendors of the earlier stage. "Had I been guilty of ornamental introductions for the mere object of show and idle spectacle, I should assuredly have committed a grievous error," Kean announced in his farewell address (1859); "but, ladies and gentlemen, I may safely assert that in no single instance have I ever permitted historical truth to be sacrificed to theatrical effect."[79] But the effect of Kean's lavish decors was hardly to turn the stage into a "school"; and the applause that greeted Planché's costumes and decors is not the response usually sought by antiquarian research.

The didacticism of the eighteenth- and nineteenth-century historical drama, like their spectacle, differs only in degree. The domestic apothegms that color Rowe's plays give way to the patriotic self-improvement that Kean smugly invokes, but the emotional center of the drama remains the same. The spectators are not engaged in learning history's lessons, however meticulously authenticated the decor, because their attention focuses primarily on the amorous intrigue. Bulwer-Lytton, in the author's preface to *Richelieu* (1839), describes what attracted him to this period in French history: "Blent together, in startling contrast, we see the grandest achievements and the pettiest agents—the spy—the mistress—the capuchin—the destruction of feudalism—the humiliation of Austria—the dismemberment of Spain."[80] But the play addresses, not the latter issues, but their agents and does so through familiar structures. De Mauprat is manipulated into rebellion by Baradas, who plays artfully upon his jealousy; the confusions are only resolved with the delivery, at the last moment, of a packet of fateful letters. Despite Bulwer-Lytton's pose of historical detachment, he concentrates on De Mauprat's unhappy passion.

Bulwer-Lytton's interest in the petty agents of grand achievements, his willingness to judge Richelieu's schemes in terms of their happy ending, and the actor-manager's attention to detail, are all equally characteristic of the great historian of the period, Macaulay. Gossipy, circumstantial, vastly detailed, and broadly optimistic, Macaulay's *History of England* owed much of its popularity to its portrayal of English history as a romance of liberty. Like the historical novelists and dramatists, Macaulay enjoyed juxtaposing petty agents to grand achievements.[81]

The sense of the thoroughgoing pettiness of history's agents is clearly latent in the passivist historiography of Rowe, and when dramatists sought to bring history's actors to life, they did so without Macaulay's redeeming irony. Richelieu's Machiavellism and patriotism sit awkwardly with each other. The dramatists' lip service to historical detachment founders in pathos. Tennyson's son tells us of his father's attitude to Mary Tudor: "She had, my father thought, been harshly judged by the popular verdict of tradition, therefore he had a desire to let her be seen as he pictured her in his imagination. Hence he was attracted to the subject. He pitied the poor girl, who not only was cast down by her father from her high estate, but treated with shameless contumely by the familiar friends of her childhood."[82] *Queen Mary* was published in 1875, performed in 1876; Tom Taylor had anticipated the appeal of Mary five years earlier. In the preface to his historical drama, *Twixt Axe and Crown,* he admitted the same worthy goal: "In these days of historical rehabilitation there are few objects of popular execration on whose behalf a plea, 'in confession and avoidance,' may be more fairly urged, than on that of 'Bloody Mary.'" But like Tennyson's, Taylor's revisionism consists in the evocation of pathos: "In attempting to present a view of Mary's character making more demand on popular sympathy than has usually been ventured on in the case of this harshly-judged queen, I have but worked out the conclusion of Mr. Froude, who, decidedly Liberal and Protestant as are his sentiments, has been unable to resist the evidence that Mary was, in many respects, of a loving and womanly nature—warped by evil counsels, but struggling towards the light, as her weak vision apprehended it."[83] Both playwrights approach history ostensibly as historians—setting the record straight—but they soon show their true colors. Tennyson "pitied the poor girl"; Taylor discovered her "loving and womanly nature" in the "evidence" compiled by Froude. Their aesthetic remains affective and pathetic; their historiography remains passivist. The historical figure is dramatized as victim, of her evil counselors or of her unhappy childhood.

Instead of restoring Mary's reputation, these historical dramatists simply heightened her pathos. History's agents are its victims. This attitude persists in English historical drama. Robert Bolt's history plays are no less affective in design than those of a century before. The theme of *Vivat! Vivat, Regina!* (1971) is, Bolt declares in his introduction, "Power. . . . Above all the unnaturalness of Power, the impermissible sacrifice of self which Power demands, and gets, and squanders; to what purpose?" The victims here are Elizabeth and Mary Queen of Scots— the first, obsessed with statecraft and living to a horrible old age in a state of emotional starvation; the second, wildly impulsive, living out a short, passionate life in utter irresponsibility. The dichotomy is familiar. Like

Banks, Bolt is contemptuous of politics because of a distaste for a chaotic present:

> I would claim, like Shakespeare, to be concerned for my own times. But I am not sure that I relish them. 'Things fall apart; the centre cannot hold.' Indeed they do; I fear it can't. And I don't like it. And have a love of old things, old buildings, books, pictures, and music, which I suspect is reprehensible. Are they really, as they seem to me, more human than our new things, or older merely? There is no going back to them in any case. . . . I wish the present were more human, though, that people were not so distressed and things were made with more respect.[84]

Bolt's antitechnological wistfulness, like Banks's pastoralism or the Victorians' "historical rehabilitation," turns to the past as an image of stability outside of politics. By treating the past as "more human" than the present, Bolt completely renounces the humanist notions of the continuity of experience that led Jonson, Chapman, and Dryden to see historical drama as potentially useful. The tradition died hard, as we have seen in its persistence in the eighteenth-century drama. But the partisanship that caused the prohibition of *Gustavus Vasa* contributed also to the rise of the ideal of historical detachment from the squabbles of one's own time. Peter Whalley, in 1746, inveighed against partisan history writing in *An Essay on the Manner of Writing History:* "To be *exact, honest,* and *impartial* is what we have a Right to demand in an *Historian.*" But Whalley's impartiality quickly slides into sentimentalism: "An *Historian* should endeavour to give us the most engaging Views of Mankind, to set them in the most amiable Light; that his Readers may be induced, by a Spirit of Benevolence, to the Practice of the same virtues."[85] Although his language is unimpeachably postmodern, Bolt, too, looks at the past through rosy lenses.

Bolt's failure to find any contemporary resonance in his historical story beyond the pathos of power is defined by his claim to be, "like Shakespeare, concerned for my own times." This challenges the whole impetus of historical drama after the seventeenth century away from applicability and towards more coherent, consistent, accurate, and self-contained models of the past. But while Shakespeare evokes and confounds conjecture and speculation about the past, Bolt expresses and evokes regret. The past is irretrievable and different; like Kemble and Kean, Bolt stresses its differences in terms of "old things." Bolt identifies his "own times" with his own sense of loss. His echo of the humanist ideal is hollow.

The precedent of Shakespeare is as unhelpful to Bolt as to the whole series of English dramatists who approached English history after the turn of the seventeenth century. Those of his contemporaries, like Jonson and Chapman, who shared none of his mistrust of humanist history, failed in their efforts to generate a more modern, secular historical drama. Later dissatisfaction with the confinements of "civil history" led Ford to dramatize as wholly fictive the appeal of a charismatic notion of monarchy. But his dialectical confrontation lacks the balance of Shakespeare's simultaneous engagement of secular and religious attitudes towards the past. The balance shifted towards a nostalgic providentialism in *Henry VIII;* however un-Shakespearean his heroic form may be, Orrery rejects political history just as decisively. The desire of Restoration playwrights to stage activist historical parallels during the Exclusion crisis led them back to Shakespeare, but Dryden and Lee's ideas of tragic decorum subverted their historical intentions.

The decorums of history, too, altered the nature of historical drama. In the age of the Royal Society, Bacon's popularization of secularized history achieved full authority. History educated the statesman through the examination of power politics: cause and effect were to be studied scientifically, without moral judgment. The effect of the historian's new authority in the drama is immediately apparent in the figure of the villain-statesman, and in the dramatists' insistence, from the Restoration to the present, that passion is wholly antipathetic to power. The historian may help to paint the scene in Victorian historical drama; the dramatist, equally a specialist, develops ahistorical intrigues of love. Later developments in historiography have done little to change the English dramatist's abdication of the national past. From Banks to Bolt, the unifying element of English historical drama is the pathos of power.

II

REDEEMING TIME

DRAMA IN THE GREAT AGE
OF HISTORY

4

Progress and Providence

SCHILLER AND STRINDBERG

In the late eighteenth century, while English audiences continued to delight in *Jane Shore* (now presented with comic or spectacular afterpieces), "imitation of Shakespeare" had become in Germany and France a gauntlet to be hurled at the feet of the ossified classicism identified with Gottsched and Voltaire. "Shakespearo-Manie," as Grabbe called it, generated not only celebration of the English playwright's deviations from classical decorum and emulation of his "Gothic" excesses, but also "new life" for his English history plays.[1] Schiller, the Sturm-und-Drang playwrights, and critics like the Schlegel brothers identified Shakespeare's public-playhouse stagecraft with ideas of freedom that were charged with political as well as theatrical significance. A generation later, French Romantic dramatists locked swords with a far more imposing classical tradition in a struggle whose violence is still surprising. The strident tones of Stendhal's dialectic in *Racine et Shakespeare* (1823) and Victor Hugo's preface to *Cromwell* (1827) anticipate but hardly account for the riots that accompanied the first performance of *Hernani* (1830). Political as well as theatrical factors dictated Shakespeare's enlistment on the side of liberty. While the revolutions and counterrevolutions of seventeenth-century England effectively stifled the native tradition of historical drama, the French Revolution, especially as witnessed through German eyes, led to cult adulation of Shakespeare's history plays. Where no indigenous tradition of historical drama existed, Shakespeare was invoked to fill the gap. The adoption was only temporary for Friedrich and A. W. Schlegel who eagerly awaited the German dramatist who would present the German nation with a mirror of its past.[2] A leading candidate for the role of German Shakespeare was Schiller. While he soon lost his luster in the Schlegels' eyes, his *Wallenstein* trilogy forces an audience to experience with almost Shakespearean complexity the struggle of dramatizing the past.

The grandiose cycles of German history plays planned by authors like Ludwig Tieck foundered. In a far different context, the only European dramatist to undertake the ambitious scheme of dramatizing a whole nation's history was August Strindberg. Like the Romantics, Strindberg infused his history plays with a spirit of rebellion against both formal and historiographical decorums, as firmly entrenched in Scandinavia in the late nineteenth century as in France a century before.[3] Strindberg inconoclastically attacked the naive patriotism of the popular histories he used as his sources and planned instead a cycle of history plays that would reflect the working out in Swedish history of his own highly idiosyncratic ideas about divine providence.

The issue of providence, explicit in the plays of Strindberg and (as we have seen) of persistent, if vestigial, interest to English dramatists, lurks behind Schiller's preoccupation in *Wallenstein* with fate. Schiller's trilogy and Strindberg's history plays are linked by their extensive questioning of human agency: questioning that leads, in both cases, to rejection of the claims of historical discipline in favor of assessments of action that are ultimately religious in nature, tending towards mysticism. The tension between the truth of history and the truth of poetry is explicit throughout *Wallenstein,* enunciated in the prologue and dramatized in the wholly fictitious presences of Max and Thekla. Idealism and realism—to use Schiller's own highly charged terms—struggle for dominance right up to the end of the vast trilogy. Schiller achieves in *Wallenstein* a balance between modes of understanding the past that is reminiscent of Shakespeare, not on the explicit level of imitation, but on the level of a shared mistrust of both political and providential readings of history. But Schiller sustains this balance only in *Wallenstein*: in *Maria Stuart* his interest narrows to concentrate on the issue of the queen's private repentance and redemption. In *Die Jungfrau von Orleans* he flouts recorded history by giving his Saint Joan a glorious death on the battlefield. In his final years Schiller was attracted, like Massinger and Ford, to famous impostors: both the *Warbeck* and *Demetrius* fragments emphasize the private, ahistorical nobility of their protagonists.

Strindberg's history plays reflect the changing attitudes of a prolific, Protean career. From the cynical skepticism of *Mäster Olof* (subtitled in a revised manuscript version, "What is Truth?"), his first history play, through to the theatrical reflexivity of a late play like *Gustav III,* Strindberg continually demonstrated the inadequacy of secular, nationalistic history as a means for understanding human action. After the Inferno crisis, Strindberg's skepticism about history developed into a private, wholly providential rejection of political assessments of past actions, accompanied by a view of the Swedish monarchs as puppets manipulated—for their own souls' good—by transcendent "Powers." Scientific history, as practiced by Ranke, Mommsen, and others in the nineteenth century, had little attraction for Strindberg, scientist though he fancied himself to be. The clarity, particularity, and complexity of Continental history writing led Wagner to reiterate with increasing vehemence the notion that history itself was hostile to drama and fundamentally undramatic ("Oper und Drama," 1852). The tension between historical fact and dramatic form is explicit in Strindberg's history plays as it is in *Wallenstein*. Both Schiller's philosophical idealism and Strindberg's dogmatic providentialism embody attempts, on the dramatist's part, to lay exclusive claim to the higher truth.

i

As a professor of history at Jena from 1789 to 1791, Schiller was a practicing historian as well as a historical dramatist. The research he undertook for his most important and sustained piece of history writing, *The History of the Thirty Years' War* (1791–93), laid the groundwork for the *Wallenstein* trilogy, and he continued to consult the original source material available to him during the eight years he spent working on the three plays. As history, Schiller's *Thirty Years' War* has not been admired: Ranke ignored it in his *Geschichte Wallensteins* (1869); Golo Mann, a recent biographer of Wallenstein, characterizes Schiller dismissively as a German practitioner of Butterfield's "Whig interpretation of history."[4] For von Srbik and other historians who cherish Schiller, the *Wallenstein* trilogy, and not the narrative history, is his great historiographical achievement.[5] As historian, Schiller fits within the humanist tradition, practicing history as art, not science. His account of the death of Gustav Adolf moralizes it: "Aber durch welche Hand er auch mag gefallen seyn, so muss uns dieser ausserordentliche Schicksal als eine That der grossen Natur erscheinen. Die Geschichte, so oft nur auf das freudenlose Geschäft eingeschränkt, das einförmige Spiel der menschlichen Leidenschaft aus einander zu legen, sieht sich zuweilen durch Erscheinungen belohnt, die gleich einem kühnen Griff aus den Wolken in das berechnete Uhrwerk der menschlichen Unternehmungen fallen, und den nachdenkenden Geist auf eine höhere Ordnung der Dinge verweisen." ("By whatever hand he fell, his extraordinary destiny must appear a great interposition of Providence. History, too often confined to the ungrateful task of analyzing the uniform play of human passions, is occasionally rewarded by the appearance of events, which strike like a hand from heaven into the nicely adjusted machinery of human plans and carry the mind to a higher order of things.") The dismissal of history's "ungrateful task" in favor of a "higher order of things" looks back to the providentialism of Bossuet's universal history and ahead to *Wallenstein*. Schiller's desire is to see Gustav Adolf's death as resonantly tragic: his "protecting genius" ("schützender Genius") saved him from "the inevitable fate of man—that of forgetting moderation in the intoxication of success, and justice in the plenitude of power" ("dem unvermeidlichen Schicksal der Menschheit, auf der Höhe des Glücks die Beschiedenheit, in der Fülle der Macht die Gerechtigkeit zu verlernen").[6] The hand of providence points an ethical lesson.

Schiller was also immersed in more recent historians: Montesquieu, Hume, and Robertson provided him with the historical perspective of the Enlightenment—"Ironic," as Hayden White says, but nonetheless animated by an idea of progress.[7] The *History of the Thirty Years' War* culminates triumphantly in the signing of the Peace of Westphalia; when we take into account the influence of Kant upon Schiller, this event gains in significance. In his philosophical essays, Schiller espouses a dialectical view of history as the record of the struggle between nature and freedom, most explicitly in "Über das Erhabene": "Die Welt, als historischer Gegenstand, ist im Grunde nichts anders als der Konflikt der Naturkräfte unter einander selbst und mit der Freiheit des Menschen, und den Erfolg dieses Kampfes berichtet uns die Geschichte" ("The world, as a subject of history, is basically nothing more than the conflict of natural forces with each other and with the freedom of man, and history reports to us the result of this struggle").[8] So far, Schiller informs us, nature has enjoyed more success than "autonomous reason" ("selbständigen Vernunft"); the Peace of Westphalia, however, is an important step in the right direction. Intrusive ironic commentary like that of Gibbon does not figure in Schiller's narrative history: in *Wallenstein* irony is the central strategy in the play's encouragement of dialectical speculation. Wallenstein's unawareness of the evolutionary process of which he is part generates a whole dramatic structure that is, according to Alfons Glück, "inordinately complicated, full of hidden meanings, ironic hints, philosophical paradoxes."[9]

Schiller employs historical irony most ruthlessly in the final acts of *Wallensteins Tod;* the strategy owes something to his intensive study of Sophocles' *Oedipus* and Shakespeare's *Macbeth* at the time of composition. Wallenstein rejects Countess Terzky's premonitions of his death by offering a historical parallel:

> Es machte mir stets eigene Gedanken,
> Was man vom Tod des vierten Heinrichs liest.
> Der König fühlte das Gespenst des Messers
> Lang vorher in der Brust, eh sich der Mörder
> Ravaillac damit waffnete. Ihn floh
> Die Ruh, es jagt' ihn auf in seinem Louvre,
> Ins Freie trieb es ihn, wie Leichenfeier
> Klang ihm der Gattin Krönungsfest, er hörte
> Im ahnungsvollen Ohr der Füsse Tritt,
> Die durch die Gassen von Paris ihn suchten—
>
> (*WT,* v.iii.3490–99)

> It always used to make me wonder, what
> Is read about the death of that fourth Henry.
> The king had sensed the spectre of the dagger
> Long in his heart before the murderer
> Ravaillac armed himself with it. Repose
> Fled from him, he was haunted in his Louvre
> And driven to the open air; the bells
> At his wife's coronation tolled as for
> A funeral; his ear foreheard the footfalls
> That sought for him throughout the streets of Paris.[10]

"Does your inner voice say nothing?" asks the countess; "Nothing. Be at peace," says Wallenstein ("Sagt dir die innre Ahnungstimme nichts?" "Nichts. Sei ganz ruhig."—*WT,* v.iii.3500–3501). Wallenstein's obliviousness to his own danger is emphasized here by this instance of his historical blindness: the analogy he draws between Henry IV of France and himself is an utterly inappropriate one. While, in Schiller's view, the French king died a martyr to the cause of national unity and religious liberty in France, Wallenstein's vague political plans and indiscriminate religious toleration ("Missal or Bible! / I don't care" ["Messbuch oder Bibel! / Mir ists all eins"], he tells the Protestant burgomaster of Eger, *WT,* iv.iii.2598–99), are merely self-serving. Henry's prescience plays off against Wallenstein's willful ignorance; Henry's status as a naive genius in the essay "Über naive und sentimentalische Dichtung" points up Wallenstein's remoteness from reality.[11] Unlike Henry, Wallenstein hears the music of the victory celebration simply as festive sound. The irony here is blunt and straightforward, as is the sequence of omens—the broken chain, the menacing configuration of the stars—that Wallenstein perversely misinterprets. The forces of nature—Buttler's desire for revenge fits the category—close in, but Wallenstein deludes himself into the illusion of freedom. As with Chapman's Byron, the failure of Wallenstein's historical perception epitomizes his tragic blindness.

But the reference to Henry IV has a broader resonance: it serves to place Wallenstein historically as well as to designate his folly. The context evoked is that of the sixteenth- and seventeenth-century struggle for religious liberty. We are asked to compare the two heroes in terms of their contributions to the cause. Henry failed, assassinated by a fanatic; Wallenstein fails, paralyzed by his own indecisiveness. In his great soliloquy early in Act I of *Wallensteins Tod*, Wallenstein presents himself as struggling against the force of custom, "das ewig Gestrige," "eternal yesterday" (*WT*, I.iv.208), in men's hearts. From this perspective, Wallenstein is, like Henry, a step on the way to the new order of toleration symbolized for Schiller by the Peace of Westphalia—just as the prologue to the trilogy suggests that the Peace of Westphalia is representative of an old order now drawing to a close. Thus the ironies multiply: Wallenstein is unlike Henry in his blindness, but like him in his anticipation of a world order whose time has not yet come. The whole riddle of the play is latent in the crossed purposes of the parallel.

Because Schiller confines the action of his three plays to the last four days of Wallenstein's life, he uses allusive reference of this kind to remind his audience of the temporal and geographical sweep of the Thirty Years' War. The banquet scene (*DP*, IV.i–IV.vii) demonstrates this technique. When Isolani greets Max Piccolomini with wine, Terzky presents him with the all-important loyalty oath that the drunken generals will be tricked into signing later. Isolani's jokes revolve around the early days of the war: the party is as lavish as those at the "Heidelberger Castle" (IV.i.1916); the lands and "princely hats" (line 1918) of those who came to rule Bohemia after the battle of the White Mountain are "on the block for bids" (line 1920). We are forced to remember the origins of war at this moment of crisis: Frederick's decision to leave the splendors of Heidelberg and accept the crown of Bohemia provides the background for Isolani's jokes. What links the two situations is an image of vanity: Frederick's presumption led to his fall. More explicitly, Wallenstein can parallel Frederick in his ambition to win—if only for his daughter—the Bohemian crown. The names Isolani lists—Eggenberg, Slawata, Lichtenstein, and Sternberg—are those of imperial loyalists who rose through Frederick's fall; he proposes stripping them of the possessions they gained through Frederick's dispossession. The pattern of rise and fall, vanity and dispossession, that informs the structure of the whole play is here reinforced by historical allusion. The drunken banquet and the conspiracy of Illo, Terzky, and Isolani will be remembered by the audience at the end of *Wallensteins Tod:* "This generation / Cannot enjoy itself except at table," says Wallenstein of that final banquet ("Dies Geschlecht / Kann sich nicht anders freuen als bei Tisch," (*WT,* v.iv.3522–23).

More complex in its resonances is the moment in which the Cellarmaster and Neumann discuss Frederick's coronation chalice, demanded by the revelers in *Piccolomini* iv.5. Like Gordon in the last two acts of *Wallensteins Tod,* the Cellarmaster disapproves of excess: "They're aiming way too high" ("Sie wollen gar zu hoch hinaus"), he grumbles as a seventieth bottle of wine is ordered (*DP,* iv.v.2048). Reluctantly he rinses the splendid cup and explains its symbolism to Neumann: on it is represented Bohemia's electoral right and freedom of religion, guaranteed by Emperor Rudolph's charter. But now, he explains

> Doch seit der Grätzer über uns regiert,
> Hat das ein End, und nach der Prager Schlacht,
> Wo Pfalzgraf Friedrich Kron und Reich verloren,
> Ist unser Glaub um Kanzel und Altar,
> Und unsre Brüder sehen mit dem Rücken
> Die Heimat an, den Majestätsbrief aber
> Zerschnitt der Kaiser selbst mit seiner Schere.
>
> (*DP,* iv.v.2094–2100)

> Since this Grätzer is our ruler
> All that has ended now, and since the Battle
> Of Prague, where Frederick Palatine lost kingdom
> And crown, our church has lost its pulpit and
> Its altar, and our brothers with their backs
> Behold their homeland, while the Emperor clipped
> Himself the royal charter with his shears.

Neumann praises the Cellarmaster for his knowledge of the "annals of your country" ("Eures Landes Chronik," line 2102). As he hands the cup over to a servant, Neumann takes it and describes the second panel, which depicts the famous defenestration:

> Sieh doch, das ist, wie auf dem Prager Schloss
> Des Kaisers Räte Martinitz, Slawata
> Kopf unter sich herabgestürzet werden.
>
> (lines 2108–10)

> Just look, we have the Emperor's councillors,
> Martinitz and Slawata, at the Palace
> In Prague, heads down and falling from the window.

As the cup is borne into the banquet, the Cellarmaster's recollections enable us to take the long view:

> Schweigt mir von diesem Tag, es war drei
> Und zwanzigste des Mais, da man eintausand
> Sechshundert schrieb und achtzehn. Ist mirs doch,
> Als wär es heut, und mit dem Unglückstag
> Fings an, das grosse Herzeleid des Landes.
> Seit diesem Tag, es sind jetzt sechzehn Jahr,
> Ist nimmer Fried gewesen auf der Erden—
>
> (lines 2112–18)
>
> Do not recall that day. It was in May,
> The twenty-third, when we were writing sixteen-
> Hundred- and-eighteen. To me it seems
> Like yesterday. On that unhappy day
> It all began, the great heart's sorrow of
> My country. Sixteen years have passed since then
> With never any peace upon the earth—

To the Cellarmaster these events, so explicitly dated and located in the past, are as present as today (not, as Passage translates *heut,* "yesterday"). Just at the moment when Wallenstein's generals openly display their disloyalty to the emperor by toasting Bernard of Weimar, the Cellarmaster reminds us that we are only sixteen years deep into what will be a thirty years war. The pattern of betrayal represented by the cup is by no means complete.

By juxtaposing the Cellarmaster's painful recollections of past freedoms to the generals' drunken party, Schiller suggests a paradoxical tension between the Bohemians' legitimate desire for liberty and peace and Frederick's presumption. Such contradictions abound in the play: as Walter Hinderer has pointed out, Wallenstein's plan to use the army to force peace upon the emperor is itself self-contradictory.[12] The Bohemians' rebellion brought them only deeper enslavement; Frederick's ambition for a crown lost him not only Bohemia but Heidelberg as well. Schiller emphasizes these historical ironies at this point in the play in order to point out not only the futility of the scheme—the loyal generals are not deflected from their course by their signatures on the fraudulent document—but also the futility of all aspiration and ambition. The vision of the play is uncompromisingly bleak: Max's dreams of freedom and peace, like the Bohemians', are doomed; Wallenstein's ambitions for an earthly crown, like Frederick's, necessitate his fall. Only Octavio wins a crown at the end.

In this scene, Schiller evokes a rich historical context in such a way as to heighten the difficulty of understanding its complicated issues. By presenting the sources of the conflict in the form of paradoxes, paradoxes that for the most part share a tragic pattern of rise and fall, he indeed succeeds, as Herbert Lindenberger says, "in making the union of history and tragedy seem complete."[13] Like the Sphinx in *Oedipus,* history asks riddles whose solution engenders the ironies of tragedy. Wallenstein's delusion of his own greatness derives, like the whole Thirty Years' War, from a fall from a window.

Schiller forces us to make such connections from the very first. The prologue to the trilogy, despite its occasional nature, is not separable from the play itself.[14] Rather, the demands it makes upon an audience, shifting as it does from discussion of the physical structure of the Weimar theater (newly remodeled) to wide-ranging speculation on history and art, prepare us for the demands of the three plays to follow. The remodeling of the Weimar theater, which the prologue commemorates,[15] becomes in this context a paradoxical image of stasis and flux at once: rejuvenated ("er hat sich neu verjüngt," line 5), it remains old ("Und doch ist dies der alte Schauplatz noch," line 10). Schiller insists upon the continuity of tradition that rebuilding represents; but the theater's stability as a temple of art and cradle of genius is threatened by the evanescence of mimetic art itself. Sculptors and poets leave monuments behind that can endure thousands of years ("nach Jahrtausenden noch leben," line 35), but the actors' art is a struggle against the passage of time itself ("Drum muss er geizen mit der Gegenwart, / Den Augenblick, der sein ist, ganz erfüllen," lines 42–43).

Cast as praise of the worthy, selected audience, these remarks lead the poet on to wider speculation about time. The rebuilding of the theater begins a new era in theatrical fashion: but at the same time the poet's decision to forsake the narrow drama of middle-class life ("des Bürgerlebens engen Kreis," line 53) is a rejuvenation of tradition, not a complete break with the past. Noble subjects, however, are appropriate to a lofty scene; and Schiller goes further by explicitly identifying the audience's own historical circumstances as a context that demands high art ("Nicht unwert des erhabenen Moments / Der Zeit, in dem wir strebend uns bewegen," lines 55–56). Thus, like the theater, we too stand on the threshold of a new era: we too, like the actors, must strive to be completely worthy of the moment that is ours.

This shift of emphasis, from theater out to audience and then out into the audience's world, rounds back on itself: as the century comes to its end, reality itself becomes art ("Wo selbst die Wirklichkeit zur Dichtung wird," line 62). The struggle for liberty that the French Revolution represents to Schiller demands nobility of spirit in both realms. The issues of tradition and renewal, implicit in the image of the rebuilt theater, are explicitly raised again in the collapse of the old order ("Die alte feste Form," line 71) embodied over the last 150 years by the Peace of Westphalia. Yet here another surprising shift of emphasis takes place: the audience, gathered to celebrate the theater's victory over time and challenged to meet the lofty demands of its own time, is also asked to make an historical analogy between its times and those of the Thirty Years' War. By allowing our imaginations to play upon the problems of the past, we can face the future with confidence: as we view the dismal circumstances of war that led to the dear fruit ("teure Frucht," line 73) of peace in the past, we can become fit for the like achievement. In Schiller's defense of the high purpose and relevance of his play, echoes of humanist ideas about the value of history resound: the past can teach the aristocratic audience to bring stability out of the chaos of the present, as the framers of the Peace of Westphalia did and as the theater does through the actors' heroic endeavor.

Thus the play is not mere historical analogy; rather, in suggesting a parallel between past and present, Schiller also takes pains to stress differences. If our age resembles the past, it, like the rebuilt theater, has profited from it as well. Schiller's highly particular description of the devastation of war that we must imagine (lines 79–90) emphasizes the difference; but as past and present merge in theatrical tradition, so too do they blur in historical thought. Against this dark background ("finstern Zeitgrund," line 91) Schiller introduces, not by name, the figure of Wallenstein in a series of conventional, tragic epithets:

> —den Schöpfer kühner Heere,
> Des Lagers Abgott und der Länder Geissel,
> Die Stütze und den Schrecken seines Kaisers,
> Des Glückes abenteuerlichen Sohn,
> Der, von der Zeiten Gunst emporgetragen,
> Der Ehre höchste Staffeln rasch erstieg,
> Und, ungesättigt immer weiter strebend,
> Der unbezähmten Ehrsucht Opfer fiel.

(lines 94–101)

—the creator of bold armies,
The idol of the camp and scourge of countries,
The prop and yet the terror of his emperor,
Dame Fortune's fabulous adopted son,
Who, lifted by the favor of the times,
Climbed rapidly the highest rungs of honor
And, never stated, striving ever further,
Fell victim to intemperate ambition.

The clarity of this pattern gives it a timeless dimension: it applies as well to any number of tragic heroes as to Napoleon or Wallenstein.[16] Even as Schiller imposes on history the pattern derived from art, he suggests the difficulty of purely historical understanding of the past. His sources—as he discovered when writing the history of the war—are biased: Wallenstein is hard to understand because partisan purposes distorted contemporary accounts ("Von der Parteien Gunst und Hass verwirrt / Schwankt sein Charakterbild in der Geschichte," lines 102–3). Wallenstein is best understood as a conventional tragic figure—in whose fate the stars have a considerable share ("unglückseligen Gestirnen," line 110).

The shifts of focus and emphasis in the prologue show Schiller to be suggesting a complementary, reciprocal relationship between the discipline of history and the art of the theater. Wallenstein's image wavers in history, and the prologue promises us, for tonight anyway, only his shadow ("Schattenbild," line 114). The tragic pattern has been firmly placed in our minds, but we are now asked to do some research: by understanding his army, we can come to understand his crime ("Denn seine Macht ists, die sein Herz verführt, / Sein Lager nur erkläret sein Verbrechen," lines 116–17). Before the poet will plunge us into the tragedy proper, we must first immerse ourself in the theater of the past ("Auf jene fremde kriegerische Bühne," line 127). Nor is this the last surprise of the prologue: solemn and ennobling as are the occasion of the play, its subject, our duty as a worthy audience and as citizens of a world on the threshold of great change, what we will see is a comedy in bumptious rhyme. All gloom will be subsumed in the cheerful world of art ("das heitre Reich der Kunst," line 134): Life may be serious, but art is joyous ("Ernst ist das Leben, heiter ist die Kunst," line 137).

By forcing us to ponder the relative "seriousness" of life and art, by arousing and frustrating tragic expectations, by supplanting our desire for an uplifting heroic experience with a comedy in four-stress, rhyming *knittelvers*, Schiller increases the tensions between tradition and change that animate the whole prologue. And these tensions animate all three plays that are to follow, not simply the comedy that the prologue explicitly introduces. The forces of revolution and reaction are in conflict in the play, in Wallenstein's own era in history, in the late eighteenth century, and in the Weimar theater itself.[17] Thus introduced, *Wallenstein* becomes a major discussion of historical understanding and, more specifically, of the ways in which we find comprehensible patterns in the flux and chaos of life.

Thus Schiller—like Shakespeare and unlike the English dramatists who followed him—provides his audience with a highly complicated theatrical experience. The issues he raises are of both immediate contemporary interest and eternal artistic interest. When we are asked to speculate on the reasons for Wallenstein's behavior and to apportion in the process responsibility upon himself and upon his stars, we must find ourselves necessarily asking not only historical but also religious questions. But Schiller, unlike Shakespeare, does not have an immense structure of belief to which he can refer: hence the notoriously "philosophical" aspect of his vision. The world beyond is defined in aesthetic terms only, and achieved by Max and Thekla offstage: onstage we are presented with a world that works according to the grim principles of power politics.

The first scene of the first play, *Wallensteins Lager,* makes this context immediately clear. The peasant and his son enter; the boy's first line—"Father, I tell you it just won't do" ("Vater, es wird nicht gut ablaufen")—informs us right away of the dynamic of frustration that animates the whole trilogy.[18] The peasant's own response introduces into the trilogy the key motif of betrayer-betrayed: his desire to trick the soldiers with their own loaded dice backfires. As befits comedy, the peasant escapes with his skin; Wallenstein, playing the same kind of double game, is not so lucky.

The opening moments of *Wallensteins Lager* make it clear enough that what we are dealing with here is not a sociological presentation of the different types of soldiers in Wallenstein's army. The army may be the seat of Wallenstein's power, but it helps us to understand his crime because the soldiers all suffer the same kind of ignorance, about the same issues, as their great general. The peasant bemoans their destruction of peacetime ways, but the soldiers extol the freedom of their life. In the seventh scene, the recruit sings of riding "free as a bird" ("Frei wie der Fink," *WL,* vii.393) as the Civilian enumerates his relationships and responsibilities: he is of good family, in line to inherit businesses and property, engaged. But the sergeant argues that he can become a "new man" ("einen neuen Menschen," line 416) and offers as an auspicious example of rising through the ranks by desert that of Buttler. The irony here is transparent, and the First Jäger follows this story up with the story of Wallenstein's poodle, which Ilse Graham sees as paradigmatic of Wallenstein's confusion of freedom with "total indeterminacy."[19] The soldiers here mistake their rootlessness for freedom. Their utter rejection of normal—civilian—standards of behavior resounds in the final song:

> Wohl auf, Kamaraden, aufs Pferd, aufs Pferd!
> Ins Feld, in die Freiheit gezogen!
> Im Felde, da ist der Mann noch was wert,
> Da wird das Herz noch gewogen.
> Da tritt kein anderer für ihn ein,
> Auf sich selber steht er da ganz allein.
>
> (*WL*, xi.1052–57)

> Then up with you, comrades, to horse, to horse,
>   To battle, to freedom riding.
> Out there a man's worth is still in force
>   And friendship still abiding.
> None other out there can take his place,
> He must stand for himself alone in space.

The poodle story shows this freedom to be illusory: Wallenstein stays out of prison by sending the dog into the ambush before him. The soldiers' freedom is undercut by their status as troops who must follow orders; the problem in the camp, as their many disputes suggest, is precisely whose orders to follow. The heroic, glorious, free, footloose life they celebrate is based upon a net of conflicting and contradictory loyalties.

If the army is presented as an amoral and destructive force, disguising its rapacity in the rhetoric of liberty and fame, the generals who command it show a similar lack of principle. Machiavellian intrigue provides the action of *Die Piccolomini:* the web of plot and counterplot forces the split between father and son that ends the play.[20] Octavio's loyalty to the emperor—which should be a virtue—leads him to betray Wallenstein, whose trust in him is foolishly absolute. Max, his loyalty to Wallenstein confronted with evidence of Wallenstein's treason, refuses to believe it ("Es kann nicht sein! kann *nicht* sein! *kann* nicht sein!" *DP*, v.i.2430) and turns his disillusioned anger against his father: "Du wärst / So falsch gewesen? Das sieht meinem Vater / Nicht gleich!" (lines 2438–40). Plot and counterplot founder in paradox.

"Trust no one here but me," Thekla says to Max when they are left alone ("Trau niemand hier als mir," *DP*, iii.v.1685). Schiller created this fictional pair of lovers to offer an alternative to the sordid intrigues of the court. Max's description of his trip with Thekla rebuts the vision of the soldier's life offered in *Wallensteins Lager:*

> Denn dieses Lagers lärmendes Gewühl,
> Der Pferde Wiehern, der Trompete Schmettern,
> Des Dienstes immer gleichgestellte Uhr,
> Die Waffenübung, das Kommandowort—
> Dem gibt es nights, dem lechzenden.
> Die Seele fehlt dem nichtigen Geschäft—
> Es gibt ein andres Glück und andre Freuden.
>
> (*DP,* 1.iv.526–32)

> The thronging hurly-burly of this camp,
> The neighing horses and the trumpets' clangor,
> The clocks monotonously set for service,
> The weapons drills, the shouting of commands,—
> The parched heart profits nothing from all these,
> This wretched business has no soul.—But there
> Are other joys and other happiness.

Max's glimpse of civilian life as humanity—"Menschlichkeit" (*DP,* 1.iv.535)—moves the imperial envoy, Questenberg; but Questenberg sees his vision as impossible: "Oh why must it be of a far, far time / You speak, not of today, not of tomorrow" ("O! dass Sie von so ferner, ferner Zeit, / Und nicht von morgen, nicht von heute sprechen!" lines 559–60). Octavio correctly interprets the unexpected violence of Max's response: his son has fallen in love with Wallenstein's daughter ("A curse upon this journey!"; "Fluch über diese Reise!"—*DP,* 1.v.589). Max makes it utterly clear in his outburst that love and politics cannot mix: "For as I love the Good, I hate you" ("Wie ich das Gute liebe, hass ich euch"—*DP,* 1.iv.577) he snaps at Questenberg. The opposition we have noticed in the English plays between love and power persists in Schiller.[21]

But unlike the English playwrights, Schiller is aware of the philosophical dimensions of this opposition. Max and Thekla are developed, not as a pathetic love interest to arouse our passions, but as an antihistorical alternative to the play's historical world. The idyllic world of love and peace that they inhabit in their scenes together serves as a counter to the real world whose pressures force them apart. Max's death in a foolhardy charge against the main strength of the Swedish army is an indictment of his father's world—a world in which loyalties come into conflict with each other, in which right and wrong blur. Max cannot juggle conflicting demands: instead he rushes off to that death under his horse's hooves that Wallenstein dreamed of for himself. That Schiller reminds us of the dream that cemented Wallenstein's absolute trust in Octavio in his account of Max's end is not coincidental: what links the two episodes is the impossibility of fixed trust, single-minded loyalty.

Schiller enlists our sympathy for Max's ethical clarity and Wallenstein's foolish trust, just as he stretches his lyric gifts to the utmost as he sends Thekla off on her pilgrimage to Max's grave. These images of transcendence challenge a merely political understanding of the action of the play. The history of the period offers a record of intrigue and duplicity: in dramatizing it, Schiller also dramatizes an attractive alternative that is abstract, philosophical, and wholly fictitious. Max and Thekla exist in the play—as Falstaff does in the *Henry IV* plays—as rebuttals of purely historical understanding.[22] The discipline of history may deny ultimate significance to human actions; the playwright offers another perspective.

In the consistency of their idealism and the purity of their love, Max and Thekla may seem the ciphers some critics deride them for being. But they reach out not only to philosophical realms but also to the play's cosmic background. The stars are a central image in the play's engagement of the issue of freedom and necessity. It is Max who sees to the bottom of Wallenstein's superstition and explains it:

> O! nimmer will ich seinen Glauben schelten
> An der Gestirne, und der Geister Macht.
> Nich bloss der *Stolz* des Menschen füllt den Raum
> Mit Geistern, mit geheimnisvollen Kräften,
> Auch für ein liebend Herz ist die gemeine
> Natur zu eng.
>
> (*DP,* III.iv.1619–24)

> O! I will never criticize his trust
> In stars and in the power of the spirits.
> It is not merely *pride* of man that fills
> Up space with spirits and mysterious forces,
> But likewise for a loving heart the common
> Nature is too narrow.

Thekla eagerly assents to his notion of astrology as an expression of cosmic harmony:

> Wenn *das* die Sternenkunst ist, will ich froh
> Zu diesem heitern Glauben mich bekennen.
> Es ist ein holder, freundlicher Gedanke,

Dass über uns, in unermessnen Höhn,
Der Liebe Kranz aus funkelnden Gestirnen,
Da wir erst wurden, schon geflochten ward.

(*DP,* III.iv.1644–49)

If that is what the star lore is, I'll gladly
Become converted to that cheerful faith.
It is a lovely thought and comforting
That over us, at heights immeasurable
The wreath of love already had been woven
Of glittering stars before we ever were.

This vision of "cheerful faith" (*heiter* describes both belief here and art in the last line of the prologue) sets up a standard by which we are asked to judge Wallenstein's own astrological conduct.

Discussion of Wallenstein's superstition tends to revolve around the exchange of letters with Goethe in which Schiller allowed his friend to persuade him into a more sympathetic attitude towards this kind of faith.[23] In their understanding of astrology as indicative of a basic harmony between the soul and the universe, Max and Thekla reflect Schiller's new approach. Thus, despite the astrologer Seni's comic appearance (we see him in *Piccolomini,* act II, dressed "in black, somewhat fantastically, like an Italian doctor"—"wie ein italienischer Doktor schwarz und etwas phantastisch gekleidet," II.i.SD), the basic tenets of his art are not completely undercut. Rather, we find ourselves again confronting a paradox: Seni, at the end of *Wallensteins Tod,* reads the signs correctly, but his master misinterprets them. "False friends" ("falschen Freunden") threaten disaster (*WT,* V.v.3610); the stars do not lie.

Wallenstein, however, does: he persistently forces interpretations from the configurations of the stars that are self-serving and arbitrary. In this way, Schiller manages to suggest that there is a tragic tension between his hero and a cosmic order that he fails to understand. By linking understanding of the stars on the highest level with the philosophical idealism of Max and Thekla, Schiller equates Wallenstein's misinterpretations with tragic error. Furthermore, he grounds Wallenstein's error in psychological causes. Wallenstein's notion of himself as someone special, exalted, chosen by fate, derives from his boyhood experience of falling from a window and surviving. The duchess dates his dabbling in black arts from the occasion of another fall:

Doch seit dem Unglückstag zu Regenspurg,
Der ihn von seiner Höh herunter stürzte,

Ist ein unsteter, ungesellger Geist
Argwöhnisch, finster, über ihn gekommen.
Ihn floh die Ruhe, und dem alten Glück,
Der eignen Kraft nicht fröhlich mehr vertrauend
Wandt er sein Herz den dunkeln Künsten zu,
Die keinen, der sie pflegte, noch beglückt.

(*WT,* III.iii.1402–9)

But since that day of woe at Regensburg
That sent him plunging downward from the heights,
A restive, uncompanionable spirit,
Suspicious and morose, has come upon him.
Tranquility deserted him, and, trusting
No more his former fortune or his strength,
He turned his heart to those dark skills which never
Blessed any man who cultivated them.

Wallenstein's study of the stars reveals at bottom a lack of faith; he has been shattered by his original betrayal by the emperor.[24] Unlike Max and Thekla, Wallenstein is out of touch with cosmic rhythms: his belief in Octavio, his blatantly propagandistic reading of the omen of the three moons in *WT,* IV.iii.2611–18, his refusal to be bothered by the portents that announce his death all point out the hollowness of his astrological professions.[25]

Schiller uses the stars, then, not only to evoke the atmosphere of oracular foreboding necessary to tragedy, but also to suggest behind Wallenstein's evasions and misreadings the existence of a higher order of which he is only dimly aware. His inchoate plans for peace suggest a similar groping towards a poorly apprehended Utopian vision.[26] If the two Piccolominis represent opposite poles—Octavio the political man, doing his duty as he sees it; Max the ethical man, destroyed by conflicting imperatives—Wallenstein vacillates between them. His shattered idealism conceals itself behind serviceable superstition; his distaste for intrigue leads to conduct of unmitigated deviousness.

The whole network of paradoxes in the three plays stretches out from a center at Wallenstein himself. To the historian's considerable problem in assessing the actions of Wallenstein, Schiller adds the difficulty of seeing Wallenstein's elusiveness as paradigmatic. For Wallenstein comes at the end of the play to embody human action itself: the dismay with which he views the transformation of possibility into actuality during his soliloquy in the first act of *Wallensteins Tod* is universal, not specific. The "dread of vital process" (Ilse Graham's words) that pervades *Wallenstein* is rather a dread of both historical and dramatic structuring and containing of life.[27] Wallenstein wishes to preserve intact the innumerable possibilities of action that he can imagine: to act at all is to eliminate the freedom to explore other possibilities. Speculation delights him: but in both history and drama we know men by their actions. Action proceeds from choice, and Wallenstein would prefer not to choose at all:

> Beim grossen Gott des Himmels! Es war nicht
> Mein Ernst, beschlossne Sache war es nie.
> In dem Gedanken bloss gefiel ich mir;
> Die Freiheit reizte mich und das Vermögen.
> War's unrecht, an dem Gaukelbilde mich
> Der königliche Hoffnung zu ergötzen?
> Blieb in der Brust mir nicht der Wille frei,
> Und sah ich nicht den guten Weg zur Seite,
> Der mir die Rückkehr offen stets bewahrte?
> Wohin denn seh ich plötzlich mich geführt?
> Bahnlos liegts hinter mir, und eine Mauer
> Aus meinen eignen Werken baut sich auf,
> Die mir die Umkehr türmend hemmt!
>
> (*WT*, I.iv.146–58)

> By Heaven's mighty God! I never meant it
> In earnest, never fixed it as decided.
> I did no more than to enjoy the thought;
> The freedom and the capability
> Engrossed my fancy. Was it wrong to take
> Delight in visions of the royal hope?
> Was not my will still free within my bosom,
> Did I not still behold the good path at
> The side that kept return still open to me?
> Where do I see myself led suddenly?
> Pathless the space behind me, and a wall
> Of my own building towers up ahead
> To block reversal of my course!

Wallenstein's dilemma is extreme: action negates freedom, because he conceives freedom as the entertainment of possibility. Such speculation begets paralysis.[28]

Thus Wallenstein's searching of the skies for confirmation of his special status, verification of his plans, takes on some attributes of compulsion. When he learns of Octavio's betrayal, he refuses to blame his art or himself for being tricked:

Die Sterne lügen nicht, *das* aber ist
Geschehen wider Sternenlauf und Schicksal.
Die Kunst ist redlich, doch dies falsche Herz
Bringt Lug und Trug in den wahrhaftgen Himmel.

(WT, III.ix.1668–71)

The stars do not deceive, but this has happened
Against the courses of the stars and Fate.
The art is true, but that false heart has brought
Lies and deceit into the very skies.

The system is so rigid as to be inapplicable to life. Wallenstein's reading of the stars as fate differs significantly from Max and Thekla's vision of the heavens as emblematic of harmony. But neither Wallenstein's sense of his own great destiny nor Max's rebellion against the limitations of military discipline and political life leads anywhere.

Beyond their deaths—linked by Wallenstein's prophetic dream— what Max and Wallenstein have in common is their craving for freedom, however differently it finds expression. Unlike the other characters— Buttler, Gordon, and especially Octavio—they both see that the current chaos of war and intrigue can give way to a vision of peace and freedom. John Neubauer sees their quest as historical: "Among the characters of the play, only Wallenstein and Max seek an order that would give to the fragmented world of the Thirty Years War an encompassing meaning." But they are doomed by their historical context: the world is not ready for peace.[29]

If Max and Wallenstein differ from their compatriots by attempting to live as though life had some higher significance, their failure provokes serious questions about the significance of history and of tragedy. The struggle depicted in *Wallenstein* between individual aspirations towards complete freedom and a context of historical and cosmic necessity con- tinues, as the prologue reminds us, in the minds of the audience. Thus the triumph of reaction at the end of the play is not horrifying or inap- propriate to tragedy—as Goethe and Hegel thought—but instead a challenge thrown to the first audience, and every audience since.[30] For the failures of aspiration in this play are presented as *past* failures. Max and Wallenstein are limited psychologically as well as historically: we do not share Max's extreme youth or Wallenstein's crippling self-doubt. The prologue forbids us to see the brutal irony of the play's ending as final, although Schiller alters history—Octavio's promotion actually came five years after Wallenstein's death, and recognized other services to the empire—to make the irony as brutal as possible. Max's charge retards the advance of the Swedish column, making the murder of Wallenstein superfluous; the honors Octavio wins are similarly empty, for Max's death ends the newly ennobled house of Piccolomini. In this atmosphere of utter futility we are asked to identify Octavio with Pontius Pilate ("Your hand remains entirely clean," snarls Buttler as Octavio piously rejects responsibility, "You have made use of mine"—"Eure Hand ist rein, Ihr habt / Die meinige dazu gebraucht"—*WT*, v.xi.3785–86), but it is only from the perspective of the Weimar audience, a century and a half later, that we can see the deaths he causes as sacrifices. Eventually the war did end, and the audience can look back over the era of peace and stability ushered in by the treaty of Westphalia.

The resolution of *Wallenstein* is thus outside the play: the vision of peace and order that Wallenstein and Max attempt to formulate imbues the prologue in the vision of the renovated theater. But in Schiller's own time as in Wallenstein's time, the audience must make a choice between progress and reaction.[31] By suggesting that noble action was impossible or doomed in the past, Schiller does not mean to suggest that it will be impossible in the future.

Thus the obtrusive theater history of the prologue is important to understanding the end of the trilogy. Schiller's dialectical manipulations of freedom and necessity, art and nature, are left to the audience to resolve, as Hinderer suggests when he describes the play as a *Lehrstück*.[32] As we reexperience the confusions of Wallenstein—even to the extent of being deceived by him ourselves—and the aspirations of Max and Thekla, we are immediately engaged in the activity of evaluating human conduct in the past. And, in light of the prologue, we are asked to learn from this activity how to apply historical perspective to our own situation in the present: the analogy to the French Revolution permits later analogies as well.[33]

The clarity with which Schiller forces his audience to speculate on the past, the richness and intricacy of dramatic structure, the philosophical ambition of *Wallenstein*, command admiration. But the thrust toward a religious, otherworldly rejection of history that is here confined to the love intrigue of Max and Thekla comes to dominate Schiller's later history plays. Clearly disillusionment at the failure of the French Revolution to meet the challenge that Schiller, when writing *Wallenstein*, thought it could is an important factor in this retreat. In a famous poem on the turn of the century—"Der Antritt des neuen Jahrhunderts"— Schiller explicitly counsels escape:

In des Herzens heilig stille Räume
Muss du fliehen aus des Lebens Drang;
Freiheit ist nur in dem Reich der Träume,
Und das Schöne blüht nur im Gesang.[34]

Into the heart's blessed quiet places
You must flee the stress of life;
Freedom is only in the realm of dreams,
And beauty blooms only in song.

By relocating freedom exclusively in the realm of dreams, Schiller gives himself up wholly to the perspective of his lovers—as he quite literally does in the short poem "Thekla," which explains, outside of the context of the play, Thekla's victory over death. The alterations to history in *Wallenstein* work to increase tension between the world of politics and its ideal alternatives: in *Maria Stuart* and *Die Jungfrau von Orleans,* alterations stress the heroine's transcendent triumphs.

In Schiller's case as in Shakespeare's, then, the mistrust of historical discipline that enriches mature historical drama eventually prevails. The idealism of Schiller's later plays, like the benign providentialism of Shakespeare's *Henry VIII,* amends history's flaws, clarifies ambiguities, illuminates continuities. But this process entails a belittlement of any claim to truth that history itself might make. By arranging a confrontation between Elizabeth and Mary, by giving Johanna a better, more satisfying, death than history records, Schiller makes explicit his idealistic distaste for the chaos and ugliness of the past. In contrast, the ending of *Wallenstein* forces the audience to experience this distaste: if there is any consolation or validity to be found in the deaths of Max, Thekla, and Wallenstein, we must find it ourselves.[35] The letters and essays in which Schiller explained his attitudes towards *Wallenstein* are not part of that experience. The letters record Schiller's personal dislike of Wallenstein and his dismay at the inchoate abundance of the *Stoff* of history: that he managed once to transform this frustration into drama is his triumph.

ii

"We have plenty of books about 'God in nature,'" August Strindberg complained in his second *Blue Book* (1908), "but about God in history we have few. Herder and Johannes von Müller are perhaps the only. Otherwise, all history is godless and therefore worthless" ("'Gud i naturen' har man månge böcker om, men Gud i historien har man få. Herder och

Johannes von Müller äro kanske de ende. Eljes är all historia gudlös och därför värdelös"). In the same essay, "The Impossibility of Writing History" ("Historieskrifningens omöjlighet"), Strindberg decried the biases of "pragmatic history" and the unreliability of source material, ending with praise of Caliph Omar, who had destroyed the library at Alexandria "because it was superfluous now that men had the Koran" ("det var öfverflödigt när man ägde Koran").[36] Strindberg's acute interest in the relationship between recorded history and revealed truth led him in the years immediately following his Inferno crisis in Paris (1894–96) to plan a cycle of Swedish history plays stretching from Saint Erik to Gustav IV Adolf. The whole cycle was never finished; when Strindberg stopped writing historical dramas in 1908, he had left behind twelve plays devoted to Swedish history and four plays he dubbed "world historical plays," part of another uncompleted scheme.[37] In both the Swedish and the world historical sequences, Strindberg intended to show the working out in history of the divine will. He described the process in a series of essays that appeared in *Svenska Dagbladet* (20 February–30 May 1903) as notes towards a book that would be entitled "The Mysticism of World History"("Världshistoriens Mystik"). In the essays, Strindberg outlined his theory of history as a "colossal game of chess with a solitary player moving both white and black" ("ett kolossalt schackparti av en ensam spelare som leder både witt och svart"),[38] a theory that clearly reflects his own highly personal experience of providence in Paris. The theological emphasis of Strindberg's post-Inferno history plays offers a simple answer to the question that reverberates through his first great play, the prose version of *Mäster Olof* (1872): "What is truth?"[39]

Mäster Olof sets a precedent for Strindberg's later work. The subsequent historical dramas are, like the rest of his vast output, passionately personal, radically inconsistent in quality and tone, rigidly dogmatic and broadly syncretistic. But *Mäster Olof* stands alone as the only significant historical drama from before the Inferno years.[40] Most of the historical plays were written between the years 1898 and 1902, during the period of immense productivity that followed Strindberg's return from Paris and his study of Shakespeare in Lund.[41] Out of this "spring flood" (twenty-two plays in four years) came eight plays devoted to Swedish kings and four to world historical figures—Luther, Socrates, Moses, and Christ.[42] The Swedish history plays came in two streams: *The Saga of the Folkungs, Gustav Vasa, Erik XIV,* and *Gustav Adolf* were all written between the summer of 1898 and the autumn of 1899. They apply the lessons of *To Damascus I* and *II* and *Crimes and Crimes,* both written early in 1898, to historical figures. After a break of two years, Strindberg returned to

Swedish history with *Charles XII, Engelbrekt, Christina,* and *Gustav III,* all written between June 1901 and March 1902, along with *To Damascus III, Swanwhite,* and *A Dream Play.*

The spring of 1903 saw publication of "The Mysticism of World History," and Strindberg rather mechanically dramatized its precepts in *The Nightingale of Wittenberg, From Wilderness to Ancestral Lands, Hellas,* and *The Lamb and the Beast* in October and November 1903. Strindberg's involvement with the Intimate Theater followed, as did the great chamber plays, and the playwright did not return to Swedish history until, in anticipation of his sixtieth-birthday celebration, he wrote *The Last Knight, The Regent,* and *The Earl of Bjälbö,* in the late summer and fall of 1908.

The copiousness of this work is overwhelming, as is its variety in tone and technique. As the only major dramatist to devote as much of his attention to his nation's history as Shakespeare, Strindberg demands comparison to his English forebear. In fact, he insisted upon it. In his *Open Letters to the Intimate Theater,* Strindberg repeatedly proclaims himself a student and an admirer of Shakespeare. *Julius Caesar,* with its presentation of Caesar as "merely a human being" ("endast en människa"), inspired the antiheroic stance of *Mäster Olof.*[43] Episodic construction, historical and biblical parallels, boisterous crowd scenes, all the hardware of Shakespearean imitation comes into play in the historical dramas.[44] But the degree of conscious imitation of Shakespeare is more pronounced in Strindberg than in Romantic drama; his repeated invocation of the world-as-stage motif testifies that Strindberg found in Shakespeare a mirror of his own monistic syncretism. "Shakespeare is a providentialist just as the ancient writers of tragedies were," Strindberg declares in his discussion of *Julius Caesar,* "so he does not neglect the historical but lets divine justice be meted out to the point of pettiness" (*IT,* p. 118; "Shakespeare är providentialist som antikens tragöder voro, därför försummar han icke det historiska, utan låter den högsta rätten skipas ända till småaktighet," *ÖB,* p. 114). He discovered echoes of Jakob Boehme's "mystic oneness" (IT, p. 218; "all-enhet," *ÖB,* p. 217) in *All Is True,* the alternative title of *Henry VIII;* Strindberg's belief in Swedenborg's theory of correspondences between the visible and invisible worlds led him to pursue biblical and historical analogies with an almost Elizabethan delight. Parallel developments in different civilizations—for example, the simultaneous appearance of Moses and Buddha in 1300 B.C.—provide proof, in the 1903 essays, that a conscious mind directs the course of history.

But Strindberg's fascination with parallels and correspondences dates from well before his conversion to Swedenborgian syncretism. Biblical reference shapes the action of *Mäster Olof,* written when Strindberg was a self-avowed atheist and free-thinker. The first scene of this early play anticipates much of Strindberg's later development. Our first view is of Olaus Petri (the eponymous Mäster Olof) among schoolchildren, rehearsing his *Comedy of Tobias,* "the oldest extant Swedish play on a Biblical subject," as Walter Johnson points out.[45] The effect of this little play-within-the-play is complex: first, it establishes for *Mäster Olof* a powerful image of the cloister, with fruit trees in bloom, which is set against the hero's decision to enter public life. But the play that the students are reading is "a little comedy about the children of Israel and the Babylonian captivity" (1.i: *VT,* p. 25; "en liten comedia om Israels barn och babyloniska fångenskap," *HD,* p. 7), according to Olof, its author; as playwright, he presides over the enactment of the plight of a people in bondage, played out by Swedish children whose souls are in bondage to the Roman church. Thus, the first of many antinomies in the play—the contemplative opposed to the active life—is enhanced by biblical resonance. The entrance of Lars Andersson provides more antinomies: "I'm playing" (*VT,* p. 25; "Jag leker," *HD,* p. 7), responds Olof when Lars asks what he is doing. Lars urges him on: "A greater task awaits you" (p. 26; "Större arbete åligger dig!" p. 7); Olof's play of Tobias becomes mere play, opposed to work. The making of pairs continues: "I'm still too young," Olof cries ("Jag är för ung ännu!"), and the old man responds with a lengthy quotation from Jeremiah.[46]

In the first scene of *Mäster Olof,* Strindberg already reveals the techniques he will use throughout his career, in both historical and nonhistorical plays. There is, first, the symbolic use of setting; second, the evocation of biblical (sometimes mythological as well) parallels to the action on stage; third, the explicit and repeated definition of the conflict as a clash of opposites. Here cloister clashes with city, freedom with bondage, youth with age, player with prophet. As in *Fröken Julie,* which takes place on Midsummer Eve, Strindberg in *Mäster Olof* begins his action on a significant holiday: it is Pentecost eve, and images of the fire that inspired the apostles abound. "I once had the flame of faith," says Olof, "and it burned beautifully, but the gang of monks put it out with their holy water when they tried to drive the devil out of my body." "That was a fire of straw," says Lars; as Strindberg was to argue explicitly after his Inferno crisis, everything contains its own opposite (*VT,* p. 26; "O ja, jag hade en gång trons låga och han brann härligt, men munkeligan släckte av henne mid sig vigvatten, då de ville läsa djävulen ur kroppen på mig!" "Det var halm som skulle fladdra ut," *HD,* p. 7).

Olof is not only prophet and apostle, however; throughout his portrayal
there are echoes of identification with Christ: "I see an angel who comes
to me with a cup; she walks on the evening sky over there; her path is
blood red, and she has a cross in her hand" (*VT*, p. 27; "jag seg en ängel
som kommer emot mig med en kalk [i.e., chalice]; hon går på aftonskyn
därborta, blodröd är hennes stig, och hon har ett kors i handen," *HD*, p.
8). Later, in the tavern scene (II.i), Olof protects the prostitute from the
wrath of the mob: "Why don't you cast stones?" he asks them; "True,
you haven't any" (II.i:*VT*, p. 50, "Varför kasten i icke sten? Det är sant, i
ha'n inga!" *HD*, p. 18). This somewhat playful reenactment of the episode of the woman taken in adultery builds to real poignancy when the
black monk, Mårten, who throughout the play dogs Olof's steps and
embodies the forces of reaction, brings Olof's mother onto the stage.
"Beside herself" (*VT*, p. 54; "utom sig" *HD*, p. 19) she rushes out; Olof
"turns and runs toward the door which is slammed shut by Mårten,"
crying "Mother! Mother!" then "he runs out through the other doorway; the stage becomes dark" (*VT*, p. 54; "[vänder sig om och springer
mot dorren, som slås igen av Mårten] Moder! Moder! [Han springer ut
genom andra dorren, det mörknar på scenen,]" *HD*, p. 19). The door that
Mårten interposes between Olof and his mother reminds us of the closed
door at the church in Strängnäs in act I, which the bishops interpose
between the people and their Pentecostal mass. Olof defies their orders
and celebrates mass anyway; but—like Ibsen's Brand, that youthful idealist who so powerfully agitated the young Strindberg—he cannot be
reconciled with his mother. She dies cursing him and trusting the
monks, who repay her trust by marking the doorway of her house falsely
with the mark of the plague.

    The ending of the play, too, is designed to remind us of its begin-
ning; the setting is again symbolic, as Gert and Olof stand in pillories by
the door of Stockholm's Great Church. The sexton and his wife comment on Olof's extreme youth and on the coincidence that Olof must die
the very day his pupils—the students from the first scene—are to be
confirmed. They march by their teacher with flowers; one of them,
Vilhelm, lays his at Olof's feet. "Take care of my daughter, and never
forget the great day of Pentecost" (v.ii:*VT*, p. 119; "Tag hand om min
dotter, och glöm aldrig den stora pingstdagen!" *HD*, p. 48), says Gert as
they lead him to execution; Lars Sparre, the national marshal, urges Olof
to recant, invoking Olof's debts to the clergy, the burghers, the con-
gregation, and the confirmands. Finally he invokes Olof's wife—last
seen conversing with the prostitute as one "unhappy woman" to another
(v.i)—and urges his obligations to society: "Let me open this door

which will lead you out into the world again; humble your spirit while it is still flexible, and thank God who still gives you time to serve humanity" (*VT*, p. 120; "Låt mig öppna denna dörr, som skall leda er åter ut i världen, böj edert sinne medan det ännu är mjukt och tacka Gud, som ännu ger er tid att verka för mänskligheten!" *HD*, p. 49). The opposites here of open and closed doors, freedom and bondage, youth and age, are baffling: Olof recants in despair: "I am lost" (p. 121; "Jag är förlorad," p. 49). Strindberg hammers home the irony with the entrance of Vilhelm, who has not heard the news and who celebrates Olof's imminent martyrdom by reminding him of the teachings that set the students free "from the cruel punishments," and "opened the heavy monastery doors"; far off in the church the dying Gert (better informed) cries "Renegade!" (*VT*, p. 122; "Avfälling!" *HD*, p. 49); Olof collapses, crushed, and the curtain falls.

In addition to biblical parallels and recurrent images like the closed doors, references to events outside Sweden at the time of Olof's Reformation give density to the play. Luther, Huss, Zwingli, and other reformers figure as precedents for Olof and the even more Brand-like Gert. Olof's conversation with the nobleman (III.i) puts events into a European perspective. Fresh home from France, the nobleman extolls the virtues of Francis I, the free-thinker, and deplores the "fuss" ("bråka") in Germany. These countries are experiencing a crisis of civilization: "I'm not talking about Sweden," he continues, "for it isn't civilized" (III.i: *VT*, p. 72; "Jag talar nu inte om Sverige, ty det är intet kulturland," *HD*, p. 27). Only the restoration of the aristocracy will save Sweden, he concludes. Olof asks him if, as a free-thinker, he believes that "Balaam's ass could talk" (*VT*, p. 73; "Bileams åsna kunde tala?" *HD*, p. 28); but as the play develops, the king adopts the strategy of the foolish nobleman and not that of Mäster Olof.

It is mainly on this final, political level of allusiveness that we can see in *Mäster Olof* the influence of the young playwright's reading in the positivist history of Thomas Buckle, the literary criticism of Taine and Brandes, the evolutionist writings of Spencer, and the pessimist philosophies of Hartmann and Schopenhauer. The various versions of *Mäster Olof*—from the prose version of 1872 to the *Mellandramat* of 1875, the verse version of 1876, and the dreamlike *Efterspelet*, or "afterpiece," of 1877—show these influences to greater or lesser degrees.[47] But the allusive technique, the drawing of parallels, persists throughout and becomes a hallmark of Strindberg's dramaturgy: "That is my strength!" he declares of "parallel action" in the *Open Letters* (p. 59; "parallelismer [det är min force!]," *ÖB*, p. 53). What Strindberg found in Buckle and Taine at this period was what he sought in vain through his Inferno period and rediscovered in Swedenborg and Eastern religion afterward: a system that would give to human activity some kind of ultimate meaning. Buckle's notion that history functioned according to natural laws, just as science did, and that these laws could be formulated appealed to Strindberg, whose own ambitions to be recognized as a scientist—which led him to try to synthesize gold out of base metal during the Inferno period—were never to be satisfied. Thus the struggle between reaction and reformation in *Mäster Olof* is a reflection of the painful progress of humanity from one level of "truth" to another. "It *wasn't* a lie, but it has become a lie," Olof cries of his mother's belief in the old ways: "When you were young, mother, you were right. When I get old, well, then I may be wrong. One doesn't grow with time" (II.ii: *VT*, p. 60; "Det *var* icke en lögn men det har blivit. När du var ung, moder, hade du rätt, när jag blir gammal, ja, då har jag kanske orätt! Man växer inte i kapp med tiden!" *HD*, p. 22). The ending of the play, with its harsh ironies, insists upon Olof's "coming of age" in this highly negative sense; he too becomes old and becomes a liar.

Thus while *Mäster Olof* reflects the young playwright's assiduous readings, the curious combination of pessimism and positivism it offers is Strindberg's own. Here as in his later works he shows himself quite capable of subscribing to radically conflicting attitudes simultaneously without betraying awareness of any inconsistency. In the case of *Mäster Olof*, Strindberg's determination to show his hero as unheroic, as an unworthy instrument of a natural evolutionary process, forces him to elevate the fanatic Gert into a spokesman of truth at the end. But while Strindberg clearly felt that Olof should be perceived as a backslider (one early version of the play is entitled "En Avfälling"), it is hard to take Gert's judgment as final given the wildly relativistic context of the rest of the play.

Yet Strindberg's attempts to portray his unheroic hero, as Shakespeare did Julius Caesar, at home, leads to some of the most characteristic scenes in *Mäster Olof*, the squabbles between Olof and his wife and mother. The second scene of act III opens with this domestic activity: "Kristina is standing by a window watering flowers; she chats with the birds in a cage as she does so. Olof is sitting writing; with an expression of impatience he looks up from the papers toward Kristina as if he wanted her to be quiet" (III.ii: *VT*, p. 82; "Kristina står vid ett fönster och vattnar blommor; under tiden jollrar hon med fåglarna i en bur. Olof sitter och skriver; med en min av otåglighet ser han upp från papperet och bort till Kristina liksom ville han tysta henne," *HD*, p. 32). The day is, significantly, Midsummer Eve; as Olof awaits news of the king's dealings with the Estates, his family life becomes a paradigm of the state of the realm. Kristina, whom he has "released from bondage" (*VT*, p. 84; "ur träldomen," *HD*, p. 33), is incapable of understanding her husband's highly abstract work, but her groping towards truth leads her to quarrel with Olof's mother. "What did you say to her?" asks Olof as his mother storms out; "I don't remember," Kristina replies, "but there were a lot of things I had never dared to think, but that I must have dreamed while my father kept me in bondage" (p. 88; "Jag minns inte nu, ty det var en hel mängd saker, som jag aldrig vågat tänka, men som jag måtte ha drömt under det min far höll mig i sitt slaveri," p. 35). Just as Olof's marriage exacts its cost by alienating his mother—who recapitulates her action of act II by once again slamming the door on her son and a woman she deems a prostitute—so do we learn at the end of the scene that the agreement arrived at between king and people undercuts Olof's work by permitting the persistence of the old faith. Kristina's joy at Olof's appointment as rector of the Great Church, like the people's joy in the Maypole and music provided by the king, dramatizes the scope of Olof's failure to effect real change. Her inability to understand Olof, like her inchoate craving for freedom and her weakness when Olof offers it, is emblematic; like the students in the first scene, Kristina embodies the people. So, too, does Olof's mother, whose reactionary clinging to the old beliefs baffles him.

Despite its cumbersome length and frequent stridency, *Mäster Olof* is a powerful play primarily because of Strindberg's use—as in this scene and throughout the play—of domestic detail to epitomize larger historical issues. Through indirect reference to public events, Strindberg evokes a context of social change that is played out on stage in domestic terms: Olof's first Lutheran sermon in the Great Church takes place offstage; what we see is Kristina's decision to marry him immediately thereafter, even though she has not heard and does not understand his preaching. Olof's quarrels with his mother and brother are similarly both familial and political. The intense personal emotions that tinge these scenes animate the characters' symbolic roles as spokesmen of aspects of Swedish society. By providing biblical parallels as a scriptural counterpoint to the action itself, by insisting upon the significance of the holidays upon which decisions are made, Strindberg suggests a complex connection between domestic, historical, and religious levels of human activity.

The naturalistic dramas that occupied Strindberg's attention during the years after *Mäster Olof* show the playwright's struggle to infuse domestic actions with sacramental or mythic significance. Miss Julie reenacts Salome's dance and John the Baptist's beheading; in *The Father*, the Captain plays out Hercules in the toils of Omphale, Agamemnon in Clytaemnestra's nets. When Strindberg again turned to historical material in the summer of 1898, it is no surprise to see him making, in *The Saga of the Folkungs*, what Birgitta Steene dismisses as "an obsolete attempt to see history *sub specie aeternitatis*."[48]

The play chronicles the misfortunes of Magnus the Good, who piously endures his wife's and mother's adulterous intrigues, his son's conspiracy against his throne, his excommunication and his loss of Scania, all to expiate the crimes of his ancestors. "Poor lamb," cries the Madwoman who interrupts the disastrous victory celebration of the second scene, "you live among wolves and dragons, but the flame of your innocence blinds you so you see only the glow of your innocence. You see only love and friendship, faithfulness and goodness, where you sit up to your neck in falseness and evil, and where all the vices, even sodomy, flourish" (1.ii:*SF*, p. 47; "Stackars lamm, du lever bland ulvar och drakar, men din osklydighets ljus bländar dig så du ser endast skenet av din egen renhet. Du ser endast kärlek och vänskap, trohet och dygder, där du sitter till halsen i falskhet och ondska, och där alla laster till och med Sodoms blomstra," *HD*, p. 58). Magnus's sacrifice became visually explicit in the Intimate Theater's production of the play, as Strindberg later complained:

> När mina Folkungar skulle ges, fann jag titelrollen maskerad
> som Kristus; jag förklarade för honom att Magnus Eriksson,
> som visserligen i Norge kallades Magnus den Gode, icke var
> någon Kristus, och jag bad aktoren icke bära korset på
> ryggen som Frälsaren till Golgata. Men han visste bättre, ty
> han hade i sin barndom sett Udhes tavlor (Kristus
> Folkskoleläraren o. s. v.). Och så blev det vid det.
>
> (*ÖB*, p. 133)

> When my *Saga of the Folkungs* was going to be produced,
> I found the actor playing King Magnus decked out
> as Christ. I explained to him that Magnus Eriksson, who
> admittedly was called Magnus the Good in Norway, was no
> Christ, and I asked the actor not to carry the cross on his
> back as the Saviour did on His way to Golgotha. But he
> knew better, for in his youth he had seen Udhe's paintings
> (Christ the teacher, etc.). So that was that.
>
> (*IT*, pp. 136–37)

Despite the playwright's protestations, the scene in which Magnus carries his cross forty times around the church—"just as many as the number of days our Saviour fasted in the wilderness," says the Gray Friar (act IV:*SF*, p. 81)—is full of explicit references. "Father, forgive them and us, for they know not what they do" (*SF*, p. 84; "förlåt dem och oss, ty de veta icke vad de göra," *HD*, p. 74), exclaims Beatrice, Magnus's daughter-in-law, as she wipes his brow with her handkerchief.

Surrounded by disloyal and evil friends and family, harassed by the false prophecies of his sister Birgitta, Magnus is more reminiscent of the persecuted penitents of *Inferno* and *To Damascus* than of Strindberg's vision of Christ; hence his disapproval of the actor's decision. But despite his desire to "place the question" of Magnus's sacrifice "on a classical and Christian foundation" (*IT*, p. 250; "att ställa frågan på antik och kristlig grund," *ÖB*, p. 241), the classical gets short shrift, as the penitential pattern of the play is purely Christian. "It is fulfilled!" cries Magnus, kneeling beside the bodies of his son and daughter-in-law, victims of the plague, as the victorious enemy army approaches and the curtain falls ("Det är fullkomnat!" *HD*, p. 83.) For the simplistic identification that Strindberg deplored, the playwright may well have to take some blame.

The suffering goodness of Magnus, certainly, is the play's center and also its greatest flaw. The hardware of the Romantic drama—vigorous crowd scenes, a procession of flagellants, comic byplay among the adulterers and conspirators—and a lively quarrel between Magnus and Birgitta do not sufficiently break up the monotony of misfortunes that Magnus piously bears. Strindberg telescopes the events of some fifteen years so that they will pile up upon each other; the result is less concentration than superfetation. His identification with the central figure is so absolute—and Magnus's identity with the autobiographical penitent of *To Damascus* is so clear—as to forbid questioning of the piety that providence so remorselessly tests. For Martin Lamm this process makes the play "Strindbergian" ("Strindbergsk");[49] as an attempt on Strindberg's part to recast his idiosyncratic spiritual autobiography in historical terms, the play is only too successful.

This complete identification of the hero's sufferings with the playwright's own gives way in *Gustav Vasa* and *Erik XIV*, written in spring and summer of 1899, to the portrayal of enigmatic central characters, whose relation to providence is problematic. Parallelisms, which merely elaborated the amorous intrigue in *The Saga of the Folkungs*, here come to the fore as a means of dramatic construction. Strindberg saw these two plays as part of a Vasa saga, completing the story he had begun twenty-seven years before with *Mäster Olof*; like the early play, these reenact on multiple levels—domestic, political, religious—the experience of the past.

The first scene of *Gustav Vasa* is as energetic, concentrated, and evocative as the best of Strindberg's nonhistorical drama. Måns Nilsson and his wife await the arrival of Gustav Vasa in their home in Dalarna; this setting is, again, significantly decorated, with "large simple paintings representing Gustav Vasa's adventures in Dalarna" (act 1:*VT*, p. 155, SD). Immediately set up is a tension between the images of Gustav Vasa as the legendary folk hero of the dalesmen and as the king who melted down the church bells to pay his debts to Lübeck. Nilsson harps upon the romantic past, while his wife reminds him of more recent injustices; as the children enter, dressed in mourning, it becomes clear that Nilsson has in mind a history lesson for the king. He has coached them to say "We're mourning our beloved Pastor Jon of Svärdsjö" (act 1:*VT*, p. 157; "Vi sörja vår älskade lärare," *HD*, p. 88). "There's no need to tell the children that the king had his friend beheaded two years ago," says Nilsson (*VT*, p. 157; "Onödigt är det däremot att säga barnen det kungen lät taga sin väns huvud för två år sen!" *HD*, p. 88); he wants the king to recognize his falling-off from what he used to be. "His life's a miracle story: of how God led him from the Danish captivity up to Dalarna, children," says Måns Nilsson, "of how after many dangers he finally freed his country from bondage" (*VT*, p. 158; "Hans liv, barn, är en mirakelhistoria, huru Gud förde honom ur fångenskapen hos Juten upp till Dalarne; och huru han genom många farligheter slutligen befriar sitt land ur träldomen," *HD*, p. 88). The biblical overtones here enhance Nilsson's reverence for Gustav as a "wonderman of God" ("Guds underman"), a type of Moses as well as a hero of Dalarna. Throughout the first act, however, Gustav Vasa plays the role of a remote, inscrutable, and bloody providence.

For he does not appear to sit at the side of his friend; rather as the dalesmen gather and remind Nilsson of their grievances ("That must be forgotten!" he cries, "Everything must be forgotten!" *VT*, p. 160; "Det måste glömmas! Allt måste glömmas!" *HD*, p. 89), the king, in his stead, sends Herman Israel, the moneylender from Lübeck, and Mäster Olof, his private secretary. One at a time, the dalesmen are sent out to what they think will be a private audience with the king; Olof asks leading questions about conditions in Dalarna that the remaining dalesmen attempt to evade. Finally, when only Måns Nilsson and Anders Persson remain, the bloody coats of the first three dalesmen—Ingel Hansson, Nils of Söderby, and Master Stig—are thrown on the table. Olof interprets the evasions of Nilsson and Persson, now terrified, as repudiations of the dalesmen's complaints; Herman Israel marvels at his cleverness, and, in the act's crowning irony is mistaken by the children for the king as he sits in the high seat. "Lovely, lovely," says Mäster Olof; "This is the famous and mighty councillor Herman Israel, who along with Cord König and Nils Bröms saved your king from Danish captivity and provided him with the means to carry on our war for freedom" (*VT*, p. 171; "Vackert! Vackert! Detta är den berömde och mäktige rådsherren Herman Israel, som jämte Cord König och Nils Bröms räddade er konung ur danska fångenskapen och skaffade honom understöd till befriersekrigets förande," *HD*, p. 94). The act comes full circle: the Mosaic phrases attached to Gustav by old Måns Nilsson are now applied to the moneylender, the melter of the bells. Liberation and bondage are confounded; the dalesmen are crushed as, proclaiming their rebellion against the king and allegiance to Christian of Denmark, they are interrupted by the reentry of Mäster Olof, who informs them that king Christian is now a prisoner of the Swedes.

The sense of patterns repeating and playing off against each other that characterizes this first act persists through the whole play. The play's ending mirrors this first scene: as Gustav and Mäster Olof anxiously wait in the palace for their overthrow, we hear drumbeats like those that accompanied the bloodbath in Dalarna. It is Gustav Vasa, not Måns Nilsson, who remembers his early ties: "Think of it—I can hear them tramping as they march through the city gates. And they're the Dalesmen, my Dalesmen! Life is cruel! Hear it? One two—one two—do you think I'll get out of this?" (act v:*VT*, p. 231; "Tänk, att jag kan höra deras tramp ända hit när de marschera genom tullen. Och det är dalkarlarne, mina dalkarlar! Livet är grymt!—Hor du: takt å tu!—takt å tu!—Tror du jag kommer ur detta?" *HD*, p. 121). As the steps of wooden shoes come nearer, Gustav reckons on his fingers his victims: "Ingel Hansson, Master Stig, Nils of Söderby! God is just!" (p. 232). But the event concludes startlingly as Engelbrekt enters, "merrily drunk" ("glatt berusad"): the same Engelbrekt whose meeting with Gustav on skis long ago was depicted in the paintings on Måns Nilsson's wall. What Gustav thought was armed rebellion against him is actually a gathering of the dalesmen against the traitor Dacke, the dalesmen sound their horns in honor of the day (Midsummer Day, the anniversary of Gustav Vasa's entrance into Stockholm), and the king raises his hands: "O God, Thou has punished me, and I thank thee!" (*VT*, p. 233; "O Gud, du har straffat mig, och jag tacker dig!" *HD*, p. 122). Engelbrekt's name resounds with significance: in the first scene, Måns Nilsson called the coincidence between the names of Engelbrekt the skier and Engelbrekt the great liberator of a century before, "the finger of God" (act 1:*VT*, p. 158; "Guds finger," *HD*, p. 88); the king, too, stumbles over the name: "Eng—el—brekt?" (*VT*, p. 232; *HD*, p. 122). Both the first and final scenes depict the twists and turns of justice: politic and bloody in the first, divine and comic in the last.

Before he appears on stage in the third act, Gustav Vasa is described as remote, colossal, inspired. His linkage with Moses and his status as folk hero of the dalesmen has been made explicit in the first and second acts. Jacob Israel describes him in terms that show his cosmopolitan culture: "And he looks like one of Michelangelo's prophets . . . Isaiah, I think! And, in truth, God the infinite One is with him" (II.i:*VT*, p. 176; "och han liknar en av Buonarrotis profeter . . . jag tror Jesajas! Och i sanning, Gud, den högste, är med honom," *HD*, p. 97). When Erik and his drunken counselor, Göran Persson, are arrested in a tavern brawl at the end of II.ii, again it is Jacob Israel who notes the moral: "Always this giant hand, which one never sees, only feels" (II.ii:*VT*, p. 189; "Alltid denna jättehand, som man aldrig få se, blott känna på," *HD*, p. 103). Thus when we see Gustav on stage at last in the beginning of the third act, it comes as no surprise that the "most striking" painting on his wall "depicts 'God visiting Abraham in the grove of Mamre'" and that "The Abraham closely resembles the king" (act III:*VT*, p. 190; "På väggarne målningar ur Gamla Testamentet; den mest i ögonen fallende föreställer 'Herren Gud besöker Abraham i Mamre lund.' Denna bild av Abraham har ett starkt tycke av konungen," *HD*, p. 103). Prince Erik, in the tavern scene (II.ii), introduces another complex of allusion through which we are to understand his father: "He threw his Hungarian hammer at me as the god Thor throws his at the trolls," he tells Göran; "You know, sometimes when he comes, in his large felt hat and blue cloak, carrying his boar's spear like a walking stick, I think it's the God Odin himself" (II.ii:*VT*, p. 183; "kastade han sin ungerska stålhammare efter mig, som guden Tor kastar sin efter trollen. . . . Vet du, ibland när han kommer i sin stora filthatt och blå kappan och bär sitt vildsvinsspjut som käpp, då tror jag det är guden Odin själv," *HD*, p. 100). Old testament giant, Norse god; yet this grand figure, when we finally see him, is harassed by the instability of the realm, by the profligacy of Prince Erik, by his mother-in-law's intransigent clinging to the old faith, by Herman Israel's duplicity.[50]

The king's miseries are reflected in the miseries of those who surround him: Herman Israel's son betrays Lübeck and is sent by his father to his death; Olof is forced to confront his past by his son Reginald. "I even predicted this hour when my son would come to me and say: Here I am as you have made me," he says with resignation (IV.ii:*VT*, p. 221; "Jag förutsade till och med denna stund, då min son skulle stå fram för mig och säga: Se här är jag sådan du gjort mig," *HD*, p. 117). Like the paintings in the old dalesman's house, the sons of the various fathers in the play force a confrontation between past dreams of glory and present confusion.[51] There is even a further level of suggestion in the explicit way in which Strindberg models the royal interview between Gustav and Erik upon that between Henry IV and Prince Hal in III.ii of *1 Henry IV*, with Göran Persson in the role of Falstaff, the chief among the prince's "bad companions" (act III:*VT*, p. 195; "dåliga sällskap," *HD*, p. 105).

Gustav Vasa's effort to understand his sins as a father and relate them to the sins of his son is part of his larger effort to come to know his relationship to divine providence. Whereas Magnus in *The Saga of the Folkungs* understands fully his role as sacrificial expiant of the family curse, Gustav Vasa finds himself confronted by a God as remote and awesome as himself. Since the execution of Jon of Svärdsjö, he tells Herman Israel:

> Sedan dess är min frid ute! Mina egna se på mig som de icke gjorde förr—Min maka, min älskade Margareta . . . vänder sig bort, då jag vill kyssa hennes rena panna, och—kan du drömma det!—i går, vid middagsbordet, satt hon ach betraktade min hand på ett sätt, som om hon sett blod på den!
>
> (*HD*, p. 106)

> I've had no peace of mind. My own family look at me as they never did before. My wife, my beloved Margareta . . . turns away when I want to kiss her pure forehead, and—can you imagine this? Yesterday, at the dinner table, she sat watching my hand as if she saw blood on it!
>
> (act III:*VT*, pp. 197–98)

This Strindbergian intrusion of the uncanny into the domestic highlights the problem of Gustav's bloodguilt, which has been emphasized from the first by the children's mourning costumes and the bloody coats of the dalesmen. As Gustav is forced to send the last two—Anders Persson and Måns Nilsson—off to the block, he prays, as he tells Herman Israel is his custom, for divine guidance: "Oh, eternal God, who directs the destinies of peoples and princes, enlighten my understanding and strengthen my will so that I may not pass judgment unjustly!" (act III:*VT*, p. 205; "O, evige Gud, some styrer folks och furstars öden,

upplys mitt förstånd, och stärck min vilja att jag icke må döma vrång
dom!" *HD*, p. 110). His attempts to bring his rough justice into line with
divine justice founder on the impenetrability of God Himself: Barbro,
the child who was to greet the king in the first act, meets him at the end of
IV.i, pleading for mercy on the innocent widow of Måns Nilsson.
Shaken, Gustav wonders

> Jag kan säga mig, att Herrans hand har lagt sig tung över
> mig, utan dock att jag förstår varför. Ty, om Gud talar
> genom samvetet och bönen, så har han intalat mig att handla
> såsom jag handlat. Varför min lydnad nu straffas, fattar jag
> icke; men jag böjer mig för den högre visdomen som går
> over mitt förstånd!
>
> (IV.i:HD, p. 115)
>
> I can say to myself that the hand of the Lord is resting
> heavily on me, but why I don't understand. If God speaks to
> me through my conscience and my prayers, He has
> persuaded me to act as I have acted. Why my obedience
> punishes me now, I don't grasp; but I bend before the
> higher wisdom, which surpasses my understanding.
>
> (IV.i:VT, p. 216)

The king must undergo a Swedenborgian audit, a balancing of accounts,
before the play's end.

The king comes to Olof in IV.ii in despair; "If I sinned as David, you
were my Nathan!" he cries (*VT*, p. 223; "Har jag syndat som David, så var
du Nathan!" *HD*, p. 117). Master Olof chronicles the king's mistakes and
failures—the astute observer might recall that the real Olaus Petri was
the author of a history of Sweden that Gustav Vasa caused to be suppressed—and concludes: "If I were to summarize all that's blameworthy
in the great king, it would be lack of piety!" (my translation). Gustav has
lacked, Olof goes on, defining piety, "the consideration the stronger
man, even if he is a man chosen by Providence, must have for the feelings
of weaker men, when these have sprung from a childlike and therefore
pious spirit" (*VT*, p. 224; "skulle jag nu sammanfatta allt vad klandervärt
finnes hos den store konungen, så vore det brist på pietet!" "Pietet ar den
hänsyn den starkare, även om han är en Forsynens man, måste visa mot
de svagares känslor, där dessa äro utsprungna ur ett barnsligt och därför
fromt sinne," *HD*, p. 118).[52] This moment is the turning point for Gustav
Vasa: like Engelbrekt (*VT*, p. 225), he is given the mission of uniting
Sweden; to avoid his death, Gustav must humble himself and offer to

negotiate with Nils Dacke, leader of the rebels. "Who is this mysterious man who's never seen?" asks the king; "Perhaps a miracle man of God— in his way!" answers Olof (*VT,* p. 226; "Vem är denna hemlighetsfulla man, som aldrig synes?" "Kanske en Guds underman, på sitt sätt!" *HD,* p. 119). Thus we are prepared to associate the approaching footsteps in the fifth act with Dacke, the mysterious agent of divine vengeance; the surprise that greets Engelbrekt greets a deliverance that answers Gustav's humility and repentance.

This miraculous deliverance tends to validate Gustav's special status as a "wonder man of God": if the theology of *Gustav Vasa* is the same as that in *The Saga of the Folkungs,* its dramatization is not. In the earlier play, we are asked merely to observe Magnus's humility; in the later one, we see a proud, titanic figure humble himself. The insistence that the central character learn or exemplify "piety" does not carry forward into Strindberg's next historical play, *Erik XIV.* Here the mad young king and his friend, Göran Persson, face with increasing frustration and in- comprehension the inscrutable ways of providence. In the final act of the play, with the realm about to topple—dramatically figured in the frenzied wedding-banquet to which, in the absence of the nobility, Erik has invited the riffraff of the streets—the two are forced to look back over their past actions. "Do you know what my biggest weakness was?" asks Erik; "No," replies Göran, "I know absolutely nothing, understand nothing, and so I'm done for" (IV.iii:*VT,* p. 323; "Vet du vad mitt största fel var?" "Nej, jag vet numera absolut intet, förstår intet, och därför är jag slut," *HD,* p. 151). Göran confesses to having "dreamt" ("drömde") he had a mission to protect the realm: "But I must have been mistaken" ("Men jag måtte ha mistagit mig"). The conversation rises to a higher plane: Erik asks, "Have you ever noticed, Göran, that there are matters we don't understand, and may not understand?" ("Har du aldrig märkt, Göran, att det finns saker som vi icke förstå, och som vi icke må förstå?"). The two always thought that what they were doing was right; but in the final analysis, Göran points out, "Who knows? Imagine how little we know!" (*VT,* p. 323; "Ja, säg det!—Tänk vad ve veta litet!" *HD,* p. 151).

This moment of helpless skepticism, an utter philosophical impasse, arises naturally out of the design of the play, in which every action taken by Erik proves disastrous and every piece of advice given by Göran comes too late. As is Strindberg's usual practice, the first scene establishes a dominant image: Erik's childish frustration fills the stage with a shower of miscellaneous household items—nails, a hammer, a flowerpot, a chair, shoes, pillows, clothes—hurled down from above by the unseen king.

The scene, which has the same setting as the last act of *Gustav Vasa,* demands comparison with the opening of the play about Erik's father. Where the unseen Gustav is bloody and swift in his justice, Erik reacts to Karin's conversations with Max and Göran with a comic tantrum. The reversals that dog his plans have the effect of making him ridiculous: when he learns that Elizabeth of England has turned down his marriage proposal, he throws the crown he has just been showing Karin over the balustrade and pelts the Stures, bearers of bad news, with the items littering the stage. He reviles Elizabeth as a "whore" (act 1:*VT,* p. 274; "en gathora," *HD,* p. 130), and when Nils Gyllensterna refuses to assassinate Leicester, he kicks some of the remaining objects and collapses, laughing and weeping.

The spectacle of Erik completely incapable of controlling himself or those around him extends to graver matters as well. Confident of marriage to Elizabeth, he readily permits Duke John to make the politically dangerous marriage to Catherine of Poland. "The stupidest thing in my life!" he cries when he realizes the implications, "Haven't you ever noticed how everything I touch becomes stupid and twisted?" (*VT,* p. 277; "Den största dumheten i mitt liv!" "Har du icke märkt, att allt vad jag lägger hand vid blir dumt och bakvänt?" *HD,* p. 131). Even more humiliating is his appearance before the Hall of State on, ironically, Pentecost eve. Göran's manipulations have led the Stures into the treasonable action of saluting Duke John at the bridge by Gripsholm Castle—a castle that Strindberg invests with added significance as the Stures pretend to confuse it with Nyköping and Håtuna, sites of earlier betrayals. All Erik has to do is read the speech Göran has written: a conviction is sure to follow. Then his children enter: they want to see "the king," Erik in his royal robes—"the theater king" (III.ii:*VT,* p. 299; "teaterkungen," *HD,* p. 141). While little Gustav admires the "rats" on Erik's ermine, Sigrid wraps her doll in the speech.[53] Erik departs; the Dowager Queen persuades Karin and the children to leave him; he returns in a ferocious temper. Without Göran's paper—and uninspired even on Pentecost eve—Erik has confused the facts and the Stures have been acquitted. Disaster succeeds disaster: Duke John escapes, Göran receives back his ring from the woman he loves, his Platonic "Idea" ("A whore, that one, too," laughs Erik, p. 306; "Haha! Det var urbilden! En gathora, den med! Håhå!" p. 144); Erik takes "divine justice into my own hands" (p. 309; "himmelska rättvisan i hand," p. 145) and helps massacre the Stures. "Can you straighten this out, Göran?" he asks at the end of the act (p. 310; "Kan du reda det har, Göran?" p. 146). The canny counselor's response is utter despair:

Nej, ty jag begriper ingenting av det hela! Ser du icke
händelserna rulla opp sig utan att vi kunna göra något åt
dem! Jag sitter stum, lamslagen, förmår inte röra ett finger
och kan endast vänta, frågande: vad skall nu ske?

(III.ii:*HD*, p. 146)

No, because I don't understand any of it! Don't you see how
the events take place without our being able to do anything
about them? I sit speechless, struck dumb; I can't move a
finger and can only wait, asking: What is going to happen
next?

(III.ii:*VT*, p. 310)

Göran's great skill can do nothing to shape Erik's uncontrolled actions;
indeed, the shaping force in the play appears only in the comic, coincidental complications that continually frustrate both.

Thus, despite some reference to the curse of the Folkungs working
itself out and a final scene in which brother once again betrays brother
(this time John tricks Charles), the play raises questions about the significance of Erik's unhappy life and reign only to refuse to answer them. But
the suggestion that there is something else—a Platonic Idea, perhaps, or
a virgin queen—that gives life meaning still remains. The balance between the chaos and strife of politics and an alternative based on love (a
word that makes even Göran "handsome" when he says it, act I:*VT*, p.
276; "vacker," *HD*, p. 131) is dramatically illustrated in the first scene of
act II: here, Göran works in the same room in which his mother, Agda,
and her child (Jacob Israel's son) eat their dinner. A partition separates
the two parts of the room as Göran deals with Svante Sture, Erik, and
Måns, Karin's father. His final interview is with Peder Welamson, the
one-eyed soldier, who readily assents to Göran's plan to kill Max, Karin's
fiancé. "Do you have a bit of cold food, mother? I'd appreciate it," he says
as the murderer leaves (act II:*VT*, p. 292; "Hor du nu en bit kallmat, mor,
så skall jag hålla till godo," *HD*, p. 138). The split-stage image sets Göran's
intrigues off against the domestic peace of the meal. Erik's wild plans and
the ruthless means needed to execute them divorce Göran from his Idea
of perfection and Erik from his own craving for the peace and beauty of
Lake Mälaren in the summertime (III.ii:*VT*, p. 308). The wedding with
Karin towards which the whole play leads is a grotesque parody—but
parody with curious resonance. Måns Knekt echoes the parable of the
great supper (Luke 14:16–24) in describing the wedding feast to Göran's mother:

Jo, mor Persson, det var en konung som skulle hålla bröllop
och han sände ut sina tjänare att kalla dem som bjudna voro,
men de ville icke komma. Då sade han till sina tjänare: gån
ut på vägarne och alla I finnen, kallen till bröllopet. Och
tjänare gingo ut och församlade alla så många de funno både
onda och goda och borden vordo alla fullsatta!

(IV.iii:*HD*, p. 153)

Well, Mother Persson, there was a king who was going to
celebrate his wedding, and he sent his servants to call those
who were invited, but they didn't want to come. Then he
said to his servants: Go out on the highways and call all
those you find to the wedding. And the servants went out
and gathered all that they found, both good and evil, and all
the places were taken!

(IV.iii:*VT*, p. 326)

This places Erik's mad gesture within an explicit Christian context; what
Duke John considers his weakness, his love of the "little people"
("småfolk") as opposed to the "little kings" ("småkonungar") Duke
Charles thinks of as his strength (*VT*, p. 328; *HD*, p. 153). Göran's dream
that king and people can stand united against the nobility falls short of
realization here: but the ending of the play insists that the struggle will
continue. "I think the world has gone mad!" cries King John as his
brother Charles departs in open rebellion; "That's what Erik thought,
too," replies Charles; "Who knows how it is . . ." (*VT*, p. 328; "Jag tror,
att världen har blivit galen!" "Det trodde Erik också! Ho vet hur det är,
. . ." *HD*, p. 154). All judgments before the last are purely provisional.

With its portrayal of an unstable king driven mad by a mad world,
Erik XIV has become the most popular of Strindberg's history plays
outside of Sweden. Most criticism tends to center on Strindberg's description of Erik as "a characterization of a characterless human being"
(*IT*, p. 256; "en karaktärsteckning av en karaktärslös människa," *ÖB*, p.
248), which seems to put the play into the mainstream of his naturalistic
drama because of its echo of the preface to *Fröken Julie*. Yet Marc Roth
has demonstrated an affinity between Strindberg's monarch and an
older theatrical convention—the player king.[54] The gross incom-
patibility between the childish, impatient Erik and the role of king that
he must play—a role complicated by its division into component parts of
political manipulator and "theater king" in robes of ermine—mirrors the
gulf in the play between ideal and real, divine and human. Erik's acute
desire to *understand* his life in relation to incomprehensible divine pur-

pose is inevitably reminiscent of Hamlet's; Strindberg himself pointed to a large number of correspondences between Erik and Hamlet, even to the extent of arguing that the historical Nils Gyllenstjerna, a vacillating timeserver in the play, was Shakespeare's model for Guildenstern (and Rosencrantz) (*IT*, pp. 79–81; *ÖB*, pp. 75–76). But while Hamlet at least is allowed some glimpse of the "divinity that shapes our ends," a solution to the riddle of action eludes Erik to the end.

The Vasa saga of *Mäster Olof, Gustav Vasa,* and *Erik XIV* constitutes Strindberg's highest achievement in historical drama; all three plays engage the audience in a vigorous and regenerative struggle to understand the past and its agents by relating national politics and personalities to some scheme, however inchoate, of ultimate significance. Through parallel construction, biblical and mythological allusion, and comic coincidences, Strindberg suggests, rather than announces, the existence of a suprahuman order best described by theatrical metaphor. The little stage imitates the great, with the playwright in the role of providence.

Through the late summer and fall of 1899 Strindberg worked at his most ambitious history play, *Gustav Adolf*—"my *Nathan the Wise*" (*IT*, p. 257; *ÖB*, p. 249), as he proudly dubbed this prodigiously lengthy and episodic piece. There is something of Lessing's pious earnestness in the way this play hammers home its moral: scene after scene demonstrates the folly of religious divisiveness and provides glimpses of a time when all religions will become one. Gustav himself comes to change from a persecutor of Catholics to a defender of toleration: Turk, Catholic, Protestant, Jew join the crowd and bedeck his coffin with flowers at the end. The first scene—which in performance would take place six hours before this—is set at Usedom on Midsummer day. The miller and his wife bluntly state the theme in the opening moments: "Even if war has raged during all the years we've been married, we've kept peace in our home— you with your Lutheran beliefs and I with my Catholic faith" (act 1:*GA*, p. 65; "i tolf år ha vi plägat hjonelag, och fastän krigen rasat i dessa år, ha vi hållit husfrid, du med din evangeliska lära och jag med in katolska tro," *GAHD*, p. 8).[55] The couple, separated and impoverished at the end of the scene, weave in and out of the play as a constant, choric reminder of the folly of intolerance.

The alternative is Strindbergian syncretism—or at least a world religion along the lines discussed at the first Hague Congress of 1899, as Ollén has suggested. "Pastor, pastor, that's our benediction!" cries Grubbe to Fabricius as they listen to the prayers of Mohammedans and Jews: "And the same Lord, the same servant! One God and the Father of all" (III.ii:*GA*, p. 148; "Präst, präst, de är ju våran 'Herren valsigne oss!'

Och samma Herre, samma tjänare! En Gud och allas fader!" *GAHD*, p. 107). Again, the funeral of Gustav is emblematic: among the ranks attending we find "Scotchmen, Frenchmen, Russians, Turks, Hungarians, Calmucks, Italians, Jews" (v.iv:*GA*, p. 225).

As Lamm has pointed out, Gustav Adolf works his way towards enlightenment as a "penitent in Inferno."[56] He sees his sufferings and setbacks—as Magnus does—as expiations of his fathers' sins, a chain of bloodguilt stretching from the days of the Folkungs through the Vasas up to his own father's massacre of the nobility at Linköping. "Why dwell on what is past?" asks the queen as he recites at length this grim saga. "Because the past comes back!" is the Strindbergian reply (IV.iv:*GA*, p. 198; "Hvärför röra i det förflutna?" "Därför att det förflutna står upp!" *GAHD*, p. 165). The suggestion that the cycle will repeat itself is never quite missing from the play: we are here and there reminded of the heir to the throne, Christina. "*Usch!*" cries the queen when she receives a gift from the Catholic Swarzenberg, "It's a rosary! Take it away! Or . . . send it to my little Christina to play with; she likes jewels!" (III.ii:*GA*, p. 159; "Fy! Det är ett radband! Tag bort det! Eller . . . skicka det till min lilla Kristina att leka med; hon tycket om juveler!" *GAHD*, p. 120). Christina's eventual apostasy undercuts all that Gustav strives for.

Not merely an expiant of the family curse, Gustav struggles through the play as an instrument of providence, working towards a divine goal of harmony and peace that he only dimly glimpses. "Does anybody here understand this?" he cries in confusion at the network of alliances and hostilities among Catholics and Protestant factions, "I don't, but just keep going," (II.iv:*GA*, p. 125; "Begriper någon det här? Jag intet, men går på bara," *GAHD*, p. 79). Finally, in IV.iv, he meets and quarrels with Frederick of Bohemia and the Palatinate, "the root and cause of this incomprehensible war" (*GA*, p. 195; "roten och opphofvet till detta obegripliga krig," *GAHD*, p. 162). His judgment is decisive, and—typical of this play—discursive:

> I var en dag konung i Böhmen, och Er konungamakt
> missbrukade I att plundern kyrkor och förfölja katoliker,
> men Er ofördragsamhet narrade Er äfven till grymhet mot
> andra protestantiska sekter än Er reformerta! För mig har I
> aldrig varit martyr, och Er landsflykt, Era lidanden har jag
> alltid funnit klara följder af Era handlingar. Jag skulle från Er
> vilja härleda hela detta rysliga krig, denna oförsonlighet och
> detta djuriska hat, som vi eljest tillskrivit fienden.
> (IV.iv:*GAHD*, p. 159)

You were once king of Bohemia, and you misused your royal power to plunder the churches and to oppress the Catholics, but your intolerance deceived you into cruelty against Protestant sects other than your own. To me, you have never been a martyr, and your exile, your sufferings I have always considered the clear results of your acts. This whole terrible war, this irreconcilability, this beastly hatred which we ascribe to the enemy really stem from you.

(IV.iv:*GA*, pp. 192–93)

From his great opponent Wallenstein, Gustav learns to see into the future: "Wallenstein has greater thoughts than I; he sees in the remote future unity, where I saw only disunity" (II.ii:*GA*, p. 106; "Wallenstein har större tänkar än jag; han ser i fjärran enheten, dar jag endast såg söndringen," *GAHD*, p. 57). "That inscrutable, dark man" (IV.iv:*GA*, p. 200; "Den ogenomtränlige, den mörke mannen," *GAHD*, p. 171) functions in this play as an unseen, educative, punitive nemesis—like Albrecht of Mecklenburg in *The Saga of the Folkungs* or the mysterious Dacke in *Gustav Vasa;* but, as the quartermaster explains to the sergeant major as they struggle to get a glimpse of him through a telescope, it is not Wallenstein but the "angel of death, the one who came with the plagues of Egypt, the one who destroyed the army of the Sennacherib . . . The Lord is against us!" (V.i:*GA*, p. 204; "Det är Herrans mordängel, samma en som kom med Egyptens plågor, samma en som ödelade Sanheribs armé . . . Herren står emot oss!" *GAHD*, p. 173). God punishes both Wallenstein and Gustav Adolf for their failure to make peace.

Thus neither Wallenstein nor Gustav Adolf can be Joshuas; the plagues of Egypt beset both sides, and both heroes die without attaining the promised land. The siege of Lützen takes place in conditions that remind Stenbock of "the last of the plagues of Egypt" (V.iii:*GA*, p. 219). Apocalyptic overtones multiply; the "great darkness" comes (*GA*, p. 221), and Gustav finally offers himself up as a Christ-like sacrifice: "What's that? The three crosses? Is it Golgotha? Into thy hands I commend my spirit, Lord Jesus!" (*GA*, p. 221; "Hvad är det? De tre korsen! Det är Golgota? I dina händer befalla jag min anda, Herre Jesu!" *GAHD*, p. 194). As an agent of providence, striving towards both religious and political unity, Gustav Adolf embodies many of the beliefs that Strindberg later delineated in "Världshistoriens mystik"—especially the idea that the goal of history is a united Europe with one single Christian faith.

The trouble with *Gustav Adolf,* as with *The Saga of the Folkungs* and, later on, with *Engelbrekt* and *The Last Knight,* is the goodness of the protagonist: these pious heroes permit Strindberg to reiterate, at great length in *Gustav Adolf,* his views without, as he does in *Gustav Vasa* and *Erik XIV,* putting them to the test. Like *Wallenstein,* which it closely resembles in structure and style as well as subject matter, *Gustav Adolf* is cumbersome to stage and has usually been performed in ruthlessly trimmed versions; but the episodic, epic sweep of the play is not its gravest problem. Rather in his recognition of Sweden's hero-king as a forerunner of his own monistic ideals, Strindberg once again succumbed to the temptation to declare the aims, rather than dramatize the workings, of providence. The result is the dogmatism and repetitiveness that mar even the play's best scenes.

After *Gustav Adolf,* Strindberg abandoned historical drama for a brief period, but with no abatement in the rate of his productivity. The second group of major historical plays, written between June 1901 and March 1902, differs markedly from the plays of two years before. We no longer find an insistence on the providential scheme in *Charles XII, Engelbrekt, Christina,* and *Gustav III:* instead Strindberg toys with notions of the world as dream and the world as play that reflect his work in October and November 1901 on *A Dream Play (Ett Drömspel).* Another important influence on these plays was Strindberg's marriage to Harriet Bosse: the turbulent ups and downs of this relationship left their mark in the rapidly shifting moods of the playwright, which in turn determined the atmosphere of each play.

Strindberg had set himself down on record as an enemy of Charles XII well before and after writing a play about Sweden's most controversial king. He decided, he told the Intimate Theater, to stage "the end of a life that was a big mistake" ("slutet på ett liv som var ett stort misstag") and to portray the king less as "the man who ruined Sweden, the great criminal, the champion fighter, the idol of the ruffians, and the counterfeiter" ("Sveriges fördärvare, den store brottslingen, slagskampen, busarnes avgud, falskmyntaren") than as "a ghost who walks the earth, who is given form by the smoke of powder, and who fades away as soon as the cannons are nailed down, the cannons with which he intended to keep world history from taking its course" (*IT,* p. 259; "en gengångare, ett spöke, som är bildad av krutrök och som dunstar bort så snart kanonerna förnaglas, dessa kanoner med vilka han ämnade hindra världshistorien gå sin gång," *ÖB,* p. 251). Strindberg's idea that a conscious will directs history towards a particular goal is clear enough here; the tragedy of Charles XII is his foolish resistance to the "powers" who direct all human life.

Gunnar Ollén has pointed out how closely Charles's situation at the beginning of the play reflects Strindberg's after his experience of the "powers" in Paris. Both returned broken to Lund, men dead to this world, both received enlightenment from Swedenborg, both were notorious woman haters.[57] Choric figures—like The Man, The Woman, The Malcontent, and Luxembourg the Dwarf—function as "disciplinary spirits," chastising and tormenting the arrogant monarch. At the end of act II, Charles lies down to sleep; The Man enters, identifying himself as Dragoon Hunger (Svält), who saved his life at Krasnokutsch and showers the "villain" ("boven"), as he calls him, with grievances. Charles awakes, calls his steward, and checks the list; there was no Dragoon Hunger number fifty-eight in Taube's regiment. "Then I have been dreaming!" he exclaims, rubbing his eyes, "That was horrible!" (act II:*QC*, p. 132; "Då har jag drömt! . . . Det var fasansfullt!" *HD*, p. 168).

The confusion of dream and reality that both the audience and Charles experience at this moment, the abstract, allegorical nature of such characters as The Man, and the unifying musical motif of the saraband of Bach, "the king of the Land of Sorrows and Pain" (act III:*QC*, p. 136; "konungen i Sorgenland och Smärtarike," *HD*, p. 169) all testify to the influence of Maeterlinck on Strindberg's later plays. "Basically a mood drama," is Birgitta Steene's assessment of *Charles XII*;[58] but, as we have seen in *Mäster Olof*, symbolic settings and characters who function as emblems of Sweden's sorrows are essential aspects of Strindberg's historical dramaturgy from the first. Here they are pushed to the limit of expressiveness. The ravaged landscape of the first scene—a village destroyed by the plague just after the disaster of Poltava—gives us a visual image of what Charles has done to Sweden. The Man returns to the ruins of his cottage: "I suppose the whole country looks like this!" he observes, "A ruin, a scrap heap"—and, looking at the tree with a lone apple on it—"with a rotten apple on top." "That ought to be shaken down," agrees the Coastguard (act I:*QC*, p. 108; "Så her ser val hela riket ut! . . . En ruin, en skräphög—och et ruttet äpple i toppen. . . ." "Som borde skakas ner!" *HD*, p. 157). The apple represents Charles himself, and it has its own scriptural reference: Sweden is not merely a ruined country, but a ruined paradise. All of act IV is set in "a large garden": silent, shabby people, "horrible to look upon" (act IV:*QC*, p. 156; "hemske at åse," *HD*, p. 178), gather at the gates as Charles learns of the bankruptcy of the realm; Görst smells them, but no one on stage sees them; as the royal party leave the garden, "shabby figures steal in, silent, ghostlike, curious, and fingering everything" (*QC*, p. 158; "ruskiga figurer smyga in, tysta, spöklika, nyfikna, och fingra på allt," *HD*, p. 179). The intrusion into Charles's willed isolation of the ragged populace accompanies his fall; in act IV he is also forced to confront his greatest enemy—woman.

It is easy to dismiss Charles's confrontations with the women in his life—Emerentia, Ulrika Eleonora, Katarina—as manifestations of Strindberg's own obsessions. Charles's rejection of love is linked, however, to the main political issue in the play: the end of absolutism. The two are confused in Charles's confession to Ulrika Eleanora:

> Alla förmän kännas som despoter. De skulle så gärna vilja vara't, alla, om de fingo, om de kunde! (*Paus.*) Ja, ni kvinnor! Jag har stått utanför fönstret och sett in i hemmen, därför såg jag mer än andra, ty de som äro innanför se blott sitt.—Det ljuvaste, det bittraste!—Kärleken på ett hår lik hatet! (*Paus.*) Nu somnar jag! Sömnen det bästa! näst bästa. (*Han somnar. Sarabanden spelas i fjärran.*)
>
> (act IV:*HD*, p. 177)

> All people in power seem to be despots. They would all like to have power, all of them, if they might, if they could! (*pause*) Yes, you women! I have stood outside windows and looked into homes; that's why I saw more than others, because the ones who are inside see only their own . . . The most delightful, the most bitter! . . . Love is almost identical with hate! (*pause*) Now I shall go to sleep! Sleep, the best there is! The next best! (*He falls asleep. The saraband is played in the distance.*)
>
> (act IV:*QC*, p. 152)

This speech effects a powerful linkage between Charles's self-exclusion from domestic life—outside the window—and his status as king of a sorrowing land, evoked by the saraband played by the dwarf he has indifferently cast off. "Are you going to put your head in a lap and let her clip the hair of your strength?" he chastises Swedenborg when the mystic protests that the unfaithful Emerentia is an "angel" (act IV:*QC*, p. 155; "Skall du lägga ditt huvud i ett knä och låta klippa din styrkas hår?" *HD*, p. 178). To Charles, the choice for Swedenborg is between "a woman" on the one hand and "king and country" on the other; "Always a woman comes and takes away my best man!" he complains (*QC*, p. 155; "Alltid kommer en kvinna och tar bort min bästa man," *HD*, p. 177). The soldier-king sees everything in terms of war: his hatred of women, his mistrust of the domestic, and his obliviousness to the ghostly presences that inhabit his ruined realm all derive from the same source.

Strindberg is careful to place Charles's despotic isolation in a context that is not merely domestic or Swedish; representatives of three of the four estates—the clergyman, burgher, and peasant—rejoice when the news comes at the end of act III that Louis the XIV of France is dead. Discussing his last history play, *The Earl of Bjälbö*, Strindberg described it as his usual practice to place "Swedish history within the frame of world history" (*IT*, p. 265; "svenska historien i världshistoriens ram," *ÖB*, p. 257). We can detect this practice in the references to Luther and Francis I in *Mäster Olof*, in Jacob Israel's mention of Michelangelo in *Gustav Vasa*, and in Erik XIV's protracted courtship of Queen Elizabeth, but it is in the later history plays that Strindberg came regularly to insist upon mention of parallel developments in other countries. For, as he pointed out in "Världshistoriens mystik," it is through observing similar developments in different parts of the world that we can guess at the purposes of history's divine hand. Thus the death of Louis XIV and the fall of Charles XII, coinciding as they do, signal the end of absolutism; but the leaders in the play, ignoring such signs and the choric voice of the people, fail to understand. "Absolutism isn't so bad, if it only gets into the right hands, eh?" suggest Gyllenborg near the end of the play (act v:*QC*, p. 161; "Enväldet är icke så dåligt, bara det kommer i rätter händer! Va?" *HD*, p. 181). Even the people realize that the end of absolutism will not lead to any real change: "Then there'll be Tuesday soup," says the dwarf, "the same as on Sunday, but with a little more water added, without butter!" (act III:*QC*, p. 140; "Så blir det tisdagssoppa, samm som på söndan, men med lite mera vatten, utan smör!" *HD*, p. 172). Providence moves, as in *Erik XIV*, in what appear to the characters to be fits and starts.

"Life is like that; what can death be like?" asks the king of Swedenborg after he learns that the dwarf, whom he has not dismissed but merely forgotten about, has been spreading slanders (act v:*QC*, p. 163; "Sådant är livet; hurudan är döden?" *HD*, p. 182). "Nature is consistent!" replies the mystic ("Natur gör inga språng!"); and Strindberg stages Charles's death as an enigma, a riddle defying solution. As the king kneels up in the trench, Swedenborg and Feif discuss him: "Have you ever understood his destiny?" asks Feif; "No, and we'll probably never understand it! I have never understood *one* human destiny, not even my own insignificant one" (act v:*QC*, p. 165; "Har du förstått hans öde någonsin?" "Nej, och vi får icke förstå't kanske! Jag har aldrig förstått *ett* människoöde, icke ens mitt obetydliga," *HD*, p. 183). The source of the shot that kills Charles just after Swedenborg tells Feif that Charles is already a dead man is a historical riddle; Strindberg makes the dilemma a religious one as well. The bullet came "from up *there*," says Swedenborg pointing to heaven; "Let us believe that!" agrees Feif. "And if it didn't, it should have come from there," is Swedenborg's melancholy conclusion, as the play ends in confusion and darkness (*QC*, pp. 165–66; *"Där* uppifrån!" "Låt oss tro det!" "Och kom den inte därifrån, så borde den ha kommit därifrån!" *HD*, p. 183).

But after the darkness and before the curtain falls, "finally a large lantern can be seen up in the trench." ("Men nu synes en stor lykta uppa i löpgraven.") If, as Charles says as he wads the scandalous letters, "The whole world is like this ball, a web of lies, mistakes, misunderstandings!" (*QC*, p. 163; "Hela livet är som denna boll, en väv av lögner, misstag, missförstånd!" *HD*, p. 182), the light at the end and the coincidence of Louis's death are glimmers of a higher order with which, like the daughter of Indra in *A Dream Play*, we can only be reunited after the purification of death.

Strindberg's deployment of the phantasmagoric staging effects of *A Dream Play* and *To Damascus* in *Charles XII* is a radical change from his usual practice of dramatizing history with scrupulous naturalism. The procession of flagellants in *The Saga of the Folkungs* and the beggar's banquet in *Erik XIV*, while eerie in effect and symbolic in import, are nonetheless grounded in historical truth; the same cannot be said for the ghostly presences who enter Charles's garden or for the purely allegorical presences, like The Man and The Malcontent, who dog Charles's steps throughout the play. The confrontation between Strindberg's continuing interest in history and the insight, recorded in his diary the day he finished *A Dream Play* (18 November 1901), that "The whole world is but a semblance (= Humbug or relative emptiness),"[59] pushes *Charles XII* towards the severe questioning of the value of historical truth that we have seen in Shakespeare and Ford. The shot and the light at the end of the play leave us stretched out between the twin poles of the unknowability of providence and the unreliability of fact.

Despite his continued obsession with life as an illusion, Strindberg never repeated the radical experiment of *Charles XII*; it was left to Pirandello to pose the conundrum of history's illusive truth in *Henry IV*. Strindberg's next historical play, *Engelbrekt*, failed in its premier performance at the Svenska Teater 3 December 1901 and has been roughly used by critics ever since. Again the problem is the pious protagonist; "Engelbrekt is one of Sweden's most beautiful memories, and I felt I should keep his character as high and as pure as Schiller had kept his William Tell," was Strindberg's explanation to the Intimate Theater (*IT*, p. 253; "Engelbrekt är ett av Sveriges vackraste minner, och jag ansåg mig böra hålla karaktären så hogt och så rent som Schiller gjort med sin Vilhelm

Tell," *ÖB*, p. 245). Like *Wilhelm Tell, Engelbrekt* is more a folk play than a fully realized historical drama.[60] Following what had become his regular practice, Strindberg draws attention to parallel European developments in this play as well, and the national liberator whose rise and fall coincide with Engelbrekt's is, not surprisingly, Joan of Arc. The newly revived debates about Scandinavian union at the turn of the century provided *Engelbrekt* with some topicality; Strindberg asserted, "I had the right to make his wife a Dane" in the absence of evidence to the contrary, "which I thought was a very fine device for making the disunity concrete" (*IT*, p. 255; "hade jag rättighet gifta honom med en Danska, vilket jag ansåg vara ett mycket gott grepp såsom förkroppsligande det nationella splitet," *ÖB*, p. 246). His enthusiasm for this "Brutus the Elder, but with a plus" ("Brutus der äldre, med men ett plus") is, however, not contagious.

The naive, episodic *Engelbrekt* celebrates a national hero; *Christina*, on the other hand, is a vigorous debunking. Strindberg preferred the scandalous gossip about Queen Christina that he found in his popular sources to more sober accounts; in "The Impossibility of Writing History," he fulminated against whitewashing, declaring it absolutely certain that "Charles XII was mad, and Christina a — — —."[61] Thus it is no surprise that the play depicts her reign as a series of love affairs. In the first scene, before the tomb of the great Gustav Adolf and on the anniversary of his death, she selects a new lover, Klaus Tott, and discards the old one, Magnus de la Gardie. She treats people like dolls—"Exactly! Big dolls!" (act I:*QC*, p. 30; "Just det! Stora dockor!" *HD*, p. 220) she agrees with Magnus—oblivious to a background of peril summed up in the presence of Whitelocke, Cromwell's ambassador. Christina's irresponsibility takes on European overtones: "No one will murder me! Everybody loves me!" she tells de la Gardie. "You know, Charles I of England said exactly the same thing!" he replies, "amazed" (*QC*, p. 30; "Inte mordar någon mig! *Alles liebt mich!*" "Vet du att Karl den förste i England sade precis detsamma?" *HD*, p. 220). Christina's lapse into German here (in the original, not in Johnson's translation) as she reckons her popularity in Sweden forces us to make a connection between her heartless, manipulative love affairs and her exploitation of the Swedish treasury. "I have never felt that I was Swedish," she cries, justifying her expropriations to Carl Gustav at the end of the play, "and I have hated Sweden as my mother hated it!" (act IV:*QC*, p. 78; "Jag har aldrig känt mig som svenska, och jag har hatat Sverige som min mor har gjort det," *HD*, p. 240). But Carl Gustav has to wonder, as all her lovers have wondered before: "Have you had any meaning in your meaningless actions, or are you improvising?" (*QC*, p. 78; "Har du verkligen haft någon mening med din meningslösa framfart, eller improviserar du?" *HD*, p. 240). Her unmasking herself as a German "nemesis" (p. 77; p. 240) avenging the depradations of the Thirty Years' War—like her costuming of herself as Pandora at the beginning of the last act—is self-consciously theatrical in the extreme.

The vision of Christina as a coquettish, cruel "Bohemian cabaret artiste" has less to do with the gossipy sources that Strindberg enjoyed reading than with his troubled relationship with Harriet Bosse. As Gunnar Ollén puts it, Strindberg wrote the role of Christina not only *for* Harriet Bosse, but also *about* Harriet Bosse.[62] Thus the charges that her lovers direct at her fecklessness take on an edge of savage bitterness. "Just wait, you'll find out . . . yes, you will . . . as everybody does who plays with a force of nature, a creative force that has its source at the roots of the tree of life" (act III:*QC*, p. 49; "Vänta en gång får du känna . . . Ja, det får du, du som alla, vilka lekt med naturkraft, skaparmakten, som her sina källor vid världsträdets rötter," *HD*, p. 228). Her youngest lover, Klaus Tott, is more severe: "Whore, you mean!" he cries when she calls herself his "queen of hearts," (act IV:*QC*, p. 73; "Din hjärtens dam! Skäka, menar du?" *HD*, p. 238). Oxenstjerna, the elderly chancellor, is more forgiving: "You are like an artist—just as careless, just as carefree, just as thoughtless" (act III:*QC*, p. 62; "Du är så lik en konstnär, en artist . . . lika slarvig, lika sorglös, lättsinnig," *HD*, p. 233). While Strindberg dramatized his conflicting attitudes to Harriet Bosse in the different men of the play, he also made it clear that she should play the role: Christina's affectation of childish helplessness, her ready slipping into the role of "little Kerstin," is tailored to the gifts of the tiny Bosse—not to those of the tall, mannish Queen Christina of history or of Manda Björling, who eventually came to play the role in the premiere at the Intimate Theater in 1908. Bosse finally took the part in 1926, at the Lorensbergsteater in Göteborg, dazzling the critic Birger Baeckström with her display of female "diableri."[63]

The idea that Christina should be characterized as a feckless player-queen based upon Strindberg's not-so-feckless player-wife is at the heart of the play's highly reflexive theatricality. As the realm crumbles about her, Christina worries lest her abdication interfere with her ballet: forced to cancel it because of unrest in the streets, she nonetheless appears in her Pandora costume in the final act. She self-consciously plays out the role of bearer of the box, sending de la Gardie first to Bourdelot with a ring inscribed, "Not without hope," and then back home—as he puts it, to "my wife . . . my vulture, and let her hack at my liver," (act IV:*QC*, p. 68; "Icke utan allt hopp!" "—till min—maka—min gam och låta hacka min lever," *HD*, p. 236). If Magnus plays the role of Prometheus here, Klaus Tott, cast in the part by Christina, offers a symbolic reading of Epimetheus: "You have soiled my soul that I gave into your keeping . . . you have brought me into a whirlpool of unknown desires . . . you have led my thoughts into paths they must not go . . . and to break off I must kill my body to release my spirit into purer air," (act IV:*QC*, p. 75; "du har orenat min själ, som jag nedlade hos dig . . . du har infört mig i en virvel av okända begär . . . du har lett mina tänkar in i banor dit de icke få gå . . . Och för att avbryta förbindelsen med dessa lägre regioner måste jag döda min kropp och släppa ut anden in renare lufter," *HD*, p. 238). This interpretation of the myth is highly Strindbergian—perhaps too Strindbergian, as Martin Lamm complained of the whole play. As he leaves her, Tott corrects Christina's version of the story: "You said, 'faithful' hope, but in the story it says 'false' hope" (*QC*, p. 75; "Du sade det 'trofasta' hoppet, men i texten står det 'bedrägliga' hoppet!" *HD*, p. 239). The box contains nothing but tricks. And Christina's *Masque of Pandora* is a debacle: as the wall opens at her command, "One sees instead of the expected tableau a crowd of strange people, all of them motionless, silent, pale-faced" (*QC*, p. 72, "Man ser i stället för den väntade tablån—en skara underligt folk, alla orörliga, tysta, bleka i ansiktet," *HD*, p. 238). Whitelocke, watching from the musicians' gallery, makes the connection clear between Christina's world of games and court entertainments and Charles I's world of masques.

"That she did not want to get married I think natural," said Strindberg of Christina, "and that she who had played with love was caught in her own net is, of course, highly dramatic" (*IT*, p. 258; "Att hon icke ville gifta sig finner jag naturligt, och att hon som lekt med kärleken blir fast i sina egna garn är ju högst dramatiskt," *ÖB*, p. 250). Throughout *Christina* Strindberg deploys puns on the words *kärlek* ("love") and *leka* ("to play").[64] "Do you think she's playing with me?" Klaus Tott asks Magnus de la Gardie (act III:*QC*, p. 46; "Tror du hon leker med mig?"). "Playing?" comes the answer, "Can a woman do anything else? Why, love is a game!" ("Leker. Kan en kvinna göra annat? Kär*leken* är vel en lek!" p. 226; emphasis in the original). The games Christina plays isolate her not only from her suffering people, but from the suffering she inflicts upon the very real passions of her lovers. Like Charles XII at the window, she views love from a cold remove. Her outburst of pro-German, anti-Swedish bitterness at the end of the play reveals a defensive reason behind her game playing.

Christina, finally, is no longer playing games. Recognizing and expressing the self-hatred that led her to play Nemesis, she agrees with

Carl Gustav that she may have found Sweden "too limited" (act IV:*QC*, p. 78; "för trångt," *HD*, p. 240); where she goes next concerns "no mortal" ("ingen annan dödlig"). Christina's withdrawal from the world of love games into her "forefather's faith" (*QC*, p. 79; "sina faders tro," *HD*, p. 241) is a kind of transcendence. In the first scene of the play she disgraces the tomb of her father by coquetting with Tott on the anniversary of his death; in the last scene, she shames Oxenstjerna and Carl Gustav by invoking his memory. She answers the counselor's menacing questions about rumors of her conversion angrily: "Are you threatening me? Then I appeal to the spirit of my great father; I, too, for he gave his life, not for a faith forced upon anyone, but for freedom of faith, for tolerance!" (*QC*, p. 80; "Hotar ni? Då vädjar jag till min store faders ande, jag också, ty han gav sitt liv, icke för trostvång, utan för trosfrihet, för tolerans!" *HD*, p. 241). The two bow their heads and cannot reply.

The emergence of the "real" Christina, German and Catholic, is the end towards which all the playacting leads; but in Strindberg's next play, *Gustav III*, role and monarch wholly fuse. The historical Gustav III was a playwright as well as the author of far-reaching social and cultural reforms; he had to his credit (in collaboration with the poet Kellgren) a *Gustav Vasa* and a *Drottning Christina*. Strindberg, therefore, makes this monarch the consummate player: at the mirror in the audience room in act II, he adjusts his appearance and demeanor to suit each new arrival. "The exit was not quite as happy as the entrance!" is Pechlin's review of the king's dramatic interruption of the conspirators' meeting in act III, "But that happens to even the best of actors!" (act III:*QC*, p. 242; "Sortien var icke like lycklig som entrén! Men sådant händer de största skådespelare!" *HD*, p. 266). The elaborate interlocking intrigues that make up the plot of the play are blatantly theatrical as well: Lamm was the first but not the last to see in the arch dialogue and arbitrary turns of plot an influence of the historical comedies of Scribe.[65] In Gustav's court, the game is not love but revolution.

To Strindberg, Gustav III was a topsy-turvy figure: "full of contradictions, a tragedian who plays comedy in life, a hero and a dancing master, an absolute monarch who is a friend of liberty, a man who strives for humanitarian reforms, a disciple of Frederick the Great, Joseph II and Voltaire" (*IT*, p. 259; "full av motsägelser, en tragiker som spelar komedi i livet, en hjälte och en dansmästare, en envädig frihetsvän, en humanitetssträvare, en Frekrik den Stores, Josef II:s och Voltaires lärling" *ÖB*, p. 250). The context that Strindberg provides for these paradoxes is one of rushing, breathless social change, of news and new ideas, epitomized in the first act by the bustling activity at the Holmberg bookstore. "Has the paper come?" are the first words of the play, as Papillon, the news-hungry valet of the king, hastens into the shop (act I:*QC*, p. 193). Rumors from all over the world fill the air, some true (the French estates are meeting in Paris; Washington has been elected president) some not (the king is imprisoned and about to be deposed). As a kind of talisman presiding over this riot of information is Gustav III's law of freedom of the press; but Voltaire's praise of this statute, Holmberg reminds Horn, "didn't prevent his Majesty from having Halldin here condemned to death, because he wrote against the liquor law. And he had me in jail for fourteen days on bread and water because I printed the article" (act I:*QC*, pp. 194–95; "icke hindrade högstdensamme att låta döma Halldin där till döden, därför att han skrev mot brännvinet, och han lät mig sitta fjorton dar på vatten och bröd förr att jag tryckt skriften," *HD*, pp. 245–46). The juxtaposition of the "old" law (which Gustav later limited) to new repressions and the rumors of the king's imprisonment that as the act continues give way to clearer knowledge of his victory over the Anjala conspiracy evoke about Gustav III a world of paradox and confusion.

These paradoxes build to a climax in the final act, Gustav's fête champêtre at Drottningholm. Here the king—who earlier in his revolution of 1772 "played Brutus and destroyed the Caesars in homespun" (act II:*QC*, p. 232; "spelade Brutus och störtade vadmals-Caesarna," *HD*, p. 262)—finds himself cast in the role of Caesar. Lady Schröderheim, costumed as the fury Megara, warns him: "Oh, great Caesar, beware the Ides of Mars!" (act IV:*QC*, p. 248; "O, store Caesar, akta dig för Idus Martii," *HD*, p. 269). In the final scene, as the assassin Anckarström, hiding in the closet, fails in his objective because the queen enters by chance, Gustav senses his escape from danger: "I was born with a caul and with Caesar's luck," he muses, (act IV:*QC*, p. 265; "Jag är född med segerhuva och med Caesars lycka," *HD*, p. 276). "Caesar's luck," ventures the queen, "Wasn't there someone called Brutus?" ("Caesars lycka . . . var det inte någon som hette Brutus?") As Anckarström lurks in the background, the king applauds with delight. Strindberg leaves it to his audience to recall that the historical Gustav III was assassinated at a masked ball 16 March 1792; he himself observed with some satisfaction that he finished writing the play on the 110th anniversary of this event.[66]

But the identification with Caesar is double-edged: for if Gustav is the tyrant Julius Caesar to the conspirators, he is also Caesar Augustus. "Soyons amis, Cinna, c'est moi qui t'en convie" ("Let us be friends, Cinna; it is I who ask it of you," act III:*QC*, p. 241), he says to Pechlin at Huvudsta, lapsing into the role of Corneille's Auguste. Corneille's play *Cinna* deals with Auguste's unveiling of an assassination plot against him, and is full of paradoxes and antithetical turns of phrase and argument in its discussion of tyrannicide. The fête champêtre to which Gustav, playing Auguste, invites Pechlin's Cinna, is thus identified with the sacrifice at the Capitol: "Tu veux m'assassiner demain, au Capitole," says Corneille's Auguste later in the scene from which Gustav takes his lines (v.i.). At the party itself, Gustav greets Bellman as Horace; "Augustus!" replies the poet.

It is fitting that Gustav's linkage with the Caesars should be literary as well as historical, that the actor-king should play parts written by both Shakespeare and Corneille. But Gustav's playacting takes place against a backdrop of European politics, as the first scene emphasizes and as the arrival of the news of the fall of the Bastille at the party in act IV hammers home. "And that's why my guests are celebrating, in my Versailles?" asks Gustav as he learns of the capture of the French king (act IV:*QC*, p. 253; "Och det är därför mina gästa jubla, i mitt Versailles?" *HD*, p. 271). The coincidence of this fall of an absolute monarch with Gustav's schemes to reintroduce absolutism leads Armfelt to exclaim, "What a paradox! What a trick!" (p. 253; "Vilken paradox! Vilken skälmstycke!" p. 271) but the ultimate paradox resides in the audience's knowledge that the Caesar Gustav plays will turn out to be Shakespeare's, not Corneille's.

In addition to evoking this rich historical and literary context for *Gustav III,* Strindberg deploys his usual technique of staging the problems of the realm in domestic terms. Gustav analogizes his difficulties establishing dominion over his Danish wife to the problem of suppressing Danish influence in the kingdom. Schröderheim thinks that the king is referring to these troubles when he suggests that ill-matched couples should divorce; tricked by Gustav into divorcing his wife, he ends the play in misery, as she does. The implied parallel between the Schröderheim marriage and the king's marriage leads also to paradox: Lady Schröderheim realizes that her wit and beauty resided only in the flattery of men and ends her part in the play "unmasked . . . because the comedy is over, and no one applauds" (act IV:*QC*, p. 259; "demaskerad— ty, komedin är slut; och ingen applåderer," *HD*, p. 273). But it will be Gustav's fate to die with his mask on.

The proliferation of parts that the king plays—the two Caesars, Gustav Vasa (when he gathers an army of dalesmen to expel the Danes), Isaac to Jakob Anckarström's Esau—finally confounds him. Fersen and deGeer discuss the constant masquerade of court life; the king learned to lie early, as a child, Fersen explains, "since then he has lied so much he doesn't know who he is himself" (act IV:*QC*, p. 260; "Och sen har han så ljugit bort sig att han vet inte själv vem han är," *HD*, p. 274). Unlike

Christina, who stops playing games at the end of her play, Gustav goes on playing. "The queen is the strongest piece in the game and has the function of protecting the king" (act IV:*QC*, p. 265; "Drottningen är den starkaste pjäsen i spelet och har till uppgift att skydda kungen," *HD*, p. 276), he jokes. The remark is particularly ironic because throughout the final moments of the play Anckarström has been prevented from shooting him because the queen has stepped into the line of fire: Gustav, the player-king, spends his final moments on stage moving in and out of danger in a way that specifically, visually, suggests the final moves in a game of chess. Anckarström's face at the window reminds us that the last move, which we will not see staged, must be checkmate.

The extreme reflexivity and self-consciousness of *Christina* and *Gustav III* reflect not only the artificiality of the courts of these monarchs but also a change of attitude towards history on Strindberg's part. The providential model that informed *Gustav Vasa* and *Erik XIV* has given way to a vision of history as a game—a vision Strindberg worked his way toward in these last two plays and described explicitly in "Världshistoriens Mystik," a year later. For the tragic uncertainty about the relationship between hero and providence that animates the earlier plays, Strindberg came to substitute a basically comic vision. "History can look grim," he wrote, "but we, who see the beginning of a happy ending, know that it's not" ("Historien kan se grym ut, men är det icke det veta vi nu, som sett början till ett gott slut").[67] The second *Blue Book* (1908) dismisses all recorded history as a pack of lies in contrast to the reliability of science or of revealed truth. "People who study are stupid" ("Dum är den som studerar!") Strindberg pronounced in a brief essay entitled "Lie-history" ("Lögn-historia"); by ridiculing the historian's claim to be able to distinguish fact from falsehood, Strindberg effected a complete rejection of history's claim to any kind of truth. Pragmatic history, as he called it, is so shot through with biases—political or religious—as to be utterly worthless. Citing Gustav Vasa's suppression of Mäster Olof's Swedish history he cries:

> . . . svenska konungarne gjorde som Assyriens och Babyloniens: De forgudade sig! Då frågar man sig: Hvad tjänar då till att skrifva historia och att läsa den?[68]
>
> . . . Swedish kings did the same as the Assyrians and Babylonians—they made themselves into gods! So ask yourself: what purpose does it serve to write history or read it?

The curious combination of mystic faith and flippant skepticism that we find in the *Blue Books* appears also in "Världshistoriens mystik" and in the plays it inspired.

The Nightingale of Wittenberg is the most important of these world historical dramas, and it dramatizes an example that figures importantly in "Världshistoriens Mystik"—that of Martin Luther, "Germany's strongest throat"—as a man of providence ("forsynens man," p. 365). Like the essay, the play insists upon the importance of the connections between events that reveal the hand of God in history: Doctor Faustus brings news to the young Luther boys of the discovery of a whole new world. The year is 1492; the parallel event, again, provides a metaphor that dominates the rest of the play. "My best, most beautiful, and perhaps my last drama!" enthused Strindberg; but critical consensus has tended to agree with Martin Lamm, who noted the play's "dizzying proximity to parody."[69]

The other world historical plays—devoted to Moses, Socrates, and Christ—lack even the comic vitality of the *Nightingale of Wittenberg*. The first, *Through Deserts to Ancestral Lands,* is an achievement on the order of a Sunday school pageant; *Hellas* offers domestic disputes between Socrates and Xanthippe as well as scenes in which Cartaphilus (a Jewish shoemaker) and Lucillus (a Roman) discuss whether Israel or Rome has been given the kingdom of the future. Characters with the same names recur in *The Lamb and the Beast* and discuss the messianic claims of the Galilean and the fall of Rome. The utterly pedestrian, wholly mechanical dramaturgy of these plays is not merely attributable to Strindberg's usual ups and downs. The history plays written between 1899 and 1902 reflected the playwright's groping towards a comprehensive theory of world history; but the theory that he arrived at in "Världshistoriens Mystik" is one that stifles drama. While the theory of correspondences upon which the essay is based lends lively resonance to Strindberg's best historical plays, the conclusion that history can best be understood as a "colossal chess-game with a solitary player" reduces all human activity to triviality. Thus the game and play motifs in *Christina* and *Gustav III* suggest the total illusiveness of action, and Charles XII stumbles somnambulistically through a world of dreams before being struck down from above. Questioning of providence's purposes, and constant tension between human and divine ideas of justice, set *Mäster Olof, Gustav Vasa,* and *Erik XIV* apart from this later group of plays. In *Charles XII, Christina,* and *Gustav III* we encounter instead innovative and energetic theatrical experimentation, a lively, wholly modern engagement of the Renaissance riddle of the world as theater and as dream.

Gustav III pushes reflexivity to its limits; in light of this play's final image of life as a game and of Strindberg's failure to bring his theories to life in the world historical plays, the playwright's decision to complete his cycle of Swedish history plays in 1908 is surprising. Not surprising is

the static, episodic quality of these late plays. Preparations for the celebration of Strindberg's sixtieth birthday reminded him of the great
theatrical success of *Gustav Vasa* ten years before, and in *The Last Knight*
and *The Regent* he sought to dramatize the fall of Sten Sture and the rise
of Gustav—events immediately preceding those dramatized in *Mäster
Olof*.[70] Just as these plays complete a cycle by leading into Strindberg's
first major work, so too does Strindberg's last historical play, *The Earl of
Bjälbö*, which takes us back to the very beginnings of the Folkung dynas-
ty. *The Last Knight* and *The Regent* are companion pieces: Strindberg
pointed out in a note to *The Regent* that this play mirrors the other in its
settings. The effect, as he describes it, is a kind of counterpoint:

> Samma sceneri som i "Sista riddaren", men i omvänd
> ordning. Denna från musiken lånade kontrapunktistiska
> form, vilken jag begagnat i Damaskus I, medför den effekt,
> att hos ahöroraren väckas minnen från de olika lokalerna, där
> de förut spelats, och därigenom verkar dramat såsom
> passerande langt fram i livet med mycket bakom sig;
> ackumlerade förnimmelser stå upp, ekon från bättre tider
> genljuda, mannaålderns hårda allvar står fram, de slagne
> räknas, krossade förhoppningar erinras, och dramat "Siste
> Riddaren" står som ungdomsagan till Rikesförestandarens
> tunga kämpadat.
>
> (*HD*, p. 313)

> The same settings as in *The Last of the Knights*, but in reverse
> order. This contrapuntal form which I have borrowed from
> music and used in *To Damascus I* has the effect of awakening
> in the theatergoer memories of the various places in which
> earlier actions took place, and thereby the drama has the
> effect of happening much later in life with a great deal
> behind it; accumulated impressions arise; there are echoes
> from better times; the hard reality of maturity dominates;
> the defeated are counted; crushed hopes are recalled, and the
> drama of *The Last of the Knights* serves as the saga of youth
> in contrast to the heavy struggle of *The Regent*.
>
> (*LK*, p. 99)

Thus, the "symmetrical repetition" of *To Damascus*—"The simplest
form of construction," according to Luciano Codignola[71]—offers what
promises to be a rewarding perspective from which to view the process of
historical change. But the plays themselves do not fulfill this promise:
Sten Sture is another Magnus the Good, another Engelbrekt. His mo-
notonous goodness in the face of betrayal and persecution draws neither

admiration nor pity. And in *The Regent*, Strindberg's portrayal of Gustav Eriksson (later to become Gustav I Vasa) lively as it is, suffers from an overabundance of patriotic enthusiasm and hero worship. "Good brass music," was Martin Lamm's judgment of this last, and it still stands.[72]

As grim and misanthropic as Strindberg's *Blue Book* pronouncements about the futility of history is *Earl Birger of Bjälbö*, his last history play. Strindberg justified at length the liberties he took with his sources in this play: to Birgitta Steene, his remarks to the Intimate Theater "suggest to what an extent the historical drama had become sheer routine for him." For Gunnar Ollén, the last history plays fail because of Strindberg's lack of identification with his protagonists; Lamm, however, sees in the humbling of the arrogant Earl Birger by the powers yet another Strindbergian self-portrait.[73] Whatever the cause, weariness and fatigue color this play from its opening scene—in "dull, gloomy weather" (act I:*LK*, p. 185; "Gråväder, halvskumt," *HD*, p. 339)—on All Souls' Day to its final scene in the Earl's study, "dark and cold" (act v:*LK*, p. 239; "mörk och kall," *HD*, p. 362). In keeping with custom, the holiday with which Strindberg opens the play epitomizes its situation: his usefulness spent, the earl is a walking dead man. "You're done, Birger," says Ivar Blå as he outfoxes the old man, "and you'll destroy your beautiful story if you keep at it" (act v:*LK*, p. 241; "Du är slut, och du förstör din vackra historia om du går på!" *HD*, p. 363). He suggests retirement, and as Birger's son Magnus abolishes his father's position, the former earl comes to agree: "My saga is over," he cries, learning of Karl Folkung's death and forgiveness:

> Jag är trött, på alltsammans; och nu går jag—jag far till Visingö!—jag skall gå på skogen, se på sjön, tänka över vad jag levat, söka försoningen med det förflutna och berede mig till det kommande!
>
> (act v:*HD*, p. 365)

> I am tired of everything, and now I'll go—I'll go to Visingö. I'll walk in the forest, look at the lake, think about what I have lived through, try to be reconciled with the past and prepare myself for what is ahead.
>
> (act v:*LK*, p. 246)

The earl's retirement to an island in the center of Lake Vättern figures Strindberg's periodic retreats to the Stockholm archipelago and provides a fitting epilogue to his prolific struggle with history.

Like the dramatists before him, Strindberg had to confront the exclusive claim to custodianship of the past made by the well-established, highly secular discipline of history. Despite its young author's lip service to Buckle's pseudoscientific positivism in his account in *The Red Room* of the genesis of *Mäster Olof,* even this early play reveals, in its use of biblical and historical parallels, the dissatisfaction that would plunge Strindberg into his Inferno crisis twenty years later. Strindberg's subsequent achievement in historical drama was made possible by his embrace— sometimes an uncomfortable one—of a medievalized providentialism that insisted that past events revealed the record of the hand of God. This sense of overriding purpose—working in tandem with Strindberg's desire to depict the great ones of the past as flawed, inconsistent, "charac- terless" people and to provide them with vigorous, colloquial dramatic speech devoid of archaisms—makes his greatest history plays collisions of modern and antique ways of looking at people and looking at the past. Strindberg shares with Shakespeare an endorsement of the medieval model that is nonetheless conscious of its obsolescence. Schiller's prob- lems with astrology show how radical Strindberg's solution to the di- lemma of historical drama in the modern age was.

Wallenstein intrigues us primarily as a cipher, as an embodiment of the failure of history to know or judge human behavior in any mean- ingful way. So too, as we shall see, do the Danton of Büchner's *Danton's Death* and the Lorenzo of Musset's *Lorenzaccio.* The questions Wallen- stein asks, like those of Lorenzo and Danton, go unanswered; no divine hand shapes his destiny. His obsession with fate, with the stars, is a despairing denial of a constantly threatening shapelessness. Strindberg's denial of the apparent randomness of life is not despairing but absolute. Convinced by his readings of world history that a divine hand ordered human affairs, Strindberg could dismiss the apparent inconsistencies and incoherences of fact as mere appearances, or, more vigorously, as lies.

The peril in Strindberg's closed system—as in Schiller's idealism— is solipsism. The play worlds of *Christina* and *Gustav III* are almost completely self-referential; the victories of Thekla and Max are stated, not dramatized. To confute our sense that life in Strindberg's last histo- ries is only a game, we have the playwright's assertion that a supernatural player manipulates the pieces to some higher purpose; Schiller demands that we put Wallenstein into a proper evolutionary perspective. The playwrights' assertions of philosophical or religious systems are not easy to endorse. Strindberg's finest history plays—*Mäster Olof, Gustav Vasa, Erik XIV,* and *Charles XII*—are those that, like *Wallenstein,* subject to rigorous questioning the very act of making assertions about the ways we can hope to understand the past.

5

The Revolution of the Times

MUSSET, BÜCHNER, AND BRECHT

Schiller and Strindberg found philosophical and religious structures that, for them, redeemed human action from the appearance of mere inconsequentiality. These structures are highly personal repudiations of the discipline of history, especially, in Strindberg's case, of history's development into a "pragmatic" science. Over the nineteenth century, historical research had come to enjoy enormous prestige and authority, authority that Strindberg, from his cosmic perspective, was able to mock. Other dramatists accepted history's overriding secularism and looked at the past without imposing a cosmic frame: three of them are Alfred de Musset, Georg Büchner, and Bertolt Brecht. All three engage, in their historical dramas, the idea of revolution, but they do so in radically different ways. History baffles Musset: his *Lorenzaccio* depicts an assassination that fails to effect any kind of change—political, moral, or even aesthetic. Büchner was, like Musset, disappointed by the failure of the Revolution of 1830, but the notorious fatalism of *Danton's Death* derives equally from the inhumanity of history itself. While studying the sources of his play, Büchner wrote to his fiancée, "Ich fühlte mich wie zernichtet unter dem grässlichen Fatalismus der Geschichte" ("I felt as though crushed by the horrible fatalism of history").[1] Words from this letter found their way into the mouth of Danton himself in the play. Musset altered history to give his Lorenzo a particularly ignominious death in the Venetian lagoon; Büchner's Danton mounts the steps of the guillotine into an abstract, but no less terrifying, void. In this context, Brecht's Utopian optimism may seem jarringly out of place. But unlike Schiller and Strindberg, and like Musset and Büchner, Brecht is remorselessly secular about history. His whole theoretical assault upon "culinary theater" has as its goal awakening the modern audience's awareness of themselves as participants in large historical processes. Revolution, in *Lorenzaccio*, is simply that: a turning of the wheel, a return to the status quo. For Büchner, the Revolution is a bloody juggernaut following implacable natural laws. Brecht aspires to nothing less than the revolutionary transformation of his whole audience into dialecticians, detached observers, scientists smoking cigars.

The Life of Galileo offers a fitting endpoint for this study because, as Brecht seldom tired of pointing out, it is formally a traditional history play.[2] As Shakespeare does, Brecht forces his audience to ponder the nature of historical understanding; like Francis Bacon, the humanist historian whom Brecht so admired that he modeled his greatest theoretical work on Bacon's *Novum Organum*, Brecht insists in *The Life of Galileo* on the immediate, practical utility of the lessons the present can draw from the past. *Verfremdung*, the key theatrical strategy in Brecht's technical repertoire, is a process of provoking historical perceptions in the audience: "Alienation thus means historicization, that means presenting events and persons as historical, and therefore as ephemeral" ("Verfremden heisst also historisieren, heisst Vorgänge und Personen als historisch, also als vergänglich darstellen").[3] What fills Musset and Büchner with horror becomes the linchpin of Brecht's dramatic historiography: the individual's emphemerality, his insignificance before the scientifically deducible and relentless "laws" of history, becomes cause for Utopian hope.[4]

The laws are of course Marxist; like Schiller and Strindberg, Brecht has a system. But where they belittle and deride mere historical understanding, Brecht paradoxically celebrates history's belittlement of individual agency. The paradox is nowhere clearer than in *The Life of Galileo*, where the classic issues of "times" and "men" are raised with a clarity even Ben Jonson would admire. The questions about human agency contained in this old debate agitate Musset and Büchner also; enemies, like Brecht, of the operatic, "culinary" theater of their age, both sought to create, in their armchair dramas—neither *Lorenzaccio* nor *Danton's Death* was written with performance in mind—an ambience in which readers would seriously engage history's basic problems. By insisting on a reintegration of the theater's traditional functions of entertainment and instruction, Brecht repudiated the conventions of armchair theater as brusquely as he flouted those of commercial opera house and playhouse. For Musset and Büchner, however, as for their doomed protagonists, there seemed to be no other choice.

i

After the failure of his *Nuits Vénitiennes* at the Odéon in December 1830, Alfred de Musset, then twenty years old, bade farewell to the "ménagerie" of the theater, "pour toujours."[5] Yet he continued writing plays, which appeared from 1832 on in the various volumes of *Armchair Theater* (*Un spectacle dans un fauteuil*); the first volume of the second book, published in 1834, contained the most remarkable specimen of the French Romantic drama, *Lorenzaccio*. What Victor Hugo in his manifestoes, Ludovic Vitet in his resolutely untheatrical *scènes historiques,* and Benjamin Constant in his polemic *Quelques réflexions sur la tragédie de Wallenstein* (1809) had demanded in the war against classicism appeared most fully realized in a play not designed for the stage.[6] Episodic in construction, entailing the development of three complementary plots, featuring large, spectacular crowd scenes in which comic and serious, high and low style mingle, unified throughout by a language charged with metaphor, *Lorenzaccio* is not only "Shakespearean" in Stendhal's limited sense but also reminiscent of the original.[7] While *Wallenstein* was first performed as an important theatrical event in the renovated Weimar theater, *Lorenzaccio* was not performed until 1896, when Sarah Bernhardt created the title role: with a few provincial exceptions, from then until 1952 the part of Lorenzo was traditionally played by an actress. Gérard Philipe, at the Théâtre Nationale Populaire in Avignon in that year, directed and acted the part in a production that sought to restore to the play its political significance and to Lorenzo his masculinity.

The strange stage history of the play suggests its fundamental challenge both to French classical dramaturgy and to the grandiose aspirations of the Romantic drama. The duplicity of Lorenzo—his affectation of effeminacy and debauchery, on the one hand, and the heroic liberalism of his desire to be a "modern Brutus," on the other—is directly experienced by the audience, rather than explained by the dramatist. Thus our first glimpse of Lorenzo pimping for his cousin the duke in the first scene of the play is not explicitly repudiated until the famous dialogue with Philippe Strozzi in III.iii. But even here the two Lorenzos merge: "For me, vice was a garment," he tells Strozzi, "now it has stuck to my flesh" ("Le vice a été pour moi un vêtement; maintenant il est collé à ma peau," III.iii, p. 239). Costume and flesh fuse as with the shirt of Nessus; our perplexity about Lorenzo's role-playing is not diffused by the allusion to the agonized end of Hercules. The female Lorenzos of the stage stressed the identity of the hero with his costume of "femmelette"; Gérard Philipe, reacting in the opposite direction, offered a true revolutionary, whose blow, futile in itself, held out some hope for the future.[8]

Thus the action of interpreting the character of Lorenzo and of assessing the significance of his tyrannicide—in which the play involves both the reader in his armchair and the performer preparing the role—leads to larger questioning of the utility of history or drama as means of understanding human activity. Where Wallenstein poses the same questions throughout his fascinated paralysis at the brink of possibility, Lorenzo's intoxicated dream of killing a tyrant forces him towards one decisive act. But the act itself is, by Lorenzo's own admission, incapable of liberating either Florence or Lorenzo himself: the futility of the assassination, the impotence of the noble republicans of the play, the "nonclimax" of the ending—all lead us to see the relation of act to identity and of individual action to social change or religious significance as ultimately, dizzyingly, paradoxical.[9]

Musset achieves our acute involvement in his character's riddles, not (as Schiller does) by explicitly raising philosophical questions, but instead through a rich texture of contemporary and literary allusion, through ironic juxtaposition of scenes, and through a language charged with erotic and religious images. Through this means, Lorenzo's role-playing comes to partake of multiple significance. In addition to his historically defined role as Brutus (which doubles into first and second Brutuses), Lorenzo enacts a romantic version of Hamlet, plays out the disillusionment of Musset's generation at the failure of the Revolution of 1830, and crafts his crime like a work of art.[10] In the same way, the play as a whole moves from explicit analogy to contemporary politics out into wide-ranging speculation about the nature of human action.

The explicit political applicability of *Lorenzaccio* is not surprising in light of what we have seen of *Wallenstein* or of the aspirations of the English historical dramatists of the seventeenth century, but in the context of French Romantic drama, and especially in that of Musset's work, the play's responsibility to historical discipline stands alone. For the most part, as Lioure puts it, historical tragedy served the Romantic movement primarily as a "demonstration of the vanity and absurdity of the rules" of classic dramaturgy, and as a "pretext" for lavish spectacle and pathos.[11] A countermovement to Hugo's and Dumas père's variety of immense, panoramic, decorative historical drama of love intrigue did exist in the *scènes historiques* of Ludovic Vitet, who argued in his preface to *Les Barricades* that historical facts, nakedly enacted, could both instruct and move pity and fear.[12] Vitet's *scènes* are directed towards readers, however. Not only the vast size of the cast and the excessive length of *Les États de Blois* prohibited its staging, but also the authorities, and so Vitet resigned himself to addressing to readers his huge three-volume drama of the League. But his experiment had its effect on Musset: after trying her hand at Vitet's genre in *Une conspiration en 1537: Scène historique,* Musset's mistress, George Sand, gave him the manuscript to expand as he saw fit.

Sand's piece was a series of scenes covering the last day in the life of Alexandre de Medici, focusing on the orchestration of his death by Lorenzo. While, as Musset was to do, Sand relied heavily on Varchi's *Storia fiorentina,* she presented the events of the past in such a way as to violate only the unity of place. Vitet enthused that the scenes he was to depict in *Les États de Blois* offered a closer approximation to classic regularity than those in *Les Barricades:*

> Ces nouvelles scènes sont encores purement historiques; néanmoins nous espérons qu'on y trouvera un peu plus d'unité d'action et d'intérêt dramatique que dans les précédentes. Le sujet le permettrait ainsi; les faits se trouvent disposés si heureusement par l'histoire, qu'en se bornant à en tracer le portrait fidèle, on ne saurait manquer de leur donner un certain arrangement théatrale.

> These new scenes are still purely historical; nevertheless we hope readers will find in them greater unity of action and dramatic interest than in the earlier ones. The subject would make this possible: the facts are set forth so happily by history that in limiting ourselves to faithful tracing of their portrait we could not fail to give them a certain theatrical arrangement.[13]

Similarly, Sand's design set out events in a sequence that was clear, simple, and tragic. The changes Musset executed in her manuscript have been fully documented by Dimoff.[14] In place of Sand's rigorous one-day time scheme, Musset offers the kind of relaxed chronology associated with Shakespeare: it is difficult to establish what period of time the play covers, as the marquis of Cibo's journey to Marra and back must take about a week, but there is little specific reference to the passage of time in the other plots of the play.[15] By concentrating on the assassination alone, Sand succeeded in creating from history another tragedy of blood; by adding to this skeleton crowd scenes evoking the spirit of Florence under the Medici and the subplots of the Strozzi and Cibo conspiracies, Musset created historical drama. As Charles Affron has noted, Florence comes to occupy the center of the play; Musset's goal, "ruthlessly" undertaken, is "to express the city."[16]

By setting the city of Florence at the center, Musset allows Lorenzo's tyrannicide to take place in a clearly defined historical context.

The act, in Sand's *Conspiration,* is "pure" tyrannicide, satisfying in itself and aesthetically complete at the end of the play: in Musset's play, the tyrannicide finishes the fourth act, and the fifth is devoted to chronicling its inconsequentiality as a political act. The corrupt and lassitudinous burghers of Florence do not rise and deliver themselves; the Florentine revolutionaries bicker and disperse. Only the students rise up, and they are easily defeated (v.v, p. 324). Musset not only provides a larger political context for the assassination: the context is specifically relevant to 1834 as well.[17] The revolution in July 1830—unenthusiastically mounted and quickly put down, with most casualties suffered by rioting students—lies behind Musset's (and Lorenzo's) contempt for the good, liberal citizens of Florence. But more than an attack upon the mediocrity of France during the revolution of 1830, *Lorenzaccio* offers a complex historical lesson. Rather than the defeatism seen here by Hunt, the play's abortive revolutions function to question historical meaning itself. As Hassan El Nouty argues, the play "erases" the apparent contradiction between history and drama, not by moving from better to worse or worse to better, but by remaining the same.[18] What is eliminated here is not so much a formal distinction, however, as the possibility of finding a suitable frame or endpoint by means of which to judge Lorenzo's (or the 1830 revolutionaries') success or failure. By rejecting the tidy, bloody, tragic ending of Sand's *scène historique,* Musset forces us to see the arbitrariness of both aesthetic and historical shaping of human action. In attempting to assess the significance of Lorenzo's act, we are not permitted to forget that it achieved nothing, in tragic or political terms.

This is not to suggest that the play is static; rather, throughout *Lorenzaccio* there is an overwhelming sense of the passage of time, of historical continuities and discontinuities. If the citizens of Florence keep watch over her through their windows, it is because she is susceptible to corruption, subject to change.[19] Florence's former glory and beauty haunt the play. The vanished past physically haunts Lorenzo's mother, in the shape of a studious Lorenzino who comes home early and sits down to his books. When he learns of this ghostly double, Lorenzo trembles from head to toe: "My spirit, my own? And he left when I returned?" ("Mon spectre, à moi? Et il s'en est allé quand je suis rentré?" ii.iv, p. 184). Not only did the ghost depart, but the image with which Lorenzo's mother describes his departure is another instance of a whole complex of images linking the lost past with dew: he vanished "like the morning mist" ("comme une vapeur du matin"). Later, Lorenzo tells Strozzi of the dew that drenched his arms as he vowed to become a modern Brutus; here too, Brutus and the dew merge as images of the past. Appalled by the ghost story, Lorenzo appeals to his young aunt, "Catherine, Catherine, read me the story of Brutus" ("lis-moi l'histoire de Brutus"). Levels of the past multiply: the classic past and Lorenzo's virtuous youth seem to fuse. The image of the scholarly early self of Lorenzo rebukes the cynical Lorenzo who has just debunked his learned aunt's study of Roman history with crude remarks about the rape of Lucrece. Lorenzo is doubly shadowed here by his past: the ghost of the morning is present in the form of Catherine.

Nor is Brutus a simple historical precedent. Lorenzo may be refer-ring to the Brutus who killed Tarquin and avenged Lucrece, or he may be referring to Marcus Brutus the tyrannicide.[20] The two were traditionally associated with and paralleled to each other. Plutarch tells us that Marcus Brutus consciously saw himself as following in the footsteps of Lucius Junius. The story of each Brutus ends, like Lorenzo's, with parricide. Lucius Junius establishes a republic, but in the process he sentences his sons to death. Marcus assassinates Caesar to reestablish the republic, and in so doing betrays his friend, patron, and even, rumor has it, father. Applied to Lorenzo, these highly charged precedents enhance the self-contradictory nature of his act.

If being a Brutus is in itself problematic, the way in which Lorenzo came to make this identification, as he describes it to Philippe Strozzi, reveals a shocking gratuitousness.[21] Among the ruins of the Colisseum, without knowing why, he made a vow:

> une certain nuit que j'étais assis dans les ruines du Colisée antique, je ne sais pourquoi je me levai; je tendis vers le ciel mes bras trempés de rosée, et je jurai qu'un des tyrans de ma patrie mourrait de ma main. J'étais un étudiant paisible, et je ne m'occupais alors que des arts et des sciences, et il m'est impossible de dire comment cet étrange serment s'est fait en moi. Peut-être est-ce là ce qu'on éprouve quand on devient amoureux.

> one night when I was sitting in the ruins of the ancient Colisseum, I rose up, I don't know why; I reached out towards the sky my arms drenched with dew, and I swore that one of the tyrants of my country would die by my hand. I was a good student, and I was concentrating only on arts and sciences, and it's impossible for me to say how this strange vow came to make itself in me. Maybe it's what one feels falling in love.

(III.iii, p. 231)

Lorenzo's passivity—the vow "makes itself" in him—leaves his decision mysterious. The invocation of providence— "si la Providence m'a poussé à la résolution de tuer un tyran, quel qu'il fut, l'orgueil m'a poussé aussi" ("if providence pushed me towards the resolve to kill a tyran, whoever he might be, pride pushed me there too") is highly qualified by a suggestion of randomness. In fact, Lorenzo arrives at his resolve in a backward way: "What more can I say? all the Caesars of the world made me think of Brutus" ("Que te dirais-je de plus? Tous les césars du monde me faisaient penser à Brutus"). Paradoxically, the decision to act, and to perform an action that th'oughout this scene the old republican persists in thinking of as glorious, is for Lorenzo a negation: "A statue that would come down from its pedestal and walk among men in the public square, maybe that would be like what I became the day I began living with that idea: I had to be a Brutus" ("Une statue qui descendrait de son pédestal pour marcher parmi les hommes sur la place publique, serait peut-être semblable à ce que j'ai été, le jour où j'ai commencé à vivre avec cette idée: il faut que je sois un Brutus"). The image of a walking statue suggests that identification with the heroes of the past is both inhuman and monumental. The offhand remark that follows it, "First of all I wanted to kill Clement VII" ("J'ai voulu d'abord tuer Clement VII"), and the wanton violence of decapitating the statues that precipitated Lorenzo's banishment from Rome and the selection of Alexandre as new target forces us, unlike Strozzi, to accept Lorenzo's vision of himself as a machine.[22]

The ambiguous historical precedents and the compulsive fatalism of Lorenzo derive not simply from his studies. He tells Strozzi that his sudden decision to kill a tyrant was like falling in love: his murder of Alexandre is planned as a wedding night (see II.ii, p. 172: "le jour de mes noces," and III.i, p. 210: "O jour de sang, jour de mes noces!"), a "consummation of his love" (as Gochberg puts it) for Alexandre. The historical Lorenzo's bitten thumb becomes a bitten ring finger, and the wound a "priceless diamond" ("inestimable diamant," IV.xi, p. 301).[23] Sexual energy and erotic language propel Lorenzo in his role of automaton of providence: the walking statue is not only a noble Roman but the statue that dines with Don Juan and drags him to hell. Again, we find ourselves in the realm of paradox. In order to recover his golden youthful purity— "Ma jeunesse a été pure comme l'or" (III.iii)—Lorenzo has had to plunge into a life of debauch.

The doubleness of the historical role Lorenzo wants to play—Brutus—redoubles as he immerses himself in vice. Role and self merge, and the garment of vice adheres to Lorenzo's flesh. "Brutus played the madman to kill Tarquin," Lorenzo confides in Philippe, "and what astonishes me about him is that it didn't drive him mad" ("Brutus a fait le fou pour tuer Tarquin, et ce qui m'étonne en lui, c'est qu'il n'y ait pas laissé sa raison," III.iii, p. 239). What Lorenzo has lost is, not his mind, but his past, his innocence, which despite his ecstasy in killing Alexandre—he rapturously breathes the clear night air as Scoroncolo panics—cannot be recovered. Philippe continues to play his role of single-minded liberal interpreter of the past after the murder—"Let me call you Brutus!" ("Laisse-moi t'appeler Brutus!" v.ii, p. 317)—and he points up the significance of Lorenzo's end in the Venetian lagoon: "Not even a tomb?" ("Eh quoi? pas même un tombeau?"). His desire to see Lorenzo in monumental, heroic terms disregards Lorenzo's perception of the monument, the walking statue, as dead: "I was a machine for murder, but only for one murder" ("J'étais une machine à meurte, mais à un meurtre seulement," V.ii, p. 330). Lorenzo never recovers identity with the lost Lorenzino who haunts his mother; nor does he achieve Herculean greatness despite the imagery of the clinging shirt. He reenacts only the parricides of the Brutuses and does not even win the tomb that would validate his identity in the eyes of Philippe Strozzi.

The lagoon in which Lorenzo ends is, like the walking statue, a key image in a play whose verbal texture is uncommonly dense. The ignominy of the watery grave is insisted upon by Musset, for the historical Lorenzo died eleven years after Alexandre. Inconsequentiality, uselessness, oblivion close over the Lorenzo of the play. Significant action, as defined by liberal, humanist tradition—of which Philippe is the impotent spokesman—is, in Musset's Florence, not possible.

The intensity with which Musset focuses our attention upon Lorenzo and through him upon the problem of action itself conditions the design of the play as a whole. It is true, as Grimsley has noted, that "all the characters are (like Lorenzo himself) obsessed" by dreams "in which they see themselves playing an 'ideal' role." More precisely, the basic structural pattern of the play, like the key historical image of Brutus, is doubling. Lorenzo's doubles abound. He and Alexandre appear in the first scene as twin connoisseurs of vice; dressed as friar and nun at the masked ball of the second scene, they play out a perverse unity. The eroticism of the murder, its wedding-night ambience, insists that the two become one. Yet there are other Lorenzos beyond the cousin and the ghost: the marquise of Cibo—"ce Lorenzaccio de l'autre sexe," as Hunt calls her—takes literally to Alexandre's bed, "hoping," says Gochberg, "thereby to breathe patriotism into the soul of her ruler."[24] Philippe Strozzi, to whom Lorenzo can tell his perverse, idealistic secrets, embodies the impotence of the tradition Lorenzo studied as a boy; Catherine retains her purity and reads Roman history. Pierre Strozzi, another would-be Brutus, figures the lust for vengeance; Louise Strozzi, poisoned by Alexandre, shares Lorenzo's infection. Identity loses itself in the play's hall of mirrors.

Bernard Masson has been most energetic among the play's critics in asserting that of all these doubles, Tebaldeo, the painter, embodies Musset's critique not only of Lorenzo but also of history. Lorenzo's tragedy—he passes, in Masson's terms, from mask to shadow without self-knowledge—[25] is challenged by Tebaldeo's creativity, his devotion to his art, and his piety. Tebaldeo's desire to paint Florence from the place that offers the loveliest perspective ("Je me placerais à l'orient, sur la rive gauche de l'Arno. C'est de cet endroit que la perspective est la plus large et la plus agréable," II.ii, p. 168) earns Lorenzo's scorn. Equating Florence with a notorious prostitute, he demands why the artist would paint the city but not the whore. "On ne m'a point encore appris à parler ainsi de ma mère" ("I was never taught to speak that way of my mother"), huffs Tebaldeo. He follows this with a reverent and exalted defense of art:

> Une blessure sanglante peut engendrer la corruption dans le corps le plus sain. Mais des gouttes précieuses du sang de ma mère sort une plante odorante qui guérit tous les maux.
> L'art, cette fleur divine, a quelquefois besoin du fumier pour engraisser le sol et le féconder.
>
> A bleeding wound can engender decay in the soundest of bodies. But from the precious drops of my mother's blood there grows a fragrant plant that cures all evils. Art, this divine flower, sometimes needs manure to enrich its soil and fertilize it.
>
> (II.ii, p. 169)

To Masson, this offers a redemptive perspective, pointing the way to a new existence lived outside of historical time, defined, not by politics, but by love. The dichotomy is familiar, and the appeal of Tebaldeo is strong; Masson finds other consolations in the beauty of places like the banks of the Arno, where Catherine first appears on the scene, in the country estate of the marquis of Cibo, who forgives his wife, and in Lorenzo's memories of Caffagiulo.[26] But these positive vibrations are indeed faint, and Tebaldeo's praise of art, juxtaposed to his more practical recognition that he needs to carry a dagger to ensure his personal safety, sounds slightly specious. After all, he does accept Lorenzo's commission to paint Alexandre. If he thus provides the opportunity for Lorenzo to discard the coat of mail, he has participated all unwitting in the duke's death. It is Tebaldeo, not Musset, who sentimentalizes the position of the artist in a corrupt state.

Art functions throughout the play as an analogy for significant action: Tebaldeo has not looked as deeply into the problem as Lorenzo, so he does not suffer his crippling malaise.[27] As one of many reflections of the protagonist, he illuminates one corner of the problem. But the greatest of Lorenzo's doubles is the largest: the city of Florence. At the open window after Alexandre's death, Lorenzo breathes the air and addresses the city in terms reminiscent of Tebaldeo's: "How sweet and balmy is the evening breeze! How the flowers of the field are blooming! O magnificent nature, eternal rest!" ("Que le vent du soir est doux et embaumé! Comme les fleurs des prairies s'entr'ouvrent! O nature magnifique, o éternel repos!" IV.x, p. 301). At this moment, the murder is indeed a work of art, but, as Lorenzo confutes the naive idealism of Tebaldeo in their discussion, so Florence—politically understood—confutes this flower of corruption. Florence's pure and golden past is, like Lorenzo's, irrecoverable. The play's stark ending, with Côme de Medici addressing the crowd, carries forward the satiric tone of the street scene that immediately precedes Lorenzo's final appearance. There two tutors, in tones redolent of pedantry, discuss art; the first obliges the second by reciting his sonnet in praise of liberty, but is interrupted as the students, one a Strozzi and one a Salviati, kick, scratch, and bite. These last glimpses of Florence give the lie to Tebaldeo's notion that its corrupt soul can nourish flowers. The ordering energy of art is debased into pompous, political rhetoric, epitomized by the tutor's sonnet and the political address that frame the scene of Lorenzo's death in Venice.

The grim satirical ending of *Lorenzaccio* thus denies significance in either political or aesthetic terms to Lorenzo's assassination. His death by drowning figures the utter worthlessness and inconsequentiality of action in a world as debased as Musset's Florence. Where Schiller altered history to give his Saint Joan a glorious death, Musset works the opposite alteration, giving his hero an unhistorical and inglorious end. There is no alternative perspective from which we can see the confusion and pettiness of human existence as illusory. Musset enhances, not the historical record's susceptibility to philosophical generalization, but rather the record's tendency towards chaos. Instead of—like Sand, Schiller, or Strindberg—discovering tragic, philosophical, or religious patterns in the seemingly random arrangements of historical facts, Musset insists on their randomness. The precedent of the two Brutuses and the proliferation of Lorenzo's doubles throughout the play transforms history into a hall of mirrors leading, not through the window into clear night air, but down to the lagoon and a death without a tomb.

ii

Dramatists approaching the past have traditionally invoked some balance between the foolish truths of historical fact and the higher truths of artistic and philosophical endeavor. As we have seen, these higher truths can be defined in any number of ways, with playwrights claiming authority over everything ranging from the secrets of broken royal hearts to the secrets of divine providence, and sometimes both combined. In this context, Musset's refusal to glorify Lorenzo's assassination, if only as a work of art, can be seen as a major surrender in the battle between playwrights and historians over custodianship of the past. For Musset's near-contemporary Georg Büchner (just three years his junior, but whom Musset, who also died young, was to outlive by twenty years) the traditional balance has itself shifted. On 28 July 1835, Büchner wrote to his parents about the accusations of "immorality" that had greeted the publication of his play *Danton's Death:*

> der dramatische Dichter ist in meinen Augen nichts als ein Geschichtschreiber, steht aber *über* Letzterem dadurch, dass er uns die Geschichte zum zweiten Mal erschafft und uns gleich unmittelbar, statt eine trockne Erzählung zu geben, in das Leben einer Zeit hinein versetzt, uns statt Charakteristiken Charaktere, und statt Beschreibungen Gestalten gibt. Seine höchste Aufgabe ist, der Geschichte, wie sie sich wirklich begeben, so nahe als möglich zu kommen. Sein Buch darf weder *sittlicher* noch *unsittlicher* sein, als die Geschichte selbst; aber die Geschichte ist vom lieben Herrgott nicht zu einer Lectüre für junge Frauenzimmer geschaffen worden, und da ist es mir auch nicht übel zu nehmen, wenn mein Drama ebensowenig dazu geeignet ist.
>
> (*SW*, 2:443)

> in my eyes, the dramatic poet is nothing but a historian, and stands *above* the latter in that he creates history for us a second time and directly, instead of giving a dry narrative, plunges us into the life of an era, giving us characters instead of characteristics, presences instead of descriptions. His highest endeavor is to come as close as possible to history as it really happened. His book can be neither *more* moral nor

less moral than history itself; but the good lord did not make history into appropriate reading for young ladies, and I don't take it badly that my drama is equally unsuitable to that purpose.

Büchner seems to assent to Ranke's definition of the historian's task as telling things as they really were, without humanist moralization or application. But Büchner goes further than Ranke in asserting that the goal of historical objectivity is better met by dramatists who can force their readers to experience immediately the personalities and problems of the past.

Büchner's assumption that his audience will be made up of readers rather than theatergoers carries with it tacit recognition of the continuing attractiveness of idealized history on the stage. Like Vitet, Büchner argues for a presentation of facts so detailed that it can only succeed in the study. Echoes of Vitet can be heard not only in the letter; much to Büchner's annoyance, the play was first published as *Dantons Tod: Dramatische Bilder aus Frankreichs Schreckenherrschaft*. Whether translated as "tableaux" or "images," the *bilder* of the subtitle are reminiscent of Vitet's *scènes historiques.* Some critics posit a closer connection between Büchner and Musset's tradition of armchair theater with contentions that Büchner "probably read" *Lorenzaccio* at the time he was writing *Danton's Death*.[28] But Büchner goes beyond Musset's challenge to Vitet in his assertion, in keeping with his scientific and medical training, of total objectivity. Thus Büchner seems to fulfill Victor Hugo's demand for a form of drama that rejects the idealizations and symmetries of classicism and mirrors life in all its aspects, especially those that Hugo calls "grotesque." *Danton's Death,* as Wolfgang Wittkowski puts it, "realizes" the program of the Romantic drama.[29]

The rebelliousness of *Danton's Death* is not merely aesthetic, however. It is worth remembering that Büchner wrote the play while in hiding as a consequence of his revolutionary political activities. In this respect he is radically different from the apolitical Musset. Thus, the biographical fallacy creeps far more often into attempts to understand Büchner's brief but complex life and work. The letter of 28 July, for example, can be accepted at face value as a declaration of historical principle; or it can be seen, with equal conviction, as a disingenuous attempt on the part of a twenty-two-year-old playwright to excuse rough language that he knows will offend his parents and others as they read his play. But the problem runs deeper: the lassitude, nihilism, and despair of Danton have been read as a mirror of Büchner's own "disillusionment" with revolutionary activity. Or Danton has been seen as a failure, whose half-revolution is to be condemned from Büchner's thoroughly revolutionary standpoint.[30] Erwin Kobel and Wolfgang Wittkowski argue that political readings of the play overlook Büchner's consistency with the philosophical and religious thought of his time, his interest throughout his life in reform and renewal. On the other hand, what intrigues Maurice Benn about Büchner is his radical rejection of messianic idealism and "all the other forms of chiliasm and utopianism so rife in the Europe of his time."[31]

Central to all the critical dispute about *Danton's Death* is disagreement about the letter of 10 March 1834, addressed to Büchner's fiancée, in which the young author complains about history:

> Ich studirte die Geschichte der Revolution. Ich fühlte mich
> wie zernichtet unter dem grässlichen Fatalismus der
> Geschichte. Ich finde in der Menschennatur eine entsetzliche
> Gleichheit, in den menschlichen Verhältnissen eine
> unabwendbare Gewalt, Allen und Keinem verliehen. Der
> Einzelne nur Schaum auf der Welle, die Grösse ein blosser
> Zufall, die Herrschaft des Genies ein Puppenspiel, ein
> lächerliches Ringen gegen ein ehernes Gesetz, es zu erkennen
> des Höchste, es zu beherrschen unmöglich. Es fällt mir nicht
> mehr ein, vor den Paradegäulen und Eckstehern der
> Geschichte mich zu bücken. Ich gewöhnte mein Auge ans
> Blut. Aber ich bin kein Guillotinemesser. Das *muss* ist eins
> von den Verdammungsworten, womit der Mensch getauft
> worden. Der Ausspruch: es muss ja Aergerniss kommen, aber
> wehe dem, durch den es kommt,—ist schauderhaft. Was ist
> das, was in uns lügt, mordet, stiehlt? Ich mag den Gedanken
> nicht weiter nachgehen. Könnte ich aber dies kalte und
> gemartete Herz an deine Brust legen!
>
> (*SW*, 2:425–26)

I have been studying the history of the Revolution. I felt as though crushed by the horrible fatalism of history. I find in human nature a hideous sameness, and in human relations an ineluctable force, granted to all and to none. The individual mere foam on the wave, greatness mere chance, the power of genius a puppet show, a laughable struggle against an iron law; recognizing it of the utmost importance, mastering it, impossible. I no longer intend to bow down before the parade horses and bystanders of history. My eyes are accustomed to the sight of blood. But I am no guillotine blade. "*Must*" is one of the curses with which man is

baptized. The saying: "It needs must be that offenses come,
but woe to him by whom the offense cometh" is appalling.
What is it in us that lies, murders, steals? I can't pursue this
thought any further. If only I could lay this cold and
tortured heart on your breast!

The problem with resting an interpretation of Büchner's work (not
merely *Danton's Death*) on this letter is clear enough. There is nothing
methodical, systematic, or coherent about this outburst. The extreme
youth of Büchner shows through in the rapid shifts of mood: from
worldly cynicism to grandiose posturing to romantic despair Büchner
regales his fiancée with a whole range of immediate unreflective responses. This letter, like the letter to Büchner's parents, has been both
enshrined as a canonical text in establishing Büchner's world view and
sentimentalized as the young playwright's "agonizing study of
history."[32]
     What is compelling about the letter is its passion about history
itself: Büchner's extreme rejections of individualism reveal the fierce
resistance that history's "horrible fatalism" and "iron law" has had to
overcome. Büchner portrays himself to his parents as a cold and objective
scientist; with his fiancée he shares horror at the very idea of "human
nature." Far better trained than Strindberg in the techniques of science,
a qualified doctor at the age of twenty-three, Büchner sought like him the
laws that determined human behavior. *Danton's Death* represents an
early phase of a life's work that would culminate in the lecture on cranial
nerves that Büchner delivered in Zürich in 1836. He prefaced his physio-
logical discussion with a rejection of "teleological" natural philosophy,
as practiced in England and France. "Nature," he argued instead, "does
not behave according to ends. . . . Everything that exists exists for its
own sake. Seeking the law of this existence is the goal of what I call the
philosophical approach, the opposite to the teleological."[33] For Strindberg, the laws of nature revealed behind them the divine hand. Büchner's
natural laws are ends in themselves. On a personal level, as we have seen,
Büchner responded to his discovery with horror.
     In *Danton's Death* he set out to dramatize the annihilation of indi-
viduality that appalled him in his reading of history. The title of the play
ironically echoes that of the last play in Schiller's idealistic trilogy; in
Brecht's terms, Büchner here offers a *Gegenstück*, or "counterplay," to
Wallenstein's Death and by extension a repudiation of Schiller's treatment there of the issues of freedom and necessity. Danton's death, unlike
Wallenstein's, grows not so much out of his particular doings and misdo-

ings as out of the necessary dynamics of the Revolution itself. "The Revolution is like Saturn," says Danton, quoting literally one of Büchner's sources, "it devours its own children"[34] ("die Revolution ist wie Saturn, sie frisst ihre eignen Kinder," I.v, p. 23). Like nature—St. Just argues when the Convention seems likely to spare the Dantonists— the Revolution follows laws of its own: "Man is destroyed when he comes into conflict with them," (II.vii, p. 40; "der Mensch wird vernichtet, wo er mit ihnen in Conflict kommt," p. 45). "Is it so astounding," he asks, "that the great flood of revolution tosses up its dead at every bend and turn?" (p. 41; "Ist es da so zu verwundern, dass der Strom der Revolution bey jedem Absatz, bey jeder neuen Krummung seine Leichen ausstösst?" p. 46). Floods, volcanoes, epidemics are equally indifferent.

St. Just's speech in II.vii gives expression to a ruthlessly scientific attitude towards the progress of the Revolution and the passage of time. Like Büchner in the letter of 10 March, but without his horror, St. Just describes the utter insignificance of individual action in history. The laws of development that the Revolution follows function on an individual level as well. The strangely lyrical speech of the whore Marion (I.v) traces the growth of her own sexuality. Social visits from a pretty young man led to visits "between two sheets" ("zwischen zwei Bettüchern):

> Das gieng so fort. Aber ich wurde wie ein Meer, was Alles
> verschlang und sich tiefer und tiefer wühlte. Es war für mich
> nur ein Gegensatz da, alle Männer verschmolzen in einen
> Leib. Meine Nature war einmal so, wer kann da drüber
> hinaus? Endlich merkt'er's.
>
> (pp. 21–22)

> And so it went on. But I became like the sea that swallows
> down everything and sinks deeper and deeper into itself. The
> only fact that existed for me was my opposite, all men
> melted into one body. It was my nature, what choice did I
> have? Finally he noticed.
>
> (p. 16)

Marion's sexual appetites awaken like the Revolution's thirst for blood; her nature, like the sea, figures St. Just's "great flood." Both drown the individual: Marion, sitting at a window, sees her pretty young man carried by in a basket, "his hair was wet—he had drowned himself" ("seine Locken waren feucht, er hatte sich ersäuft"). Despite the brief interruption, Marion's life goes on: "I am always only one thing, an unbroken longing and grasping, a flame, a stream" ("Ich bin immer nur eins. Ein ununterbrochenes Sehnen und Fassen, eine Gluth, ein Strom"). Marion's inexorable pursuit of pleasure has its religious dimension as well: "the person who enjoys the most, prays the most" ("wer am Meisten geniesst, betet am Meisten"). The only break in this drive is her moment at the window.

It is a moment of arrest that anticipates the two scenes in which Robespierre and Danton, too, look out windows and reflect on the passage of time. In I.vi, Danton confronts Robespierre. The argument quickly escalates into a philosophical discussion; after Danton's departure, shaken by his Epicurean attack upon the idea of virtue, Robespierre, alone, looks out the window. He senses outside a vast and menacing potentiality:

> Die Nacht schnarcht über der Erde und wälzt sich im wüsten Traum. Gedanken, Wünsche kaum geahnt, wirr und gestaltlos, die scheu sich vor des Tages Licht verkrochen, empfangen jetzt Form und Gewand und stehlen sich in das stille Haus des Traums. Sie öffnen die Thüren, sie sehen aus den Fenstern, sie werden halbwegs Fleisch, die Lippen murmeln.—Und ist nicht unser Wachen ein hellerer Traum, sind wir nicht Nachtwandler, ist nicht unser Handeln, wie das im Traum, nur deutlicher, bestimmter, durchgeführter?
>
> (I.vi, p. 28)

> Night snores over the earth and tosses itself about in dreamful dreams. Thoughts, desires, scarcely imagined, confused and formless, that crept timidly from the light of day, take shape now and steal into the silent house of dreams. They push open the doors, they look out of the windows, they become half flesh and blood, their limbs stretch in sleep, their lips murmur—And is our waking anything but a dream, a clear dream? Are we not all sleepwalkers? What are our actions but the actions of a dream, only more clear, more definite, more complete?
>
> (p. 23)

The transformation of half-formed thoughts into action is nightmarish; the clarity of the waking dream of life is merely illusory. "Whether the thought will grow into deed, or the body imitate it," Robespierre concludes, "is a matter of chance" ("Ob der Gedanke That wird, ob ihn der Körper nachspielt, das ist Zufall"). The development of inchoate thought into action is a process governed only by the law of chance. Like Marion's desires, Robespierre's night thoughts take shape of their own accord, sensuously stretching and murmuring at the window of the fierce moralist's conscience.

Danton, too, has his moment by the window. "For Robespierre it is the future which assumes a threatening shape," Gerda Bell points out, "for Danton it is the past."[35] The night seems to shriek "September!" at the architect of the September massacre:

> Unter mich keuchte die Erdkugel in ihrem Schwung, ich hatte sie wie ein wildes Ross gepackt, mir riesigen Gliedern wühlt'ich in ihrer Mähne und presst ich ihre Rippen, das Haupt abwärts gedrückt, die Haare flatternd über den Abgrund. So ward ich geschleift.
>
> (II.vii, p. 41)
>
> The globe of the world writhed under me as it lept from its course; I had grabbed hold of it like a wild horse, I clutched at its mane with giant arms and dug into its ribs, my head turned aside, my hair streaming across the abyss, and I dragged along.
>
> (p. 36)

Danton's image of history as a runaway horse fulfills rather than counters Robespierre's vision of the random incarnation of thought into action.[36] The world leaps from its course as events follow directions undreamed of by Danton, whose heroic action in September—"You saved the country," says Julie—engendered the Terror. Danton's guilt about the massacre becomes a thoroughgoing despair:

> Ja das hab'ich. Das war Notwehr, wir mussten. Der am Kreuze hat sich's bequem gemacht: es muss ja Aergernis kommen, doch wehe dem, durch welchen Aergernis kommt. Es muss, das war diess Muss. Wer will der Hand fluchten, auf die der Floch des Muss gefallen? Wer hat das Muss gesprochen, wer? Was ist das, was in uns hurt, lügt, stiehlt und mordet? Puppen sind wir von unbekannten Gewalten am Draht gezogen; nichts, nichts wir selbst! Die Schwerter, mit denen Geister kämpfen, man sieht nur die Hande nicht, wie im Mährchen.
>
> (p. 41)
>
> Yes, I saved it; it was self-defense, we had no choice. That man on the Cross made it easy for Himself: "It must needs be that offenses come; but woe to that man by whom the offense cometh." That *must!* That *must* was *mine!* Who will

curse the hand on which that curse of *must* has fallen? Who
spoke of that *must?* Who? What is this in us that lies,
whores, steals, and murders?—What are we but puppets,
manipulated on wires by unknown powers? We are nothing,
nothing in ourselves; we are the swords that spirits fight
with—except no one sees the hands—just as in fairy tales.

(pp. 36–37)

Robespierre looks out the window, a vessel waiting to be filled; Danton
looks back in a horror that directly echoes his young creator's at the
compulsion that filled him, that transformed his thought into action.
The compulsion to lie, whore, steal, and murder is as inescapable as the
woe that follows it. Robespierre too will be dragged down by the wild
horse: the Revolution will devour him just as it eats its first generation of
children in *Danton's Death*. To Hans Mayer, Robespierre's doom is the
key to understanding Büchner's tragic determinism; all political action is
a hopeless struggle against the "must."[37]

   The biblical text that forces us to see both Danton and Robespierre
as bringers of offense to the world is clearly central to Büchner's view of
history. The drives that compel them come from without, as the two
window scenes suggest; Marion's window speech locates compulsion in
sex. The offense text from the Sermon on the Mount similarly locates the
origins of evil: but the paradox of offense is resolved for Christians
through Christ himself. Büchner, however, accepts that offense must
come, but denies the redemptive sacrifice. Inverse images of Christ
abound in the play: for Danton he is the finest Epicurean ("Es giebt nur
Epicuräer und zwar grobe und feine, Christus war der feinste," I.vi, p.
27), making it easy for Himself on the cross. Robespierre responds to
Camille's indictment of himself as a "bloody Messiah" (p. 25; "blut
Messias," p. 30) as to a personal betrayal ("And so you, too, Camille?";
"Also auch du, Camille?") with Roman overtones. But his dream of
redemption is equally vain:

> Wahrlich des Menschensohn wird in uns Allen gekreuzigt,
> wir ringen Alle im Gethsemanegarten im blutigen Schweiss,
> aber es erlöst Keiner den Andern mit seinen Wunden.—
> Mein Camille!—Sie gehen Alle von mir—es ist Alles Wüst
> und leer—ich bin allein.

(p. 31)

> Truly the Son of Man is crucified in us all; we all wrestle
> in bloody agony in our own Gardens of Gethsemane;
> but not one of us redeems the other with his wounds.

—O Camille!—They are all leaving me—the world
is empty and void—I am alone.

(p. 25)

Both Robespierre and Danton confront a world in which offense is
compulsory and redemption impossible. Wittkowski's argument that the
play itself generates renewal by chastising its audience and that the playwright steps in to fill the gap, becoming a new Moses and Messiah,
resolves the paradox, but in the Christian terms that Büchner, however
reluctantly, has repudiated.[38]

The traditional metaphors of life as a game and the world as a stage
through which the providentialism of Strindberg finds expression animate the language of *Danton's Death*. But where the image of a great
chess game leads Strindberg to postulate the existence of a solitary
player, Büchner introduces his play with an image of a card game that
leads nowhere. The play's first scene, in a drawing room, offers a split
image: Danton and Julie watch as Hérault-Séchelles and some ladies
play cards. "Sieh die hübsche Dame, wie artig sie die Karten dreht!"
Danton exclaims:

Ja wahrhaftig sie versteht's, man sagt sie halte ihrem Manne
immer das coeur und andern Leuten das carreau hin. Ihr
könntet einen noch in die Lüge verliebt machen.

(1.i, p. 9)

See the pretty lady, she plays her cards sharp enough. They
say she always deals the *coeur* to her husband and the *carreau*
to everyone else. You could make anybody fall in love with a
lie.

(p. 3)

Just as the growth of the Revolution's appetites is paralleled to the
growth of Marion's sexuality, so the game of cards figures, to Danton,
the game of sex. The coarse pun—which only works in French—brings
both game and sex down to the lowest level.[39] As Hérault-Séchelles
loses in his "amorous adventure" (p. 4; "verliebtes Abenteuer," p. 10),
Danton and Julie arrive at a stalemate. "You know me, Danton" ("Du
kennst mich, Danton"), says Julie: "Know one another? We'd have to
crack open our skulls and drag each other's thoughts out by the tails"
("Wir müssten uns die Schädeldecken aufbrechen und die Bedanken
einander ans den Hirnfasern zerren") is the end of Danton's reply. Mean-
while, Hérault-Séchelles makes suggestive gestures to one of the ladies.
Failures of communication, even on the physical level, are depicted in
both encounters; Danton's despairing desire to know Julie and Hérault-

Séchelles' lassitudinous lechery comment on each other. Even Danton's cynical despair is undercut by the degenerate setting. There is only one way out: "Julie, I love you as I love the grave" (p. 3; "Nein Julie, ich liebe dich wie das Grab," p. 9); the mingling of sex and death is complete.

The split-stage technique continues in the first scene as Camille and Phillipeau enter and engage Hérault-Séchelles in political conversation. Danton and Julie remain to one side. The language of revolution replaces the language of lechery in Hérault-Séchelles' mouth; Danton's weariness reduces both to the same level. "Danton, you must lead the attack at the next Convention," cries Camille, attempting to arouse his friend's interest. "I must, you must, he must," conjugates the revolutionary (p. 6; "Danton du wirst den Angriff im Convent machen." "Ich werde, du wirst, er wird," p. 11). Danton's separation both from the card playing and from the Revolution tends to equate the two. Hérault-Séchelles makes the identification complete, as Camille, after Danton leaves, insists that Danton will come to join the struggle against Robespierre: "It would only be a pastime with him, like playing chess" (p. 6; "Ja, aber bloss zum Zeitvertrieb, wie man Schach spielt," p. 12).

If the metaphor of the game only serves to heighten the sense of the hopelessness and futility of political and amorous activity in I.i, the metaphor of the theater works much the same way in I.ii. The struggle between Simon, the malapropic prompter, and his wife over their daughter's prostitution makes a grating commentary on the pretensions of the Republic. Simon misuses names of the theater's noble figures and misquotes lines from tragedy as he reviles his wife.[40] For her, the decision to send the daughter out into the streets is simple common sense: "She's a good girl and supports her parents," (p. 7; "sie ist ein braves Mädchen und ernährt ihre Eltern," p. 13). The onstage audience that has gathered to observe Simon's grotesque performance as a wronged Roman father sides with the mother: "What has she done? Nothing! It's her empty belly makes her whore and beg," (p. 8; "was es sie? Nichts! Ihr Hunger hurt und bettelt," p. 14). Against the inflated rhetoric and theatrical posturing of Simon, the human compulsion of hunger stands out in sharp relief. "Kill!" cry the crowd as they rush on a young man with a handkerchief.

The first two scenes juxtapose the Dantonists in their Epicurism to the needs of the crowd; it is hard for an audience to weigh them in the balance and not find them wanting. The confrontation of rhetorical posturing with basic human needs is central to the whole play.[41] Simon's inflated theatrical verbiage has as little effect upon the necessities of life as Danton's fiercest and most heroic self-defense does upon the impetus of the Convention. Camille's indictment of theater in 11.iii clarifies Büchner's attack upon the conventional, idealized theater. "Consistency" is the audience's cry of praise for a clumsy marionette; "ideal" its pronouncement on a "minor sentiment" dressed up in coat and trousers; "what art!" they exclaim over the fiddling of an opera. Regularity, symmetry, and order oppose the basic energy of life:

> Sie vergessen ihren Herrgott über seinen schlechten
> Copisten. Von der Schöpfung, die glühend, brausend und
> leuchtend, um und in ihnen, sich jeden Augenblick neu
> gebiert, hören und sehen sie nichts. Sie gehen in's Theater,
> lesen Gedichte und Romane, schneiden den Fratzen darin
> die Gesichter nach und sagen zu Gottes Geschöpfen: wie
> gewöhnlich!
>
> (11.iii, p. 37)

> They forget their Lord God because of his bad imitators.
> And they see and hear nothing of the creation round about
> them and in them that glows, and surges, and glitters, and is
> born anew with every moment. All they do is go to the
> theatre, read poetry and novels, and grimace like the
> characters they find in them, and then say to God's real
> creations: How commonplace!
>
> (p. 32)

Camille's depiction of the theater as a barren Galatea offers, in Janis L. Solomon's words, a "secularized vision of the world as theater" directly related to the posturing, "historical role-playing," and internal power struggles of the Revolution. Robespierre's "obsessive drive to impose his own order upon life" mirrors the falsehoods of nineteenth-century theater with its unreal symmetries and consistencies. What are "laughable delusions" in the prompter Simon become "potentially destructive forces" on the stage of history.[42]

Büchner thus makes of the theater of his day an image of falsehood and delusion; by carrying the theatrical metaphor into the actions of his historical figures, he manages to trivialize their heroic posturing. Robespierre's depiction of himself, at the window, as an empty room waiting to be inhabited by thought easily translates into the image of the marionette praised for its consistency of character. Similarly, his willingness to play Messiah or Cato, like his service to virtue, is a mechanical denial of life. Danton, confronting him in 1.vi, chides him for his clean conscience: "Conscience is a mirror that monkeys torment themselves in front of" (p. 21; "Das Gewissen ist ein Spiegel vor dem ein Affe sich quält," p. 27). With considerable coarseness, Robespierre is reduced to the status of the monkey in military uniform who struts, salutes, and plays the trumpet before the market stall in *Woyzeck*.

The persistent trivialization of human activity through both brutally reductive language and ironic reference to the *theatrum mundi* motif enforces an audience's consent to Danton's weariness. But this is not to say that Danton is Büchner's mouthpiece: rather, as Kobel has argued, it is the dialectical configuration of Danton and Robespierre that holds the key to Büchner's thought. Neither the stoic Robespierre in his pride and vanity nor the Epicurean Danton in his ennui and despair can effect any change in the situation.[43] For Büchner stubbornly insists that the persistence of pain and suffering in the world must shatter any philosophical system. "Consider this, Anaxagoras," says Payne as he proves the nonexistence of God to his fellow prisoners, "why do I suffer?" (III.i, p. 44; "Merke dir es, Anaxagoras, warum leide ich?" p. 48). Critics sharply divide on whether to take Payne's dogmatic atheism seriously; Payne may well be a fool, but his question resounds through the play and strikes at the very heart of all revolutionary idealism. The failure of both Danton's earlier heroics and Robespierre's Terror to relieve suffering points to the utter futility of both systems.

Payne describes his questions as "the very bedrock of atheism" ("der Fels des Atheismus"):

> Das leisteste Zucken des Schmerzes und rege es sich nur in einen Atom, macht einen Riss in der Schöpfung von oben bis unten.
>
> (III.i, p. 48)

> The least quiver of pain, in even the smallest of atoms, makes a rent in the curtain of your creation from top to bottom.
>
> (p. 44)

The rending of the veil of creation is a powerful image; Danton echoes Payne's language in his own confession of atheism later in the play. Again, it is the reality of suffering that transforms creation into the self-annihilation of nothingness:

> Die Schöpfung hat sich so breit gemacht, da ist nichts leer, alles voll Gewimmels. Das Nichts hat sich ermordet, die Schöpfung ist seine Wunde, wir sind seine Blutstropfen, die Welt ist das Grab worin es fault. Das lautet verrückt, es ist aber doch was Wahres daran.
>
> (III.ix, p. 61)

Creation has spread itself so far that there is nothing empty
any more, multitudes everywhere. This is the suicide of
nothingness, creation is its wound, we its drops of blood,
and the world the grave in which it rots.—Mad as that
sounds, there is some truth in it.

(p. 56)

The negation of negation creates a bloody positive. The play's drive
towards theological speculation is grounded in human pain.

Büchner's desire to generalize the Revolution, his attempt to extract
from history a natural law that will accommodate the mystery of pain—a
mystery that continued to agitate him even on his deathbed—sets him
apart from Musset. The resonances of Lorenzo's action are primarily
aesthetic; confronting Danton's inaction, Büchner puzzles over the
whole purpose of the universe. And the puzzle remains vexatiously un-
solved. The critical controversy about Büchner's real intentions in *Danton's Death* makes that clear enough: it is as difficult to endorse wholeheartedly a Christian view of Büchner, like that of Wittkowski or Kobel,
as it is to assent to facile declarations of the young playwright's nihilism.

For if there is no answer to the problem of suffering in the play,
neither is there a trivialization or dismissal of human love. The suicide of
Julie and the madness of Lucile, both wholly fictive, pose a strong pathetic challenge to the grim world around them. "Tell him he won't have
to go alone" IV.i, p. 60; "Sag ihm er würd nicht allein gehn," p. 64), says
Julie to the boy whom she sends to Danton with a lock of her hair; the
separateness that Danton complained about in the first scene will be
overcome in death. Lucile's madness leads her to an act of heroic defiance
as she cries "Es lebe der König" ("Long live the King"), and is led off
"Im Namen der Republik" ("In the name of the republic") at the play's
very end. The presence of the women in the play is anomalous in more
ways than one. They stand out most conspicuously as exceptions to
Büchner's policy of scrupulous closeness to his sources. Unlike the men
in the play, the women are close to nature; in the case of Marion, they can
embody it. Ideal presences, sources of pathos, mysterious and inscrutable, the women bring a much needed tragic relief into the play.[44] "I
won't be going alone; thank you, Julie," says Danton at the prison
window, gazing at the stars (IV.iii, p. 62; "Ich werde nicht allein gehn,
ich danke dir Julie," p. 67).

Lucile and Julie exist outside the world of history and redeem their
men with their love. The redemption is of a highly literary kind: Lucile's
Ophelian madness makes Camille into a Hamlet; Julie's suicide is osten-

tatiously romantic. Büchner's recoil from the horrors of history is cushioned by the faded conventional presences of saints and whores.[45] Refusing to sentimentalize the Revolution, debunking the revolution-aries' heroic posturing, decrying the artificiality and emptiness of the contemporary stage, Büchner sentimentalizes women instead. Marion and the wives represent two sides of the same coin: spontaneous, direct, in touch with nature, women are exempt from the self-consciousness that cripples men. Paradoxically, in madness, in suicide, in desire, they can set themselves free.

Büchner's near obsession with necessity puts *Danton's Death* in the mainstream of post-Renaissance historical drama. Like Schiller, and like the English playwrights of the seventeenth and eighteenth centuries, he counters history's grim necessity with pathetic appeal. His antihistorical women find freedom as Max and Thekla do, through the death and madness that figure an escape from the historical contexts in which they are, in the last analysis, intruders. Curiously, for one so outspoken in his anti-idealism, Büchner cannot apply the iron law of necessity to men and women alike. The men's agonized questioning of the role of political activity in an incomprehensible and uncontrollable world is assuaged through women's love.

Musset avoids this kind of vitiation by omitting the almost obliga-tory love interest from his play, but he also omits the wide-ranging theological speculation that makes *Danton's Death* as much a play about history as a history play. Musset concedes the futility of political action and with a certain lyrical flair drowns his hero in the Venetian lagoon. To Büchner, the futility of individual political action is a horrible possibility that must be questioned to the very end. Discovering what kind of world would permit the continuance of human suffering despite revolutionary efforts to eliminate hunger and want shatters the playwright as much as it does his disillusioned characters.[46] As an individual, Danton effects as much real change as Lorenzo, but he acts in a context of irrevocable natural laws. Lorenzo achieves a kind of freedom in the gratuity of his act; Danton's revolution and Danton's death are both necessities.

The treatment of history as necessity that we first saw in Shake-speare's *Henry VIII* is nowhere bleaker. Schiller's idealism, Strindberg's providentialism, Musset's lyricism, all help wash down history's bitter pill. To Strindberg as well as Büchner life may seem an incomprehen-sible, brutal game, but Büchner cannot share with Strindberg the op-timistic teleology that makes the game endurable. The sense of the impla-cable necessity of source material that horrifies Büchner distinguishes *Henry VIII* from Shakespeare's mature history plays. The English playwrights of the late-seventeenth and early-eighteenth centuries, in their passivism, pastoralism, and pathos expressed a feeble protest at humanist history's monopoly over the truth of the past. Schiller and Strindberg reargued the Platonic precedence of philosophical truths over historical. For Musset and Büchner, only love, undetectable in *Lorenzaccio* and tacked on to *Danton's Death*, can resist the historian's annihilating authority.

Such a vision of nineteenth-century history writing as a monolith grimly determined to expunge the individual from the record of past time is simplistic, but so too is Büchner's letter to his fiancée. Herbert Lindenberger buttresses his description of nineteenth-century opera as offering an experience of "history as sheer power" with a quotation from Hegel: his "world-historical individuals" are those who can "grasp . . . a higher universal, make it their own purpose, and who realize this purpose in accordance with the higher law of the spirit." "By the nineteenth century," Lindenberger comments on this passage: "the historical process rather than the individual had become the chief carrier of heroic action."[47] Where there is no grasp of the higher law, as in Musset and Büchner, the individual's action becomes vain and meaningless. But, as Strindberg's world historical plays prove, dramatizing the activities of individuals in tune with the higher laws can be a tedious and unrewarding enterprise. Through music, as Lindenberger points out, opera can evoke the heroic magnitude of historical process itself; without music, Strindberg's efforts are relegated by Walter Johnson to the "minor form" of "imaginary conversation."[48]

Büchner sought but did not find the natural law that would permit the forward rush of historical necessity to make sense; Strindberg found God in history as well as in nature, but "The Mysticism of World History" made few converts. Both expressed disillusionment with the massive circumstantial detail and moral detachment of early modern history writing, embodied in the shocking combination of arrogance and modesty in Ranke's claim to tell everything "as it really happened," nothing more and nothing less. Both playwrights see in this kind of history an annihilation of the individual, or, more precisely, an abrogation of the playwright's right to create great individuals or dramatize heroic actions. Strindberg's world historical plays are among his feeblest dramatic works. If we deny Büchner Danton's systematic nihilism—"The world is chaos. Nothingness is the world-god yet to be born" (IV.v, p. 67; "Die Welt ist das Chaos. Das Nichts ist der zu gebärende Weltgott," p. 72)— we cannot deny him Danton's despair.

What seems to be needed is a way of looking at historical necessity that is optimistic, like Strindberg's, but scientific rather than reactionary and providential. Hegel turned on his head, in short. What seems to be needed is a way of looking at theater that insists upon the primacy of performance rather than the armchair and that confounds the falsehoods and complacencies of the kind of dramaturgy Büchner despised in its own arena, the stage. Rather than regret the impossibility of heroic action in the modern world, we should recognize that "heroism" and "greatness" are catchwords of a power structure whose time has long since passed, and that significant action must be redefined as mass action. Taken at his own estimation, Bertolt Brecht fills these needs and forces the recognitions necessary to revive a truly historical drama.

iii

The central fact in Brecht's *Life of Galileo* is the main character's—one dares not call him a hero—recantation of his doctrine of the motion of the earth before the Inquisition. Although, as we shall see, Brecht's responsiveness to events of his own time led this incident to carry radically different moral burdens over the twenty years the playwright devoted, off and on, to this play, the scene of Galileo's recantation retained substantially the same structure in the play's successive versions. The scene is full of striking examples of Brecht's technique of *Verfremdung* (most frequently translated "alienation"): the broad variety and controversy in explications of this term do not negate the fact that *V-effekts* in the theater are strong, simple, easy to feel. Defining them is another matter; as is usual with his own discussions of his work, Brecht tells us both too much and too little. "Verfremden," we recall, "heisst also historisieren" ("Über Experimentelles Theater," *GsW* 15:302; "Alienation thus means historicization"). "Bei der Historisierung," he explained later in *Der Messingkauf,* second postscript, "wird ein bestimmtes Gesellschaftssystem vom Standpunkt eines anderen Gesellschaftssystem aus betrachtet," (*GsW,* 16:653; "Through historicizing, an entire social system can be observed from the viewpoint of another social system"). Thus Brecht's central dramatic strategy—making the familiar strange and the strange familiar; heightening misunderstanding until understanding peaks (*GsW,* 15:360–61)—implies a whole body of historical thought, although a *V-effekt* can be, on stage, a soliloquy, an aside, or a brightly lit sign announcing the title of a song.[49] Through close analysis of the recantation scene we can make a start at grasping both the technique and the related historical perspective.

It goes without saying that Brecht does not stage the recantation of

Galileo itself. Despite a sign or projection announcing that this is the narrative content of the scene, what an audience sees is the small group of Galileo's supporters, augmented by his daughter, awaiting news. This is a very primitive sort of alienation, promising one thing and delivering another. But the shift in emphasis is significant: what the scene dramatizes is, not Galileo's abjuration, but its effects; similarly, the play as a whole insists that we see the consequences of this act as still present, shaping our own time. A recitation, sung by children dressed as choirboys in productions supervised by Brecht, follows the title and further stresses the immediate relevance of the scene:

> Und es war ein Junitag, der schnell verstrich
> Und der war wichtig für dich und mich
> Aus Finsternis trat die Vernunft herfür
> Ein'ganzen Tag stand sie vor der Tür.

> June twenty-second, sixteen thirty-three
> A momentous day for you and me.
> Of all the days that was the one
> An age of reason could have begun.[50]

Both the English version—slightly distorted because of the translators' commendable desire to preserve the rhyme-scheme of Brecht's *knittelvers*—and the original stress the importance of this swiftly passing June day for "you and me." We could have been led out of darkness into light; an age of reason, like Christ, stood at the door. The translation does not reflect Brecht's offhand echo of the Bible here; his works abound in scriptural reference.[51] Both versions make clear the possibility of revelation on this particular day; but the scene's title, projected on the screen, removes the possibility even as it is being offered. So, too, do the choirboys' robes: a future generation, eager for light and reason, the boys are clad in the dark garments of reaction and repression.

Clearly the effect of all of this is not to eliminate suspense; telling the story first and then suggesting that things might have been otherwise in actually staging it is a tried and true method of heightening tension. Brecht is ruthless in drawing out the hopes of Galileo's supporters in this scene. As they fret, reassuring themselves of Galileo's courage and consistency, Galileo's daughter, Virginia, prays for her father's salvation. The effect is, as Charles R. Lyons has put it, "contrapuntal": Virginia's "frenzied prayers" play off against the anxiety of the scientists.[52]

The language of the scene is charged: the Little Monk refers to Galileo's touchstone, the pebble that figures his faith in reason. The remark recalls Galileo's argument with Sagredo in scene 3. To demon-

strate his belief in "the gentle force of reason," Galileo drops a little
stone: "Kein Mensch kann lang zusehen, wie ich einen Stein fallen lasse
und dazu sage: er fällt nicht. Dazu is kein Mensch imstande" (pp. 34–35;
"Nobody can watch me drop a pebble and say: it doesn't fall. Nobody
can do that," p. 24). Sagredo's response to the demonstration is a grim
foreboding: he smells burnt flesh. "When you said you believed in proofs
I smelled burnt flesh" (p. 27; "Als du sagtest, du glaubst an Beweise, roch
ich verbranntes Fleisch," p. 39). Wondering why a stone drops is symptomatic of the curiosity and scepticism of the new age celebrated by
Galileo in scene 1; when the stone is mentioned again, in scene 6, it takes
on a color of menace from the disagreement with Sagredo. Waiting for
the decision of Clavius, the Vatican astronomer, Galileo drops his pebble
during a long and patently irrational defense of scripture delivered by a
Very Thin Monk. "You dropped something" sneers a Scholar; "It didn't
drop, Monsignor, it rose," is Galileo's response, a proleptic parody of the
repudiation of reason that will come later on in scene 13 (p. 45; "Hinauf,
Monsignor, es ist mir hinaufgefallen," p. 61). Both scene 3 and scene 6
anticipate the retraction itself; it is as inevitable as the pebble's fall. Scene
6 concludes with the first appearance of the Cardinal Inquisitor; Virginia's prayers remind us of the Inquisition too. "Let her pray," says
Federzoni, "She's all mixed up since they talked to her" (p. 82; "Lass sie.
Sie ist ganz verwirrt, seit sie mit ihr gesprochen hat," p. 111). The main
terms of the play's debate—the power of reason and the suppression of
reason by power—resonate in the scene's language.

Brecht uses the set in a similar way. Before us we see two significant
objects, the little Priapus in the garden, and right by it, the sundial. The
Little Monk quotes a poem by Horace, "in which it is also impossible to
change anything" (p. 82; "in dem man auch nichts ändern kann," p. 110),
with regard to Galileo's search for the truth. But it is the sundial, rather
than the enduring, unchanging Priapus, that dominates the rest of the
scene; in the 1956 Berliner Ensemble production of the play, a flaming
sun with a clockface superimposed on it filled the rear wall of the stage.
An image of stability is countered by an image of change; Galileo's
assistants watch the sundial as Virginia continues to pray.[53]

The stage is set with emblematic clarity; the language of the scene
resounds with ironic echoes of earlier scenes, and it will come to anticipate the language of the play's last scenes as well. The techniques of
Shakespeare's Elizabethan theater—"Ein Theater voll von V-Effekten!"
("A theater full of V-effekts!") is the enthusiastic pronouncement of the
Dramaturg in the Messingkauf (GsW, 16:586)—are all mustered: repetition, anticipation, proleptic parody, emblematic properties, dramatic

irony. The richness of the scene rests upon Brecht's careful earlier invest-
ment of words and things with symbolic charges that can now detonate.
The "traditional modes of exposition" that Fuegi sees in the play pay off
in the recantation scene; the tradition they draw upon is Shakespearean.[54]

Not only is the recantation not dramatized: it is ostentatiously not
dramatized. The most startling coup de theatre in the scene is the three-
minute pause, during which the assistants look at the sundial, Andrea
and the Little Monk with hands over their ears, waiting for the bell that
will announce Galileo's public abjuration, while Virginia prays "louder
and louder" (p. 83). It is unlikely that any actors, even Brecht's own
company, could sustain this pause for the full three minutes. But the
effect, as the shadow on the sundial slowly moves past five o'clock, is one
of a strange and almost intolerable suspension of time. Again, the stage
picture is emblematic: the scientists watch the sun while Virginia prays.
The sun, too, has earned symbolic value in the play; Galileo's blindness
stems from his researches into sunspots—research in which he publicly
engaged in scene 9 when Ludovico brought the news that Barberini, a
mathematician, was to be the new pope. Full of optimism about the new
age this betokens, Galileo quarrels with Ludovico and sends him away:
"In silence they begin their examinations. When the flaming image of the
sun appears on the screen Virginia in her bridal gown runs in" ("*Sie
beginnen schweigend die Untersuchung. Wenn das flammende Abbild der
Sonne auf dem Schirm erscheint, kommt Virginia gelaufen, im Brautkleid*")
is the stage direction at the end of scene 9 in this version—Brecht labored
to heighten the pathos here over the three versions of the play. "You've
sent him away!" she cries, and faints (p. 70; "Du hast ihn weggeschickt,
Vater!" p. 93). "I've got to know" ("Ich muss es wissen"), murmurs the
scientist, wholly absorbed in the sun's image, while "Andrea and the
Little Monk rush to her aid." The watching of the sundial in scene 13
replays this single-minded obsession with truth, while Virginia's prayers
in the foreground remind us of its cost.

Rülicke-Weiler, Brecht's assistant for the Berliner Ensemble production of the play, sees the opposition in the scene as one of past and
future: the past in Virginia, the future in the scientists.[55] This is one of
several possibilities. For the ironies multiply. The activity of the scientists—observation—follows the method of the new age, just as Virginia's prayers are typical of the old. As the shadow on the dial moves to
three minutes past five, they rejoice, "wildly happy" (p. 83, SD;
"überglücklich," p. 112). But their observation, their precise measure-
ment of the passage of time, is doomed to disappointment. While they

frolic in their error, Brecht heightens the incongruity of the moment: the Little Monk kneels down in tears and thanks the Lord.

Past and future clash with considerable deliberate awkwardness in the scientists' use of traditional Christian apocalyptic language to describe the impossible consequences of Galileo's—now to them impossible—recantation. "It would have been as if morning had turned back to night," says Federzoni; "As if the mountain said: I'm water," echoes Andrea (p. 84; "Als ob es am Morgen wieder Nacht würde, wäre es gewesen." "Als ob der Berg gesagt hätte: ich bin ein Wasser," p. 112). Both announce ecstatically the birth of a new age; their joy peaks in Andrea's vision of suffering mankind lifting up his head and saying "I can live": "All this is accomplished when one man gets up and says NO!" (p. 84; "So viel ist gewonnen, wenn nur einer aufsteht und Nein sagt!" p. 112). The new creation is a negation; the word that ushers in the new age is no. The delusion of Galileo's followers has multiple dimensions: historically, they are wrong—Galileo did in fact recant; theatrically, the projection at the beginning of the scene and the choral passage have emphasized this fact. Their language with its biblical overtones founders in paradox, a paradox visually represented in the Little Monk's apparently kneeling to join Virginia in prayer.

Their error is equally a scientific error. The observation of the sundial makes this clear, as does Andrea's series of conclusions:

> Also: es geht nicht mit Gewalt! Sie kann nicht alles!
> Also: die Torheit wird besiegt, sie ist nicht unverletzlich.
> Also: der Mensch fürchtet den Tod nicht!
>
> (p. 112)

> You see: They can't do it with force! Force isn't everything.
> Hence: Stupidity is defeated, it's not invulnerable! Hence:
> Man is not afraid of death!
>
> (p. 83)

There is something inhumane, not to mention illogical, about this sequence. It is easy enough for Andrea not to fear Galileo's death. At the end of the scene before this, the robing of the Pope, the Inquisitor suggests that torture will not be necessary: "Mr. Galilei is well versed in instruments" (p. 81; "Herr Galilei versteht sich auf Instrumente," p. 108). His examination becomes a parody of a physics experiment; Andrea's exaltation, a total misapplication of the laws of force.

Finally the bell of St. Mark's sounds, putting an end to the delusive age of reason. Virginia stands, thanking God for her father's salvation; the text of Galileo's recantation is read offstage. In place of Andrea's vision of "mankind" rising up, Virginia does so. Darkness falls on the stage—the audience experiences the blackness, hears the tolling of the bell, ponders the recantation. Brecht has arrested the movement of the scene twice: first, during the three minutes of muttered prayers during which a new age might have begun, and, second, during the blackout that follows the news of the recantation. Both moments are assaults upon the audience, designed, not to produce relaxed reflection—as Brecht sometimes argued of his theater—but rather to induce passionate involvement in the tempting dream of an age of reason free from fear of death. Despite the comedy of the scientists' foolish hopes, their disillusionment is made palpable in the real darkness.

The lights come up again on Federzoni's grumbling complaints and Andrea's "loud" reproach: "Unhappy the land that has no heroes!" (p. 84; "Unglücklich das Land, das keine Helden hat!" p. 113). This line accompanies Galileo's return, "completely, almost unrecognizably, changed by the trial" ("*beinahe bis zur Unkenntlichkeit verändert durch der Prozess*"). The stage directions remind us of his bad eyesight as he moves "uncertainly" to a footstool: the pathos of the broken, blinded scientist is almost unbearable as Andrea flings insults at him: "Get him a glass of water," Galileo says calmly (p. 85; "*Ruhig:* Gebt ihm ein Glas Wasser!" p. 113). As Andrea drinks, we hear the text of the recantation again: another interruption in the movement of the scene, another assault upon the sensibilities. Federzoni and the Little Monk take Andrea off, and Galileo finally speaks: "No. Unhappy the land that needs a hero." ("Nein. Unglücklich das Land, das Helden nötig hat.") The "no" has been spoken, and it is a crushing negation.

But the scene is not over yet: a reading from Galileo's *Discorsi* follows. It is impossible for an audience not to identify the falling horses, dogs, cats, and crickets of the discussion of durability, and the logic leading up to the conclusion that human giants are impossible and that "large and small machines" are not equally durable, with the fall of Galileo and his failure to achieve superhuman size and durability. Falling bodies recur throughout the play. Galileo's pebble, whose self-evident falls cannot be denied, has lent scientific inevitability to Galileo's own fall. The scientists in scene 13 have merely misread the laws that will govern the Inquisitor's experiment. In the final version of the play, the dropping pebble links up with the apocalyptic language that ushers in the new age in the choral passage that introduces the last scene:

Hütet nun ihr der Wissenschaften Licht
Nutzt es und missbraucht es nicht

Dass es nicht, ein Feuerfall
Einst verzehre noch uns all
Ja, uns all.

(p. 128)

May you now guard science' light
Keep it up and use it right
Lest it be a flame to fall
One day to consume us all.

(p. 98)

The confusion of light and darkness, falling and rising, creation and negation, evoked throughout the play by the symbolic devices and language we have seen at work in scene 13 is resolved in the atomic bomb.

The impact of the bombing of Hiroshima on Brecht and Charles Laughton as they reworked the *Life of Galileo* for American production in 1945 is notorious. Brecht's view of Galileo changed "overnight" ("von heute auf morgen," "Anmerkungen zu *Leben des Galilei*," *GsW*, 17:1106). In the 1938–39 version of the play, written while Brecht was in exile in Denmark, Galileo's recantation was a maneuver that permitted him to keep working, despite the repressions of the authorities. For Ernst Schumacher, this play resembled Brecht's essay on the "Five Difficulties of Writing the Truth" in Nazi Germany, and Galileo was the embodiment of the wily survivor.[56] The applicability of the history play changed with the passage of time. After Hiroshima, Brecht came to regard Galileo's recantation as the "original sin" ("Erbsünde," *GsW*, 17:1109) of science. Without, he boasted, a single alteration to the structure of the play, Brecht and Laughton transformed Galileo from a Schweykian evader of oppression into a gluttonous, sensual, insensitive coward. "As a technical as well as a social phenomenon, the atom bomb is the classic culmination of his scientific achievement and his social failure," Brecht wrote in 1947 ("Die Atombombe is sowohl als technisches als auch soziales Phänomen das klassiche Endpunkt seiner wissenschaftlichen Leistung und seines sozialen Versagens," *GsW*, 17:1109). From unheroic hero to goat: Brecht balances Galileo's great new age speech in the first scene with the murderous self-analysis ("mörderische Analyse," as Brecht called it) of the fourteenth scene. A new age could have begun; that it did not is now Galileo's fault.

The overlay of this highly personal reading of Renaissance history on a dramatic structure that was originally basically optimistic lends to the play much of its complexity, but it has also led to persistent difficulties of interpretation. These difficulties came to the surface when rehearsals for the Berliner Ensemble production, with Ernst Busch to play Galileo, began in 1955: Busch insisted that Galileo was less a great criminal than a victim of circumstances. Out of the "dialectic" of the conflict between actor and director—dutifully recorded by Rülicke-Weiler—emerged the final version of the play.[57] But Brecht cut the plague scenes from this last version, as he did from the Laughton version: Alfred D. White has suggested that the complex, dialectical Galileo who is both hero and goat is therefore relegated to "armchair theater." "The reader," he points out, "is expected to cope with more contradictions in Galileo than is the audience."[58] Some of these contradictions are the result of revision, rehearsal, and the passage of time rather than of design, as White suggests, but their accretion is not mere chance.

Contradiction and *dialectic* are key words in Brecht's dramatic theory: while his application of Marxist terms to drama is at times playful, there is no doubt about the profound impact of Marx upon Brecht's thought about theater. Just as Brecht urged his actors to "historicize" characters (*Neue Technik der Schauspielkunst, GsW,* 15:347), he was enabled through his reading of Marx to "historicize" all that bothered him about the contemporary "culinary" theater. His attack upon the "eternal laws of the theater" ("ewigen Gesetze des Dramas")—in, for example, "A Little Private Tuition for My Friend Max Gorelik"—("Kleines Privatissimum für meinen Freund Max Gorelik," *GsW,* 15:471) is part of a revolutionary attack upon the whole notion of human nature. Far from being unalterable and eternal, human nature, to Brecht, is wholly determined by society and changes by jumps. In Brecht's sense, the fatalism and pathos of historical drama before Brecht can be easily seen as culinary: the suffering queens of Banks and Rowe, the idealized Max and Thekla, the persecuted penitents of Strindberg—all reach out for empathy as emblems of humanity's struggle with fate. To Brecht, this kind of appeal is intolerable: the whole goal of his theater—whether he is calling it epic, scientific, or dialectical—is to shatter complacent acceptance of the human condition. His attack on the audience is an attempt to transform them into historians, fascinated by the process of change; in his theater, he declares: "the spectator no longer flees from the present into history; the present becomes history." When the present becomes history it becomes ephemeral, changeable; the audience, perceiving its own condition as relative and alterable, is capable of taking action: "The criticism of society is revolution," Brecht declares; "that's down-to-earth, executive criticism."[59]

Brecht came to Marx as to a kind of revelation: "When I read *Das Kapital* by Marx," he said in 1926, "I understood my plays." Because of his intelligence and interests, "this Marx was the only spectator for my plays that I had ever seen."[60] All of Brecht's later polemical and theoretical writings have the goal of molding an audience to fit this ideal. Early on, Brecht admired the audiences of sporting events, especially boxing matches ("Mehr guten Sport," *GsW*, 15:81–82); later, in the *Short Organum*, his most coherent single critical work, the audience became the optimistic children of the scientific age, transformed by contemporary theater into "a cowed, credulous, hypnotized mass."[61] Brecht's desire to liberate these children from their bondage—a bondage figured in the choirboys of *Galileo*—remained consistent throughout his career. Whether the audience is to be transformed into Marxist historians, into Marx himself, into bettors at a boxing match, or into scientists, it is to be transformed. The audience in the culinary theater is lulled into passivity by identification with the sufferings of characters on stage; the audience in Brecht's theater must adopt, above all, "the critical attitude." And, as we have seen, *Kritik* is revolution.[62]

This is not to say that an audience, after seeing *Galileo*, will rush out into the streets. Rather, as we have observed, the effect of scene 13, typically Brechtian, is to bludgeon an audience with successive coups de theatre into an acute and almost intolerable sense of paradox and contradiction. In Marxist terms, this should lead to an awareness of the basic contradictions inherent in capitalist society; what we experience in theatrical terms is an extreme ambivalence about Galileo, and his role in history, which is heightened rather than dispelled—despite the playwright's "own opinion"—by the murderous self-analysis of scene 14.[63] In attempting to think over Galileo's apparently paradoxical role in history, we are invited to think about our own.[64]

In his "reverence for *historicity*, as distinct from historical source-material," as Keith Dickson puts it, Brecht strives to stress the immediate relevance of his history play, frequently at the expense of fact. His "meanest trick," to quote Dickson again, "on his historical model" is a falsification of Galileo's "private life . . . in order to make him 'more negative as a human being' and thus elicit a more critical response from the audience."[65] Thus Virginia, a most benign presence in the life of the historical Galileo, becomes grim wardress of his prison in Brecht's play, her happiness destroyed by her father's single-minded pursuit of knowledge. Galileo himself is wholly secularized: his aggressive rationalism is far from historical as he is transformed into a "precursor of scientific socialism" in the first Galileo play and a traitor to that cause in later versions.[66] The emphasis on "you and me" as children of science in the choral passages brings the play's relevance home to the audience.

History has been used this way before in the drama. Schiller's prologue to *Wallenstein*, as we have seen, greets its audience as a special group gathered on the threshold of a new age, an age of revolutionary progress, and identifies this age with a new kind of theater, the restored theater at Weimar. Further, the trilogy itself presents us with a central character whose self-contradictory behavior demands ambivalent—even dialectical?—response. Brecht is acutely aware of his idealistic predecessor; both give to theater a central role in the coming of a new age.[67] Brecht derided *Galileo* as "technically a great step backwards, like *Senora Carrar's Rifles*. All too opportunistic."[68] In terms of its program for the audience, *Galileo* steps back even further into traditional historical drama. In his optimistic faith in reason, his use of history as a light to illuminate the present, Brecht reminds us not only of Schiller but also of Jonson.

But it is Bacon who lurks behind much of Brecht's play: he borrowed from the English civil historian Galileo's definition of science, whose "only purpose is to lighten the toil of human existence" (p. 94; "die Mühseligkeit der menschlichen Existenz zu erleichtern," p. 125). Brecht's attack upon contemporary theater echoes directly, as Reinhold Grimm has pointed out, Bacon's scorn of "*idola theatri*" in his *Novum Organum*.[69] Science for Brecht erred in diverging from the clear-sighted natural philosophy advocated by Bacon; Galileo carries the blame. Some critics have found a contradiction between Brecht's Marxism and his considerable enthusiasm for Baconian humanism: "a good Marxist," suggests Frank K. Borchardt, might "have felt obliged to subordinate Galileo to some inescapable social or economic laws."[70] In Brecht, says Michel Zéraffa, "*le destin de l'homme, c'est l'homme* et non pas . . . le destin" ("the destiny of man is man, and not . . . destiny"; emphasis and ellipsis in the original).[71] Discussing the way "historical conditions" should be staged in the new theater for a scientific age, Brecht adopts a humanist perspective:

> Die *historischen Bedingungen* darf man sich freilich nicht denken (noch werden sie aufgebaut werden) als dunkle Mächte (Hintergründe), sondern sie sind von Menschen geschaffen und aufrechterhalten (und werden geändert von ihnen): was eben da gehandelt wird, macht sie aus.
> *(Kleines Organon, GsW, 16:679)*

The "historical conditions" must of course not be imagined (nor will they be so constructed) as mysterious Powers (in the background); on the contrary, they are created and

maintained by men (and will in due course be altered by
them); it is the actions taking place before us that allow us to
see what they are.

(Willett, *Short Organum*, p. 190)

The dispelling of illusion, the banishment of dark powers from the stage,
the portrayal of human action as it really happens are all central features
of Bacon's program for a reformed stage.[72]

If Brecht's Galileo, like Bacon and Schiller, stands at the beginning
of the play on the threshold of an age of reason, at the end he has
destroyed the possibility of that age coming to pass. But only in his own
time: the opportunity he botched was, like Wallenstein's, a particular
one. In a sense, scene 15, in which Andrea takes the *Discorsi* across the
border to the northern countries, puts the ball squarely in the audience's
court. "No one can fly through the air on a stick," he calls back across the
border to the children left behind. "Unless it has some sort of machine
attached to it. Such machines don't exist yet. Maybe they never will
because man is too heavy" (p. 98; "Auf einem Stock kann man nicht
durch die Luft fliegen. Er müsste zumindest eine Maschine dran haben.
Aber eine solche Maschine gibt es noch nicht. Vielleicht wird es sie nie
geben, da der Mensch zu schwer ist," p. 131). The reference to the airplane
here is shocking; we know this is where the science that forsook Baconian ideals has led. Andrea's optimism recalls the "new age" speech of the
first scene, but his remark about the heaviness of man also recalls the
sheer physical bulk of Galileo. Galileo's fatness is the visual image of the
sensual greediness that engendered both his recantation and his con-
tinuation of the *Discorsi;* it is another apparent paradox, like the problem
of durability in small and large machines in the reading before the curtain
at the end of scene 13. This reading, with its resonance out from the
theory of falling bodies to the Fall and to falling bombs, dominates the
latter part of the play.

The associative method of dramatic construction—with its parallel
scenic units and repeated key words—which gives to Andrea's final
speech its curious mixture of promise and menace, is Shakespearean.
Despite his repudiation of Shakespeare's ideology and his attempts to
"sociologize" Shakespeare, Brecht saw the Elizabethan theater as a
model for his own.[73] A course of dramatic study suggested in a diary
entry of 26 October 1941 begins with Shakespeare's histories:

Der Realität am nächsten erschienen mir immer solchen
Stücke wie die *Shakespear*schen Historien, die
Dramatisierungen von Chronikkapiteln. Da ist keine "Idee,"

da wird kein Plott geformt, da ist kaum Aktualität. Es ist nur eine Durchleuchtung von Verbürgtem mit gelegentlichen Korrekturen nach der Richtung "anders ist kaum denkbar." Kurse über Dramatik müssten beginnen mit einem Vergleich etwa der *König Johan* mit der Chronik aus der er vermütlich geschöpft ist. Fortsetzung: die *Strindberg*schen Königsdramen. Selbstverständlich wäre zu studieren, wo die Glorifizierung oder Deglorifizierung praktisiert wird.[74]

Such plays as Shakespeare's histories always seemed to me the closest possible to reality, dramatizations of chapters from the chronicles. There is no "Idea," no structured plot, hardly topicality. It's only an illumination of well-known material with appropriate corrections in the direction of "otherwise is hardly thinkable." Drama courses ought to begin with a comparison of something like *King John* to the chronicle it's probably made from. To continue: Strindberg's royal dramas. Obviously what should be studied is where glorification or deglorification is used.

The "appropriate corrections" Brecht makes to the life of the historical Galileo tend strongly in the last version towards "deglorification." Brecht's description of the history plays as formless and without ideas is disingenuous; his use of Shakespearean repetition and metaphor makes clear his understanding of how much ideology apparently unplotted, episodic forms can bear. *Galileo* has a dominant idea—the scientist's "original sin"—a highly symmetrical and balanced structure and an abundance of topicality. The comparison study between *King John* and the chronicles would make immediately clear how little that play can be considered a mere illumination of the familiar. In discussing Shakespeare, Brecht is continually misleading and self-contradictory in this way. His good Marxist view of the Renaissance makes him deplore Shakespeare's ideology even as he rifles Shakespeare's theater's fascinating store of *V-effekts*.[75]

Brecht's imperialistic co-optation of Shakespeare's techniques—possibly *vandalism* is a better word—is always accompanied by rejection of Shakespeare's ideology.[76] But technique, as we have discovered, cannot for Brecht be understood without recognition of its ideological content. The theatrical *Gestus* always has social and historical implications. Thus, Brecht's admiration of Shakespeare as a "chef-dramaturg" in his own image, who would, according to the Philosopher in *Messingkauf,* be "Realist" enough to recognize that *King Lear* must be completely reworked to be staged in our time (*GsW*, 16:592), may have its own particular ideological components.

What is vexatious to Western critics about Brecht is the fact that plays that they find deeply moving have been written according to political principles that they find repellent. Eastern critics are annoyed, on the other hand, by inconsistencies with, even repudiations of, official doctrine in both the forms and the attitudes of the plays. Hence the tendency to celebrate Brecht as a poet in spite of his beliefs—popularized mostly by Martin Esslin—on the one side, and to confer upon Brecht monumental "classic" status on the other. Ideologically, as we have seen, Shakespeare has posed similar problems: his nostalgia for an ordered, bounded, hierarchical, circumscribed worldview led to the enshrinement of that nostalgia as *the* Elizabethan world picture; the anguished questionings and horrible sufferings of characters in the plays led equally to canonization of Shakespeare's absurdist despair. The stage techniques they both use also compound this confusion. Shakespeare tempts audiences to believe that the actions they witness are morally intelligible and aesthetically complete; then he revokes this comfort. Cordelia dies. Brecht's *V-effekts,* like Shakespeare's moralized spectacles, force from an audience double responses.

The recantation scene in *Galileo* demands a double response of great intensity, which can be described in terms of Brecht's favorite pattern of "Not . . . But": not darkness, but light; not "pure research," but morally sensitive rational inquiry. The alternatives are offered even as they are taken away. We live in darkness, not in light; scientists are "inventive dwarfs" (scene 14, p. 94; "erfinderischer Zwerge," p. 126), not moral giants. Brecht shares with Shakespeare, not an ideology, but an attitude towards ideology: systems exist to be explored, "sounded,"[77] confuted, and repudiated even as they are embraced.

The process is intensely dramatic, explicitly theatrical. By offering the audience an image of the rational Utopia that might have been and roughly taking it away, even mocking it, Brecht uses the age of reason in *Galileo* much as Shakespeare uses the haunting image of Eden in the Henry IV plays. Eden is always present in Shakespeare's histories because it is always lost; Brecht's new age haunts Galileo as an unrealized, but tantalizingly realizable, potential. A whole range of beliefs current in their society allowed Shakespeare's original audiences to respond with full complexity to Henry V's short-lived conquest of the "world's best garden"; Brecht has to train his audience as he goes along. But the techniques are similar—and similar, too, to the way Strindberg invests the actors in his histories with figural significance. Biblical reference, historical parallels, repetition of scenic patterns, language rich in sustained metaphor: time and again we have seen these techniques employed to shape history while still preserving a sense of its unruliness.

iv

The unruliness, the intractability of the past, the impossibility of writing historical drama without Idea, shaped plot, or topicality is its fascination. To assent wholly to the past's intransigence is to adopt in some way the post-Shakespearean English playwrights' assertion of history's total estrangement from virtue. Brecht will have none of the separation of private and public realms this implies; this is what offends him most in Schiller. Brecht enjoys the rawness of raw material: history's clutter of stuff does not alienate him as it did Schiller, nor is he oppressed like Büchner by the idea that whatever laws the study of history reveals are reductive, natural laws indifferent to human pain.

Brecht's Galileo, unlike Musset's Lorenzo or Büchner's Danton, is a revolutionary who had a chance to lessen human suffering. He lessened his own suffering instead. But as we view the play, we question whether Galileo's self-assessment, his assertion of the unique power he wielded at that moment in history, is valid. The three-minute pause in scene 13 also demands that we consider how "one man's steadfastness might have had tremendous repercussions" (p. 94; "Unter diesen ganz besonderen Umständen hätte die Standhaftigkeit eines Mannes grosse Erschütterungen hervorrufen können," p. 126). The subjunctive is significant: suspended between the Not and But of Brecht's theater experience, we are asked to consider not so much alternative pasts as alternative futures.

Alternative pasts dominate much of the drama we have been studying: the English playwrights' challenge of the past of public record with a past of private love, suffering, and intrigue continues to tempt historical drama's practitioners. But the classical art of Schiller and the systematic "deglorification" of Strindberg point in the same direction: their transhistorical, universal systems also negate the rough and messy record. No alternatives offer themselves to Musset and Büchner: the lagoon and the runaway horse figure their despair. By formulating a theatrical means of presenting the past as alterable and ephemeral, Brecht could crowd his stage with alternatives. Aristotle, in his *Poetics,* argued that tragic poets draw their plots from history because what has already happened must be possible. Brecht, in his continuing dialectical ballet with Aristotle, countered by insisting upon the improbability, the utter unnecessariness, of actions in the past.

This is as true of *Mother Courage and Her Children,* Brecht's "worm's eye view"[78] of the Thirty Years' War, as it is of *Galileo,* a "great man" historical drama with a world-historical individual at its center. Galileo's failure to grasp the full nature of his social and historical context begets his fall; it is as appalling a blindness as Mother Courage's stubborn persistence in following the war that gives her a livelihood but devours her children. The contradictions are again polarized with naked theatricality. Helene Weigel's silent scream at the end of scene 3 as Mother Courage hears the shots of the firing squad that kills Swiss Cheese assaults an audience as strenuously as the three-minute pause in *Galileo.* We are again given an emblematic stage picture: the body of the son is brought in and laid before the mother. She retains possession of the wagon, for which she had haggled so long, and must deny her son. The wagon dominates the stage throughout the play; the audience is asked to calculate its cost.

What makes Brecht's stage pictures as potent and evocative as Shakespeare's is both playwrights' willingness to take an audience's most cherished expectations—about "motherhood" here, about "kingship" in Shakespeare—and exploit them by simultaneously raising and disappointing them. The collision between our desire to see Galileo as a hero or martyr and Brecht's refusal to dignify the cowardly traitor with these names creates the tension that drives the play. As historical dramatists, both playwrights play upon an audience's desire that the past make sense, that history inform the present and the present inform the future. But Falstaff rises again, stealing Hal's glory; France, the chorus to *Henry V* reminds us, will be mismanaged and lost. The pattern of reform and recovery—redemption—is complete; but time marches on. A new age of reason might have begun if Galileo had said no. To usher in a new age now, we must say no to the idea that a single individual, a great man, can make a difference. Maybe Galileo could have done so in Brecht's Renaissance; now we must act in a mass.

Brecht's and Shakespeare's lessons thus are critiques of the processes by which we derive lessons from the past. What distinguishes Brecht and Shakespeare from run-of-the-mill dramatists like Rowe is that they engage their audiences in their own passionate scrutiny of the imaginative activity of understanding the past. The tension between the chaos of life, as we experience it, and the order of history, as we reflectively learn from it, is at the surface of their drama. Politics is the area of experience where this tension is greatest, where the human capacity for imposing order is most severely tested. Political action, for both, is the paradigm of human action.

This is not a formulation that sits easily with most of the playwrights in this study. Historical scholarship has shown them that politics is a morass of internecine squabbling, petty vendettas, meaningless equivocations, insincere negotiations. From this it would follow that human action is similarly small; without God, Strindberg reminds us, history is worthless. Hence the dramatist's fear of scientific history in the nineteenth century and his rivalry with humanist history in the seventeenth led to assertions of authority over the unknowable, undocumented regions of the human heart. Brecht and Shakespeare, on the other hand, historicize history as a discipline in itself. Shakespeare questions both providential and humanist ways of looking at the past. Brecht rewrites the history of science in order to make us rethink its future.

No dramatist since Jonson has approached the past with this moral fervor, with the conviction that things not only could have been different, but *should* have been. The English historical dramatists discussed in part one and the major dramatists we have just finished examining reveal instead an acceptance, however querulous, of the historian's authority over the past, a loss of interest in politics as petty and meaningless, and an assertion of ahistorical, artistic "truth." Thus it is tempting to descend from the peak of Bardolatry and ascend a peak of Brechtolatry: at last we have found the elusive "German Shakespeare." Imitation of Shakespeare led to the adoption of wooden formulae of easy pastoral pathos in English historical drama; imitation of Shakespeare's technique led for Brecht to his adoption, almost in spite of himself, of Shakespeare's evenhanded mistrust of all ideological certainties.

But if our study of Shakespeare, Brecht, and a whole host of other dramatists has taught us anything, it is to suspect such tidy formulations. Shakespeare transformed history into romance in *Henry VIII;* Brecht moved on to the more congenial form of the parable play. Neither wrote history plays for long. Creating great historical drama is a tightrope act; the strain of balancing the warring demands of dramatic form and historical data soon begins to tell. There is, in addition, an analogous tension in the discipline of history itself, expressed in the classic distinction between mere chronicle, the record of facts, and true history, which organizes the facts according to principles that may be called either scientific or literary.[79] Thus the historical dramatist, working from a usually published source, works from a predigested version of the past. But the immediacy of drama—the fact that it traffics in bodies on stage, or, in Büchner's words, gives us "characters instead of characteristics"—forces the dramatist to reexperience the gulf between the historian's "dry narrative" and the living bodies that once peopled the dead past.

This is hard work. The very "presence" of dramatic form itself makes the dramatist feel closer to life's energies than the historian, while, ever since the beginnings of secular history writing in the seventeenth century, historians have been seen as the custodians of "truth," guardians of the past and teachers of its lessons. Pushed to an extreme, this attitude led to the passivist pathetic tragedy of eighteenth-century England. Dramatists like Rowe explore the passions, their particular province; historians engage in dispassionate research. For Brecht, this is an odious division of labor; properly speaking, all the children of the scientific age, playwrights and audiences alike, must become historians. Nor does the division satisfy the dramatists we have studied in part two. Schiller may despise the *Stoff* of history, but he does not, like Rowe, ignore it: *Wallenstein* testifies to the intensity of his struggle. Strindberg's providentialism may be wholly personal, but it is not, like Rowe's, sensationalistic. The rejection of providentialism and its analogues by Musset and Büchner forces from both a shocked recognition of the worthlessness of history without God—a far cry from the benign theodicies of the early-nineteenth-century stage. Brecht's historicism permits him to elude the historian's authority by seeing the discipline itself as relative, socially conditioned, and ephemeral.

Shakespeare treats the chronicles with considerable freedom: their claim to truth is no stronger than his own. This is as true of *Henry VIII*, for all its weaknesses, as it is of the great Lancastrian plays. Brecht too faces the specter of the historian on an equal footing: he is one too. We all are. Or at least we should be: for the problem with Brecht, of course, is that the audience he hoped to create for his plays never materialized. The children of the scientific age remained enthralled by empathy, by the vision of unchanging, suffering human nature, even in Brecht's own Theater am Schiffbauerdam. What Shakespeare could achieve before the great age of history, Brecht was not wholly able to achieve at its close.

Thus the question of imitation of Shakespeare that unites this study of historical drama becomes, aptly, a question that, in historical drama, so quickly founders in paradox. Perhaps the English playwrights can be excused the staggering banality that imitation of Shakespeare conferred upon their historical dramas: after all, as Benjamin Bennett puts it, they "obviously could not dream of becoming the English Shakespeare."[80] What attracted the Germans, the French Romantics, and Strindberg as a luminous potentiality continues to be for the English dramatist an image of potentiality so utterly fulfilled as to necessitate Shakespeare's transformation into a force of nature and domestication into a household god. But as we have seen most clearly in the case of Brecht, honest imitation of

Shakespeare's techniques must entail an adoption of Shakespeare's multiplex perspective upon human experience and his suspicion of ideologies. Imitating Shakespeare forced Schiller to put his idealism to its toughest test; imitating Shakespeare helped Strindberg to evolve his own providentialism and give it expression in full dramatic form. Shakespeare was a gauntlet Büchner threw at Schiller—just as Stendhal flung him at Racine—and his unclassical episodic structure and crowd scenes gave both Büchner and Musset a means to express the horrible randomness of life. Brecht makes it clear that Shakespeare has not outlived his usefulness. In confronting the human need to make sense out of experience—exemplified in history—with the human experience of life as chaotic, surprising, and even senseless, Shakespeare not only offers the tools, but also defines the dramatist's task.

Notes

Introduction

1. R. G. Collingwood, *The Idea of History* (New York: Oxford University Press, 1956), pp. 282–302.

2. Francis Bacon, *De Augmentis,* in *Works,* ed. James Spedding, Robert Leslie Ellis, and Douglas Denon Heath, 15 vols. (Boston: Taggard and Thompson, 1860–64), 9:211.

3. Donald J. Wilcox, *The Development of Florentine Humanist Historiography in the Fifteenth Century* (Cambridge, Mass.: Harvard University Press, 1969), p. 105. See also Nancy S. Struever, *The Language of History in the Renaissance* (Princeton: Princeton University Press, 1970), and Richard Lanham, *The Motives of Eloquence: Literary Rhetoric in the Renaissance* (New Haven: Yale University Press, 1976), pp. 190–205.

4. In the essay "Historieskrifningens omöjlighet" ("The Impossibility of Writing History") in August Strindberg, *En Ny Blå Bok* (Stockholm: Björck and Börjesson, 1908), pp. 555–63.

5. Translated by and quoted from Leonard Krieger, *Ranke: The Meaning of History* (Chicago: University of Chicago Press, 1977), pp. 129, 269.

6. Lawrence Stone, "History and the Social Sciences in the Twentieth Century," in *The Future of History: Essays in the Vanderbilt University Centennial Symposium,* ed. Charles F. Delzell (Nashville: Vanderbilt University Press, 1977), p. 6.

7. Quoted from *Wagner on Music and Drama,* ed. Albert Goldman and Evert Sprinchorn, trans. H. Ashton Ellis (New York: E. P. Dutton, 1964), p. 145.

8. Herbert Lindenberger, *Historical Drama: The Relation of Literature and Reality* (Chicago: University of Chicago Press, 1975), p. 62.

9. Hayden White, *Metahistory: The Historical Imagination in Nineteenth-Century Europe* (Baltimore: Johns Hopkins University Press, 1973), p. 280.

10. "Verfremden heisst . . . historisieren," in Bertolt Brecht, *Gesammelte Werke,* 20 vols. (Frankfurt: Suhrkamp, 1967) 15:302; Roland Barthes, "Brecht, Marx, et l'histoire," *Cahiers de la Compagnie Madeleine Renaud / Jean-Louis Barrault* 21 (1957): 23. (Unless otherwise specified, translations are mine.)

11. See Lindenberger, *Historical Drama,* p. 51, for a discussion of Galileo as hero of a "martyr-play."

12. Hayden White, *Tropics of Discourse: Essays in Cultural Criticism* (Baltimore: Johns Hopkins University Press, 1978), p. 99.

1. Shakespeare's Dramatic Historiography

1. *1 Henry IV* and all other Shakespeare plays are quoted from William Shakespeare, *The Complete Works: The Pelican Text Revised,* Alfred Harbage, gen. ed. (Baltimore: Penguin, 1969). All subsequent act, scene, and line references cited in the text are from this edition.

2. Mark Rose's analysis of *Shakespearean Design* (Cambridge, Mass.: Harvard, Belknap Press, 1972) draws its language from the visual arts, with the triptych as a primary analogy. Bernard Beckerman describes the plays' centers as "climactic plateaux," to distinguish them from the explosive turning points of well-made plays, in *Shakespeare at the Globe* (New York: Collier, 1966), pp. 40–45. Hereward Price's idea of mirror-scenes has been highly influential: see his "Mirror-scenes in Shakespeare," in *J. Q. Adams Memorial Studies,* ed. J. G. McManaway et al. (Washington, D.C.: Folger Library, 1948), pp. 101–13, and *Construction in Shakespeare,* University of Michigan Contributions in Modern Philology (Ann Arbor: University of Michigan Press, 1951).

3. See, for example, John Russell Brown's discussion of the 1951 Royal Shakespeare Company production of the play, in which he describes the scene as giving "a still center in personal affection, to the round of wars, distrust, and self-aggrandizement," in "Theatrical Research of Shakespeare and His Contemporaries" (*Shakespeare Quarterly* [hereafter cited as *SQ*] 13 [1967]: 451–61), or Arthur Colby Sprague's comments on the Welsh scene in *Shakespeare's Histories: Plays for the Stage* (London: Society for Theatre Research, 1964), pp. 64–65. Robert B. Pierce, curiously, comments on "the charming domesticity of the rebel camp" in *Shakespeare's History Plays: The Family and the State* (Columbus: Ohio State University Press, 1971), p. 183. The tendency seems to be to treat the scene as a kind of intermission. Rose, in his discussion of the play, insists upon the centrality of II.iv and neglects III.i (*Shakespearean Design,* pp. 81–82).

4. James E. Hirsh notes parallels in structure between the final scene of *1 Henry IV* and III.i of *Richard II;* in both, the Welsh dilemma suggests that "the work goes on; holiday has not yet arrived. Henry presumably recalls that past but is still condemned, at least by Shakespeare, to repeat it" (*The Structure of Shakespearean Scenes* [New Haven: Yale University Press, 1981], p. 131). News of Glendower's death accompanies Henry's last, and weariest, reiteration of his wish to march upon the Holy Land in *2 Henry IV:* "And were these inward wars once out of hand, / We would, dear lords, unto the Holy Land" (III.i.108).

5. James Black, "*Henry IV:* A World of Figures Here," in *Shakespeare: The Theatrical Dimension,* ed. Philip C. McGuire and David A. Samuelson (New York: AMS Press, 1979), p. 176. This is not utterly unqualified, for Black sees in the play a "pendulum of spoken thesis and seen antithesis" (p. 172).

6. The discrepancy in the account is pointed out by Kenneth Muir in *The Sources of Shakespeare's Plays* (New Haven: Yale University Press, 1978), pp. 91–103, with no comment on whether the jumbling is Hotspur's, Glendower's, or Shakespeare's.

7. Quoted in Arthur Granville Bradley, *Owen Glyndwr and the Last Struggle for Welsh Independence* (New York: G. P. Putnam's Sons, 1901), pp. 121–22.

8. W. Garmon Jones, "Welsh Nationalism and Henry Tudor," *Transactions of the Cymmrodorion Society,* 1917–18, p. 32: "Henry appealed to the ancient historic memories of the age, to the past that is ever present with the Celt; he was 'mab y darogan,' in whom the prophecies were to be fulfilled; he was the long-promised hero who was to deliver the race from the intolerable yoke of the Saxon; he was the prince in the true Brutus succession, the descendant of Cadwaladr who was to wear the iron crown of

Britain." Jones provides a good discussion of the king's Welsh propaganda; for a more general discussion of Henry's "Britishness," see Henry A. Kelly's account of the genesis of Tudor myth in *Divine Providence in the England of Shakespeare's Histories* (Cambridge, Mass.: Harvard University Press, 1970).

9. Black, *"Henry IV,"* p. 179.

10. Geoffrey Bullough points out that the sources give an earlier date for the Tripartite Indenture, but Hotspur is still not part of it: *Narrative and Dramatic Sources of Shakespeare* (London: Routledge and Kegan Paul; New York: Columbia University Press, 1962), 4:165. Peter Saccio, in *Shakespeare's English Kings: History, Chronicle, and Drama* (New York: Oxford University Press, 1977), regrets this transposition: *"2 Henry IV* is thereby left a little thin in political substance," he complains (p. 52).

11. Robert P. Merrix and Arthur Polacas, "Gadshill, Hotspur, and the Design of Proleptic Parody," *Comparative Drama* 14 (1980): 299–311. See also John Shaw, "The Staging of Parody and Parallels in *1 Henry IV"* (*Shakespeare Survey* 20 [1967]: 61–73), for another way of describing the device: "It works without strain theatrically as a kind of 'double exposure' instantaneously modifying and ultimately enriching the playgoer's experience of the play" (p. 71). Lawrence L. Levin mentions Bardolph's nose as an inverse parody of Hotspur's confrontation with Glendower in "Hotspur, Falstaff, and the Emblem of Wrath," *ShakS* 10 (1977): 58.

12. Emrys Jones, in *Scenic Form in Shakespeare* (Oxford: Clarendon Press, 1971), describes the use of this kind of "scenic paradigm" drawn from tradition: "when converting his source material into scenic form, the dramatist must already possess the rudiments of a dramatic vocabulary, a repertory of expressive figures and devices which can be used in new combinations according to his needs" (p. 23). The idea that the mystery plays may provide such a repertory is more fully argued by Jones in *The Origins of Shakespeare* (Oxford: Clarendon Press, 1977): "it is the mystery plays that are our first history plays" (p. 85). See also Glynne Wickham, *Shakespeare's Dramatic Heritage* (New York: Barnes and Noble, 1969).

13. Morality play elements in Falstaff were first pointed out by John Dover Wilson in *The Fortunes of Falstaff* (Cambridge: Cambridge University Press, 1944) and were emphasized by E. M. W. Tillyard in *Shakespeare's History Plays* (London: Macmillan, 1946), p. 265, passim. Bernard Spivack expands this treatment in "Falstaff and the Psychomachia," *SQ* 8 (1957): 449–59, and in *Shakespeare and the Allegory of Evil* (New York: Columbia University Press, 1958). More recently, Alan C. Dessen has explored intensively the morality tradition's staying power: see *Elizabethan Drama and the Viewer's Eye* (Chapel Hill: University of North Carolina Press, 1977); "The Intemperate Knight and the Politic Prince: Late Morality Structure in *1 Henry IV,"* *ShakS* 7 (1974): 147–71; and "Homilies and Anomalies: The Legacy of the Morality Play to the Age of Shakespeare," *ShakS* 11 (1978): 243–58.

14. *Woodstock: A Moral History,* ed. A. P. Rossiter (London: Chatto and Windus, 1946), p. 227; Saccio, *Shakespeare's English Kings,* p. 52.

15. The Welsh chronicler Ellis Griffith tells a cautionary story about Glendower's assumption that he, and not Owen Tudor and his line, was the promised deliverer of Wales. The abbot of Valle Crucis, out for an early morning stroll in the hills, met Glendower. "'You are up betimes, Master Abbott,' said Owen. 'Nay, sire,' came the answer, 'it is you who have risen too soon—by a century!'" Quoted from Glanmor Williams, *Owen Glendower* (London: Oxford University Press, 1966), p. 60.

16. See Richard David's account of the Royal Shakespeare Company 1975 production, directed by Terry Hands, in which Worcester's "sour presence" added "fatality" to the scene, in *Shakespeare in the Theatre* (Cambridge: Cambridge University Press, 1978), p. 5.

17. Joseph A. Porter, *The Drama of Speech Acts: Shakespeare's Lancastrian Tetralogy* (Berkeley and Los Angeles: University of California Press, 1979), p. 115. For Porter the conversation between Mortimer and his wife dramatizes "the proliferation of tongues in the Babel story" (p. 53). David Woodman describes the potency of Glendower's incantations in *White Magic and English Renaissance Drama* (Rutherford, N.J.: Farleigh Dickinson University Press, 1973), p. 47. For another view of Glendower as benign and potent, see Anthony Harris, *Night's Black Agents: Witchcraft and Magic in Seventeenth-Century English Drama* (Manchester: Manchester University Press, 1980), pp. 139–40.

18. Robert B. Pierce sees the affirmation here as unqualified: "Hal stands above the bodies of Hotspur and Falstaff, the two half-men whom he has transcended" (*Shakespeare's History Plays,* p. 195). Black finds a pat resolution impossible. Alvin Kernan, too, discusses some of the problems that the morality substructure of the ending of *1 Henry IV* raises rather than resolves: "Hal may be Lusty Juventus, counselled by Vices and Virtues, gradually learning to be the true prince and the savior of the commonwealth, but Vices and Virtues like Falstaff and Hotspur speak with such ambiguous voices that it is difficult to tell which is which, and 'the mirror of all Christian kings' is so complex a character, and the nature of rule so mixed a business, that we are left wondering whether the restoration of the kingdom represents a triumph of morality or of Machiavellian politics" (*The Playwright as Magician: Shakespeare's Image of the Poet in the English Public Theater* [New Haven: Yale University Press, 1979], p. 116). James Calderwood offers some interesting speculation on the theatrical implications of the ending in *Metadrama in Shakespeare's Henriad* (Berkeley and Los Angeles: University of California Press, 1979), in which Falstaff figures "as a rebel against realism" who "threatens a secession of the theatrical from the mimetic aspects of the play" (p. 88). Edward Pechter's speculations are more concrete in their application to the theater: "In the vulgar hawking terms of modern mass entertainments: if you liked part one, you'll love part two" ("Falsifying Men's Hopes: The Ending of *1 Henry IV,*" *MLQ* 41 [1980]: 230).

19. See especially John Doebler, *Shakespeare's Speaking Pictures: Studies in Iconic Imagery* (Albuquerque: University of New Mexico Press, 1974), and Martha Hester Fleischer, *The Iconography of the English History Play* (Salzburg: Salzburg Studies in English Literature, 1974), for discussion of visual aspects (in addition to authors cited before, like Price, Rose, Dessen, Emrys Jones, and Wickham). Alice-Lyle Scoufos discusses traditional Christian imagery in *Shakespeare's Typological Satire: A Study of the Falstaff-Oldcastle Problem* (Athens: University of Ohio Press, 1979). More sophisticated is Howard Felperin's treatment of morality materials in *Shakespearean Representation: Mimesis and Modernity in Elizabethan Tragedy* (Princeton: Princeton University Press, 1977): "the older models embedded in the plays cast life as a drama of salvation and damnation, and the repudiation of those older models guarantees that there will be no clear-cut cases of salvation and damnation. The older models raise the questions; their repudiation insures a multiplicity of responses to them" (p. 65). For a more theoretical approach, see Albert Cook, *Shakespeare's Enactment: The Dynamics of Renaissance Theater* (Chicago: Swallow Press, 1976).

20. Emrys Jones discusses the relationship between *The Serpent of Division* (a prose tract by Lydgate), *Gorboduc,* and their possible influence on the *Henry VI* plays in *Origins,* p. 124.

21. Hereward Price uses the image: "Shakespeare's art is polyphonic, or it would, perhaps, be better to say prismatic; he decomposes his truth into many shades of color" (*Construction,* p. 36).

22. Emrys Jones, *Origins,* p. 282.

23. Herschel Baker offers the best discussion of the problems of providentialism in the seventeenth century: see *The Race of Time* (Toronto: University of Toronto Press, 1967), pp. 59–70, and *The Wars of Truth: Studies in the Decay of Christian Humanism in the Earlier Seventeenth Century* (Cambridge, Mass.: Harvard University Press, 1952), pp. 12–25. C. A. Patrides, in *The Grand Design of God: The Literary Form of the Christian View of History* (London: Routledge and Kegan Paul, 1972), argues that English historians had "such a preference for explicit formulations of the providential theory of history that indirect statements were avoided or, if made, were amended as soon as possible" (p. 73). See also Robert Hanning, *The Vision of History in Early Britain: From Gildas to Geoffrey of Monmouth* (New York: Columbia University Press, 1966). For the contributions of antiquaries to the debate, see May McKisack, *Medieval History in the Tudor Age* (Oxford: Clarendon Press, 1971).

For good discussions of Shakespeare's position in this complicated picture see Moody E. Prior, *The Drama of Power* (Evanston, Ill.: Northwestern University Press, 1973), and M. M. Reese, *The Cease of Majesty* (London: Arnold, 1961). Reese expresses the dilemma this way: Tudor historians tried "to hold simultaneously theories of history and society that were on the one hand practical and on the other hand providential" (p. 56). Also useful is Karen Hermassi's treatment of Shakespeare in terms of *The City of God* in *Polity and Theatre in Historical Perspective* (Berkeley and Los Angeles: University of California Press, 1977). John Wilders handles the issue of the Elizabethan world picture and Tillyard's Tudor myth gracefully in *The Lost Garden: A View of Shakespeare's English and Roman History Plays* (London: Macmillan, 1978), pp. 53–78, as does Pechter in "Falsifying Men's Hopes." Robert Merrix argues in "Shakespeare's Histories and the new Bardolators" (*SEL* 19 [1979]: 179–96) that repudiation of Tillyard has gone far enough. Eamonn Grennan argues for a closer linkage of Shakespeare with the humanist historians in "Shakespeare's Satirical History: A Reading of *King John*," *ShakS* 11 (1978), 23–37, and "'This story shall the good man teach his son': *Henry V* and the Art of History," *Papers in Language and Literature* 15 (1979): 370–82.

24. See especially Henry A. Kelly, *Divine Providence,* and Peter Saccio, *Shakespeare's English Kings.* Wilders offers a telling quote from Hall on the matter of portents: "But such conjectures for the most part, be rather of mens phantasies, then of divine revelacion" (*The Lost Garden,* p. 69).

25. See, for example, Aubrey Williams's discussion of the persistence of the world-as-theater image in *An Approach to Congreve* (New Haven: Yale University Press, 1979), pp. 19–57. Chief debunkers of Tillyard are Kelly—"the providential aspect of the Tudor myth as described by Mr. Tillyard is an ex post facto Platonic Form" (*Divine Providence,* p. 298)—and Robert Ornstein in *A Kingdom for a Stage: The Achievement of Shakespeare's History Plays* (Cambridge, Mass.: Harvard University Press, 1972). Merrix points out in "Shakespeare's Histories" that if Ornstein sees Tillyard as inordinately influenced in his theories by England's experience of the Second World War, Ornstein's work shows an inordinate influence of the American experience of Vietnam. The most flexible engagement of the issues raised by the critics of Tillyard, Irving Ribner (*The English History Play in the Age of Shakespeare* [New York: Barnes and Noble, 1965]), and Lily B. Campbell (*Shakespeare's "Histories": Mirrors of Elizabethan Policy* [San Marino, Calif.: Huntington Library, 1958]) has been that of Wilbur Sanders, who raises important questions in *The Dramatist and the Received Idea* (Cambridge: Cambridge University Press, 1968). See also David L. Frey, *The First Tetralogy: Shakespeare's Scrutiny of the Tudor Myth* (The Hague: Mouton, 1976).

26. See J. R. Mulder, *The Temple of the Mind: Education and Literary Taste in*

Seventeenth-Century England (New York: Pegasus, 1969), and B. N. DeLuna, *Jonson's Romish Plot* (Oxford: Clarendon Press, 1967), for discussions of the general practice of parallel-drawing.

27. See Baker, *The Race of Time,* p. 89.

28. "His typical scene is a miniature play with its internal logical structure, its beginning, middle, and end" (Price, *Construction,* p. 21).

29. Wilders: "The winner in this game of deception is Hal, who deliberately impersonates the prodigal son and feigns the false impression he knows his subjects have formed of him in order that, eventually, they will be convinced by his equally contrived reformation" (*The Lost Garden,* p. 90). Thomas F. van Laan, in *Role-Playing in Shakespeare* (Toronto: University of Toronto Press, 1978), offers a more orthodox view of Hal and Falstaff as "players": "Falstaff's is a world for playing roles for pleasure, as many as possible, and the more innovative the better; the emphasis falls on the skill of the playwright-actor. In the heroic world, however, such role-playing would be unequivocally evil. There the ideal consists of finding one's proper role from an approved list of existing possibilities and striving to fulfill it satisfactorily by obeying its dictates. In Falstaff's world, all roles are possible because none is crucial. In the heroic world, only certain roles can be tolerated, and one of them, that of king, matters more than all the others" (p. 150). Side by side these two confirm Grennan's lively image: "Shakespeare is constantly catching his audience in a noose of equal and opposite sympathies" ("Satirical History," p. 34).

30. Grennan describes the Chorus as the voice of "official history," translating the play to the audience and "in reality censoring what they see and how they interpret it" ("'This Story . . . ,'" p. 371); see also Edward I. Berry, "'True Things and Mock'ries': Epic and History in *Henry V,*" *JEGP* 78 (1979): 1–16: "*Henry V,* then, is epic history only if we accept the phrase as oxymoron" (p. 16).

31. See Bullough, *Narrative and Dramatic Sources,* for the sources themselves; Marie Axton, in *The Queen's Two Bodies* (London: Royal Historical Society, 1977) discusses *Lear* in the context of Gorboduc, Brute, and other predecessors, pp. 137–42.

32. Felperin, *Shakespearean Representation,* p. 94: "The air of contrivance that hangs about the Gloucester action is pervasive and it smells of morality." See also Susan Snyder, *The Comic Matrix of Shakespeare's Tragedies* (Princeton: Princeton University Press, 1979), and Michael Goldman, *Shakespeare and the Energies of Drama* (Princeton: Princeton University Press, 1972)—each of whom devotes an interesting chapter to the frustration of comic impulses in *King Lear*—and the richly suggestive *King Lear in Our Time* of Maynard Mack (Berkeley and Los Angeles: University of California Press, 1972).

33. Sanders, *The Dramatist,* p. 76.

34. Ibid., p. 117.

35. From the *Apologie for Actors,* as quoted by David Riggs in his valuable study *Shakespeare's Heroical Histories:* Henry VI *and Its Literary Tradition* (Cambridge, Mass.: Harvard University Press, 1971), p. 8; see also Riggs's discussion of Heywood, pp. 8–14.

36. Hamlet makes the same assumption: Claudius recognizes his guilt from the play, but does not, like the proverbial murderers and tyrants of Sidney's theory, reform; he becomes more dangerous.

37. See Grennan's distinction between Pistol's "outlawed comedy" and the Chorus's "official history" ("'This Story . . . ,'" p. 379); see also Edward I. Berry, "'True Things. . . .'" Marie Axton argues that "the eloquent disagreements of critics over its tone seem to me to underline the very real ambiguity which is the essence of figural history. A performance of the play will depend upon faith, not so much

in the historical person of Henry V as in the body politic" (*The Queen's Two Bodies,* p. 114).

38. The idea of "reenactment" comes from R. G. Collingwood's *The Idea of History* (New York: Oxford University Press, 1956), pp. 282 ff. Grennan argues that we *do* perform such reenactment and gain "some final insight into the natures of the two principal and, as it turns out, complementary 'makers' of history—the king, maker of *res gesta,* and the official historiographer, maker of *res scripta*" ("'This Story . . . ,'" p. 371).

39. Evelyn May Albright, "The Folio Version of *Henry V* in Relation to Shakespeare's Times," *PMLA* 43 (1928): 722–56, and "Shakespeare's *Richard II* and the Essex Conspiracy," *PMLA* 42 (1927): 686–720. Albright's readings of the plays and of the political situation were challenged by Ray Heffner in "Shakespeare, Hayward, and Essex," *PMLA* 45 (1930): 754–80. The paper war between them is neatly summed up by Peter Ure in his edition of *Richard II* (London: Methuen, 1956).

40. Richard Levin, in *New Readings vs. Old Plays* (Chicago: University of Chicago Press, 1979), sees Fluellen's salmons as pure red herrings and devotes his considerable skill to debunking "King James versions" that find contemporary parallels in unlikely plays. His skepticism is refreshing, but Shakespeare's joke would not have much point if it were directed at a modern scholarly practice and not a habit in which members of his audience, sometimes sloppily, indulged.

41. James Winny, in *The Player King: A Theme of Shakespeare's Histories* (New York: Barnes and Noble, 1968), argues that critical problems about Henry's conscience show that Shakespeare is losing interest in history: "At the point where uncertainty over established values begins to obtrude upon Shakespeare's interest in man's political identity, the matter of the English chronicles can no longer provide the groundwork of his imaginative interest" (p. 214). But Shakespeare's whole career shows that kind of uncertainty; and Ornstein's portrayal of Henry as a self-satisfied prig is also unsatisfactory. Calderwood calls Harry's a "corporate royalty" (*Metadrama,* p. 160) and says, rather wistfully, "I do not suppose that Shakespeare was entirely happy with Harry, but I think he may have regarded him as an ideal English king without feeling he was an ideal character" (p. 142 n. 6).

42. Ornstein, *A Kingdom for a Stage,* p. 211. See also James Spedding, "Who Wrote Shakespeare's *Henry VIII?*" *Gentleman's Magazine* 34 (1850): 115–30; Peter Alexander, "Conjectural History, or Shakespeare's *Henry VIII,*" *Essays and Studies by Members of the English Association* 16 (1930): 85–120; A. C. Partridge, *The Problem of* "*Henry VIII*" *Reopened* (Cambridge: Cambridge University Press, 1949); R. A. Foakes, ed., *Henry VIII* (Cambridge, Mass.: Harvard University Press, 1957); Frank Kermode, "What is Shakespeare's *Henry VIII* About?" *Durham University Journal* 11 (1948): 48–55; Howard Felperin, "Shakespeare's *Henry VIII:* History as Myth," *SEL* 6 (1966): 225–46. An interesting discussion of the authorship problem can also be found in Clifford Leech, *The John Fletcher Plays* (London: Chatto and Windus, 1962), pp. 154–57.

43. For a good discussion of disguised kings, see Anne Barton, "The King Disguised: Shakespeare's *Henry V* and the Comical History," in *The Triple Bond,* ed. Joseph G. Price (University Park: Pennsylvania State University Press, 1975), pp. 92–117, and "He That Plays the King: Ford's *Perkin Warbeck* and the Stuart History Play," in *English Drama: Forms and Development* (Essays in Honour of Muriel Clara Bradbrook), ed. Marie Axton and Raymond Williams (Cambridge: Cambridge University Press, 1977), pp. 69–93.

44. E. M. W. Tillyard, "Why Did Shakespeare Write *Henry VIII?*" *Critical Quarterly* 3 (1961): 27.

45. See Foakes's introduction to his *Henry VIII* edition, pp. xliii ff.

46. Ornstein finds "titillating jests" about the king's conscience wholly unworthy of the author of *Henry V* (*A Kingdom for a Stage*, p. 220).

47. See, for example, Edward I. Berry, "*Henry VIII* and the Dynamics of Spectacle," *ShakS* 12 (1979): 229–46; Larry S. Champion, "Shakespeare's *Henry VIII*: A Celebration of History," *South Atlantic Bulletin* 44 (1979): 1–18; Ronald Berman, "*Henry VIII*: History and Romance," *English Studies* 48 (1967): 112–21; H. M. Richmond, "Shakespeare's *Henry VIII*: Romance Redeemed by History," *ShakS* 4 (1968): 334–49; in addition to other authors cited above.

48. Ornstein describes the portrayal of Buckingham as a "masterpiece of artistic equivocation" (*A Kingdom for a Stage*, p. 210), designed by Fletcher "to intrigue and tantalize his audience, not to explore the mysterious paradoxes of human personality" (p. 209).

49. Felperin, "Shakespeare's *Henry VIII*," p. 231. The evidence for the alternative title is printed in Foakes, ed., *Henry VIII*, pp. 180ff.

50. Frank V. Cespedes, in "'We are one in Fortunes': The Sense of History in *Henry VIII*" (*English Literary Renaissance* 10 [1980]: 413–38), calls this "historical irony" (p. 416); Tom McBride sees Henry as "both romantic hero and Machiavellian prince" in "*Henry VIII* as Machiavellian Romance" (*JEGP* 76 [1977]: 33).

51. Ribner, *English History Play*, p. 249; Felperin, "Shakespeare's *Henry VIII*," p. 227.

52. Isaiah Berlin, "Historical Inevitability," in *Four Essays on Liberty* (New York: Oxford University Press, 1969), pp. 41–118.

53. Hence the numerous attempts of critics to reclassify the play in terms of other genres: historical romance, masque, etc.

54. See Calderwood's paradoxical treatment of Falstaff's theatricality in *Metadrama*, pp. 73 ff.

55. Cespedes uses a traditional comic vocabulary to describe Elizabeth's birth as "a 'holiday' in the midst of history's grim and implacable business" ("'We are one,'" p. 437); see also Lee Bliss, "The Wheel of Fortune and the Maiden Phoenix of Shakespeare's *King Henry VIII*," *ELH* 42 (1975): 1–25, and Robert W. Uphaus, "History, Romance, and *Henry VIII*," *Iowa State Journal of Research* 53 (1979): 177–83.

56. For court masques, see Stephen Orgel, *The Illusion of Power: Political Theater in the English Renaissance* (Berkeley and Los Angeles: University of California Press, 1975), and Stephen Orgel and Roy Strong, *Inigo Jones: The Theatre of the Stuart Court*, 2 vols. (London: Sotheby Parke Bernet; Berkeley and Los Angeles: University of California Press, 1973): "The Caroline masque provides us with a remarkable insight into the royal point of view, whereby the complexities of contemporary issues were resolved through idealizations and allegories, visions of Platonic realities" (1:51).

57. For Sidney, history, "being captived to the truth of a foolish world, is many times a terror from well-doing and an encouragment to unbridled wickedness" (*A Defense of Poesy*, in *Miscellaneous Prose of Sir Philip Sidney*, ed. Katherine Duncan-Jones and Jan van Dorsten [Oxford: Clarendon Press, 1973], p. 90). Bacon neatly reverses the conventional elevation of poetry over history while at the same time seeming to endorse it: "So as it appeareth that poesy serveth and conferreth to magnanimity, morality, and to delectation. And therefore was it ever thought to have some participation of divineness, because it doth raise and erect the mind, by submitting the shew of things to the desires of the mind; whereas reason doth buckle and bow the mind unto the nature of things" (*The Advancement of Learning*, in *Works*, ed. James Spedding, Robert Leslie Ellis, and Douglas Denon Heath, 15 vols. [Boston: Taggard and Thompson, 1860–64], 6:203). In *De Augmentis*, he reveals his position more

bluntly: "We are much beholden to Machiavelli and other writers of that class, who openly and unfeignedly declare or describe what men do, and not what they ought to do" (*Works*, 9:211).

2. Humanist History and Theatrical Truth

1. The Privy Council ruled in June 1599 that "no English Histories should be printed unless allowed by members of the Council": B. N. DeLuna, *Jonson's Romish Plot* (Oxford: Clarendon, 1967), p. 2. For the rise of the Office of Revels, see Virginia Gildersleeve, *Government Regulation of the Elizabethan Drama* (New York: Columbia University Press, 1908), and Glynne Wickham, *Early English Stages, 1300–1660*, vol. 2, pt. 1 (New York: Columbia University Press, 1963), pp. 54–97. Appearing too late to be consulted while this chapter was being written is Annabel Patterson, *Censorship and Interpretation: The Conditions of Writing and Reading in Early Modern England* (Madison: University of Wisconsin Press, 1984).

2. Irving Ribner's list, appended to his *English History Play in the Age of Shakespeare* (New York: Barnes and Noble, 1965), includes "romantic drama employing historical figures" that makes "no attempt to accomplish the serious purposes of the historian" (p. 267); plays that draw upon the legendary or remote past, like Fletcher's *Bonduca* or Davenport's *King John and Matilda* (printed 1656), are purely fanciful and do not qualify as historical drama.

3. See *The Dramatic Records of Sir Henry Herbert*, ed. Joseph Q. Adams (New Haven: Yale University Press, 1917; rpt. New York: B. Blom, 1964), p. 18 (hereafter cited as Herbert, *Dramatic Records*). For *Perkin Warbeck*, see G. E. Bentley, *The Jacobean and Caroline Stage* (Oxford: Clarendon Press, 1956), 3:455–56; Peter Ure discusses some of the problems involved in the printers' announcement that they had published the play "observing the Caution in the License" in his edition of *Perkin Warbeck* (London: Methuen, 1968), pp. xxii–xxv.

4. See Herbert, *Dramatic Records*, p. 19; see also the discussion of the manuscript in *The Plays and Poems of Philip Massinger*, ed. Philip Edwards and Colin Gibson, 5 vols. (Oxford: Clarendon, 1976), 3:293–94.

5. Jonson told Drummond that "Northampton was his mortall enemie for beating, on a St. George's Day, one of his attenders: He was called before the Councell for his Sejanus and accused both of poperie and treason by him" (Jesse F. Bradley and Joseph Q. Adams, eds. *The Jonson Allusion-Book* [New Haven: Yale University Press, 1922], p. 115).

6. "To the Readers," in Ben Jonson, *Sejanus*, ed. Jonas A. Barish (New Haven: Yale University Press, 1965), p. 28. All quotations are from this edition, and subsequent references are cited in the text.

7. The account of Essex's involvement in the publication of Hayward's *History* can be found in Robert Lacey, *Robert, Earl of Essex* (New York: Atheneum, 1971), pp. 255–56. See also Edwin A. Abbott, *Bacon and Essex* (London: Seeley, Jackson, and Halliday, 1877). Tacitus is quoted from the *Annals of Imperial Rome*, trans. Michael Grant, rev. ed. (Baltimore: Penguin, 1971), p. 170.

8. See Marvin L. Vawter, "The Seeds of Virtue: Political Imperatives in Jonson's *Sejanus*," *Studies in the Literary Imagination* 6 (1973): 41–60, for a reading of the play that attacks the passivity of the Germanicans.

9. K. M. Burton, "The Political Tragedies of Chapman and Ben Jonson," *Essays in Criticism* 2 (1952): 397; Christopher Ricks, "*Sejanus* and Dismemberment," *MLN* 76 (1961): 301–8; K. W. Evans, "*Sejanus* and the Ideal Prince Tradition," *SEL* 11 (1971):

253. See also Geoffrey Hill, "The World's Proportion," in *Jacobean Theatre*, ed. John Russell Brown and Bernard Harris (New York: Capricorn, 1967): Tiberius is treated with a cautious balance between "disgust at corruption and reverence for consecrated power" (p. 124). John G. Sweeney III, in *"Sejanus* and the People's Beastly Rage" (*ELH* 48 [1981]), discusses Jonson's interest in Tiberius as a relationship of "part fascination, part expiation, fascination with the kind of self-posturing that spurns all moral principle except what it incorporates disingenuously into its self-gratifying theatricality, expiation for his selfishness with principles that seemed to him to require selflessness" (p. 79).

10. For a fuller discussion of the pattern of contemporary reference in *Sejanus*, see Matthew H. Wikander, "'Queasy to be Touched': The World of Ben Jonson's *Sejanus*," *JEGP* 78 (1979): 345–57. See also Patterson, *Censorship and Interpretation*, pp. 49–58. In a different context, Sweeney also discusses Jonson's technique of "exciting responses in order to reject them and soliciting judgments that go unsupported by dramatic action" (*"Sejanus,"* p. 68).

11. DeLuna uses *Sejanus* to prove that Jonson "had a history of being unfriendly to Essex" (*Jonson's Romish Plot*, pp. 250–52), but surely this is going at the problem backwards.

12. See Barish, *Sejanus*, p. 7.

13. Quoted in George Chapman, *The Tragedies*, ed. T. M. Parrott, 2 vols. (1910; rpt. New York: Russell and Russell, 1961), 2:591. All quotations are from this edition, and subsequent references are cited in the text.

14. DeLuna, *Jonson's Romish Plot*, p. 20n.

15. Lacey, *Robert, Earl of Essex*, p. 212; Chapman, *The Tragedies*, ed. Parrott, 2:609.

16. Quoted in G. B. Harrison, *The Life and Death of Robert Devereux Earl of Essex* (New York: Henry Holt, 1937), p. 316.

17. Burton argues this point in "Political Tragedies," as do Ennis Rees in *The Tragedies of George Chapman* (Cambridge, Mass.: Harvard University Press, 1954) and Parrott in his edition of Chapman's *Tragedies*.

18. Norma D. Solve, *Stuart Politics in Chapman's "Tragedy of Chabot"* (Ann Arbor: University of Michigan Publications, 1928), p. 148.

19. Most historians do not agree with DeLuna's assessment, in *Jonson's Romish Plot*, of Jonson's importance to the discovery of the plot. Paul Durst, in *Intended Treason* (London and New York: W. H. Allen, 1970), sees Jonson as one of many petty informers (p. 85).

20. Burton, "Political Tragedies," p. 409.

21. For a full discussion of the problems involved in dating *Mortimer His Fall*, see *Ben Jonson*, vol. 2, *The Man and His Work*, ed. C. H. Herford and Percy Simpson (Oxford: Clarendon Press, 1925), pp. 6, 214, and Leo Kirschbaum, "Jonson, Seneca, and Mortimer," in *Studies in Honor of John Wilcox*, ed. A. Dayle Wallace and Woodburn O. Ross (Detroit: Wayne State University Press, 1958), pp. 9–22.

22. *Mortimer His Fall*, quoted from *Ben Jonson*, vol. 7, *The Sad Shepherd, The Fall of Mortimer, Masques and Entertainments*, ed. C. H. Herford, Percy Simpson, and Evelyn Simpson (Oxford: Clarendon, 1941), pp. 58–59.

23. Philip Edwards, "The Royal Pretender in Massinger and Ford," *Essays and Studies* 27 (1974): 36; Anne Barton, "He That Plays the King: Ford's *Perkin Warbeck* and the Stuart History Play," in *English Drama: Forms and Development* (Essays in Honour of Muriel Clara Bradbrook), ed. Marie Axton and Raymond Williams (Cambridge: Cambridge University Press, 1977), p. 77; Jackson I. Cope, *The Theater and the Dream* (Baltimore: Johns Hopkins University Press, 1973), p. 133.

24. Thomas Drue, *The Life of the Dutches of Suffolke* (London: for Jasper Emery,

1631), sig. B3v; all quotations are from this edition, and subsequent references are cited in the text.

25. S. R. Gardiner, "The Political Element in Massinger," *ContempR* 28 (1876): 495. See also Allen Gross, "Contemporary Politics in Massinger" (*SEL* 6 [1966]): at the end of his career, according to Gross, Massinger "no longer quite trusted his king" (p. 290). Benjamin T. Spencer discusses the politics of *The Bondman* in his edition of that play (Princeton: Princeton University Press, 1932), pp. 28–43; for *The Maid of Honour,* see Eva Byrne's edition (London: R. Clay, 1927), pp. xxi–xxxii.

26. Philip Massinger and John Fletcher, *The Tragedy of Sir John van olden Barnavelt,* ed. Wilhelmina P. Frijlinck (Amsterdam: H. G. van Dorssen, 1922), p. xlix. All quotations, including the notes of the censor, are from this edition, and subsequent references are cited in the text.

27. Herbert, *Dramatic Records,* p. 19.

28. *Believe as Ye List* in *Philip Massinger,* ed. Arthur Symons, 2 vols. (London: Vizetelly, 1889), 2:383. All quotations are from this edition, and references are cited in the text.

29. Gardiner, "The Political Element," p. 503.

30. Edwards, "The Royal Pretender," p. 34.

31. Anderson, *John Ford,* p. 80. Harbage conjectured ("The Mystery of *Perkin Warbeck,*" in *Studies in the English Renaissance Drama,* ed. Josephine Waters Bennett, Oscar Cargill, and Vernon Hall, Jr. [New York: New York University Press, 1959], p. 131) that Ford's play is a reworking of an original play, of which Dekker "shaped the whole," with the pointedly Pirandellan title *Believe It Is So and It Is So.* There is no external evidence for this: Harbage, like U. M. Ellis-Fermor, finds *Perkin Warbeck* uncharacteristic of Ford and suggests Dekker's play in preference to the "mystery" of its stylistic uniqueness. For Ellis-Fermor, in *The Jacobean Drama* (New York: Random House, 1964), *Perkin Warbeck* "is likely to please best those who least appreciate the author's individual flavor" (p. 233). Peter Ure has tried to resolve the question of relationships among the three plays in his edition of *Perkin Warbeck* (London: Methuen, 1967), pp. xxii–xxv.

32. Cope, *The Theater and the Dream,* pp. 124–25. Cope also borrows from *1 Henry IV* the image of Perkin as "a carnival king whose moment of pageantry must fade with the holidays" (p. 125). In Habsburg propaganda, Frederick of Bohemia was frequently satirized as a mockery king, a ridiculous imposter.

33. T. S. Eliot, *Selected Essays* (New York: Harcourt, 1960), p. 177; Jonas A. Barish, "*Perkin Warbeck* as Anti-History," *Essays in Criticism* 20 (1970): 152.

34. Alfred Harbage, *Cavalier Drama* (London: Oxford University Press, 1936), uses the word *bookish:* he sees in Ford a "tendency to create plays as literature, to concentrate upon his own predilections and develop his own artistic ideals" (p. 162). Peter Ure, ed., *Perkin Warbeck,* cites a large body of opinion on the anachronistic quality of the play (p. xlix). All quotations are from *Perkin Warbeck,* ed. Donald K. Anderson (Lincoln: University of Nebraska Press, 1965), and references are cited in the text.

35. Donald K. Anderson, in *John Ford* (New York: Twayne, 1972), points out a "striking pattern of alternation" in the exposition of *Perkin Warbeck* (p. 90). See also A. L. Kistner and M. K. Kistner, "The Fine Balance of Imposture in John Ford's *Perkin Warbeck,*" *English Studies* 52 (1971): 419–23.

36. Barish, "*Perkin Warbeck* as Anti-History," p. 158; Peter Ure, ed., *Perkin Warbeck,* p. xxx. See also Donald K. Anderson, "*Richard II* and *Perkin Warbeck,*" *SQ* 13 (1962): 260–63.

37. Barish, "*Perkin Warbeck* as Anti-History," p. 160; Bacon, *History of Henry VII,*

in *Works,* ed. James Spedding, Robert Leslie Ellis, and Douglas Denon Heath (Boston: Taggart and Thompson, 1860–64), II:210–11.

38. See, for example, Lawrence Babb, "Abnormal Psychology in John Ford's *Perkin Warbeck*" (*MLN* 51 [1936]: 234–37), where Perkin is diagnosed as suffering from Burtonian Melancholia; Ronald Huebert argues in *John Ford: Baroque English Dramatist* (Montreal: McGill-Queen's University Press, 1977) that an interest in extreme states and delusions is characteristically "baroque" rather than "renaissance" (p. 67).

39. Donald K. Anderson argues in "Kingship in Ford's *Perkin Warbeck*" (*ELH* 27 [1960]: 177–93) that James progresses from an immature infatuation with such archaic notions as divine right to a mature appreciation of royal responsibility. Jonas Barish views the process with less delight "that a young, high-spirited prince, fired by aspirations to honour, should be forced to leave the highroad of chivalry and take refuge in the thickets of policy" (*"Perkin Warbeck* as Anti-History," p. 161). Michael Neill, in "'Anticke Pageantry': The Mannerist Art of *Perkin Warbeck*" (*Renaissance Drama* 7 [1976]), characterizes the two poles represented by Henry and Perkin with a witty paradox: "If Henry's master . . . is Machiavelli, Perkin's is Castiglione, whose *Courtier* is recognizably a denizen of the *Prince's* court" (p. 119).

40. Bacon, *History of Henry VII,* in *Works,* II:289.

41. See Michael Neill's discussion of the marriage ceremony—and ceremony in general—in *Perkin Warbeck*: "a kind of performance which can confer its own reality through the magic of ritual" ("'Anticke Pageantry,'" p. 143).

42. Clifford Leech, *John Ford and the Drama of His Time* (London: Chatto and Windus, 1957), p. 12. Leech is one of very few critics to see affinities to court culture in Ford's plays. Harbage dismisses Ford from consideration in *Cavalier Drama,* pronouncing him oblivious to court concerns, as do Gunnar Sorelius, *The Giant Race before the Flood* (Uppsala: Studia Anglistica Upsaliensa, 1966), and J. H. Wilson, *The Influence of Beaumont and Fletcher on Restoration Drama* (Columbus: Ohio State University Press, 1928).

43. Barbara Lauren argues in "John Ford: A Caroline Alternative to Beaumont and Fletcher" (*Modern Language Studies* 5 [1975]) that *"Perkin Warbeck* is perhaps the most poignant of Ford's plays because, in it, an aristocratic code of values is invoked with profound sincerity by a fraud," making it an important "self-critique" of Ford's "tendency to freeze into an apotheosis of aristocratic virtues" (p. 61).

44. The word is from David L. Frost, *The School of Shakespeare* (Cambridge: Cambridge University Press, 1968), p. 160.

45. Ribner, *English History Play,* p. 300.

46. Barton, "He That Plays the King," p. 92.

47. J. A. Bryant describes *Sejanus* and *Catiline* as "a great poet's illumination of two important segments of Roman history," in "The Significance of Ben Jonson's First Requirement for Tragedy: 'Truth of Argument,'" *Studies in Philology* 49 (1952): 213.

48. As Stephen Orgel puts it, "If we can really see the king as the tamer of nature, the queen as the goddess of flowers, there will be no problems about Puritans or Ireland or Ship Money. Thus the ruler gradually redefines himself through the illusionist's art, from a hero, the center of a court and a culture, to the god of power, the center of the universe" (*The Illusion of Power: Political Theater in the English Renaissance* [Berkeley and Los Angeles: University of California Press, 1975], p. 52). "Platonic and Machiavellian assumptions merge in a common concern with the image of the ruler. Power, say the masques, is love; rebellion, unbridled passion; the king is order and nature and peace" (Stephen Orgel and Roy Strong, *Inigo Jones: The Theatre of the Stuart Court* [London: Sotheby Parke Bernet; Berkeley and Los Angeles: University

of California Press, 1973], p. 57). See also Jonathan Goldberg's inquiry into "absolutist poetics" in *James I and the Politics of Literature: Jonson, Shakespeare, Donne, and Their Contemporaries* (Baltimore: Johns Hopkins University Press, 1983), especially his discussion of Roman plays, pp. 164–209.

49. See Neill's discussion of constancy in Ford ("'Anticke Pageantry,'" pp. 132–35); Leech devotes some concern to Ford's "quietist ideal" (*John Ford*, p. 91). Barish coins the phrase "ethical kingship" ("*Perkin Warbeck* as Anti-History," p. 168). A good discussion of the cult of love and French prose romances in the Caroline court can be found in Graham Parry, *The Golden Age Restor'd: The Culture of the Stuart Court, 1603–42* (Manchester: Manchester University Press, 1981), pp. 189–90, 203–5.

3. The Pathos of Power

1. *An Essay of Dramatick Poesie* in *The Works of John Dryden*, vol. 17, *Prose 1668–1691*, ed. Samuel Holt Monk et al. (Berkeley and Los Angeles: University of California Press, 1971), p. 8. All quotations are from this edition, and subsequent references are cited in the text.

2. Mary Thale, in "The Framework of *An Essay of Dramatic Poesy*," *Papers in Language and Literature* 8 (1972), sees this ending as a "final fillip" (p. 363). For a different reading of the dancing French, see Cedric D. Reverand II, "Dryden's 'Essay of Dramatick Poesie': The Poet and the World of Affairs," *SEL* 22 (1982): 375–93.

3. *The Works of John Dryden*, vol. 15, *Plays: Albion and Albanius, Don Sebastian, Amphitryon*, ed. Earl Miner et al. (Berkeley and Los Angeles: University of California Press, 1976), p. 65.

4. Achsah Guibbory in "Dryden's Views of History" (*Philological Quarterly* 52 [1973]: 187–204) discusses "Dryden's insistence on the relationship between the age and its literature" (p. 199).

5. Lawrence Stone, "The Results of the English Revolutions of the Seventeenth Century," in *Three British Revolutions: 1641, 1688, 1776*, ed. J. G. A. Pocock (Princeton: Princeton University Press, 1980), makes use of the metaphor of a "seismic rift" (p. 23). J. P. Kenyon, *Stuart England* (London: Allen Lane, 1978), calls the Second Dutch War a "disaster" (p. 201).

6. For a full discussion of the mirroring of epic theory in Dryden's heroic drama, see Richard Law, "The Heroic Ethos in John Dryden's Heroic Plays," *SEL* 23 (1983): 389–98.

7. Nicholas Rowe, *The Tragedy of Jane Shore*, ed. Harry William Pedicord (Lincoln: University of Nebraska Press, 1974), p. xxi. All quotations from *Jane Shore* are from this edition, and subsequent references are cited in the text.

8. French historical romances of the same period show a similar emphasis. "Souvent dans ces fades récits, les révolutions et les guerres réputés inexplicables, se trouvaient soudain éclairées par une passion *inavouée*, par une jalousie, par un désir de vengeance" ("Often in these dreary narratives, revolutions and wars thought to be inexplicable are suddenly explained by an *undisclosed* passion, by jealousy, by a desire for vengeance"), says Antoine Adam, quoted by Jean Marie Goulemot in *Discours, révolutions, et histoire: Représentations de l'histoire et discours sur les révolutions de l'Age Classique aux Lumières* (Paris: Union Générale d'éditions, 1975), p. 161. Goulemot describes in detail some of these "histoires secrètes" (pp. 162–65).

9. Richard Savage and William Woodfall, *Sir Thomas Overbury, A Tragedy* (London: for F. Newbery, 1777), act v, p. 81. All quotations from *Sir Thomas Overbury* are from this edition, and subsequent references are cited in the text.

10. See J. G. A. Pocock, *The Ancient Constitution and the Feudal Law* (Cambridge: Cambridge University Press, 1957). See also Robert Ashton, "Tradition and Innovation and the Great Rebellion," in *Three British Revolutions,* pp. 208–23, and, on the discipline of history itself, Barbara J. Shapiro, *Probability and Certainty in Seventeenth-Century England: A Study of the Relationships between Natural Science, Religion, History, Law, and Literature* (Princeton: Princeton University Press, 1983).

11. Leo Braudy, *Narrative Form in History and Fiction: Hume, Fielding, and Gibbon* (Princeton: Princeton University Press, 1970), pp. 145, 211, 268.

12. Hayden White, *Metahistory: The Historical Imagination in Nineteenth-Century Europe* (Baltimore: Johns Hopkins University Press, 1973), pp. 54–55.

13. Herbert Lindenberger, *Historical Drama: The Relation of Literature and Reality* (Chicago: University of Chicago Press, 1975), p. 62.

14. Scribe's remarks on historical drama are quoted from Frederick Brown, *Theater and Revolution: The Culture of the French Stage* (New York: Viking, 1980), p. 16. "Historical drama served him as a means of demystifying the past," says Brown, "of banalizing exalted figures and exalting banality, of having Great Shades unmask themselves before a bourgeois tribunal" (p. 15).

15. *A Defence of* An Essay of Dramatick Poesie, in *The Works of John Dryden,* vol. 9, *Plays: The Indian Emperour, Secret Love, Sir Martin Mar-All,* ed. John Loftis et al. (Berkeley and Los Angeles: University of California Press, 1966), p. 15.

16. See Gordon Pocock, *Corneille and Racine: Problems of Tragic Form* (Cambridge: Cambridge University Press, 1973), pp. 1–14.

17. Robert J. Nelson, "Classicism: The Crisis of the Baroque in French Literature," *L'Esprit créateur* 11 (1971): 185.

18. Serge Doubrovsky, *Corneille et la dialectique du héros* (Paris: Gallimard, 1963), p. 83; Robert McBride, *Aspects of Seventeenth-Century French Drama and Thought* (London: Macmillan, 1979), p. 20.

19. Pierre Corneille, *Writings on the Theatre,* ed. H. T. Barnwell (Oxford: Basil Blackwell, 1965), p. 8.

20. Orrery, dedicatory verses to *Pompey,* by Katherine Philips, quoted from K. M. Lynch, *Roger Boyle: First Earl of Orrery* (Knoxville: University of Tennessee Press, 1965), p. 116.

21. Saint-Évremond quoted from Marie-Odile Sweetser, *Les conceptions dramatiques de Corneille* (Geneva: Droz; Paris: Minard, 1962), p. 145.

22. Jean Racine, *Bérénice,* ed. Léon Lejealle (Paris: Larousse, 1960) p. 22. On Corneille's *modernisme,* see Sweetser, *Les conceptions dramatiques,* especially p. 92; see also André Stegmann, *L'héroisme Cornélien: Genèse et signification,* vol. 1, *Corneille et la vie littéraire de son temps* (Paris: Colin, 1968), and Marie-Odile Sweetser, *La dramaturgie de Corneille* (Geneva: Droz, 1977). For discussions of *Bérénice* as an attack on Corneille, see Sweetser, *Les conceptions dramatiques,* pp. 153–56; McBride comments on its "extremely rich historical background" (*Aspects,* p. 63).

23. Richard Sennett, in *The Fall of Public Man* (New York: Vintage, 1978), argues a wide-ranging shift from public to private during the eighteenth century. One could add to the change in French and English drama a similar shift of focus in the Spanish drama: a play like Calderon's *Constant Prince* is far more introspective and ethical in its treatment of history than one like Lope de Vega's *Fuenteovejuna.*

24. *The Conquest of Granada,* and the essay "Of Heroique Plays" in *The Works of John Dryden,* vol. 11, *Plays: The Conquest of Granada, Marriage-A-La-Mode, The Assignation,* ed. John Loftis and David Stuart Rodes (Berkeley and Los Angeles: University of California Press, 1978): Epilogue, p. 201; the discussion of Almanzor's origins,

p. 11. All quotations from *The Conquest of Granada* are from this edition, and subsequent references are cited in the text.

25. See Laura Brown, "The Ideology of Restoration Poetic Form: John Dryden" (*PMLA* 97 [1982]), on Almanzor: "But by formal fiat—the imposition of a fortuitous romance resolution on the hero's extravagant career—this radical challenge is turned to the service of royalist stability" (p. 402).

26. *The State of Innocence and Fall of Man, an Opera,* in *The Dramatic Works of John Dryden,* ed. Sir Walter Scott and George Saintsbury, 8 vols. (Edinburgh: William Patterson, 1882), 5:133. L. C. Knights, in "Restoration Comedy: The Reality and the Myth" (1946; reprinted in *Restoration Drama,* ed. John Loftis [New York: Oxford University Press, 1966], pp. 3–21) decried the triviality of the comedy of the age without noting the heroic play's frequently literal dependence upon contemporary philosophy for the matter of abstract debate. Anne Righter, "Heroic Tragedy" (in *Restoration Theatre,* ed. John Russell Brown and Bernard Harris [New York: Capricorn, 1967]), quotes cynical remarks by rakes like Sedley to support her arguments (p. 137); Bruce King's *Dryden's Major Plays* (Edinburgh: Oliver and Boyd, 1966) attempts to show that the intention of the plays is deflationary and mock-heroic. Anne Barbeau, on the other hand, in *The Intellectual Design of Dryden's Heroic Plays* (New Haven: Yale University Press, 1970), sees the plays as ambitious Christian histories, "charting the pilgrimage of mankind to the new Jerusalem" (p. 81). Geoffrey Marshall, *Restoration Serious Drama* (Norman: University of Oklahoma Press, 1975), treats the plays in terms of "designs of stress" between ethical demands and feelings (see especially pp. 119–26). More recently, Derek Hughes, in *Dryden's Heroic Plays* (London: Macmillan, 1981), offers a reading of the plays that sees them as Christian cautionary tales about the limits of human potential.

27. A point of view current in the first half of the twentieth century: quoted here is C. V. Deane, *Dramatic Theory and the Rhymed Heroic Play* (London: Oxford University Press, 1931), p. 221.

28. "A Discourse concerning the Original and Progress of Satire," in John Dryden, *Essays,* ed. W. P. Ker, 2 vols. (Oxford: Clarendon Press, 1926), 2:38. For the relevance of ideas of history painting to Dryden's poetry, see George McFadden, *Dryden: The Public Writer, 1660–1685* (Princeton: Princeton University Press, 1978), pp. 233–40.

29. Guibbory, "Dryden's Views of History," p. 202.

30. *Heads of an Answer to Rymer,* in Dryden, *Works,* 17:185–93. Dryden's evaluation of Rymer quoted from 17:414.

31. Preface to *All for Love,* in Dryden, *Dramatic Works,* ed. Scott and Saintsbury, 5:326. "The Grounds of Criticism in Tragedy" in the preface to *Troilus and Cressida* by Dryden, in *Dramatic Works,* ed. Scott and Saintsbury, 6:263.

32. For a discussion of the importance of the shift to blank-verse tragedy in Dryden, see Arthur C. Kirsch, *Dryden's Heroic Drama* (Princeton: Princeton University Press, 1965). Eric Rothstein's argument is in *Restoration Tragedy: Form and the Process of Change* (Madison: University of Wisconsin Press, 1967).

33. *A Short View of Tragedy,* in *The Critical Works of Thomas Rymer,* ed. Curt A. Zimansky (New Haven: Yale University Press, 1956), pp. 161–63. All quotations from Rymer are from this edition, and subsequent references are cited in the text.

34. Letter to Dennis quoted from Dryden, *Works,* 17:414.

35. Dacier, Dennis, and Voltaire quoted from Trusten Wheeler Russell, *Voltaire, Dryden, and Heroic Tragedy* (1946; rpt. New York: AMS Press, 1966), pp. 20, 63, 110. Gordon Pocock, *Boileau and the Nature of Neo-Classicism* (Cambridge: Cambridge

University Press, 1980), p. 97. For Boileau's response to Corneille, see Sweetser, *Les conceptions dramatiques*, pp. 161–64. William Myers, *Dryden* (London: Hutchinson, 1973), p. 9. For discussion of Dryden's "strong sense of cultural relativity," see Robert D. Hume, *Dryden's Criticism* (Ithaca, N.Y.: Cornell University Press, 1970), p. 67.

36. Orrery's *Henry V* (v.51–66) quoted from *The Dramatic Works of Roger Boyle*, ed. W. S. Clark, vol. 1 (Cambridge, Mass.: Harvard University Press, 1937). All quotations from *Henry V* and *The Black Prince* are from this volume of this edition, and subsequent references are in the text.

37. Clark quotes these anecdotes and the French courtier's letter in his edition of Orrery's *Dramatic Works*, 1:25–29. Clark himself finds Orrery "Frenchified" (1:73), his plays stiff with "Gallic inactivity" (1:91).

38. Lynch, *Roger Boyle*, p. 146. This view differs from that of Allardyce Nicoll, who finds that for a "gentleman of letters" such as Orrery, "poetry and the drama sank to the level of a playful essay, a game to be indulged in for a brief hour or two" (*A History of Restoration Drama, 1660–1700* [Cambridge: Cambridge University Press, 1940], p. 19). Laura Brown also downplays the complexity of Orrery's career: for her, he and Davenant "reveal the obliviousness of the illusory royalist self-confidence of the 1660s" (*English Dramatic Form, 1660–1760* [New Haven: Yale University Press, 1981], p. 25).

39. Marshall, *Restoration Serious Drama*, p. 35: "The plays never present moral problems which seem to stem in any way from the framework of society" (p. 35).

40. Susan Staves, *Players' Scepters: Fictions of Authority in the Restoration* (Lincoln: University of Nebraska Press, 1979): "One function" of heroic drama "seems to have been to assuage the guilt of the postwar generation over its abandonment of the legitimate monarch" (p. 110). For Staves, these plays reflect a "gradual assimilation of changing political ideology, especially of a changed understanding of the right relationship between sovereigns and subjects" (pp. 109–10).

41. "The rules of the contest are so explicit that they constitute a catalogue of prescriptions for exemplary behavior" (Brown, *English Dramatic Form*, p. 7).

42. J. Douglas Canfield, "The Significance of the Restoration Rhymed Heroic Play," *Eighteenth Century Studies* 13 (1979): 58–59. For Mrs. Evelyn's remarks on *The Conquest of Granada*, see *The London Stage, 1660–1800*, 5 pts. in 11 vols., *Part One, 1660–1700*, ed. William Van Lennep, with a critical introduction by E. L. Avery and A. H. Scouten (Carbondale: Southern Illinois University Press, 1965), p. 177. See also John M. Wallace, "Dryden's Plays and the Conception of a Heroic Society," in *Culture and Politics from Puritanism to the Enlightenment*, ed. Perez Zagorin (Berkeley and Los Angeles: University of California Press, 1980), pp. 113–34, and Eugene M. Waith, *Ideas of Greatness* (London: Routledge and Kegan Paul, 1972), p. 207.

43. Dryden, *Dramatic Works*, ed. Scott and Saintsbury, 7:1. See also George F. Whiting, "The Condition of the London Theatres, 1679–83" (*Modern Philology* 25 [1927]): for him, "partisan zeal in the audience and on stage" are responsible for the Union of the Companies (p. 206); he divides playwrights into Whig and Tory groups that do not reflect the true turbulence of the period in "Political Satire in London Stage Plays, 1680–83" (*Modern Philology* 28 [1930]: 29–43). Rose Abel Wright, *The Political Play of the Restoration* (New Haven: Yale University Press, 1926), offers a good discussion of censorship; Robert D. Hume's discussion of the crisis is flexible and responsive in *The Development of English Drama in the Late Seventeenth Century* (Oxford: At the Clarendon Press, 1976), pp. 340–79.

44. The stage history of *The Massacre of Paris*, including its revivals during Jacobite uprisings, is from Nathaniel Lee, *Collected Works*, ed. A. C. Cooke and R. Stroup, 2 vols. (Baton Rouge: Scarecrow, 1954), 2: 3. For discussion of the suppres-

sion of *Lucius Junius Brutus,* see John Loftis's edition of the play (Lincoln: University of Nebraska Press, 1968), p. xii. Janet Aikins, in a paper delivered at the 1983 MLA Convention, discussed *Lucius Junius Brutus* in light of Filmer.

45. Shadwell quoted in *Dryden: The Critical Heritage,* ed. James and Helen Kinsley (London: Routledge and Kegan Paul, 1971), p. 157. Roswell G. Ham, *Otway and Lee: Biography from a Baroque Age* (New Haven: Yale University Press, 1931), p. 206.

46. *The Vindication of* The Duke of Guise, in Dryden, *Dramatic Works,* ed. Scott and Saintsbury, 7:148. All quotations from the *Vindication* and from *The Duke of Guise* are from this edition, and all subsequent references are in the text.

47. The parallel was often drawn in the 1640s too: for example, Edward Symmons observed in *A Loyall Subjects Beliefe* (1643); "Who that hath observed in the French story, the waies and doings of them that call'd themselves the Holy League in the days of Henry the third but must needs say, that the practice of some association in this our nation against their soveriegn doth most notably in many particulars go parallel with them" (quoted by J. M. Salmon in *The French Religious Wars in English Political Thought* [Oxford: Clarendon Press, 1959], p. 88). The explicitness of this parallel may have been important to Dryden's abandonment of the project in the early 1660s. While there may be, as John Loftis argues, "more use of historical event, and more accurate reporting of it, than may at first appear" in Dryden's heroic plays with their Spanish and Portuguese stories, Dryden eschewed the drawing of topical parallels in his early plays (see *The Spanish Plays of Neoclassical England* [New Haven: Yale University Press, 1973], p. 179).

48. Thomas d'Urfey, *Sir Barnaby Whigg, or, No Wit Like a Woman* (London: for Joseph Hindmarsh, 1681), sig. A2v.

49. "The curtain falls," says William Myers of the ending of *All for Love,* "on the play's only convincing representatives of human values, dead but forever (at least in art) enthroned, while an enigmatic, traditionless, inhuman authority advances to take possession of the world" (*Dryden,* p. 45); Henry in *The Duke of Guise* becomes similarly inhuman; Guise and Marmoutier become similarly "enthroned."

50. John Crowne, *Henry VI, The First Part* (London: for R. Bentley and M. Magnes, 1681), sig. A2v.

51. Nahum Tate, *The History of Richard II* (London: for Richard Tonson and Jacob Tonson, 1681), sig A2v. Tate expresses a degree of compunction about the abuse to history he feels he performed in whitewashing Richard: "*The Arbitrary Courtiers of the Reign here written, scarcely did more Violence to the Subjects of their Time, then I have done to* Truth, *in disguising their foul Practices. Take even the* Richard *of* Shakespear *and* History, *you will find him Dissolute, Careless, and Unadvisable: peruse my Picture of him and you will say as Aeneas did of Hector (though the Figure there was alter'd for the Worse and here for the Better)* Quantum mutatis ab illo!" (sig. A2v). The suppressions of these plays are discussed in Van Lennep, ed. *The London Stage, 1660–1800: Part One, 1660–1700,* p. lxiii. See also Robert Müller, "Nahum Tate's *Richard II* and Censorship during the Exclusion Bill Crisis in England," in *Poetic Drama and Poetic Theory,* vol. 26, ed. James Hogg (Salzburg: Institut für Englische Sprache und Literatur, 1975), pp. 40–51, and Christopher Spencer, ed., *Five Restoration Adaptations of Shakespeare* (Urbana: University of Illinois Press, 1965), p. 2.

52. John Banks, *Vertue Betray'd* (London: for R. Bentley and M. Magnes, 1681), sig. A4r. All quotations are from this edition, and subsequent references are cited in the text.

53. There are certainly more than in the first half of the century. S. N. Bogorad, in "The English History Play in the Restoration" (Ph.D. diss., Northwestern Univer-

sity, 1946), arrived at a count of twenty English-history plays between 1660 and 1700; but five of these are pure romance, and three are adaptations of Shakespeare. J. P. Vander Motten, in "The Dramatic Uses of History in the Restoration Period," concurs that there were few plays and describes them as "manifestly unhistorical" (*Studia Germanica Gandensia* 18 [1977]: 15–29). Nicholas Jose, in *Ideas of the Restoration in English Literature, 1660–71* (Cambridge, Mass.: Harvard University Press, 1984), suggests that "serious dramatists" of the Restoration "were intent on revivifying and refining the great and pertinent political histories of the Elizabethan stage" (p. 44); the gulf between intention and act is readily visible in the difference between the plans and the plays of Dryden and Orrery.

54. Ronald Berman, "Nature in Thomas Otway's *Venice Preserv'd*," *ELH* 36 (1969): 532, 543.

55. Colley Cibber, *An Apology for the Life of Colley Cibber*, ed. B. R. S. Fone (Ann Arbor: University of Michigan Press, 1968), p. 190. Steele quoted in James Sutherland, *English Literature of the Late Seventeenth Century* (Oxford: Clarendon Press, 1969), p. 77.

56. John Banks, *The Unhappy Favourite*, ed. Thomas Marshall Howe Blair (New York: Columbia University Press, 1939), 1.i; p. 1. All quotations are from this edition, and subsequent references are cited in the text.

57. Lessing quoted and translated in Rothstein, *Restoration Tragedy*, p. 98. See also Adolphe Rietmann, *The Earl of Essex and Mary Stuart* (Wetzikon: Wirz, 1915): "Banks is a dreary and illiterate writer whose blank verse is execrable" (p. 6).

58. Sutherland, *English Literature*, p. 77. For Hans Hochhuli, Banks moves "vom Höfischen zum Bürgerlichen, vom Love-Honour Idealismus zur Pity-Duty Empfindsamkeit, vom Phantastischen zur Wahrscheinlichkeit, vom freilassenden Fernen zum bindenden Nahen, vom erhabenen heroischen Stil zur Vertrauliche" ("From the courtly to the bourgeois, from love-honor idealism to pity-duty sentimentalism, from the fantastic to the realistic, from the freedoms of the exotic to the constrictions of home, from the noble heroic style to the familiar"—*John Banks, Eine Studie* [Berne: A. Francke, 1952], p. 95). The claim is grandiose, but Banks's move from public to private is reflected in it.

59. Rothstein, *Restoration Tragedy*, p. 98. For Laura Brown, Banks achieved a "skillful and surprising equation of English history and private pathos" (*English Dramatic Form*, p. 97), in which "royalty" serves as a "uniquely pitiable situation, and aristocracy becomes synonymous with misfortune" (p. 96).

60. Rymer, *Critical Works*, p. 163.

61. For a discussion of Rowe's plays as "theodicies," see J. Douglas Canfield, *Nicholas Rowe and Christian Tragedy* (Gainesville: University Presses of Florida, 1977). But one should beware, as Christopher Hill warns, of wholehearted acceptance of Rowe's providentialism: "Although 'providential' theories of history did not lose their vogue" in the late seventeenth century, "the fact that partisans of both sides in the civil war used such arguments weakened their effectiveness" (*Some Intellectual Consequences of the English Revolution* [Madison: Univeristy of Wisconsin Press, 1980], p. 44). For Rowe's partisanship, see Annibel Jenkins, *Nicholas Rowe* (Boston: Twayne, 1977), especially her discussion of *Tamerlane*, pp. 37–52.

62. Canfield's reading of the play is persuasive and influential, and he sees the ending as unqualified: "At the end, her own Way of the Cross, patterned as it is upon the Atonement, has brought her, deserted and derided, to her own Calvary of expiation and to a final *at-onement* with her husband and her God" (*Nicholas Rowe*, p. 168).

63. Jenkins, *Nicholas Rowe*, p. 116. She is an epitome of "Christian heroism" to Canfield (*Nicholas Rowe*, p. 176). Laura Brown emphasizes the disjunction between

Jane's sin and the moral design of the play: "She is particularly exemplary because she is not only innocent but perfectly virtuous" (*English Dramatic Form,* p. 153).

64. *Lady Jane Grey,* in Nicholas Rowe, *Dramatic Works,* 2 vols. (London: for T. Jauncy, 1720), 2:17. All quotations are from this edition, and subsequent references are cited in the text.

65. Alfred Jackson, "Rowe's Historical Tragedies," *Anglia* 54 (1930): 324, 326.

66. William Havard, *King Charles the First: An Historical Tragedy* (London: for J. Watts, 1737), sig. A3r. All quotations are from this edition, and subsequent references are cited in the text.

67. *The London Stage, 1660–1800,* 5 pts. in 11 vols., *Part 3, 1729–1747,* ed. A. H. Scouten (Carbondale: Southern Illinois University Press, 1961), 2:643. In *Charles the First: An Historical Tragedy,* by W. G. Wills (Edinburgh: Blackwood, 1873), the pathos is heightened by another authentic quote (again the only one in the play). The king's final speech is one word: "Remember."

68. In his edition of *Jane Shore,* Harry William Pedicord mentions these "hastily printed 'lives' of Jane Shore" (pp. xviii–xix). For lists of this kind of material, see *English Theatrical Literature, 1559–1900,* ed. J. F. Arnott and J. W. Robinson (London: Society for Theatre Research, 1970), pp. 367–87.

69. John Bancroft, *The Fall of Mortimer* (London: for J. Millan, 1731), sig. A2r. For a full discussion of stage satires of Walpole, see Bertrand A. Goldgar, *Walpole and the Wits: The Relation of Politics to Literature, 1722–42* (Lincoln: University of Nebraska Press, 1976), pp. 30–32, and John Loftis, *The Politics of Drama in Augustan England* (Oxford: Clarendon Press, 1963), pp. 105–6.

70. Henry Brooke, *Gustavus Vasa, or, The Deliverer of His Country* (London: for R. Dodsley, 1739). All quotations are from this edition, and subsequent references are cited in the text. For a full discussion of the licensing act and its impact, see (in addition to Loftis, *Politics of Drama*) L. W. Conolly, *The Censorship of English Drama, 1737–1824* (San Marino, Calif.: Huntington Library, 1976), and Calhoun Winton, "Dramatic Censorship," in *The London Theatre World, 1660–1800,* ed. Robert D. Hume (Carbondale: Southern Illinois University Press, 1980), pp. 286–308.

71. Joseph M. Levine argues in "Ancients, Moderns, and History: The Continuity of English Historical Writing in the Later Seventeenth Century" (in *Studies in Change and Revolution: Aspects of English Intellectual History, 1640–1800,* ed. Paul J. Korshin [New York: Scolar Press, 1972]) that both sides in the Ancient and Modern dispute "thought" that history's primary function was "the education of the statesman. Both considered it, at its best, a branch of literature" (p. 51).

72. *Courtnay, Earl of Devonshire, or The Troubles of the Princess Elizabeth* [author unknown] (London: for Nicholas Coxe, [1705?]), sigs. A4r, A3v.

73. Sheridan's prologue in Richard Savage, *Sir Thomas Overbury,* sig. A3v.

74. William Robertson quoted in Thomas P. Peardon, *The Transition in English Historical Writing, 1760–1830* (New York: Columbia University Press, 1933), p. 27.

75. Henry Hallam, *Constitutional History of England,* 3d ed. (London: John Murray, 1832), 2:310–11.

76. Braudy, *Narrative Form,* pp. 20, 13, 35; Peardon, *The Transition,* p. 108. Peardon discusses in some detail the impact of Macpherson's Ossianic "discoveries" on historians in the eighteenth century; some indulged in primitivistic adulation of the Celtic past (pp. 112–13).

77. See Leo Hughes, *The Drama's Patrons: A Study of the Eighteenth-Century London Audience* (Austin: University of Texas Press, 1971), pp. 114–15.

78. J. R. Planché, *Recollections and Reflections* (London: Tinsley Brothers, 1872), 1:56–57.

79. Kean quoted in John William Cole, *The Life and Theatrical Times of Charles Kean* (London: Bentley, 1860), 2:382.

80. Edward Bulwer-Lytton, *Richelieu* (London: Robert Dewitt, 1875), p. 16. The similarity with the historiography of Eugène Scribe is evident. Curtis Dahl, in "History on the Hustings: Bulwer-Lytton's Historical Novels of Politics" (in *From Jane Austen to Joseph Conrad,* ed. Robert C. Rathburn and Martin Steinman, Jr. [Minneapolis: University of Minnesota Press, 1958], pp. 60–71), finds an abundance of contemporary topicality in Bulwer-Lytton's novels.

81. See Peter Gay, *Style in History* (New York: Basic Books, 1974), for a fuller discussion of Macaulay: "His greatest sin, venial rather than mortal, is complacency, and he had some reason even for that" (p. 138).

82. Hallam Tennyson, *Alfred Lord Tennyson: A Memoir by His Son* (New York: Macmillan, 1898), 2:178. Tennyson's *Harold, Becket,* and *Queen Mary* composed a trilogy that "pourtrays the making of England," according to Hallam Tennyson's account; as such, the project won the praise of the eminent historian J. A. Froude— "No one since Shakespeare has done that"—quoted, with similar testimonials, by Hallam Tennyson, 2:181.

83. Tom Taylor, *Historical Dramas* (London: Chatto and Windus, 1877), p. 135. Roy Strong, in *Recreating the Past: British History and the Victorian Painter* (New York: Thames and Hudson, 1978), discusses the tendency of Victorian painters to be "preoccupied with the vanishing and transitory nature of monarchy" in a context of "gradual extension of the franchise" (p. 45). Thus, queens hitherto perceived as dangerously popish could be pitied, leading to a cult of Mary Queen of Scots as "*the* heroine above every other from the British past" (p. 129). Like Mary Tudor, she could now be safely seen as "a calumniated woman, and an injured princess" (p. 131).

84. Robert Bolt, *Vivat! Vivat, Regina!* (New York: Random House, 1971), pp. ix, xxiv.

85. Peter Whalley, *An Essay on the Manner of Writing History* (London: Cooper, 1746), pp. 11, 18.

4. Progress and Providence

1. Christian Dietrich Grabbe's essay "Über die Shakespearo-Manie" (1827) is discussed by Friedrich Sengle in *Das Historische Drama in Deutschland: Geschichte Eine Literarischen Mythos,* 2d ed. (Stuttgart: Metzler, 1969), pp. 164–65. For Schiller, Shakespeare's power was not merely Gothic, but also Scythian: he used the phrase "rohen, skythischen Pracht" in the first foreword to *Die Räuber;* see the discussion of Gothicism in the Sturm-und-Drang in Paul Steck, *Schiller und Shakespeare: Idee und Wirklichkeit* (Frankfurt: Peter Lang, 1977), pp. 56–67. Philip Edwards discusses the "new life" of Shakespeare's histories in *Threshold of a Nation: A Study in English and Irish Drama* (Cambridge: Cambridge University Press, 1979): "At the end of the eighteenth century, Shakespeare's English history plays, which had contributed powerfully to England's national awareness at the end of the sixteenth century, began a new life, profoundly important and long-lasting, in developing a sense of national awareness in other countries" (pp. 191–92).

2. "In diesem Spiegel lasse uns der Dichter schauen, sei es auch zu unserm tiefen Shammerötten, was die Deutschen vor Alters waren, und was sie wieder werden sollen" ("In this mirror let the poet show us, though it might be to our deepest blushes of shame, what the Germans were in days of old, and what they should be again"), urged August Wilhelm Schlegel in his last Vienna lecture (quoted from Sengle, *Das*

Historische Drama, p. 101). Friedrich Schlegel's views are more abstruse, and he recommended an allegorical historical drama; see Sengle, *Das Historische Drama,* pp. 101–3.

3. For Strindberg's predecessors in historical drama, see Gerda Rydell, *Adertonhundratalets historiska skådespel i Sverige före Strindberg* (Stockholm: Bonnier, 1928).

4. Golo Mann, "Schiller als Geschichtsschreiber," in *Schillers Werke* (Frankfurt: Insel, 1966), 4:893: "Von dieser protestantischen Geschichtsauffasung—der Whig-Geschichtsauffassung, wie sie neuerdings genannt wurde—ist Schillers Geschichtsphilosophie eine deutsche Spielart" ("Of this Protestant view of history— the Whig view of history as it has recently been named—Schiller's philosophy of history is a German offshoot").

5. Heinrich von Srbik in his great historiographical study *Geist und Geschichte vom Deutschen Humanismus bis zur Gegenwart* (Salzburg: Otto Müller, 1950) praises *Wallenstein:* "nicht nur grösste Dichtung, es ist auch grosse geschichtswissenschaftliche Tat" ("Not only great poetry, but a great historiographical achievement"—1: 156). Theodor Schieder comments on von Srbik's judgement: "Aber es ist fast einer Ironie zu nennen, dass zuletzt der Dichter über den Geschichtsschreiber einen letzten Sieg errungen hat, wenn nun der Wallenstein der Tragödie und nicht der seines Geschichtswerkes als 'geschichtswissenschaftliche Tat' gepriesen wird" ("But it is almost ironic to notice that for the last time Schiller the poet has won a final victory over Schiller the historian, since now it is the Wallenstein of the tragedy and not of the historical work that is praised as 'historiographical achievement' "—"Schiller als Historiker," in *Begegnungen mit der Geschichte* [Göttingen: Vanderhoeck und Ruprecht, 1962], p. 58). Schieder sees Schiller as succeeding in finding out the truth about Wallenstein in poetic rather than historical terms: "Aber Schillers geistiges Interesse blieb an ihm haften und wenn er die *historische* Wahrheit nicht rein und unverfälscht finden konnte, so hat er ihn schliesslich im Lichte der *poetischen* Wahrheit verständlich gemacht" ("But Schiller's spiritual interest remained constant, and if he could not see the *historical* truth about Wallenstein as pure and unfalsified, he did finally make him comprehensible in the light of *poetic* truth," p. 58). In English, see Benno von Wiese, "Schiller as Philosopher of History and Historian," trans. Christopher Middleton, in *Schiller: Bicentenary Lectures,* ed. F. Norman (London: University of London Institute of Germanic Languages and Literatures, 1960), pp. 83–103. Von Wiese's fullest discussion of Schiller's historical work is in *Friedrich Schiller,* 4th ed. (Stuttgart: J. B. Metzler, 1978), pp. 341–94.

6. *Geschichte des Dreissigjährigen Krieges,* in *Schillers Werke: Nationalausgabe,* vol. 18, *Historische Schriften, Zweiter Teil,* ed. Karl-Heinz Hahn (Weimar: Böhlaus, 1976), pp. 279, 191. Translation quoted in the text is from Friedrich Schiller, *History of the Thirty Years' War,* trans. A. J. W. Morrison (New York: Harper Brother, 1846), pp. 264, 178.

7. Hayden White, *Metahistory: The Historical Imagination in Nineteenth-Century Europe* (Baltimore: Johns Hopkins University Press, 1973), p. 54.

8. "Über das Erhabene," quoted from von Wiese, *Friedrich Schiller,* p. 394. The translation is from E. L. Stahl, *Friedrich Schiller's Drama: Theory and Practice* (Oxford: Clarendon, 1954), p. 73. Stahl discusses the influence of Kant on Schiller's theory of history (pp. 73–87), as does Hans Vowinckel, in *Schiller: Der Dichter der Geschichte: Eine Auslegung des* Wallenstein (Berlin: Junker und Dünnhaupt, 1938), pp. 23 ff. See also R. D. Miller, *The Drama of Schiller* (1963; rpt. Harrogate: Duchy Press, 1966): "This world is characterised above all by a principle which conflicts with that of freedom, the principle of 'necessity,' and throughout Schiller's plays the image of the

puppet is repeatedly employed to symbolize this principle opposed to human dignity" (p. 5). "After the early plays," however, "Kantian idealism no longer forms the main source of Schiller's dramatic inspiration" (p. 45).

9. "Ausserordentlich kompliziert, voll verborgener Sinnbezüge, ironischer Anspielungen, philosophischer Zweideutigkeiten"—Alfons Glück, *Schillers* Wallenstein (Munich: Fink, 1976), p. 10.

10. *Wallenstein* quoted from *Schillers Werke: Nationalausgabe,* vol. 8, *Wallenstein,* ed. Hermann Schneider and Lieselotte Blumenthal (Weimar: Böhlaus, 1949). English translation is quoted from Charles Passage's verse translation in *Wallenstein: A Historical Drama in Three Parts* (New York: Ungar, 1958). All quotations are from these editions, and subsequent references are cited in the text; line numbers are the same in both. *Wallensteins Lager* is abbreviated as *WL, Die Piccolomini* as *DP, Wallensteins Tod* as *WT*.

11. See Herbert Meyer, "Heinrich IV von Frankreich im Werk Schillers: Ein Beitrag zum Verständnis der Wallenstein-Figur," *Jahrbuch der deutschen Schillergesellschaft* 3 (1959): 94–101. "Der naturnahen, instinktsicheren, klar seinen Weg gehenden Gefühlsmenschen Heinrich steht für ihn offensichtlich der naturferne, zwiespältige Verstandemensch Wallenstein gegenüber" ("Close to nature, sure in his instincts, serenely going his way, Henry, the man of feeling, stands for him in obvious opposition to Wallenstein, far from nature, divided against himself, the man of reason," p. 100).

12. Walter Hinderer, *"Wallenstein,"* in *Schillers Dramen: Neue Interpretationen,* ed. Walter Hinderer (Stuttgart: Reclam, 1979), pp. 136–37.

13. Herbert Lindenberger, *Historical Drama: The Relation of Literature and Reality* (Chicago: University of Chicago Press, 1975), p. 78.

14. See Walter Müller-Seidel, "Episches im Theater der deutschen Klassik: Eine Betrachtung über Schillers *Wallenstein,"Jahrbuch der deutschen Schillergesellschaft* 20 (1976): "Es ist üblich, diesen Prolog zu behandeln, als gehöre er nicht zum Werk" ("It is customary to treat this prologue as though it did not belong to the work," p. 349).

15. For a full account of the remodeling, see Gertrud Rudloff-Hille, *Schiller auf der deutschen Bühne seiner Zeit* (Berlin and Weimar: Aufbau, 1969), pp. 107–10.

16. Kurt May, in "Schillers *Wallenstein*" (in *Form und Bedeutung: Interpretationen deutscher Dichtung des 18. und 19. Jahrhunderts* [Stuttgart: Klett, 1957]), discusses the general, typical nature of this introduction of the protagonist (p. 179).

17. Hinderer, *"Wallenstein,"* pp. 133–34. For Marxist readings of Schiller's relation to the revolutions of the times, see Karl-Heinz Hahn, "Schiller und die Geschichte," in *Friedrich Schiller: Zur Geschichtlichkeit Seines Werkes,* ed. Klaus L. Berghahn (Kronberg: Scriptor, 1975), pp. 25–54, or Horst Hartmann, Wallenstein: *Geschichte und Dichtung* (Berlin: Volk und Wissen, 1969), to whom *Wallenstein* is a complex historical drama "dass die Grundwidersprüche der gewählten historischen Periode mit erfasst und für das zeitgenössische Publikum fruchtbar gemacht werden" ("that grapples with the basic contradictions of the historical period selected and makes them productive for the contemporary audience," p. 106). Glück rejects readings of the play like Hartmann's or Hegel's that see Wallenstein as a national hero, working for unity and peace (*Schillers* Wallenstein, pp. 212–32).

18. John Neubauer, "The Idea of History in Schiller's *Wallenstein,"* (*Neophil* 56 [1972]), sees the design as virtually cyclical: "The closing symbolic gesture is anticipated by the opening sentence of *Wallensteins Lager*" (p. 451).

19. Ilse Graham, *Schiller's Drama: Talent and Integrity* (New York: Barnes and Noble, 1974); for Wallenstein, she argues, "to act is to walk into a trap, resolutely facing backwards" (p. 138).

20. See Clemens Heselhaus, "Wallensteinisches Welttheater," *Der Deutschunterricht* 12 (1960): "So ist das ganze *Piccolomini*-Drama ein Gespinst von Intrigen, die ineinander und gegeneinander arbeiten" ("Thus the whole drama *The Piccolomini* is a net of intrigues, working in and against one another" p. 58).

21. William F. Mainland, in *Schiller and the Changing Past* (London: Heinemann, 1957), describes *Maria Stuart* as offering a "serious satire" of Machiavelli's *Principe* through the character of Elisabeth (p. 70). The rejection of politics in the later play has much the same effect as in *Jane Shore:* see E. L. Stahl, "The political crime perpetrated by Elisabeth and her followers becomes the occasion for Maria's moral regeneration" (*Friedrich Schiller's Drama*, p. 110). Elisabeth is not, of course, a villain-statesman; nor is Octavio, although some critics, like John Rothman, treat him as one. See "Octavio and Buttler in Schiller's *Wallenstein*," *German Quarterly* 27 (1954): "the ultimate responsibility for the murder of Wallenstein rests with Octavio" (p. 115).

22. Unlike Falstaff, of course, the lovers point to something better: as Gerhard Storz puts it, "Die Beseligung durch die Liebe bezeugt sich als Entdeckung der hohen Werte: des Friedens, der Gesittung, der Lauterkeit, der Andacht" ("The blessing won through love testifies to a discovery of lofty values: of peace, of morality, of purity, of prayer"—*Der Dichter Friedrich Schiller,* 4th ed. [Stuttgart: Klett, 1968], p. 289). "Die Liebeshandlung war von Schiller schon in seinen frühesten Entwürfen, wie die Briefe zeigen, der politischen Handlung 'entgegengesetzt' worden" ("As the letters show, even in Schiller's earliest plans the love plot was to be 'set in opposition' to the political plot," p. 275).

23. See Emil Staiger, *Friedrich Schiller* (Zurich: Atlantis, 1967), pp. 32–33; for discussion of the critical controversy provoked by astrology in the play, see Glück, *Schillers* Wallenstein, pp. 47–53.

24. "Der Fürstentag zu Regensburg hat sein Vertrauen in die Welt, mit der er immer siegesgewisser umgehen zu dürfen glaubte, erschüttert" ("The princes' meeting at Regensburg shattered his faith in the world, his belief that he would always be able to get by, sure of victory"—Staiger, *Friedrich Schiller,* p. 34). For Hinderer, the meeting at Regensburg is "der Angelpunkt aller probleme Wallensteins . . . bei dem Wallensteins Vertrauen in den Kaiser, in sich, und in der Welt traumatisch erschüttert worden war" ("the turning-point of all of Wallenstein's problems . . . through which Wallenstein's faith in the emperor, in himself, in the world, was traumatically shattered"—"*Wallenstein,*" p. 160). See also Glück, *Schillers* Wallenstein, pp. 43–46.

25. "Wallenstein handhabt die Sterndeutung als Mittel der Propaganda" ("Wallenstein manipulates astrology as a means of propaganda"). Glück, *Schillers* Wallenstein, p. 86.

26. Heinz Ehrig, in *Paradoxe und Absurde Dichtung: Über die Formproblematik von "Geschichte" und "Held," dargestellt an Textbeispielen von Schiller, Kleist, und Beckett* (Munich: Fink, 1973), describes three phases in Schiller's view of universal history: from "goldne Alter" ("golden age") to "künstliche Welt" ("synthetic world")—"der Beginn der Geschichte menschlicher Selbstverwirklichung" ("The beginning of the history of human self-realization")—to "die Utopie 'Idylle'" (pp. 97–99). See also von Wiese, "Schiller as Philosopher," pp. 341 ff.

27. Graham, *Schiller's Drama,* p. 279. Goethe explained the problem succinctly: "in dem Augenblick, da er die Freiheit übertritt, fühlt er, dass er einen Schritt zur Knechtschaft tue" ("In the moment of stepping over to freedom, he feels that he has taken a step towards slavery"—quoted by Hinderer in "*Wallenstein,*" p. 154).

28. To Benjamin Bennett, Wallenstein's paralysis shows Schiller to be "aiming at a tragedy of self-consciousness"—"Wallenstein's mystical groping and inaction, his vision of freedom and his inevitable ruin, are an intellectual pattern by which the

spectator is made aware of the constant tragic potential inherent in his own self-consciousness" (*Modern Drama and German Classicism: Renaissance from Lessing to Brecht* [Ithaca: Cornell University Press, 1979], pp. 183, 198–99).

29. Neubauer, "The Idea of History," p. 455. "If the world of Shakespeare's tragedies is 'out of joint,' in *Wallenstein* we miss the Archimedean reference point around which it was dislocated: there are no bearings, no overarching structure with respect to which one could piece together the confusing fragments of the play's world" (p. 454). In his famous letter to Augustenburg (13 July 1793), Schiller described seventeenth-century man as "noch nicht reif . . . zur bürgerlichen Freiheit, dem noch so vieles zu *menschlichen* fehlt" ("not yet ready for civic freedom, lacking so much that is human"—*Briefe*, ed. Erik Jonas [Stuttgart: Deutsche Verlags Anstalt (1892)], 3: 333).

30. Hegel found the ending out of keeping with his generally optimistic reading of the play: "Leben gegen Leben; aber er steht nur Tod gegen Leben auf, und unglaublich! abscheulich! der Tod siegt über das Leben!" he exclaimed in his essay on *Wallenstein*, "Dies ist nicht tragisch, sondern entsetzlich! Dies zerreisst das Gemüt, daraus kann man nicht mit erleichterter Brust springen!" ("Life for life; but he sets up death against life, and, unbelievable! horrible! death is victorious over life! This is not tragic, but terrifying! This tears the soul to pieces; no one can rise up from this with a lighter heart!"—"Ueber *Wallenstein*," in *Sämtliche Werke: Jubiläumsausgabe,* ed. J. Glockner [Stuttgart: Frommann, 1958], 20:458). "Der Fall ist auch wohl einzig," Goethe wrote to Schiller 18 March 1799, "dass man, nachdem alles, was Furcht und Mitleid zu erregen fähig ist, erschöpft war, mit Schrecken schliessen konnte" ("The case is probably unique: that, after exhausting every possible means of arousing pity and fear, one is capable of concluding with terror"—*Der Briefwechsel zwischen Schiller und Goethe,* ed. Emil Staiger [Frankfurt: Insel, 1966], p. 744). Heselhaus sees a lack of consolation in all of Schiller's endings: "kein Fortinbras, kein Areopag, kein Freiheitsengel" ("No Fortinbras, no Areopagus, no angel of Freedom") consoles us after this "tiefsten Demaskierung" ("most profound unmasking"—"Wallensteinisches Welttheater," p. 71). For Herbert Singer, in "Dem *Fürsten* Piccolomini" (*Euphorion* 53 [1959]: 281–302), this ending closes the circle and returns the audience to the beginning. Others, however, have seen more than a full measure of pathos in the ending—for example, see Kurt May—at the end we marvel "dass sie beide [Max und Wallenstein], jeder in seiner Art, zu gross waren oder zu gut, um sich in der gemeinen Wirklichkeit zu erhalten" ("that they both, each in his own way, were too great or too good to be confined to ordinary reality"—"Schiller's *Wallenstein,*" pp. 241–42). Emil Staiger offers the pathos of Octavio. "Der neue Titel errinert ihn nur an den verlust des Sohns. Ein einsames Alter steht ihm bevor" ("The new title only reminds him of the loss of his son. A lonely old age stands before him"—*Friedrich Schiller,* p. 356).

31. Neubauer: "The play raises the dilemma shared by Wallenstein's and Schiller's age, whether to continue with loyalty towards empty traditions or take the risk of breaking with the past without full conviction of moral superiority" ("The Idea of History," p. 457).

32. Hinderer, "*Wallenstein,*" p. 166.

33. See Hartmann, *Wallenstein,* pp. 61–63. For a different view, see Ehrig: "Für Schiller folgt daraus: die Erfahrungen mit dem fatalen Ausgang der Französischen Revolution als ein realhistorischen Paradigma haben zwar nicht das Ideal einer freien Gesellschaft zerstört, aber ihre aktuelle Unmöglichkeit erwiesen" ("For Schiller it follows thus: the experience of the fatal consequences of the French Revolution as a paradigm of true history did not destroy the ideal of a free society, but merely pointed out its current impossibility"—*Paradoxe und Absurde Dichtung,* p. 72). Hahn offers a

broader perspective: "Es war demnach ein sehr aktuelles Problem seiner eigenen Zeit, nämlich die gesellschaftliche Emanzipation des Bürgertums, das der Historiker Schiller zum Gegenstand seiner Untersuchungen machte, das er in seinen historischen Anfängen zu fassen und seinen eigenen Zeitgenossen zu verdeutlichen versuchte" ("It was consequently a very pressing problem of his own time, namely the emancipation of the bourgeoisie, that Schiller the historian took as subject of his research and attempted to grasp and clarify to his own contemporaries at the outset of his career"—"Schiller und die Geschichte," p. 33).

34. "Der Antritt des neuen Jahrhunderts," quoted from Friedrich Schiller, *Sämtliche Werke*, ed. Gerhard Fricke and Herbert G. Göpfert (Munich: Carl Hanser, 1965), 1:459.

35. For Mainland, Schiller's "feelings were repelled by most of the material" (*Schiller and the Changing Past*," p. 49). The letters mark his struggle to find "an idiom" that would give "some order, some dignity, some general relevance" to the "narrow purposes of men as he perceived them in the records and rumours of the chronicles" (p. 53). For Neubauer, Schiller's effort is a failure: "Though a historical drama, *Wallenstein* gives us no clue as to the meaning of history. In a literal sense, its history is mute and meaningless" ("The Idea of History," p. 459).

36. "Historieskrifningens omöjlighet," in *En Ny Blå Bok* (Stockholm, Björck and Börjesson, 1908), p. 563.

37. For a good summary of these plans, compiled from manuscript sources, see Walter Johnson, *Strindberg and the Historical Drama* (Seattle: University of Washington Press, 1963), pp. 11–17.

38. The image of the chess player is quoted from "Världshistoriens Mystik" in August Strindberg, *Samlade Skrifter*, ed. John Landquist, vol. 54, *Efterslåtter* (Stockholm: Bonnier, 1920), p. 353.

39. The question "What is truth?" recurs also in the margins of the manuscripts and serves as a subtitle in the fifth revised manuscript; see Barbara Lide, "The Young Idealist and the Fat Old Clown: Development of the Tragicomical in Strindberg's *Mäster Olof*," *Scandinavian Studies* 51 (1979): 13–24.

40. *The Secret of the Guild* (1880) and *Lord Bengt's Wife* (1882) are also early historical plays, taking the form of "well-made" comedies. Walter Johnson ascribes their thoroughgoing conventionality to Strindberg's desire to furnish his first wife with flattering popular vehicles in her acting career; see his chapter "Two Plays for Siri," in *Strindberg and the Historical Drama*, pp. 56–72.

41. Martin Lamm describes Strindberg's readings in Shakespeare during these years in *August Strindberg*, 2d ed. (Stockholm: Bonnier, 1948), pp. 252–56.

42. The phrase and the count are Gunnar Ollén's in *Strindbergs Dramatik* (Stockholm: Sveriges Radio, 1961): "Dramerna kom som en springflod" (p. 261).

43. August Strindberg, *Samlade Skrifter*, ed. John Landquist, vol. 50, *Öppna Brev till Intima Teatern* (Stockholm: Bonnier, 1919), p. 237. English translation quoted from *Open Letters to the Intimate Theater*, trans. Walter Johnson (Seattle: University of Washington Press, 1966), p. 246. All quotations are from these editions, and subsequent references will be cited in the text as *ÖB* and *IT*.

44. See Joan Bulman, *Strindberg and Shakespeare: Shakespeare's Influence on Strindberg's Historical Drama* (London: Jonathan Cape, 1933); Harry V. E. Palmblad, "Shakespeare and Strindberg," *Germanic Review* 3 (1928): 71–94, 168–77; and Birgitta Steene, "Shakespearean Elements in the Historical Plays of Strindberg," *Comparative Literature* 11 (1959): 209–20, for accounts of direct borrowings and influences.

45. Walter Johnson, in a note to his translation, *The Vasa Trilogy: Mäster Olof, Gustav Vasa, Erik XIV* (Seattle: University of Washington Press, 1959), p. 128. All

English quotations are from this translation. Swedish quotations are from August Strindberg, *Skrifter*, vol. 10, *Historiska Dramer*, ed. Gunnar Brandell (Stockholm: Bonnier, 1946). Subsequent references from both are cited in the text as *VT* or *HD*.

46. Harry G. Carlson discusses this first scene in *Strindberg and the Poetry of Myth* (Berkeley and Los Angeles: University of California Press, 1982), p. 38. See also p. 216: "Olof's literary, artistic concern with the freeing of the people of Israel from the slavery they must endure at the hands of their Babylonian captors is transformed into a real concern for the spiritual freedom of his own people."

47. For a full account of the genesis of *Mäster Olof*, see Carl Reinhold Smedmark, Mäster Olof *och* Röda Rummet (Stockholm: Almquist and Wiksell, 1952). Harry V. E. Palmblad gives a good account of the young playwright's reading in *Strindberg's Conception of History* (New York: Columbia University Press, 1927), pp. 3–39; Martin Lamm's first account of the different versions remains useful: see *Strindbergs Dramer*, vol. 1 (Stockholm: Bonnier, 1924), pp. 85–176. Evert Sprinchorn argues that the play parallels the Paris Commune of 1871: "Since it would have been folly to write a play dealing directly with the uprising, Strindberg resorted to the stratagem of mirroring the present in the past" (*Strindberg as Dramatist* [New Haven: Yale University Press, 1982], p. 186). Sprinchorn stresses Strindberg's youthful radicalism in his discussion of the play, pp. 185–91.

48. Steene, "Shakespearean Elements," p. 220. All English quotations are from *The Saga of the Folkungs and Engelbrekt*, trans. Walter Johnson (Seattle: University of Washington Press, 1959); references are cited in the text as *SF*; Swedish quotations are from *HD*.

49. Martin Lamm, *Strindbergs Dramer*, vol. 2 (Stockholm: Bonnier, 1926), p. 124.

50. Harry G. Carlson explores the figural importance of the identities of Gustav Vasa in "Christian Ritual and Mythic Pattern in *Gustav Vasa*," in *Strindbergs Dramen im Lichte neuerer Methodendiskussionen: Beiträge zum IV Internationalen Strindberg-Symposium in Zürich 1979*, ed. Oskar Bandle, Walter Baumgartner, and Jürg Glausner (Basel: Helbig and Lichtenhahn, 1981), pp. 83–96.

51. Sprinchorn discusses the contrapuntal father-and-son motif in the play's structure in *Strindberg as Dramatist*, pp. 196–97.

52. Johnson's translation: "If I were to summarize all that's blameworthy in the great king, I'd lack respect" (*VT*, p. 224) makes no sense in the context of the king's response and the play's meaning. While the antecedent of *det* is syntactically unclear, Olof is talking about the king's, not his own, lack of *pietet*.

53. Karin calls Erik "Paleface" ("Blodlös") and that is also the doll's name. To Michael W. Kaufman, in "Strindberg's Historical Imagination: *Erik XIV*" (*CompD* 9 [1975]), this conveys an image of Erik as "an abandoned doll, passively borne by forces he can neither control nor understand" (p. 327).

54. See, for example, Johnson's introduction to the play in his translation, p. 257. Marc A. Roth discusses "characterlessness" in theatrical terms in "Strindberg's Historical Role-Players" (*Scan* 18 [1979]: 123–39). Sprinchorn also decries "seeing the play as character drama" (*Strindberg as Dramatist*, p. 205). But his reading is thoroughly political: "Strindberg would have agreed with Mao Tse-Tung that 'the people, and the people alone, are the motive force in the making of world history'" (p. 210).

55. English quotations from *Gustav Adolf*, trans. Walter Johnson (Seattle: University of Washington Press; and New York: American-Scandinavian Foundation, 1957). *Gustav Adolf* is not included in *HD*; Swedish quotations are from Strindberg, *Historiska Dramer*, vol. 2 (Stockholm: Geber, 1903). All quotations are from these editions, and references are cited in the text as *GA* and *GAHD*. Both Gunnar Ollén

(*Strindbergs Dramatik*, p. 300) and Walter Johnson (*GA*, pp. 7–8) suggest that the play's plea for religious toleration reflects Strindberg's interest in the Hague Congress for International Peace of 1899. Claes Rosenquist, in "Strindberg's Thirty Years' War" (in *Strindberg und die Deutschsprachigen Länder: Internationale Beiträge zum Tübingen Strindberg-Symposium 1977,* ed. Wilhelm Friese [Basel: Helbig and Lichtenhahn, 1979]), sees the various mixed marriages in the play as reflections of Strindberg's second marriage (pp. 87–89).

56. Lamm, *Strindbergs Dramer*, 2:179: "Han är en botgörare i Inferno."

57. Ollén, *Strindbergs Dramatik*, pp. 367–68. All English quotations are from *Queen Christina, Charles XII, and Gustav III,* trans. Walter Johnson (Seattle: University of Washington Press, 1955); subsequent references to these three plays are cited in the text as *QC*. Swedish quotations are from *HD*, and references are cited in the text.

58. Birgitta Steene, *The Greatest Fire: A Study of August Strindberg* (Carbondale: Southern Illinois University Press, 1973), p. 132. George Steiner compares the world of Charles XII to "a puppet theatre full of strange, nervous marionettes" in *The Death of Tragedy* (London: Faber, 1961), p. 299. Ollén describes the play as a "musikstycke, en komposition i moll med ledmotiv och variationer, en drömspelbetonad förnylse av en ärevördiga svensk-historiska dramgenren" ("a piece of music, a composition in minor with leitmotifs and variations, a renewal, in dream-play accents, of a venerable genre of Swedish historical drama"—*Strindbergs Dramatik*, p. 368). Walter Johnson discusses the "impressionistic-expressionistic" technique of this play in his introduction (*QC*, p. 94).

59. Quoted and translated by Michael Meyer in *The Plays of Strindberg*, vol. 2 (New York: Vintage, 1976), p. 547.

60. Ollén, *Strindbergs Dramatik*, p. 382. "Måla änglar var inte hans genre," he continues: "Painting angels was not his genre." Walter Johnson describes *Engelbrekt* charitably (as he does all of the historical plays) as "a well-made folk drama and impressionistic experiment" in *Strindberg and the Historical Drama*, p. 189.

61. *En Ny Blå Bok*, p. 559: "Men att Carl XII var galen, och Kristina en — — —, det är nog säkert" ("That Charles XII was mad and Christina a — — —, that is true enough").

62. Lamm calls Kristina "en bohemkonstnärinna från en kabarett på 1890-talet" ("a bohemian artiste from an 1890s cabaret") in *Strindbergs Dramer*, 2: 300; Ollén discusses the influence of Strindberg's marriage to Harriett Bosse on the characterization in *Strindbergs Dramatik*, pp. 386–88.

63. Baeckström quoted from Ollén, *Strindbergs Dramatik*, p. 392. Ollén discusses these performances, and others on pp. 390–97.

64. Palmblad discusses Strindberg's fondness for puns in "Shakespeare and Strindberg," p. 170.

65. Lamm, *Strindbergs Dramer:* "en historisk komedi i Scribestil" (2: 341); Walter Johnson concurs, but he finds that the "Scribean" aspects of *Gustav III* serve a realistic purpose: "conveying the artificiality of a highly formalized court and the artificiality of the king's behavior" *Strindberg and the Historical Drama*, p. 215.

66. Ollén, *Strindbergs Dramatik*, p. 421; see also Marc A. Roth, "Strindberg's Historical Role-Players," p. 134. Palmblad suggests that "Strindberg's fondness for anniversaries is probably due to his study of Shakespeare" ("Shakespeare and Strindberg," p. 64), but the degree of the fondness is Strindberg's own.

67. August Strindberg, *Samlade Skrifter*, ed. John Landquist, vol. 54, *Efterslåtter* (Stockholm: Bonnier, 1920), p. 380. "Världshistoriens Mystik" occupies pages 337–401 of this edition, and subsequent references are cited in the text.

68. *En Ny Blå Bok*, pp. 782, 559.

69. Strindberg in a letter to Hugo Geber, 17 May 1904, quoted in Ollén, *Strindbergs Dramatik*, p. 441; a condensed version of Ollén's remarks on these plays, in English, appears as introduction to August Strindberg, *World Historical Plays*, trans. Arvid Paulson (New York: Twayne and American Scandinavian Foundation, 1970). Lamm, *Strindbergs Dramer*, 2:354, notes the tendency to self-parody in *The Nightingale of Wittenberg* and suggests that the Moses-Socrates-Christ trilogy is completely out of control.

70. English quotations from these plays are from *The Last of the Knights, The Regent, Earl Birger of Bjälbö*, trans. Walter Johnson (Seattle: University of Washington Press, 1956). All subsequent references are cited in the text as *LK*. All Swedish quotations are from *HD*.

71. Luciano Codignola, "Two Ideas of Dramatic Structure: Strindberg's Last Period and Pirandello's Third Period, a Confrontation," in *Strindberg and Modern Theatre* (Stockholm: Strindbergssällskapet, 1975), p. 39.

72. Lamm, *Strindbergs Dramer*, 2:417: "god mässingsmusik."

73. Steene, *Greatest Fire*, p. 138; Ollén, *Strindbergs Dramatik*, p. 503; Lamm, *Strindbergs Dramer*, 418–19.

5. The Revolution of the Times

1. Georg Büchner, *Sämtliche Werke und Briefe*, ed. Werner R. Lehmann, 2 vols. (Hamburg: Wegner, 1967–71), 2:425. All quotations are from this edition, and subsequent references are cited in the text as *SW*.

2. Ernst Schumacher discusses the Aristotelian qualities of the first version of the play in *Drama und Geschichte: Bertolt Brechts "Leben des Galilei" und andere Stücke* (Berlin: Henschel, 1965), pp. 18ff.

3. "Über experimentelles Theater," in *Schriften zum Theater*, ed. Werner Hecht, vols. 15, 16, and 17 of *Gesammelte Werke* (Frankfurt: Suhrkamp, 1967), 15:302. All quotations from Brecht's writings on theater are from this edition, and subsequent references are cited in the text as *GsW*.

4. As Keith A. Dickson puts it: "The dialectical interplay between mimesis and observation, drama and audience, was for Brecht a true image of social reality. Exposed to his form of dramatic art in the theater, the audience participates in the revolutionary process of history," *Towards Utopia: A Study of Brecht* (Oxford: Clarendon Press, 1978), p. 250.

5. Musset quoted by Robert Abirached, ed., in *André del Sarto, Lorenzaccio*, by Alfred de Musset (Paris: Gallimard, 1978), p. 8. All quotations are from this edition of *Lorenzaccio*, and subsequent references are cited in the text.

6. Pierre Gastinel, in *Le romantisme d'Alfred de Musset* (Paris: Hachette, 1933), defines *Lorenzaccio* as the perfect Romantic drama: "Ajoutons l'évocation de la foule, l'influence shakespearienne plus nette que jamais; recapitulons ces traits qui font, au drame, un physionomie particulière: pièce historique à tendances démocratiques, pièce grave et philosophique à la fois, c'est bien là ce que Victor Hugo appelle: le drame romantique, avec le rime en moins et le souci psychologique en plus" ("Add together the portrayal of the crowd, the Shakespearean influence now clearer than ever; recapitulate the features that give this play a unique physiognomy: a historical play with democratic tendencies, serious and philosophical at once; this is certainly what Victor Hugo called romantic drama, with a minimum of rhyme and a maximum of psychological interest," p. 450). See also Michel Lioure, *Le drame de Diderot à Ionesco* (Paris: Colin, 1973), who comments on Musset's curious relationship to the

theoretical writings of his contemporaries: "L'auteur du drame le plus accompli de cette période féconde en demi-réussites est aussi le plus avare de théories et de manifestes": ("The author of the most successful play in this period so rich in half-successes is also the most miserly in theories and manifestoes"). *Lorenzaccio* nonetheless epitomizes the *drame*, "exprimant à la fois la grandeur et la vérité, d'une ville, d'une âme, et d'un siècle" ("expressing at once the greatness and truth of a city, a soul, a century," p. 105). Charles Affron argues that the best of the *drames romantiques*, the most stageworthy in modern times, are those written without regard to contemporary stage conditions; see *A Stage for Poets: Studies in the Theatre of Hugo and Musset* (Princeton: Princeton University Press, 1971), p. 228.

7. For discussion of Romantic imitation of Shakespeare in France, see Eric L. Gans, *Musset et le "drame tragique": Essai d'analyse paradoxale* (Paris: José Corti, 1974). Gans argues that the Romantic drama "reproduit l'anarchie apparente de l'univers shakespearien tout en omettant ce qui en fait un univers tragique" ("reproduces the apparent anarchy of the Shakespearean universe while utterly leaving out what makes it a tragic universe," p. 37) an implicit sense of order. In *Lorenzaccio,* however, "la fragmentation scénique . . . exprimerait la cohérence purement idéale de son univers dramatique" ("the fragmentation of the scenes may express the purely ideal coherence of [the play's] dramatic universe," p. 165). For a discussion of the impact of English actors on the French stage in this period, see W. D. Howarth, *Sublime and Grotesque: A Study of French Romantic Drama* (London: Harrap, 1975), pp. 96–100. For Howarth, too, it is Musset's "sympathetic understanding of Shakespeare's *manner*" rather than mere imitation that sets him apart from his contemporaries (p. 299).

8. Full discussion of the stage history of the play is available in Bernard Masson, *Musset et le théâtre intérieure: Nouvelles recherches sur "Lorenzaccio"* (Paris: Colin, 1974), pp. 223–391. In a "Conversation sur *Lorenzaccio,*" held 26 December 1954 and printed in *Théâtre populaire* (41 [1961]: 137–41), Gérard Philipe, Henri Lefebvre, Jean Deschamps, and Roland Barthes debated the political "message" of the production. While Lefebvre saw the play as a "chant funèbre pour la mort de la liberté" ("funeral dirge for the death of liberty"), Philipe countered that the play holds out hope for the future (pp. 138–39).

9. "Musset thus raises nonart to a high symbolic level, and ends his play with a nonclimax of daring originality," says David Sices of Côme de Medici's speech (*Theater of Solitude: The Drama of Alfred de Musset* [Hanover, N.H.: University Press of New England, 1974], p. 169). For Hassan El Nouty, Musset's play describes a spiral: "La spirale de l'Histoire, que nous déchiffrons chez Musset, nous entraîne dans un tourbillon sans commencement ni fin, auquel il serait vain d'attribuer un sens, puisque, semble-t-il nous dire, les choses bougent sans changer au fond de situation" ("The spiral of history that we decipher in Musset leads us into a whirlpool without beginning or end, to which it would be futile to attribute a meaning, since, it seems to tell us, things move without changing the essentials of the situation"— "L'esthétique de *Lorenzaccio,*" *Revue des sciences humaines* [hereafter cited as *RSH*] 27 [1962]: 599–600). El Nouty elaborates his notion of a "mouvement hélicoïdal" in the play in *Théâtre et pré-cinema: Essai sur la problematique du spéctacle au XIXe siècle* (Paris: Nizet, 1978), pp. 201–9.

10. Affron notes that Brutus gives Lorenzo "two historical identities" (*A Stage for Poets,* p. 218). Leon Lafoscade enumerates the resemblances between Lorenzo and Hamlet in *Le théâtre d'Alfred de Musset* (Paris: Hachette, 1901), pp. 78–83. André Lebois, in *Vues sur le théâtre de Musset* (Paris: Aubanel, 1966), sees the play as, like *La confession d'un enfant du siècle:* "cri d'une génération sans épée, imbue de souvenirs napoléoniens et désarmée à Waterloo, réduite à la honte par la Sainte-Alliance" ("the

cry of a swordless generation, saturated with napoleonic memories and disarmed at Waterloo, reduced to shame by the Holy Alliance," p. 61). For Claude Duchet, in "Musset et la politique," *RSH* 27 (1962): "*Lorenzaccio* décrira l'affrontement tragique et nécéssaire d'une société malade et *d'un poète qui ne voulait pas être de son temps*" ("*Lorenzaccio* will describe the necessary and tragic shame of a sick society and *of a poet who did not want to be of his time,*"—original emphasis, p. 549). Herbert S. Gochberg, *Stage of Dreams: The Dramatic Art of Alfred de Musset* (Geneva: Droz, 1967), discusses the relationship between Lorenzo's murder and Musset's ideas about art (p. 197); for Robert T. Denommé, Lorenzo is a classic case of the *poète maudit:* "the poet hopes to achieve his aim by crystallizing his forbidden visions into an unforgettable poem; Lorenzaccio wants to believe that his crime will forever be impressed in the minds of men" ("The Motif of the '*poète maudit*' in Musset's *Lorenzaccio,*" *L'Esprit créateur* 5 [1965]: 144).

11. Lioure, *Le drame:* "La tragédie historique est donc une démonstration de la vanité et de l'absurdité des règles" ("Historical tragedy is thus a demonstration of the emptiness and absurdity of the rules," p. 65). "La vérité historique n'est donc pas une fin en soi, mais le prétexte à la somptuosité du spéctacle, au pathétique de l'action et au naturel du style" ("Historical truth is thus not an end in itself but a pretext for sumptuous spectacle, pathos in the plot, and simplicity of style," p. 92).

12. For discussion of Vitet, see especially Robert Baschet, "Vitet, Mérimée, Musset," *RSH* 27 (1962): 573–88, and Hassan El Nouty, "Théâtre et anti-théâtre au dix-neuvième siècle," *PMLA* 79 (1964): 604–12. For comparison of Vitet to Shakespeare, see W. D. Howarth, "History in the Theatre: the French and English Traditions," *Trivium* 1 (1966): 151–68.

13. Ludovic Vitet, *Les États de Blois,* 3d ed. (Paris: Fournier Jeune, 1829), pp. v–vi.

14. See Paul Dimoff, *La génèse de* Lorenzaccio (Paris: Droz, 1936). For further work on the creation of the play, see also Jean Pommier, *Variétés sur Alfred de Musset et son théâtre* (Paris: Nizet, 1966), Masson, *Musset et le drame intérieure,* and Joyce Bromfield, *De Lorenzino de Médicis à "Lorenzaccio": Étude d'un thème historique* (Paris: Didier, 1972).

15. Jean Nathan, editor of the Nouveaux Classiques Larousse edition of the play (Paris: Larousse, 1964) disapproves: "Le voyage du marquis et son retour à la fin de la pièce semblent indiquer que le drame se passe à peu près en une semaine. C'est presque la seule indication de Musset sur cette question qui semble ne pas l'avait beaucoup préoccupé" ("The departure of the marquis and his return at the end of the play seem to indicate that the drama takes place in a little less than a week. This is the only hint Musset offers on this issue, which does not seem to have troubled him very much," p. 30n.).

16. Affron, *A Stage for Poets,* p. 200. "The private anguish of Lorenzaccio is regularly interwoven with an anonymous urban complaint in a fugal pattern of re-statement and counterpoint which shapes the theme in time without altering its integrity" (p. 201). "Avec Musset la Ville entre, corps et âme, dans les lettres fran-çaises" ("With Musset, the city enters, body and soul, into French literature"), pro-nounces Duchet ("Musset et la politique," p. 527).

17. In addition to Duchet, "Musset et la politique," see Herbert J. Hunt, "Alfred de Musset et la révolution de Juillet: la leçon politique de *Lorenzaccio,*" *Mercure de France* 251 (1934): 70–88, and Henri Lefebvre, *Musset,* 2d ed. (Paris: Arche, 1970): "Ainsi la dramaturge donne la situation politique à Florence en 1533 comme l'analogue de la situation en France après la restauration et la révolution de 1830 (fusionnées dans une sorte de vue synthétique)" ("Thus the dramatist offers the political situation in

Florence in 1533 as an analogy to the situation in France after the Restoration and the Revolution of 1830, fused into a sort of composite picture," p. 117). A more sophisticated perspective is that of Bernard Masson, who argues: "Le dramaturge ne cherche alors ni la résurrection du passé, ni l'allusion déguisée à l'actualité, mais très exactement la superposition de deux situations politiques équivalentes et qui, dessinant la même figure, appellent le même jugement" ("The dramatist is seeking neither a resurrection of the past, nor a disguised allusion to present-day affairs, but precisely the superimposition of two political situations, which, following the same design, call for the same judgement")—("L'approche des problèmes politiques dans *Lorenzaccio* de Musset," in *Romantisme et politique 1815–1851*, Colloque de l'École Normale Supérieure de Saint-Cloud, 1966 [Paris: Colin, 1969], pp. 307–8).

18. For Hunt in "Alfred de Musset," "les leaders republicains" both in the play and in history, "sont, pour la plupart, des ganaches" ("For the most part, the republican leaders are incompetent dolts," p. 73). For El Nouty, this kind of moral judgment is forbidden by the shape of the play: "Il y a passage continuel du même en même" ("There is a continual passage from the same to the same") in history and in the play (*Théâtre et pré-cinéma*, p. 209); "l'Histoire, toujours semblable à elle-même, dessine dans un vide absurde . . . un mouvement circulaire que réproduit l'architecture de l'ouvrage" ("History, always repeating itself, sketches in an absurd void . . . a circular movement that is reproduced by the structure of the play"—"Théâtre et anti-théâtre," p. 609)—the process, needless to say, is "vertigineuse" ("L'esthétique," p. 610).

19. See Bernard Masson, *Musset et son double: Lecture de "Lorenzaccio"* (Paris: Minard, 1978), p. 85: "Mais pourquoi tant de fenêtres? . . . Car, pour les Florentins, Florence est une personne sur laquelle on garde les yeux fixes et dont on épie les moindres réactions. On se met aux fenêtres pour regarder ses souillures ou lui cracher son mépris" ("But why so many windows? . . . Because, for the Florentines, Florence is a person to watch over fixedly, spying out her slightest reactions. You go to the windows to watch her debase herself or to spit on her in scorn").

20. Lebois, *Vues sur le théâtre*, p. 75: "Quand il crie, 'Catherine, Catherine, lis moi l'histoire de Brutus'—alors qu'il est au fond de la crise nerveuse—c'est déjà du *second* Brutus qu'il s'agit" ("When he cries, 'Catherine, Catherine, read me the story of Brutus'—when he is in the depths of a nervous breakdown—it is already a case of the *second* Brutus"). Pommier (*Variétés sur Alfred de Musset*) is less certain, but more political in his interpretation: "Ainsi, qu'il s'agit du premier Brutus ou du second, la même leçon politique ou à peu près ressortait de leur histoire. Celui-là n'a pas tué le tyran, mais il a tué la tyrannie, celui-ci n'a pas tué la tyrannie, mais il a tué le tyran" ("Thus, whether it is a question of first or second Brutus, the same, or approximately the same, political lesson emerges from their stories. The first did not kill the tyrant, but he killed tyranny; the second did not kill tyranny, but he killed the tyrant," p. 153).

21. "Gratuitousness" or "the law of the *premier venu*," is, according to A. Callen (in "The Place of *Lorenzaccio* in Musset's Theatre," *Forum for Modern Language Studies* 5 [1969]), characteristic of Musset's view of "an indifferent world." In *Lorenzaccio*, "Gratuitousness is seen, then, on a larger canvas than in any other play, for its cruel laws govern the church and political life as well as individuals. . . . An indifferent world and the law of 'le premier venu' have strikingly made nonsense of idealism" (p. 228).

22. Lebois, *Vues sur le théâtre*, p. 91: "La Providence a pu le choisir . . . ; il éprouva par la suite l'automatisme de la vocation. Il est la statue de fer blanc qui marche, il ne s'appartient plus, possédé par l'idée fixe et dépossédé de soi—aliéné"

("Providence could have chosen him . . . ; he demonstrates in action the automatism of vocation. He is the walking statue of iron: he no longer belongs to himself, possessed by a fixed idea and dispossessed of himself—alienated").

23. For discussion of the murder as an "act of love" see Gochberg, *Stage of Dreams*, pp. 196–97; Sices, *Theater of Solitude*, pp. 157–58; Callen, "The Place of *Lorenzaccio*," pp. 230–31.

24. Ronald Grimsley, "The Character of Lorenzaccio," *FS* 11 (1957): 25; Hunt, "Alfred de Musset," p. 88; Gochberg, *Stage of Dreams*, p. 171. Lefebvre, too, sees the play as populated with Lorenzo's doubles, but from a Marxist perspective: "les autres personnages principaux déploient devant nous, spectateurs, les aspects du héros principal, et ses contradictions" ("the other principal characters deploy before us, the audience, aspects of the hero, and his contradictions"—*Musset*, p. 101).

25. Bernard Masson, in *Musset et son double*: "Telle est la sombre histoire du héros du Musset qui passe de la condition de masque à l'état d'ombre sans avoir jamais connu l'adhésion heureuse de soi à soi-même, l'intériorité, la conscience de soi comme être pensant et agissant librement, à la fois en dialogue avec le monde et prologeant son être intérieur par l'action" ("Such is the dark story of Musset's hero, who passes from the condition of mask to the state of shadow without ever having known the happy adherence of self to itself, interiority, the sense of self as a being that thinks and acts freely, at the same time engaging in dialogue with the world and maintaining its own internal being through action," p. 163).

26. What Tebaldeo points to is "le chemin d'une existence nouvelle vécue à l'heure non de l'histoire, mais de l'esprit et du coeur, à l'ordre non de l'ambition, mais de l'amour" ("the road to a new existence lived not by the time of history, but of the spirit and the heart, by the rule not of ambition, but of love"—Masson, *Musset et le théâtre intérieur*, p. 221). For the other consolations ("C'est peu et c'est beaucoup"), see Masson, "L'approche des problèmes politiques," p. 315.

27. As Lebois puts it (*Vues sur le théâtre*), the real question of the play is "faut-il agir? peut-on agir? à quoi bon agir?" ("must he act? can one act? what good is it to act?" p. 125); "A la vérité," says El Nouty ("L'ésthétique"), "*Lorenzaccio* offre à peu pres toutes les réponses possibles au problème de l'action" ("In truth, *Lorenzaccio* offers almost all the possible responses to the problem of action," p. 608).

28. Herbert Lindenberger argues the probability of this reading in "*Danton's Death* and the Conventions of Historical Drama," *CompD* 3 (1969): 101. See also Elisabeth Trenzel, "Mussets *Lorenzaccio*: ein mögliches Vorbild für *Dantons Tod*," *Euphorion* 58 (1964): 59–68. Trenzel is less convinced than Lindenberger.

29. "Hugo hat sein Programm nicht selbst verwirklicht. Das tat Büchner" ("Hugo himself never realized his program: Büchner did"), he declares: Wolfgang Wittkowski, in *Georg Büchner: Persönlichkeit, Weltbild, Werk* (Heidelberg: Carl Winter, 1978), p. 114.

30. Karl Viëtor, *Georg Büchner: Politik, Dichtung, Wissenschaft* (Bern: Francke, 1944) argues for Büchner's disillusionment, pp. 293–94; Georg Lukàcs, in "Der faschistisch verfälschte und der wirkliche Georg Büchner," in *Georg Büchner*, Wolfgang Martens, ed. (Darmstadt: Wissenschaftliche Buchgesellschaft, 1965), pp. 197–224, strongly challenges him. Gerhard Jancke, *Georg Büchner: Genese und Aktualität seines Werkes: Einführung in das Gesamtwerk* (Kronberg: Scriptor, 1975), attempts to resolve these contradictory interpretations (pp. 145–46). See also Jan Thorn-Prikker, *Revolutionär ohne Revolution: Interpretationen der Werke Georg Büchner* (Stuttgart: Klett-Cotta, 1978): "Der von Marx konstatierte Charakter der Halbheit der bürgerlichen Revolution wird in *Dantons Tod* ebenso deutlich begriffen und dargestellt"

("The incompleteness of bourgeois revolution, as defined by Marx, is understood and delineated in *Danton's Death*," p. 52).

31. For Erwin Kobel, the influence of Pascal is paramount: *Georg Büchner: Das dichterische Werk* (Berlin and New York: de Gruyter, 1974), pp. 4–7, 125. For Wittkowski (*Georg Büchner*), Büchner sees himself ("der Dichter") as "ideale richterliche Revolutionär und Menschheitserneuerer, der neue Moses und Messias" ("ideal judicial revolutionary and regenerator of mankind, the new Moses and Messiah," p. 237): Maurice B. Benn, in *The Drama of Revolt: A Critical Study of Georg Büchner* (Cambridge: Cambridge University Press, 1976), insists on Büchner's "metaphysical revolt" against the philosophical framework that even Marx accepted (p. 35).

32. In addition to Wittkowski, Hans Mayer emphasizes the importance of this "Ärgernis-Brief" ("offense letter"): see *Georg Büchner und seine Zeit* (Frankfurt: Suhrkamp, 1972), pp. 222–23. Benn refers to Büchner's "agonizing study" (*Drama of Revolt*, p. 67).

33. "Die Natur handelt nicht nach Zwecken. . . . Alles, was ist, ist um seiner selbst willen da. Das Gesetz dieses Seins zu suchen, ist das Ziel der, der teleologischen gegenüberstehenden Ansicht, die ich die *philosophische* nennen will," *SW*, 2: 292.

34. English text of *Danton's Death* is quoted from Georg Büchner, *Complete Plays and Prose*, trans. Carl Richard Mueller (New York: Hill and Wang, 1963), p. 19; subsequent references are cited in the text.

35. Gerda E. Bell, "Windows: A Study of a Symbol in Georg Büchner's Work," *GR* 47 (1972): 98.

36. Ulrike Paul, in *Vom Geschichtsdrama zur Politischen Diskussion* (Munich: Fink, 1974), uses the image forcefully: "Dieses: dass kein moralische und keine künstlerische Anstrengung mehr den Menschen als Herrn im Sattel der Geschichte halten kann— dies ist Büchners Geschichtsbild im 'Danton.' Die Geschichte hat wie ein wildgewordenes Ross ihren Meister abgeworfen und galoppiert" ("This is the point: no moral or artistic exertion can keep mankind as master in the saddle of history—this is the image of history in *Danton*. History, like a runaway horse, has thrown off its rider and galloped," p. 174).

37. Mayer, *Georg Büchner*, p. 219: "Der Thermidor ist das Problem des Werkes; Robespierres Scheitern der Angelpunkt" ("Thermidor is the problem of the work; Robespierre's failure the turning point"). Robespierre's downfall in Thermidor confirms that "*Dantons Tod* ist die Tragödie des Determinismus; in schrecklicher Gleichformigkeit nehmen die Ereignisse ihren Lauf; politisches Handeln des Menschen ist hoffnungslosen Versuch gegen ein 'Muss' anzukämpfen" ("*Danton's Death* is the tragedy of determinism; in terrible repetitiveness events take their course; the political activity of man is a hopeless attempt to struggle against a 'must,'" p. 221).

38. Wittkowski (*Georg Büchner*) says of *Danton's Death:* "Es will uns schrecken, sittlich-religiös richten, strafen, reinigen, erwecken—wie die Revolution. Es ist zuinnerst und vollkommen revolutionär" ("It wants to shock us, judge us in religious and moral terms, punish, purify, awaken—like the Revolution. It is first and foremost revolutionary," p. 236).

39. Mueller's translation sidesteps the pun: "She knows how to play her cards all right; deals her husband the hearts and every other man her———" (p. 3). For further discussion of Büchner's use of French wordplay see Jürgen Siess, *Zitat und Kontext bei Georg Büchner* (Göppingen: Kümmerle, 1975), pp. 10–13.

40. Walter Hinderer, in *Büchner—Kommentar zum dichterischen Werk* (Munich: Winkler, 1977), discusses the "parodistischen Elemente des Dramas: . . . sie enthüllen

die Revolution als *theatrum mundi*" ("parodic elements of the drama . . . expose the Revolution as *theatrum mundi*," p. 54).

41. For Herbert Lindenberger, this is "the tragic gap between political ideals and political actualities" that the play explores in terms of "rhetoric and anti-rhetoric": *Georg Büchner* (Carbondale: Southern Illinois University Press, 1964), pp. 41, 32.

42. Janis L. Solomon, "Büchner's *Dantons Tod:* History as Theatre," *GR* 54 (1979): 9, 12, 15, 19.

43. Kobel, *Georg Büchner,* pp. 42–43, applies Schiller's Idealist/Realist distinction to Danton and Robespierre; later, he contrasts the two in terms of Pascal's definitions of failings of Epicureans and Stoics (pp. 49–52).

44. "With the exception of Danton," says Julian Hilton, in *Georg Büchner* (New York: Grove Press, 1982), "it is notable that all the male characters in the play seem to be part of an historical process in a way the women are not, and significantly the women exercise what seem for Büchner to be the two great freedoms of natural law, suicide and making love" (p. 75). Of Lucile and Julie, Benn proposes: "one might be tempted to suspect Büchner of *idealizing* their characters in a manner inconsistent with his realistic theory" (*The Drama of Revolt,* p. 140). Lindenberger sees the "pathos" expressed by the women as "necessary to the design of the play" (*Büchner,* p. 38). Of Lucile's death, he comments, "In her willful absurdity she has assumed a kind of heroic stance." The implication is that "only in madness . . . can one perform an act that has meaning in a meaningless world" (p. 53). "Die beiden Frauengestalten des *Danton*," says Viëtor (*Georg Büchner*), "sind ein Dank des Dichters für das einzige reine Glück in seinem unstäten problematischen Dasein" ("both female presences in *Danton* are the author's thanks for the only pure happiness in his own shifting, problematic existence," pp. 148–49), introducing the element of biography.

45. To Richard Gilman, Büchner was successful in devising "an imaginative action that would rebuke history, turning it against itself and testifying to a new kind of freedom from its pitiless claims" ("Georg Büchner: History Redeemed," *Yale/Theatre* 3 [1972]: 15). There is nothing very new about the rebuke of history through pathetic appeal, as we have seen.

46. See Franz Schonauer, "Das Drama und die Geschichte: Versuch über Georg Büchner," *Deutsche Rundschau* 87 (1961): Büchner's faith in the Revolution is "vielmehr gebrochen durch den Schmerz, durch das Wissen um die Leiden des Menschen" ("utterly shattered by pain, by knowledge of human suffering," p. 544).

47. Lindenberger, *Historical Drama,* pp. 62–63.

48. Johnson, *Strindberg and the Historical Drama,* p. 245.

49. A full discussion of Brecht's historical thought can be found in Klaus-Detlef Müller, *Die Function der Geschichte im Werk Bertolt Brechts: Studien zum Verhältnis von Marxismus und Ästhetik* (Tübingen: Niemeyer, 1967). For specific discussion of "historicization," see pp. 30–45.

50. Edition cited is *Leben des Galilei* (Frankfurt: Suhrkamp, 1962), scene 13, p. 109. English translation from *Life of Galileo,* trans. Wolfgang Sauerlander and Ralph Manheim, *Brecht: Collected Plays,* ed. Ralph Manheim and John Willett, vol. 5 (New York: Random House, 1972), p. 81. Subsequent references are cited in the text to these editions.

51. "Sie werden lachen: die Bibel" was Brecht's answer when asked about the greatest influence on his work. Brecht, quoted from G. Ronald Murphy, S. J., *Brecht and the Bible: A Study of Religious Nihilism and Human Weakness in Brecht's Drama of Mortality and the City* (Chapel Hill: University of North Carolina Press, 1980), p. 1.

52. Charles R. Lyons, *Bertolt Brecht: The Despair and the Polemic* (Carbondale: Southern Illinois University Press, 1968), p. 120.

53. There is a photograph of this production reproduced in Käthe Rülicke-Weiler, *Die Dramaturgie Brechts: Theater als Mittel der Veränderung* (Berlin: Henschel, 1966), p. 223, plate 4.

54. John Fuegi, *The Essential Brecht*, University of Southern California Studies in Comparative Literature, vol. 4 (Los Angeles: Hennessey and Ingalls, 1972), pp. 169–70. Fuegi draws a Shakespearean connection on p. 177: "Once again, as had been possible in the drama of the Greek and Elizabethan periods, a single exemplary figure has been made to reflect the furthest reaches of the known universe."

55. Rülicke-Weiler discusses the scene's staging in *Die Dramaturgie Brechts*, p. 190.

56. Schumacher, *Drama and Geschichte*, pp. 70–92. The "Five Difficulties" figure in Ann Clark Fehn's discussion of the last version of the play, but here, Fehn argues, Galileo utterly fails the test: "Vision and Blindness in Brecht's *Leben des Galilei*," *Germanic Review* 53 (1978): 27–34.

57. See Käthe Rülicke, "*Leben des Galilei*: Bemerkungen zur Schluss-szene," *Sinn und Form* 9 (1957): 269–321; much of this material also appears in Werner Hecht, ed., *Materialien zu Brechts* Leben des Galilei (Frankfurt: Suhrkamp, 1968).

58. Alfred D. White, "Brecht's *Leben des Galilei*: Armchair Theatre?" *German Life and Letters* 27 (1973–74): 131.

59. "Nicht länger flüchtet der Zuschauer aus der Jetztzeit in die Historie; die Jetztzeit wird zur Historie" (*Der Messingkauf*, GsW 16:610); "Die Kritik der Gesellschaft is die Revolution. Das is zu Erde gebrachte, exekutive Kritik" (*Neue Technik der Schauspielkunst*, GsW 15: 378). Müller, in *Die Function der Geschichte*, discusses the audience of historians, p. 39. See also Schumacher's useful discussion of "historicization" in *Drama und Geschichte*, pp. 190–91.

60. "Als ich das Kapital von Marx las, verstand ich meine Stücke. . . . dieser Marx war der einzige Zuschauer für meine Stücke, den ich je gesehen hatte" *Der weg zum zeitgenössischen theater* (GsW, 15: 129). Rülicke-Weiler discusses this remark and Brecht's Marxism, in *Die Dramaturgie Brechts*, pp. 14–15.

61. From *Brecht on Theatre*, ed. and trans. John Willett (New York: Hill and Wang, 1964), p. 188; "eine eingeschüchterte, gläubige, 'gebannte' Menge" (*Kleines organon*, GsW, 16: 675).

62. "Kritische Haltung" always interested Brecht (see *Neue Technik der Schauspielkunst*, GsW, 15: 377–79, for example); the *Short Organum* discusses the beginnings of a critical attitude, GsW, 16: 678–79; see also Willett, *Brecht on Theatre*, p. 190.

63. "Wenn es jemanden interessieren sollte: Dies ist auch das Urteil des Stückeschreibers" ("If it interests anybody, this is also the playwright's opinion"— "Anmerkungen zu Leben des Galilei," *GsW* 17: 1133).

64. See Werner Zimmermann, *Brechts 'Leben des Galilei': Interpretation und didaktische Analyse* (Düsseldorf: Schwann, 1965): "der Zuschauer sieht sich immer wieder aufgerufen, über Wesen und Bedeutung der dargestellten Gegensätze und Spannungen nachzudenken und die Möglichkeiten einer Lösung zu prüfen" ("The spectator finds himself repeatedly called upon to think over the essential meaning of the contradictions and tensions set before him and to experiment with the possibilities of a solution," p. 39).

65. Keith A. Dickson, "History, Drama, and Brecht's Chronicle of the Thirty Years' War," *Forum for Modern Language Studies* 6 (1970): 257, and *Towards Utopia*, p. 93.

66. Schumacher documents the distortions, in *Drama and Geschichte*, pp. 41–57. Leroy R. Shaw complains that "by committing himself so wholeheartedly to historical relevance and by making history, the actual course of events, the subject of his work, Brecht necessarily lessened the chances of any play's surviving the moment that

had originally called it forth," in *The Playwright and Historical Change* (Madison: University of Wisconsin Press, 1970), p. 120.

67. See Günter Hartung, "Brecht und Schiller," *Sinn und Form* 18 (1966): 743–66. We may recall that Walter Hinderer dubbed *Wallenstein* a *Lehrstück*.

68. "Technisch ein grosser Rückschritt, wie *Frau Carrars Gewehre*. Allzu opportunistisch," Brecht quoted in Schumacher, *Drama und Geschichte*, p. 17.

69. Schumacher points out the debt to Bacon's definitions of science (*Drama und Geschichte*, pp. 40–41). Reinhold Grimm, "Das Huhn des Francis Bacon," in *Zu Bertolt Brecht: Parabel und episches Theater*, ed. Theo Buck (Stuttgart: Klett-Cotta, 1979), finds in Bacon "die erste philosophische Grundlegung der Verfremdung" ("the earliest philosophical basis for alienation," p. 76). Galileo, Bacon, and Shakespeare's actors merge in a remark by the Dramaturg in the *Messingkauf*: "Sie experimentierten nicht weniger als Galilei zur selben Zeit in Florenz und als Bacon in London" ("They experimented no less than Galileo at the same time in Florence and Bacon in London," *GsW*, 16: 589).

70. Frank K. Borchardt, "Marx, Engels, and Brecht's *Galileo*," *Brecht Heute* 2 (1972): 162. Dickson, however, argues that there is "no warrant for a mechanistic interpretation of history within the context of Marx's work as a whole" (*Towards Utopia*, p. 63).

71. Michel Zéraffa, "Shakespeare, Brecht, et l'histoire," *Europe* 35 (1957): 131.

72. *Galileo* becomes for some readers a humanist parallel play like those of Jonson, Chapman, and Dryden. Schumacher discusses Isaac Deutscher's notion that the play parallels the showtrials of Stalin (*Drama und Geschichte*, pp. 107ff). Betty Nance Weber argues that the play shadows "Trotsky's life and Russian history" ("*The Life of Galileo* and the Theory of Revolution in Permanence," in *Bertolt Brecht: Political Theory and Literary Practice*, ed. Betty Nance Weber and Hubert Heinen [Athens: University of Georgia Press, 1980], p. 61).

73. See Paul Kussmaul's discussion of "die soziologisierte Shakespeare" in *Bertolt Brecht und das Englische Drama der Renaissance* (Bern and Frankfurt: Herbert Lang, 1974), pp. 132–35. See also Bernard Dort, "Brecht devant Shakespeare" *Revue de l'histoire du théâtre* 17 (1965): "Alors qu'il rejette 'l'idéologie' shakespearienne, sa vision tragique de l'univers, Brecht accepte les formes du théâtre elisabéthain" ("Even as he rejects the Shakespearean 'ideology,' its tragic view of the universe, Brecht accepts the devices of the Elizabethan theater," p. 73).

74. Brecht quoted in Schumacher, *Drama und Geschichte*, p. 270.

75. "Brecht sieht die Geschichte hier als guter Marxist" ("Here Brecht sees history as a good Marxist"), says Kussmaul of Brecht's attitude to the Renaissance, *Bertolt Brecht*, p. 27.

76. It is Brecht's word, anyway; see *GsW*, 15: 179. See also W. E. Yuill, *The Art of Vandalism: Bertolt Brecht and the English Drama* (London: Bedford College, 1972), Yuill's main interest is in the adaptations, as is Rodney J. K. Symington's in *Brecht und Shakespeare* (Bonn: Bouvier, 1970).

77. Michael Goldman uses the image of the "sounding of the self" with telling force in *Shakespeare and the Energies of Drama* (Princeton: Princeton University Press, 1972).

78. Dickson, "History, Drama, and Brecht's Chronicle of the Thirty Years' War," p. 258.

79. Historians continue to debate the issue in much the same terms. "In my view," says Hayden White, "history as a discipline is in bad shape today because it has lost sight of its origins in the literary imagination. In the interest of appearing scien-

tific and objective, it has repressed and denied to itself its own greatest source of strength and renewal": see "The Historical Text as Literary Artifact," in *The Writing of History,* ed. Robert Canary and Henry Kozicki (Madison: University of Wisconsin Press, 1978), p. 62.

80. Benjamin Bennett, *Modern Drama and German Classicism* (Ithaca: Cornell University Press, 1979), p. 63.

Index

Hunt, Herbert J., 202, 205, 270n.17, 271n.18

Ibsen, Henrik, *Brand,* 163–64

Jackson, Alfred, 122
Jancke, Gerhard, 272n.30
Jenkins, Annabel, 258n.61
Johnson, Samuel, 100
Johnson, Walter, 162, 186, 222, 265nn. 37, 40, 266nn. 52, 54, 267nn. 55, 60, 65
Jones, Emrys, 26, 243n.12, 244n.20
Jones, Inigo, 63
Jones, W. Garmon, 242n.8
Jonson, Ben: and censorship, 4, 50–52, 57, 249n.5; and court masques, 63, 85; and humanist history, 4, 49–51, 56–57, 63–64, 68, 70, 84, 198, 232, 238; and Northampton, 52, 249n.5; parallel-drawing in, 54–57, 62, 66, 76; and sources, 52, 55. Works: *Catiline,* 62; *Mortimer His Fall,* 50, 62–65, 69, 250n.21; *Sejanus,* 51–58, 61–63, 83, 249n.9, 250n.10; *The Silent Woman,* 88, 92–93
Jose, Nicholas, 258n.53

Kaufman, Michael W., 266n.53
Kean, Charles, 131–32, 134
Kelly, Henry A., 243n.8, 245nn. 24, 25
Kemble, Charles, 131
Kenyon, J. P., 253n.5
Kermode, Frank, 37
Kernan, Alvin, 244n.18
King, Bruce, 97, 255n.26
Kirsch, Arthur C., 255n.32
Kirschbaum, Leo, 250n.21
Kistner, A. L., 251n.35
Kistner, M. K., 251n.35
Knights, L. C., 97, 255n.26
Kobel, Erwin, 210, 219, 273n.31, 274n.43
Krieger, Leonard, 241
Kussmaul, Paul, 276nn. 73, 75

Lacey, Robert, 249n.7
Lafoscade, Leon, 269n.10
Lamm, Martin, 169, 179, 189, 193, 195, 265n.41, 266n.47, 267nn. 56, 62, 65, 268n.69

Lanham, Richard, 241n.3
L'Astrée, 84
Laughton, Charles, 229–30
Lauren, Barbara, 252n.43
Law, Richard, 253n.6
Lebois, André, 269n.10, 271nn. 20, 22, 272n.27
Lee, Nathaniel: with Dryden, 4, 118. Works: *Caesar Borgia,* 106; *Constantine the Great,* 107; *The Duke of Guise,* 90, 98, 106–13, 116, 119, 124, 135; *Lucius Junius Brutus,* 106–7; *The Massacre of Paris,* 106–7
Leech, Clifford, 82, 247n.42, 252n.42, 253n.49
Lefebvre, Henri, 269n.8, 270n.17, 272n.24
Lessing, Gotthold Ephraim, 118, 178
Levin, Lawrence L., 243n.11
Levin, Richard, 247n.40
Levine, Joseph M., 259n.71
Lide, Barbara, 265n.39
Lindenberger, Herbert, 7, 90, 147, 222, 241n.8, 272n.28, 274nn. 41, 44
Lioure, Michel, 200, 268n.6, 270n.11
Loftis, John, 257n.47, 259nn. 69, 70
Lukacs, Georg, 272n.30
Lynch, Kathleen M., 102
Lyons, Charles R., 224

Macaulay, Thomas Babington, 5, 88–89, 132–33
McBride, Tom, 248n.50
McFadden, George, 255n.28
Machiavelli, Niccolo, 2, 50, 110, 113, 116; as humanist historian, 27–29, 33, 83–84, 124
Mack, Maynard, 246n.32
McKisack, May, 245n.23
Macready, Charles, 131
Maeterlinck, Maurice, 182
Mainland, W. F., 263n.21, 265n.35
Mann, Golo, 141, 261n.4
Marshall, Geoffrey, 97, 104, 255n.26, 256n.39
Marx, Karl, 7, 230–31
Massinger, Philip, 4; and John Fletcher, *The Tragedy of Sir John van olden Barnavelt,* 66–67. Works: *Believe as Ye List,* 51, 64, 67–69, 79, 88, 249n.4; *The Bondman,* 66; *The Maid of Honour,* 66

THE JOHNS HOPKINS UNIVERSITY PRESS

The Play of TRUTH & STATE

This book was set in Galliard text and display type
by the Composing Room of Michigan, Inc., from a
design by Martha Farlow. It was printed on 50-lb.
Sebago Cream offset paper and bound in Holliston
Roxite A with Multicolor Antique end sheets by the
Maple Press Company.